Sam,

Thanks for being a great
mentor and colleague.

— Leah

From Power to Prejudice

From Power to Prejudice

The Rise of Racial Individualism in Midcentury America

LEAH N. GORDON

The University of Chicago Press
Chicago and London

Leah N. Gordon is assistant professor of education and (by courtesy) of
history at Stanford University.

The University of Chicago Press, Chicago 60637
The University of Chicago Press, Ltd., London
© 2015 by The University of Chicago
All rights reserved. Published 2015.
Printed in the United States of America

24 23 22 21 20 19 18 17 16 15   1 2 3 4 5

ISBN-13: 978-0-226-23844-9 (cloth)
ISBN-13: 978-0-226-23858-6 (e-book)
DOI: 10.7208/chicago/9780226238586.001.0001

Library of Congress Cataloging-in-Publication Data

Gordon, Leah N., author.
    From power to prejudice : the rise of radical individualism in midcentury
America / Leah N. Gordon.
        pages cm
    Includes bibliographical references and index.
    ISBN 978-0-226-23844-9 (cloth : alkaline paper) — ISBN 978-0-226-
    23858-6 (e-book) 1. Race discrimination—United States—History—20th
    century. 2. Prejudices—United States—History—20th century. 3. United
    States—Race relations—History—20th century. I. Title.
        E185.61.G67 2015
        305.800973'09045—dc23

                                                                    2014037001

⊗ This paper meets the requirements of ANSI/NISO Z39.48-1992
(Permanence of Paper).

To my parents,
Clifford and Linda Gordon

CONTENTS

ACKNOWLEDGMENTS

It is a pleasure to thank the many people who have made writing this book possible. At the University of Pennsylvania, a wonderful group of advisors initially nurtured the book's development. I could not have asked for a more supportive and conscientious advisor than Michael Katz. He provided a model of politically engaged and socially responsible historical scholarship, and his encouragement and insight continued to sharpen my thinking well after I completed my degree. He will be sorely missed. Kathleen Hall, Sarah Igo, and Thomas Sugrue also greatly enriched my experience in graduate school and have continued to provide invaluable critiques and scholarly models ever since. The project also benefited considerably from Bruce Kulick, Adolph Reed Jr., and Barbara Savage's insights.

My colleagues at Stanford University have been especially supportive and welcoming. David Labaree has been a wonderful mentor during my time at Stanford's Graduate School of Education and has provided much feedback on the manuscript. David Tyack and the late Elizabeth Hansot were especially welcoming when I arrived in Palo Alto, and I am thankful for their lively conversation and scholarly advice. Colleagues, especially those in the Graduate School of Education, History Department, and Center for Comparative Studies in Race and Ethnicity, have made Stanford an intellectually engaging and friendly place to research and teach. I extend special thanks to Clayborne Carson, James Campbell, Prudence Carter, Estelle Freedman, Michael Kahan, Daniel McFarland, John Meyer, Jelena Obradovic, Francisco Ramirez, Sean Reardon, Mitchell Stevens, Sam Wineburg, and Caroline Winterer for their collegiality and support for the project. I am also thankful for feedback I received on presentations or portions of the manuscript from the Bay Area Consortium for the History of Ideas, Stanford's Center for Opportunity Policy in Education, Stanford's Center for Philanthropy and Civil Society, and Stanford's Higher Education Seminar.

I have also received thoughtful comments on this project while at conferences and seminars outside the Bay Area. These include annual meetings of CHEIRON, the History of Education Society, the Social Science History Association, the Organization of American Historians, and the American Historical Association. I appreciated the chance to present research related to this book at a seminar on Color-Blind Disciplining of Race Conscious Research sponsored by the Center for the Advanced Study of Behavioral Sciences and African American Policy Forum; the International Research Congress on International and National Standardization and Differentiation of Education Systems from a Historical Perspective held in Monte Verita, Switzerland; and a seminar conducted by the Research Community on Philosophy and History of the Discipline of Education: Faces and Spaces of Educational Research at the Catholic University of Leuven. Special thanks go to Glenn Adams, Andrew Abbott, Jean-Claude Croizet, Lani Guinier, Luke Harris, Carl Kaestle, Harvey Kantor, George Lipsitz, Alice O'Connor, and William Reese whose feedback on conference papers, proposal drafts, or chapters aided my thinking. Jonathan Zimmerman provided feedback and kind support throughout this project's development, as he has for so many young historians of education. I am especially thankful for his generosity. In addition, I owe a considerable debt to two wonderful historians—Hilary Moss and Tracy Steffes—who have read multiple portions of the manuscript, in some cases many times, offered invaluable insights, and provided consistent encouragement along the way. I also want to thank the colleagues and friends I met in graduate school and since who helped nurture this project in its earliest stages and have provided an invaluable academic community ever since: Gretchen Aguiar, Jeffrey Allred, Daniel Amsterdam, Deirdre Brill, Zoe Burkholder, Michael Clapper, Ansley Erickson, Brett Gadsden, Sean Greene, Sarah Manekin, Julia Rabig, Jordan Stanger-Ross, and Meredith Webber. I also want to thank Ethan Hutt, Matthew Kelley, and Jack Schneider for their diligent and insightful work as research assistants.

I extend thanks to reviewers, editors, and staff associated with the University of Chicago Press for their ongoing assistance. Andrew Jewett and an anonymous reviewer provided invaluable feedback that greatly improved the manuscript. Much thanks goes to editors Robert Devens and Timothy Mennel who guided the publication process and to Nora Devlin and other staff who handled many necessary details.

Portions of chapter 3 have appeared in Leah N. Gordon, "The Individual and 'the General Situation': The Tension Barometer and the Race Problem at the University of Chicago, 1947–1954," *Journal of the Behavioral Sciences*, 56, 1 (2012): 27–51. I extend thanks to Wiley Periodicals Inc. for permission to reprint this material.

Dissertation and postdoctoral fellowships from the Spencer Foundation/ National Academy of Education were essential to this project's completion. I also received generous support from the University of Pennsylvania's School of Arts and Science and Africana Studies Departments. I also want to acknowledge, and highlight the crucial importance of, Stanford University's generous parental leave and child care assistance policies, which allow junior faculty to simultaneously have a family and pursue an academic career.

My greatest debt is to my parents, Clifford and Linda Gordon, whose love for ideas has always inspired me and to whom I can never offer enough thanks. This book is dedicated to them. Great thanks also go to my brother, Adam Gordon, whose scholarly insights, encouragement, and good humor so often brighten my day. My husband's family, Jeanne Carpenter and Andrew Moshinskie, provided much support, especially in the book's final stages. My daughter, Miriam, son, Elijah, and dog, Brett, bring great joy to my life and daily remind me of what matters. By keeping our household running, my priorities straight, and my life balanced, my husband, Adam Contois, has helped to make this book—and all my work—possible.

ABBREVIATIONS

ACRR	American Council on Race Relations
AMA	American Missionary Association
CP	University of Chicago, Committee on Education, Training, and Research in Race Relations Papers, Special Collections Research Center, University of Chicago Library, Chicago, Illinois
GEB	General Education Board records, Rockefeller Archive Center, Sleepy Hollow, New York
JNE	*Journal of Negro Education*
JP	Charles S. Johnson Papers, Fisk University Special Collections, Fisk University, Nashville, Tennessee
LSRM	Laura Spellman Rockefeller Memorial Papers, Rockefeller Archive Center, Sleepy Hollow, New York
LWP	Louis Wirth Papers, Special Collections Research Center, University of Chicago Library, Chicago, Illinois
NAACP	National Association for the Advancement of Colored People
NAACP, LDF	National Association for the Advancement of Colored People, Legal Defense and Education Fund
NCCJ	National Conference of Christians and Jews Records, Social Welfare History Archive, University of Minnesota, Minneapolis
NCSNC	National Committee on Segregation in the Nation's Capitol
OMR	Office of the Messrs. Rockefeller Papers, Rockefeller Archive Center, Sleepy Hollow, New York
RBF	Rockefeller Brothers Fund records, Rockefeller Archive Center, Sleepy Hollow, New York

RF	Rockefeller Foundation records, Rockefeller Archive Center, Sleepy Hollow, New York
RFA	Rockefeller Family Archives, Rockefeller Archive Center, Sleepy Hollow, New York
RRD	Race Relations Department, Fisk University
RRI	Race Relations Institutes
RRIP	Race Relations Institutes Papers
RRI Summary	American Missionary Association and Race Relations Department, Race Relations Institutes Summary
SSRC	Social Science Research Council Papers, Rockefeller Archive Center, Sleepy Hollow, New York
TP	Charles H. Thompson Papers, Moorland-Spingarn Research Center, Howard University, Washington, DC

Introduction

It is only within the nexus of personality that we find the effective operation of historical, cultural, and economic factors. Unless mores somehow enter the fibre of individual lives they are not effective agents, for it is only individuals who can feel antagonism and practice discrimination.

—GORDON ALLPORT, *The Nature of Prejudice*, 1954

If beliefs per se could subjugate a people, the beliefs which Negroes hold about whites should be as effective as those which whites hold about Negroes.

—OLIVER CROMWELL COX, "An American Dilemma: A Mystical Approach to the Study of Race Relations," *Journal of Negro Education*, 1945

In the 1940s and 1950s, basic questions divided scholars and activists committed to racial justice: What exactly constituted "the race problem"? What was its primary cause? What aspects of the race problem could be changed and how? Four major conceptions of racism that had very different programmatic implications competed in midcentury social scientific and activist debate. Many agreed with Gordon Allport that the race problem was essentially psychological. The culprit, in this first view, was white prejudice, the flawed racial attitudes that might lead to discriminatory behaviors. Educational programs to improve those attitudes and planned interracial contacts to promote intergroup "understanding" constituted the best response. For many others, the problem's roots involved legal injustice, the state-sanctioned denial of African American rights as citizens. Legal desegregation, the protection of voting rights, and legislation to prevent discrimination in employment, housing, and the distribution of public services were the solutions to this second way of framing the race problem. Others embraced a third approach, social structural analysis, which had constituted the leading sociological and anthropological frameworks of the 1920s and 1930s. In these theories racial conflict was the central issue and intergroup antagonism derived from totalizing cultural systems or large-scale, inevitable social processes of migration and intergroup competition. Since these evolutionary developments would subside naturally over time, there was little government or individuals could do to intervene. For still others, like radical sociologist Oliver Cromwell Cox, the race problem's sources lay in political economy. Power, exploitation, and oppression, according to this fourth framework, created the problem and challenging the structures of capitalism was necessary to solve it.

While all four theories circulated in the 1920s, 1930s, and first half of the 1940s, a framework that I have termed *racial individualism* proved especially influential in the postwar decades. Bringing together psychological individualism, rights-based individualism, and belief in the socially transformative power of education, racial individualism presented prejudice and discrimination as the root cause of racial conflict, focused on individuals in the study of race relations, and suggested that racial justice could be attained by changing white minds and protecting African American rights. This social theory and agenda for change grew in influence between the publication of Gunnar Myrdal's *An American Dilemma* in 1944 and the passage of the Civil Rights Act in 1964.[1]

Individualistic approaches were particularly evident among postwar psychologists, sociologists, and anthropologists but also flourished among an expanding group of postwar "racial liberals" seeking to fight prejudice, ease racial tensions, and secure African American civil rights. Interwar sociologists associated with the Chicago school, social anthropologists of the Caste and Class school, and economists concerned with southern agriculture had offered robust social structural and political economic analyses of the race issue.[2] The postwar decades, in contrast, saw less attention to the structural sources of racial conflict and growing concern with white prejudice, discrimination, and African American psychology. Not only psychologists but also sociologists and anthropologists associated with the postwar behavioral sciences, an interdisciplinary field that tended to prioritize the causal importance of individual actors, focused research on racial attitudes and discrimination.[3] In the same period, many civil rights activists and proponents of improved race relations—distinct but overlapping groups—also adopted increasingly individual-centered theoretical and strategic approaches. While a Depression-era "interracial left," which included coalitions of civil rights workers, communists, socialists, laborites, religious advocates of social welfare, and New Dealers, joined forces with the "African American popular front" to root the race issue in political economy, postwar racial liberals prioritized educational efforts to reduce white bigotry, legal desegregation, and antidiscrimination legislation.[4] Beginning during the war, efforts to fight prejudice through "education, exhortation, and negotiation" expanded significantly, while concern with prejudice, discrimination, and individual rights played central roles in the fair employment and open housing movements.[5] Many factors contributed to the growth of postwar racial liberalism, and the relationship between social theory and social reform proved complex.[6] Still, racial individualism undergirded two tenets of the postwar liberal agenda on race—antidiscrimination legislation and antiprejudice education—and provided a set of rationales for the third: legal desegregation.

The legal arena also favored individualistic approaches to the race issue. A vision of Jim Crow as an intertwined political and economic system had motivated civil rights litigation in the 1930s and 1940s. After 1950, however, the NAACP dropped this view when it directly attacked *Plessy v. Ferguson* by arguing that the psychological stigma of school segregation, even if resources were equalized, violated African American rights.[7] The landmark *Brown v. Board of Education* (1954) decision did lead to the redistribution of educational resources through integration in much of the South. Nonetheless, legal scholar Lani Guinier writes that subsequent courts turned *Brown's* tendency to view "the caste system of Jim Crow narrowly, as a function of individual prejudice," and the decision's claim that "treating individuals differently based on the color of their skin was constitutionally wrong," from a "clarion call to an excuse not to act."[8] In the last three decades of the twentieth century, individualistic views of racism encouraged more conservative courts to make de facto separation legally "invisible," to solidify distinctions between race and class "that lifted unequal resource distribution out of the constitutional cannon," to prevent desegregation in cases where intentional racial animus could not be proven or had been remedied, and to retreat from affirmative action using "color-blind" logics.[9]

While historians have shown that individualistic approaches to the race issue became increasingly influential in the postwar years, we have a less clear understanding of *how* and *why* racial individualism gained the traction it did. By focusing on debates over the significance of prejudice to the "race problem," this history reveals that racial individualism's postwar development was both complicated and contested. Various causal pressures intersected in complex ways to favor individualistic paradigms and inhibit alternative views of the race issue. Constituencies with different priorities—

foundation elites, behavioral scientists, religious and educational proponents of antiprejudice education, civic groups concerned with urban racial
tensions, and diverse civil rights activists—all came to favor, or at least acqui-
esce to, individualism, though often for different reasons. Racial individualism's postwar growth was also uneven, however, since behavioralism and
antiprejudice education produced only limited enthusiasm among many
leading African American intellectuals. Understanding how individualistic
views of the race issue prevailed despite being challenged is important because racial individualism helped rationalize reform agendas that proved
insufficient against the extralegal sources of segregation and the intertwined
racial and economic mechanisms that sustained racial inequality throughout the second half of the twentieth century.[10]

The case studies in this book root intellectual history in institutions
and, in so doing, highlight the intersecting factors that shaped ideas on
the race problem. The institutional vantage point illuminates the calcula-
tions scholar-activists employed when translating theory into reform, as
well as the contested process by which racial individualism gained ground
alongside—not always in lieu of—alternative views of the race issue. The
cases here are illustrative not representative, meaning that they create win-
dows into specific influential institutions but don't claim that these institutional histories can necessarily be generalized. Rather than provide a comprehensive history of either postwar social science on the race issue or a
deep chronicle of particular disciplinary approaches to racial questions, the
institutional orientation illuminates how diverse causal pressures worked
in conjunction, how some disciplinary paradigms obscured others, and
how antiracist scholar-activists contended with the competing demands of
theory and politics.

I focus on a range of institutions that were differently situated in racialized academic hierarchies, intellectual agenda-setting networks, and aca-
demic/activist nexuses: the Rockefeller Foundation (RF), one of the most
influential philanthropies setting social scientific agendas on racial issues;
the University of Chicago's Committee on Education, Training, and Research in Race Relations (CETRRR), a race relations department at an elite
white research university whose sociologists had produced the dominant
systemic approach to race relations in the 1920s and 1930s; Fisk University's
Race Relations Institutes (RRI), a center of African American intellectual and
political life committed to linking social science and racial politics; Howard University's *Journal of Negro Education* (*JNE*), a civil rights and educational journal produced by another elite historically black institution that
had been a center of black radical thought in the 1930s; and the National

Conference of Christians and Jews (NCCJ), an organization at the forefront of the religious antiprejudice education movement. At all these institutions leading social scientists, civil rights activists, and individuals who bridged those roles debated the significance of prejudice to the race problem. Yet the Rockefeller Foundation and NCCJ's political leanings made individualism's rise expected in those settings, while interwar theoretical and political tendencies at the other sites made racial individualism's postwar successes surprising. This diverse set of institutional vantage points helps illuminate convergence among the major constituencies that supported postwar racial individualism, reveals the fate of postwar efforts to use social science to inform racial politics, and allows us to assess if and how academic segregation mattered to racial individualism's history. These sites also expose the persistence of counternarratives in African American–led intellectual spaces and the ways dilemmas associated with the scale of scientific method and feasible reform complicated "social science for social action."

Debates over the race problem in these settings share a broad history. Racial individualism and alternative theoretical and reformist approaches each flourished from the 1920s through 1939. Between 1939 and 1948, individualism grew in influence, but alternative frameworks had not yet declined. Distinct turns toward individualism and away from alternative theoretical frameworks occurred in 1948 and 1949 at the RF and CETRRR and in reformist orientations at the RRI and *JNE*. This relatively abrupt shift ushered in racial individualism's period of peak significance between 1949 and the passage of the Civil Rights Act in 1964, though theoretical alternatives continued to surface at the RRI and *JNE* in these years, and social scientists began turning attention to structural sources of African American poverty by the early 1960s.

Three sets of distinct causal dynamics shaped postwar debate on the race issue in these settings. Internalist pressures (1) included notions of scientific rigor associated with scientism (social scientific reliance on the investigative norms of the natural sciences); methodological priorities favoring individual units of analysis, quantification, and large data sets; and theoretical concerns, especially enthusiasm for interdisciplinary social relations paradigms, behavioralism, and theory generation. These were always difficult to separate from the politics of knowledge production (2), the federal and foundation funding streams and institutional hierarchies (including academic segregation) that prioritized certain scholars and research agendas over others. And finally, evolving externalist causes (3), including World War II, retreats from New Deal liberalism, shifts in civil rights legal strategy, anticommunism, and the enduring appeal of uncontroversial tolerance education, directly encouraged individualistic reformist approaches and indirectly fostered theoretical shifts toward individualism. In particular institutions, however, the three sets of causal factors reinforced one another, exposing the complicated ways the "the intellectual" and "the political" intertwined. In the elite, white-led academic networks that moved through the RF and CETRRR, political, methodological, and theoretical considerations together encouraged postwar racial individualism. During World War II and in the immediate postwar years, the jolting specter of Nazi racism, domestic racial disturbances, and the expansion of religious, educational, and civic efforts to fight prejudice and racial tensions motivated many sociologists, anthropologists, and psychologists to study prejudice. However, methodological considerations simultaneously drove scholars concerned with race to focus on attitudes. For example, researchers at CETRRR turned attention to prejudice—rather than political economy or social structure—because they wanted to aid reformers and because, while they knew how to quantify individual attitudes, they were less sure how to measure the systemic and relational sources of fraught race relations. Internalist and externalist pressures also converged in the late 1940s and 1950s, years when anticommunism, scientism, and behavioralism reinforced one another. While RF leaders were closely attuned to congressional investigations of foundation "subversion," methodological and theoretical considerations—especially commitment to theory generation, generalizability, and quantification—largely led the elite social scientists helping the RF set its scientific agendas to favor individualistic research on race. Postwar scholars thus had political, institutional, theoretical, and methodological reasons to embrace racial individualism.

Despite these intersecting pressures, theories that presented the sources of racial conflict outside individual minds did continue to circulate between 1944 and 1964, especially in the two centers of African American intellectual and political life I examine, Fisk University's RRI and Howard University's JNE. The interdisciplinary and interracial group of scholars and civil rights activists who met at the yearly Institutes and wrote in the JNE (groups that often overlapped) frequently emphasized labor exploitation, intergroup competition, political oppression, and patterns of institutionalized discrimination when describing the historical origins of racial injustice and its ongoing mechanisms. These thinkers expressed less enthusiasm for postwar behavioralism and less concern with the limits of nonquantifiable research methods than their colleagues at the RF and CETRRR. After 1949, however, in the same years that methodological and scientistic pressures produced an individualistic drift at the RF and CETRRR, postwar anticommunism, declining congressional support for New Deal redistributive social and economic policies, and the growing momentum of the NAACP's direct attack on *Plessy v. Ferguson* encouraged rapid shifts toward the rights-based components of racial individualism at the RRI and *JNE*. Between 1949 and the early 1960s, many RRI and *JNE* participants avoided translating social structural and political economic theories of the sources of the race issue into calls for change. Instead, at least in their politics, RRI and *JNE* leaders embraced racial liberalism, though faint calls for positive, social and economic rights still occasionally surfaced. Many acquiesced to popular antiprejudice education even though they understood it to be incomplete as a total strategy for progress toward racial justice. They also, with the mainstream civil rights movement, prioritized antidiscrimination legislation and legal desegregation, frequently overlooking questions their social theories continued to imply about whether rights-based approaches would be sufficient for securing racial justice and equality.

This pragmatism, evident throughout the academic settings I examine but most striking at Fisk's RRI and Howard's *JNE*, exposes tensions inherent in projects of "social science for social action" in which many midcentury thinkers placed considerable faith. Recognizing that, as sociologist Robin M. Williams Jr. put it, "the factors which are most important in producing hostility and conflict are by no means the same as those which are most important *for control purposes*," scholars found different ways to compartmentalize theoretical and political commitments.[11] In the end, many advocated reforms that did not reflect the true complexity of their scientific theories. The interests of pragmatic structuralists who "pulled their punches" converged with those of politically conservative foundation officials, advocates of interdisciplinary behavioralism, religious and educational antiprejudice workers, and the mainstream, rights-focused civil rights movement in ways that favored both racial individualism and racial liberalism.

By the early 1950s, antiradicalism, rightward shifts in American liberalism, mounting civil rights successes in the courts, and the appeal of politically innocuous educational approaches to social problems interacted with scientism, behavioralism, and a commitment to quantification to favor racial individualism, even in institutions where alternative approaches had flourished five, ten, and twenty years before. While an understanding of racism that obscured class and power relations flowered in the postwar decades—a view at odds with the interwar interracial left's emphases on the inseparability of race and class oppression—anticommunism did not work alone to reduce the reach of class-based theories of racial injustice.[12] The postwar politics of knowledge production provided researchers with theoretical and methodological reasons to focus on individuals and encouraged questions about the case-based methods, political-economic frameworks, and conflict-based structural theories that interwar anthropologists and sociologists concerned with race had frequently employed.[13] In addition, a movement against prejudice and for improved race relations, which had a less political orientation and less African American leadership than the civil rights movement, gained visibility during and after World War II with important consequences for postwar racial thought and politics. In fact, both the NAACP's strategy against *Plessy* and this antiprejudice activism ensured that "educationalization"—the American penchant for addressing complex social problems through education—played a central role in the ascent of postwar racial liberalism.[14] Antiracist scholars negotiated competing theoretical and political commitments, frequently delineating racial individualism, the social theory, from racial liberalism, the agenda for change. Ultimately, however, many embraced racial liberalism while simultaneously raising questions about racial individualism, a form of political pragmatism whose long-term consequences endure.

Racial Individualism and Its Alternatives in Midcentury Theory and Reform

The distinctions political scientist Charles Tilly draws among dispositional, systemic, and relational social theories help to elucidate the various theoretical and reformist approaches to the race issue circulating between the 1930s and the 1960s.[15] Dispositional theories, which point to an entity's "orientations just before the point of action," usually focus on individual motives, incentives, and emotions.[16] When applied to race relations, dispositional individualism suggests that individuals are the most important causal actor and unit of analysis. Most psychologists concerned with prejudice took a dispositional approach to the race issue, though some rooted prejudice in normal cognitive and emotional processes, others emphasized contextual determinants, still others tested educational interventions, and some explored the ties between prejudice and personality structure. Psychologists generally accepted social psychologist Gordon Allport's claim, however, that individuals were appropriate units of analysis because it is only through them that historical and sociological forces become visible to a scientist. From the 1920s through the 1950s sociologists like Donald Young, Robert Merton, and John Dollard and anthropologists like Hortense Powdermaker also, at times, used dispositional frameworks by turning attention to prejudice, devising attitude scales, testing college race relations courses, or examining the relationship between prejudiced attitudes and discriminatory behaviors.[17] The wartime refining of the modern social survey, a research method that quantified individual attitudes at a large scale, ensured that scholars could easily translate dispositional theories into projects considered rigorous by the standards of postwar scientism.[18]

Systemic theories, by contrast, highlighted the causal power of social processes; presented societies or economies as "coherent, self-sustaining entities"; situated events within a broader system or structure; and generally took communities, social groups, or patterns of intergroup interaction—not individuals—as the unit of analysis.[19] In the 1920s and 1930s these frameworks were popular among Chicago school sociologists and social anthropologists associated with Lloyd Warner and the Caste and Class school who generally treated societies or cultures as cohesive wholes. For example, Chicago school sociologists, often described as social ecologists, depicted the social using biological, corporeal, or ecological metaphors.[20] While some social ecologists traced patterns of racial inequality and disadvantage nationally, interwar systemic frameworks often led to detailed community studies whose rigor scholars concerned with quantification and generalizability questioned by the early 1950s.[21]

The relational approach conceptualized ongoing patterns of interaction between individuals or social groups as the key forces shaping the social order and producing change. Most evident in political economic theories of oppression and exploitation popular among the Depression-era interracial left, relational approaches, in contrast to systemic, emphasized power and did not consider the entities in question part of a cohesive structure.[22] The lines between relational, political economic frameworks and systemic, social ecological theories could blur, however, since both centrally addressed conflict. Each also emphasized the causal importance of structures, though relational theories prioritized the structures of capitalism while systemic theories pointed to more amorphous social structures. In fact, between the late 1920s and the mid-1940s, a number of Chicago-trained African American sociologists and anthropologists—a group including Charles S. Johnson, E. Franklin Frazier, St. Clair Drake, and Horace Cayton whose work contributed to the "Golden Age of Negro Sociology"—combined the systemic assumptions associated with Robert Park's social ecology with the attention to capitalist exploitation, oppression, and power relations characteristic of political economic thought.[23] Although these thinkers did not ignore prejudice per se, they treated it as a derivative factor. While in Park's theory prejudice was a component of the inevitable process of conflict that resulted from patterns of intergroup contact, in relational theories prejudice did not cause racial oppression but emerged to justify it.

While dispositional, systemic, and relational frameworks all circulated in the interwar years, in the immediate postwar era, wartime survey research, experiments in interdisciplinary "social relations," and support for research on prejudice by religious and civic groups encouraged dispositional approaches among not only psychologists but also sociologists and anthropologists. Between 1948 and the early 1960s, moreover, growing foundation support for the interdisciplinary behavioral sciences, the decline of Chicago school frameworks, and McCarthyism only made this individualistic theoretical orientation more pronounced, especially in sociology.[24] That mainstream economics and political science proved relatively quiet on racial issues in the decade and a half after Myrdal's work may also have contributed to the success of dispositional paradigms among sociologists and anthropologists in these years.[25] Although sociologists E. Franklin Frazier and Robin M. Williams Jr. worried in the late 1940s about the "atomistic" drift in their field, Drake and Cayton's *Black Metropolis* (1945) represented the denouement of the combination of systemic and political economic analysis that had characterized the African American Chicago school.[26] Instead, sociologist Robin M. Williams Jr.'s Rockefeller-funded *The Reduction of Intergroup Tensions* (1947), which dismissed large-scale analysis of economic or social structures as politically disillusioning and sought to improve antiprejudice educational techniques, exhibited the applied concerns and behavioral assumptions motivating much postwar research on prejudice and discrimination.[27] In addition, many of the most celebrated social scientific statements on race of the late 1940s and 1950s, most notably work by Theodor Adorno and colleagues and Gordon Allport that prioritized personality theory, proved widely influential among sociologists.[28] Explicitly relational frameworks, in contrast, faced substantial obstacles amid postwar antiradicalism. When, in 1948, radical sociologist Oliver Cromwell Cox published his enormous political economic treatise on American racism, *Caste, Class, and Race*, anticommunist pressures led the publisher to refuse a second printing in 1949 even though the first had sold out within the year.[29]

Theoretical, institutional, and political considerations, as we will see, all contributed to the postwar behavioral shift in research on race, but the relationship between social science and social reform was not always seamless. In some cases, especially with dispositional frameworks, the relationship appeared simple and direct. Many antiprejudice educators turned to psychologists or sociologists to inform their reform agendas; when reformers proceeded without expert advice, well meaning though frequently condescending scholars intervened; and scientists often turned scholarly attention to racial attitudes because they believed beliefs seemed easily malleable.

Especially for proponents of systemic and relational frameworks, however, efforts to use social science in the service of social action proved quite complicated. One reason for this complication, as chapter five will show with respect to school integration, was that activists often relied on more than one theoretical paradigm to champion a reform.

Linking social science and social reform also proved complicated because dilemmas of scale—in which politically available reforms were theoretically insufficient but theoretically sanctioned reforms were too grand to be politically practical—hampered efforts at scientific application.[30] Dispositional theories raised one type of dilemma of scale: the issue of inadequacy. Many scholars of prejudice, including Allport and the authors of *The Authoritarian Personality*, recognized that antiprejudice education was limited as a total paradigm for progress in race relations. Nonetheless, the popularity of this reform, which derived in part from tolerance education's political innocuousness, led scholars to advocate research on the topic even when skeptical.[31] Systemic and relational theories raised different dilemmas of scale: issues of programmatic and political feasibility. Because systemic theories envisioned the root causes of racial conflict in large-scale social, economic, or cultural forces, they implied that change in race relations would be very difficult, if not impossible, to engineer. As Robin M. Williams Jr. argued in 1947, a "total orientation" to the race problem might disillusion activists since it prompted "the feeling that intergroup tensions are so deeply embedded in the nature of our whole social system that only a major alternation of the system could bring adequate solutions."[32] In contrast, relational perspectives had more precise but also more politically controversial implications for change. Radicals called for challenges to liberal capitalism as essential components of the struggle against white supremacy while political liberals employed relational logics when proposing state engineering of labor markets, New Deal–style jobs programs, and expansive, racially sensitive welfare programs in the 1930s and mid-1940s. Both types of reform became increasingly unlikely, however, in the early Cold War era.

The midcentury projects of "social science for social action" that many activist social scientists championed were thus fraught with tensions. While the systemic and relational theories that highlighted the large scope and great complexity of the race issue were either programmatically challenging or politically impractical, scholars recognized that more easily implemented, dispositional, and even rights-based, reforms were insufficient as total programs for progress toward racial justice. The most radical critics of racial liberalism—who quickly took aim at Gunnar Myrdal's 1944 focus on prejudice and democratic rights—suggested that individualistic theories themselves had conservative political consequences. Sociologist Oliver Cromwell Cox and historian Herbert Aptheker presented Myrdal's moral dilemma thesis as a "mystification," an aspect of the ruling ideology "calculated" to perpetuate racial oppression and exploitation.[33] While postwar racial liberals like Charles S. Johnson, Charles H. Thompson, Robert Weaver, or Louis Wirth, whose theories acknowledged the limits of the liberal paradigm they favored politically, remained more restrained, using social science in the service of racial reform proved far from simple.

Scientism and Behavioralism in the Midcentury Intellectual Context

Debates over the significance of prejudice to the race problem emerged during decades of transformation and expansion in American social science. Key themes in twentieth-century American intellectual history and the history of social science—the separation of science and reform associated with arguments surrounding "scientism," the growing institutional strength of psychology, the refining of individualistic social survey methods, and expanded support for the interdisciplinary behavioral sciences amid Cold War antiradicalism—marked the terrain that nurtured racial individualism. Social reform and social science had been difficult to disentangle in the late nineteenth and early twentieth centuries, years when Progressive reformers in the United States and Europe, often with support from foundations, responded to problems associated with urbanization, industrialization, and immigration with large-scale social surveys produced for the purpose of social amelioration.[34] And yet by the first decades of the twentieth century, countervailing trends would also have important implications for the social science of race relations: the rise of "scientism," a commitment to objectivity in scientific method and purpose; the professionalization of the social sciences; and their movement into the university. Proponents of scientism favored theory development (the production of generalizable analytic frameworks especially those that identified natural, universal laws of the social world), empiricism (the application of experimental techniques associated with the natural sciences to human interaction), and objectivity as evidence of professional status.[35] Indeed, as historian Sarah Igo argues, "This putatively definitive split between amateur social investigation and scientific research performed by professionals served as the modern social sciences' legitimizing myth."[36] Early twentieth-century social scientists in the emerging disciplines of political science, history, economics, sociology, anthropology, and psychology established institutional homes in the university; developed professional organizations, journals, and credentialing processes; and rejected the reformist traditions from which many of their fields had grown as "amateur" and "value-laden."[37]

Challenges to scientism endured, nonetheless, throughout the first half of the twentieth century. Social scientific technologies moved easily between "basic" and "applied" realms as social surveys, opinion polls, community studies, and mental tests proved their utility to politicians, advertisers, industrial managers, educators, and the federal government, especially in wartime.[38] Some academics suggested that social science was inescapably ethical because scholars could not truly separate political and scientific commitments, and social science, ideally, informed public engagement in democratic processes.[39] In fact, debate over scientific purpose—in this case over whether scientists should aim to produce useful research rather than advance knowledge for its own sake—divided many of the disciplines, especially in the 1930s. These disagreements led to the establishment of organizations like the Society for the Psychological Study of Social Issues (SPSSI) and the Society for the Study of Social Problems (SSSP) that embraced politically engaged research and, in so doing, challenged mainstream disciplinary authorities.[40] Nonetheless, a version of instrumental scientism, in which scholars engaged in basic, value-free investigations that would help "leaders from other sectors of society, such as politics and business, to make better decisions and take more effective action," provided the model for scientific involvement in World War II.[41] By the early 1950s, when this view prevailed among many scholars hoping to receive some of the new federal research funding as well as among many foundation executives, scientism pushed more politically engaged visions of scientific purpose to the margins.[42]

Concerns related to the intersections of science and politics had particular implications for scholars of color examining the race issue from inside a segregated academy. While many prominent African American scholars wrote for both scholarly audiences and a broader "black reading public," many foundation leaders and white academics expected black social scientists to be inherently biased on racial issues, producing added pressure for African American social scientists to prove their objectivity.[43] In addition, philanthropists often funded black colleges as part of their social welfare not their social scientific initiatives and assumed HBCUs (historically black colleges and universities) would not produce cutting-edge research. The racialized politics of knowledge production ensured that HBCUs saw little of the defense-related federal research money that poured into leading white research universities after World War II.[44]

While debates over scientism broadly shaped the theoretical and institutional landscape in which racial individualism competed with alternative theories, the rising stature of twentieth-century psychology more directly encouraged social scientists to turn to individuals when studying the race issue.[45] Between 1920 and 1946, historically unprecedented growth "transformed psychology from an emerging academic specialty into a mammoth techno-scientific profession."[46] With ever-increasing federal and foundation support, midcentury psychologists and social psychologists discussed a host of politically charged topics, from civilian morale, to soldiers' attitudes, to the mindsets of developing nations that might "fall" to communism, though psychological expertise was especially influential on racial issues.[47]

Methodological developments also help to explain why individualistic logics became influential in postwar research on race. Quantitative attitude measures improved significantly in the 1930s and 1940s, as the modern social survey, an instrument initially developed in the Progressive Era to quantify community life for the purpose of amelioration, was refined and separated from its reformist roots. In addition to psychologists and social psychologists, many sociologists were involved in midcentury survey research. Many learned survey techniques working for Harvard's Samuel Stouffer on the colossal, War Department–sponsored *The American Soldier*.[48] While postwar surveys could examine subjective information (attitudes or self-reported behaviors) and objective statistics (income, residence, or health), the method was inherently individualistic. As historian Jean Converse shows, surveys investigated "anything that could be stored and analyzed by the individual record, as *reported by* or *observed of* individuals." Wartime and postwar survey researchers tended, however, to examine the subjective realm and were best at measuring attitudes.[49] After World War II, with significant federal and foundation support, modern social surveys moved to the institutional outskirts of universities, further helping to institutionalize the approach.[50]

In addition, beginning in the mid-1940s and accelerating by the decade's end, enthusiasm for two types of interdisciplinarity, "social relations" paradigms and behavioralism, added to the collection of intellectual and institutional forces encouraging individualistic approaches to the race issue. Established in 1946, Harvard's Department of Social Relations (DSR) replaced the university's Department of Sociology, housed half of the Department of Psychology, and sought to foster exploration of the convergences between sociology, social psychology, cultural anthropology, and clinical psychology.[51] In addition, beginning in 1949 with the Ford Foundation's behavioral sciences initiative, new funding streams encouraged not only anthropologists, psychologists, and sociologists, but also a few "political scientists, economists, and statisticians to reinvent themselves as 'behavioural scientists.'"[52] While behavioralism had a more strongly dispositional slant than social relations frameworks, advocates of both types of interdisciplinarity prioritized the intersections of psychology, culture, and society, and deemphasized the political, economic, and institutional.[53] In so doing, each directed attention away from the intersection of social structure and political economy that had flourished among interwar African American sociologists.

Postwar anticommunism also certainly encouraged racial individualism by providing added incentives for both scientism and behavioralism. In many cases McCarthyism and scientism directly supported each other. Debates over social scientific inclusion in the National Science Foundation from 1945 to 1950 and congressional investigations into the subversive tendencies of social scientists and their funders from 1952 through 1954 each gave scholars added reasons to model their methods and rhetorical style on the purportedly apolitical investigative norms of the natural sciences. These controversies also encouraged scholars to distance themselves from both political-economic analysis and politically divisive topics like race.[54] It is not coincidental, moreover, that behavioral rather than political economic approaches to racial issues came to prominence precisely as anticommunism restructured the priorities of American liberals. While behavioralism did generate some suspicion from the most ardent anticommunists, behavioral theories proved considerably more acceptable than overtly political economic frameworks.[55] Still, the relationship between the Cold War state and the human sciences was complex. Although postwar scholars of race maneuvered around increasingly taboo issues of class, economics, and statism, antiradicalism intersected with the theoretical and methodological pressures just discussed, and with a host of other political pressures (to which we turn next), in aiding the growth of postwar racial individualism.[56]

Methodological and theoretical considerations internal to the social sciences, as well as institutional and financial dynamics associated with the politics of knowledge production, helped to set the intellectual landscape of midcentury debates on race in ways that encouraged racial individualism and created obstacles for proponents of systemic and relational theories. While scientism, survey methods, and the growing stature of psychology were all evident during World War II, these dynamics gained influence in the following decade and intersected with antiradicalism and behavioralism after 1948 to further encourage racial individualism. This intellectual and institutional context was of course deeply intertwined with politics traditionally defined, as War Department support for survey research and McCarthyism's impact on foundations and universities reveals. Still, scientism and behavioralism worked independently of but in ways that converged with antiradicalism to favor theories that framed the race issue in terms of individual perpetrators and victims.

From Redistribution to Rights in the Midcentury Political Context

The evolving midcentury political landscape simultaneously shaped scientists' sense of what kinds of research were useful and what types of reforms were worth pursuing. In addition to internalist dynamics and the politics of knowledge production, traditional political pressures also marked the terrain in which racial individualism took root. These included mounting African American protests against a segregated war for freedom and democracy, increasing concerns with prejudice and domestic racial tensions, declining congressional commitment to the reformist and redistributive elements of New Deal liberalism, the movement of racial issues onto the postwar "liberal agenda," the civil rights movement's successful use of legal strategies and rights discourse in the fight against segregation, and McCarthyism. At times, as when wartime concern with prejudice encouraged antiprejudice education and research on how to improve it, externalist pressures directly shaped evolving research priorities. In other cases, when, for example, declining support for New Deal liberalism, the success of court-based civil rights strategies, and McCarthyism coincided, the midcentury political context encouraged racial individualism indirectly by discouraging alternative reformist priorities.

Relational theories that rooted racial oppression in labor exploitation, interracial competition, and class struggle—and associated agendas for change that either challenged liberal capitalism outright or envisioned an expansive state regulating its excesses and making up for its inequalities— flourished during the Depression and in the first half of the 1940s among civil rights activists, an interracial left, and New Deal liberals. How central the class struggle was to the race struggle had been a point of debate throughout African American political and intellectual life, though many African Americans had long seen access to gainful employment as an essential element of racial justice.[57] The 1930s, however, saw a "proletarian turn" in African American politics and social thought whose repercussions lasted through the mid-1940s and beyond. During the Depression, African American intellectuals sympathetic to socialism and communism emphasized the links between race and class oppression, Justice Department and NAACP lawyers included agricultural and industrial workers' demands in their legal strategies, civil rights activists associated with the Amenia Conference and the National Negro Conference linked calls for racial and economic justice, and traditionally middle-class organizations like the NAACP expanded their working-class membership. Both the African American "popular front" and the "interracial left," groups that often overlapped, situated demands for civil rights within broader calls for interracial unionization, collectivist agricultural experiments, an expanded welfare state, and, at the extremes, challenges to liberal capitalism.[58] In addition, while President Roosevelt was not progressive on racial issues, his early New Deal had a redistributive orientation, seeking to reform not just stabilize capitalism, regulate production, produce (rather than simply train individuals for) jobs, and provide social insurance.[59] Still, the interracial left was politically diverse. Many prominent scholars of race, including sociologist Charles S. Johnson, economist Robert Weaver, and sociologist Louis Wirth remained liberal in political orientation in the 1930s, but others, like political scientist Ralph Bunche, economist Abraham Harris Jr., sociologist E. Franklin Frazier, and sociologist/historian W. E. B. Du Bois, flirted with socialism.[60]

During World War II and in the immediate postwar years, the Depression-era tendency to link race and class oppression slowly began to decline. A watershed moment in the "long civil rights movement," World War II saw civil rights activists capitalize on democratic rhetoric when protesting segregation and discrimination and the social scientific interracial left consistently highlighted this theme.[61] Sociologist Charles S. Johnson, Rosenwald Fund executive Edwin Embree, and philosopher Alain Locke, to name just a few, emphasized the discrepancy between American democratic rhetoric and reality and drew parallels between the African American freedom struggle and international anticolonialism.[62] These years also saw the federal government and the courts emerge as allies for proponents of racial justice, further encouraging rights discourse and discouraging class-based approaches. Northern African American voting blocks, wartime democratic rhetoric, and African American protest eventually led the executive and judicial branch to respond directly to black demands for change. In the late 1940s, as the NAACP scored decisive victories in the struggle against disenfranchisement and segregation in higher education, transportation, and housing, Truman desegregated the military and civil service, and both the Democratic and Republican Parties issued civil rights planks.[63]

Efforts against prejudice and discrimination saw explosive growth during the war, as religious, civic, labor, and educational organizations waged a domestic "war on intolerance." Interwar intercultural educators and religious proponents of intergroup "goodwill" had used educational techniques to ease intergroup tensions, reduce prejudice, and aid the assimilation of second-generation immigrants.[64] However, both the Nazi specter and well-publicized incidents of racial violence between 1943 and 1946 made the need for activism to alleviate domestic racial tensions seem an increasingly pressing national concern.[65] Groups specifically committed to improving race relations, intergroup relations, or human relations—many requesting scientific expertise to inform their efforts—sprouted in the mid- and late 1940s, especially in northern and western cities where wartime African American migration pushed at the boundaries of already overcrowded, segregated neighborhoods.[66] A new sort of professional, the race relations practitioner, was born, along with the National Association of Intergroup Relations Officials.[67] Some advocates of improved race relations joined forces with state and local civil rights activists to pursue legal and legislative change, especially in the North and West where multiracial coalitions for unity waged successful campaigns for fair employment legislation and generally less successful campaigns for open housing in the 1940s and 1950s.[68] Still others, like the National Conference of Christians and Jews, focused largely on changing white attitudes.[69] Although many groups, like the Federal Council of Churches or the American Jewish Congress, opposed legal discrimination, segregation, *and* prejudice, there were crucial distinctions between the civil rights and race relations movements. Civil rights activists had long emphasized that antiprejudice work—such as the accommodationist politics of southern interracialists who called for improved racial understanding but accepted legal segregation—could provide an excuse for avoiding legal, legislative, and direct action strategies for change. As E. Franklin Frazier put it in a 1924 article criticizing efforts to secure racial justice by gaining white allegiance: "The Negro does not want love. He wants justice."[70] This theme emerged in wartime and postwar civil rights activists' debates about how to respond to the rise in race relations activism.

Concerns with Nazi racism and wartime domestic unity also fueled a wave of research on prejudice and the sources of racial tensions that reached a crescendo with *The Authoritarian Personality* (1950) and *The Nature of Prejudice* (1954).[71] The American Jewish Committee's Department of Scientific Research funded the Studies in Prejudice series, while many national religious groups—including the American Jewish Congress, the Anti-Defamation League, the Society of Friends, the American Missionary Association, and the Federal Council of Churches—increased their support for scholarship on the foundations of racial conflict, the sources of prejudice, and the best ways to alter racial attitudes "scientifically."[72] Moreover, foundations, religious organizations, and civic groups turned to sociologists, psychologists, and

1. "If Your Next Neighbors Are Negroes," courtesy of Fisk University, John Hope and Aurelia E. Franklin Library, Special Collections, Race Relations Institutes Collection.

anthropologists for expertise. The University of Chicago–based American Council on Race Relations (ACRR, founded 1944), the Social Science Research Council's Committee on Techniques for Reducing Group Hostility (established 1945), and the Rockefeller Foundation helped leading sociologists publish compilations of existing research to inform activist work.[73] At the request of religious, civic, or educational groups, social scientists also produced many pamphlets—some with snappy titles like *Race Riots Aren't Necessary* or *If Your Next Neighbors Are Negroes*—to educate the public about the dangers of prejudice and discrimination.[74]

Shifts in American liberalism also aided racial individualism's postwar appeal. The wartime employment boom, postwar economic growth, and new alliances between labor and the Democratic Party generated "a new kind of liberalism" that was less critical of the economic order and less redistributive in emphasis than the early New Deal.[75] Congressional support for the redistributive, statist, and reformist elements of New Deal liberalism had begun declining toward the end of the war and continued to decline after Republican victories in the midterm elections of 1946. Even liberal commitment to full employment was unreliable after World War II, as the passage of "the 'badly watered down'" Employment Act of 1946 revealed.[76]

In addition, the language with which many proponents of racial justice pursued desegregation and antidiscrimination legislation—a language of rights—increasingly had an individualistic ring. Of course rights discourse was quite malleable, since it could have negative (civil and political) or positive (social and economic) iterations. Thinkers associated with the postwar social scientific interracial left at times demanded jobs, education, health care, housing, and welfare using notions of positive rights.[77] Still, many postwar efforts to secure "civil rights" in housing and employment relied on theories that envisioned the social good arising from many individuals pursing their private goals in an unfettered marketplace, views with a long though contested history in American political culture.[78] In fact, advocates of open housing and fair employment frequently assumed that discrimination in the distribution of these resources, not insufficient supply, was the crux of the problem.[79] For example, while economist Robert Weaver clearly understood de facto housing segregation as rooted in both law and market processes, much of his work against housing segregation in the 1940s and 1950s sought to remove the legal obstacles, like restrictive covenants, to open occupancy.[80] Negative rights played a central role in state and federal efforts for "civil rights in employment" in the 1940s and 1950s as well. State fair employment laws embodied this individualism by putting the onus on the individual victim to begin the proceedings, suggesting that the only actionable racial inequality was intentionally produced, and requiring attempts at conciliation before sanctioning offending employers.[81]

The Cold War only exacerbated retreats from structural, especially political economic, explanations of racial injustice. As congressional committees searched for domestic subversion in universities, foundations, Hollywood, and even the military after 1947, statism, redistribution, and class analysis generated suspicion throughout both the academy and the civil rights movement. Certainly the Cold War provided a resource to civil rights activists, as African American intellectuals emphasized the international importance of domestic racial injustice and forged an anticommunist anticolonialism that drew links between the struggle for human rights at home and abroad.[82] In this context, postwar antiradicalism ensured that psychological and rights-based approaches to the race issue—frameworks that challenged racism without questioning capitalism—proved especially useful.

Individualistic logics also aided the postwar legal fight against de jure segregation, helping to explain why psychological and rights-based individualism, as well as assumptions about the socially transformative power of education, proved central to reformist debate among integrationist social scientists in the early 1950s. Certainly challenges to legal segregation resisted a structural impediment, though one rooted in legal and institutional structures as opposed to the economic structures Marxists discussed or the social structures Chicago school sociologists identified. In addition, much of the *Brown v. Board* legislation and subsequent implementation involved financial, organizational, and institutional considerations, especially questions of district boundaries, the use of school facilities, pupil placement, and teacher assignment. And yet psychological and rights-based individualism aided the fight against *Plessy* because the legal realm tends to rely on complaints of harm from an aggrieved individual, because NAACP lawyers needed to prove that equally funded segregated schools could never be equal, and because psychological research constituted the new evidence that allowed the case to be reconsidered. Although Charles Houston, Thurgood Marshall, and their colleagues did not advance arguments about white prejudice per se, they employed key components of postwar racial individualism in emphasizing violated rights, opportunity-based egalitarianism, intentional racial animus, and the psychological harm segregation inflicted on African American school children.[83] The postwar racial liberalism that scored a great victory in *Brown v. Board* relied, moreover, on educationalization, the long-standing American tendency to expect education to solve social problems that were too complex and expansive for schools to effectively address alone.[84] In fact, since both school integration and civil rights legislation redistributed resources but could be justified without redistributive logics, that varied social theories could be used to defend these civil rights priorities may well have enabled these civil rights gains in the politically conservative 1950s.

Aspects of the political and intellectual context converged between the end of World War II and the early 1960s in ways that encouraged the psychological, rights-oriented, and educational components of racial individualism and discouraged both systemic and relational thinking on race and redistributive or structural reform. Between 1939 and 1948, wartime support for survey research methods and growing interdisciplinary interest in noneconomic social relations paradigms intersected with subtle rightward shifts in postwar liberalism, civil rights activists' embrace of rights discourse, and expanded antiprejudice activism to encourage sociologists and anthropologists to join the growing ranks of social psychologists bringing scholarly attention to racial attitudes and discriminatory actions. After 1948, while anticommunism favored scientism and behavioralism and dissuaded proponents of racial justice from pursuing redistributive racial reforms, legal successes convinced the NAACP that attacking *Plessy* using rights-based and psychological discourses was timely. Although dispositional, systemic, and relational approaches to the race issue continued to compete after 1944, and even after 1948, they did not compete on equal footing.

My chapters explore how these contextual factors intersected to influence arguments over the significance of prejudice to the race issue in a series of institutions that nurtured the postwar social scientific interracial left but were differently situated in the politics of knowledge production. In all but one setting challenges to racial individualism surfaced but did not fully succeed. The history of these incidents of competition between theoretical and reformist paradigms illuminates the different causal pressures—scientistic, methodological, theoretical, institutional, and political—shaping postwar debate on the race issue, and shaping it differently depending on institutional location.

To situate the case studies that follow, chapter one depicts the rise of racial individualism in postwar psychology, social psychology, and sociology—and the ways the psychology of prejudice, rights-based individualism, and antiprejudice education reinforced one another. The chapter describes how sociological, anthropological, and political economic theories circulated alongside individualistic research on prejudice during the interwar years, how dispositional individualism and the political economy of race relations rested together uncomfortably in Gunnar Myrdal's *An American Dilemma* (1944), and how scientism, behavioralism, and antiradicalism shaped the psychology of prejudice and the sociology of race relations from the late 1940s through the early 1960s.

The second chapter examines the ways scientism, antiradicalism, and behavioralism intersected to shore up racial individualism at the Rockefeller Foundation (RF). Chronicling the foundation's evolving approach to the race issue between the late 1920s and the mid-1960s, chapter two traces changes in RF assumptions about the appropriate relationship between science and politics, disciplinary diversity on the race issue, and who should be involved in social scientific agenda setting. By 1950, as foundation leaders retreated from increasingly contentious racial politics, weathered investigations into their own "subversive activities," and embraced scientism, the RF supported only individualistic research on the race issue and treated the topic as a small subset of larger theoretical interest in the study of "human relations."

Chapter three investigates how two postwar dynamics—the favoring of individualistic social survey methods amid postwar scientism and urban race relations commissions' concerns with the "racial tensions"—together encouraged racial individualism at the University of Chicago's Committee on Education, Training, and Research in Race Relations (CETRRR) between 1947 and 1952. CETRRR was a surprising place for individualism to take root, since Chicago sociology produced the leading systemic approach to race relations in the 1920s and 1930s. In the postwar years, however, although some at CETRRR questioned individualistic approaches to the race issue, methodological considerations and the interests of antiprejudice activists together discouraged critics of racial individualism from pursuing alternative frameworks.

Focusing on Fisk University's yearly Race Relations Institutes (RRI), chapter four shows that racial individualism did not set the terms of theoretical debate in all postwar intellectual arenas. Given the interwar interests of RRI leader sociologist Charles S. Johnson and the social scientific interracial left who attended the yearly meetings, racial individualism was unlikely to take hold in this center of African American intellectual life. Indeed, individualistic survey methods and interdisciplinary behavioralism had only limited influence at the RRI. Still, amid declining support for New Deal liberalism, postwar antiradicalism, and civil rights successes in the courts, pragmatic scholar-activists had a hard time translating systemic and relational theories of the race issue into reform agendas. While theoretical alternatives to racial individualism endured more robustly at the RRI than at the RF or CETRRR, after 1949, RRI scholar-activists acquiesced to brands of racial liberalism about which they articulated theoretical reservations.

Chapter five highlights the importance of political pragmatism to debate on the race issue at Howard University's *Journal of Negro Education* (*JNE*). Since theories that presented race and class as inseparably intertwined flourished at Howard in the 1930s, the *JNE* was also an unexpected location for individualistic theories of or political approaches to the race issue to take root.[85] Like participants in Fisk's RRI, *JNE* authors challenged individualistic theories of the race problem from the mid-1930s through the 1960s. However, two factors encouraged racial individualism to make limited inroads at the *JNE*: the widespread popularity of psychologically informed antiprejudice education during World War II and, after 1950, the NAACP's shift in strategy against legal segregation. Chapters four and five together highlight the fate of the social scientific interracial left, the endurance of theoretical alternatives to racial individualism, and the dilemmas of scale scholar-activists who understood the race issue in terms of oppression and exploitation negotiated in the postwar decades.

An analysis of the National Conference of Christians and Jews' stance toward race relations between the late 1920s and the mid-1960s, chapter six does not describe competition between individualistic and systemic theories of the race issue. Instead, it reveals the politically conservative implications of racial individualism, especially the educational techniques it encouraged. While religious antiracists were important proponents of individualism in racial research and reform, many combined antiprejudice education with support for civil rights legislation and desegregation.[86] The NCCJ, in contrast, legitimated by scientifically imprecise theories of prejudice, used antiprejudice education to justify disengagement from more contentious political work. When "massive resistance" against *Brown v. Board* emerged between 1950 and 1956, both the NCCJ's religious purpose and its focus on educational methods helped leaders rationalize "moderation" on school desegregation.

Racial individualism was often combined with alternative theoretical and strategic approaches and faced competition, even in the years of the paradigm's growth between 1944 and 1964. Dispositional, systemic, and relational approaches to the race issue were never fully mutually exclusive. Psychologists of prejudice acknowledged the importance of context, while economists identified the ways attitudes contributed to the political economy of Jim Crow. The relationship between theory and practice, moreover, was rarely neat and direct. Theoretically sound reforms were not necessarily practical, and most activists called, at least rhetorically, for a multipronged approach to both research and reform. Alternative theoretical and even programmatic visions of the race issue also circulated in the postwar decades. Radical thinkers situated racial oppression and inequality in capitalist structures and suggested that reforms to American capitalism—and frequently global capitalism and imperialism—were necessary to programs for racial justice.[87] Although they frequently relied on rights-based individualism and opportunity-based egalitarianism to do so, many civil rights activists who leaned toward liberalism also targeted the economic manifestations of employment discrimination and housing segregation throughout the rightward moving postwar decades.[88] As we will see, the intellectual undergrounds that moved through Fisk's RRI and Howard's *JNE* nurtured theoretical challenges to racial individualism whose political implications would move onto the national stage in the decade after the passage of the Civil Rights Act of 1964.

Nonetheless, theories of and programmatic approaches to the race issue evolved between the end of World War II and the passage of the Civil Rights Act in ways that had lasting consequences for the American movement for racial justice, the American left, American education, and the variously defined pursuit of racial equality. This evolution involved the expanding popularity of both psychological assumptions about the causal importance of individual beliefs and individualistic survey research methods among postwar psychologists, sociologists, and anthropologists. Sociologists simultaneously began expressing uncertainty about how to rigorously measure "the general situation" in which race relations developed. In the reformist arena, the postwar years saw many activist scholars and civil rights workers emphasize prejudice, individual acts of discrimination, and violated rights, a rhetorical shift that made racialized inequality and the extralegal sources of segregation difficult to fight. The most extreme manifestation of postwar racial individualism involved growing support for scientifically legitimized antiprejudice education, efforts that gained popularity among religious, civic, and educational workers beginning during World War II and fell within a long history of educationalizing social problems.[89] Post-*Brown* civil rights litigation and legislation did redistribute educational resources by integrating many southern schools and directed much federal educational funding to poor and minority children.[90] Nonetheless, conceptions of racism rooted in postwar racial individualism—which reduced racial oppression to prejudice, highlighted questions of intent, and dismissed evidence of inequality of results as inconsequential—had negative consequences. These ideas obstructed educational equalization, blocked much desegregation outside the South, helped roll back southern desegregation, and aided color-blind iterations of racial conservatism in the last three decades of the twentieth century.[91]

Because racial individualism was a framework that many who favored justice and equality supported, because its conservative potential was often hard to see, and because even those who recognized its limitations often acquiesced to its core elements, the paradigm's postwar growth deserves careful examination. The intersecting intellectual, institutional, and political pressures that contributed to the narrowing of debate on the race issue in the two decades following World War II, and the reasons why many scholar-activists who rejected racial individualism in theory felt compelled to support it in practice, are the subject of the chapters that follow.

ONE

Attitudes, Structures, and "Levers of Change": The Social Science of Prejudice and Race Relations

Gunnar Myrdal's training in economics and experience constructing Sweden's welfare state led many to expect a political-economic analysis from *An American Dilemma: The Negro Problem and Modern Democracy* (1944). To a large extent Myrdal delivered. The race problem's roots, he suggested, lay squarely in political economy. African American status as a statistical minority and the fact that "practically all the economic, social, and political power is held by whites" created a situation, Myrdal held, in which "Negroes do not by far have anything approaching a tenth of the things worth having in America."[1] The economist emphasized systemic and relational factors—exploitation, disenfranchisement, and the intricate, violent politics of white supremacy—when explaining African Americans' low economic, political, and social status. His major recommendations for change followed this combination of social structural and political economic logic, as the social engineer called not only for effectively enforced civil rights laws but also for state-led economic planning, industrial restructuring, and political mobilization of northern African American communities.[2]

However, the postwar trajectory of the ambitious synthesis exposes how a study focused squarely on the politics and economics of racial injustice came to be remembered as an investigation of the white conscience. Despite the weight of Myrdal's evidence, the book would be best known for "the American dilemma" thesis, which held that the conflict between the American creed of democracy and equality and the reality of racial discrimination created a mental and moral crisis for white Americans.[3] Myrdal chose the individualistic framing because he wanted to emphasize that the race problem's roots lay in white America to a public used to equating "the race problem" with "the Negro problem," because he worried about offending his sponsors, and because his experience in wartime Sweden made the political importance of irrationality difficult to overlook.[4] The effects of this choice were far-reaching. A clear example of the contested but decisive ascent of racial individualism, many postwar social scientists, religious and civic activists, and philanthropists paid attention to Myrdal's psychological and moral framing and overlooked the political and economic analysis at the heart of the volume.[5]

Myrdal's work came to be known as a study of the white conscience in a particular intellectual, institutional, and political landscape. To situate the case studies that follow, this chapter chronicles the growth of individualistic paradigms for conceptualizing the race issue, and the contexts that nurtured them, in the fields where that growth was especially pronounced: psychology, sociology, and the interdisciplinary behavioral sciences. Racial individualism slowly emerged in psychology and sociology in the 1920s and 1930s, in step with a relatively small antiprejudice education movement whose reformist efforts were often justified by and helped to legitimize research on prejudice. The interwar years also, however, saw the robust flowering of systemic and relational frameworks, especially in sociology and anthropology, which largely overshadowed racial individualism's interwar development. While Myrdal sought to integrate dispositional, systemic, and relational frameworks, his volume represents a turning point in racial individualism's expansion, as psychological and rights-based individualism reinforced each other and drew attention away from his political economic theorizing. In the decade and a half following *An American Dilemma*, the individualism so celebrated in Myrdal's analysis of the race issue took root in academic debate more broadly. Personality-based theories of prejudice gained widespread popularity among psychologists, sociologists associated with structural functionalism presented prejudice and discrimination as aberrations to consensual social norms, and interdisciplinary social relations and behavioral sciences frameworks drew scholarly attention away from political economy.

During and immediately following World War II rightward shifts in American liberalism, advances in survey research, accelerating scientism, the presence of émigré scholars, and antiprejudice activism—and then, after 1949, McCarthyism and behavioralism—intersected to alter scientific agendas on the race issue. In addition, theoretical shifts toward personality theory in psychology and from social ecology to structural functionalism and large-scale quantitative work in sociology favored individualistic approaches to racial research.[6] While in many cases a rightward moving political context made individualistic theories of the race issue increasingly useful in the civil rights struggle, the relationship between social theory and social reform was not always clear-cut. The impracticality of large-scale political economic restructuring led activist-scholars away from reforms that reflected systemic and relational logics. At the same time, the psychology of prejudice did not always support racial liberalism as seamlessly as liberal integrationists might have hoped.

The Psychology of Prejudice and
the Sociology of Race Relations, 1920–44

Research on prejudice expanded in the 1920s and 1930s as psychologists, sociologists, educators, and religious workers responded to the discrediting of theories suggesting prejudice was instinctive, to advances in attitude testing methods, and to religious and educational reformers' ameliorative interests. Although in the first two decades of the twentieth century many social scientists had viewed prejudice as a natural and instinctive response to racial difference, two interwar theoretical developments raised new questions. Columbia University cultural anthropologist Franz Boas's view that racial differences were culturally and historically not biologically determined gained widespread acceptance among racially liberal social scientists, while John Broadus Watson's behavioralist views of psychology suggested that children's beliefs and behaviors were not innate but shaped by stimuli. Both theoretical developments left many scholars searching for explanations for racial prejudice, inequality, difference, and conflict that reached beyond the rejected biological and instinct-based explanations.[7] In addition, beginning in the Progressive Era and continuing through World War I, northern urban reformers sought to assimilate "provisionally white" southern and eastern European immigrants, responded to spikes in nativism, and worried about interracial conflict as the Great Migration accelerated.[8] In this context, psychologists, social psychologists, and sociologists interested in prejudice addressed the sources, nature, and malleability of racial attitudes and built on innovations in quantitative attitude scaling techniques.[9] In contrast, sociologists and anthropologists of race relations (often in dialogue with work by economists, historians, and political scientists concerned with sharecropping, Jim Crow, and southern white supremacy) examined patterns of intergroup interaction and the social, cultural, economic, and political structures that influenced them.Although many scholars of prejudice addressed how the social or cultural context shaped attitudes, the study of prejudice, in contrast to the sociology or anthropology of race relations, required individual units of analysis. Moreover, while interwar studies of prejudice often tested and legitimated educational interventions, the sociology and anthropology of race relations frequently suggested that larger-scale, and often less precisely defined, reforms were needed.[10]

Advances in attitude-based survey research methods encouraged not only psychologists but also many sociologists and anthropologists to focus on racial attitudes in the interwar years. Scholars distinguished attitudes from instincts, ideas, and feelings. They also disagreed about the relationship between private attitudes and publicly expressed opinions and argued about whether attitudes reliably predicted behavior. Nonetheless, survey-based attitude research expanded considerably among academics and pollsters working for government and private corporations during and after World War I.[11] Surveys in contrast to other types of statistical research were organized around "the individual record" and, since it was easier to find large enough "N's" for the study of individuals rather than communities, cities, or corporations, surveys usually measured individual people or households.[12] The refining of attitude scales in the late 1920s, 1930s, and early 1940s— especially advances by Emory Bogardus, L. L. Thurstone, Rensis Likert, R. F. Sletto, and Louis Guttman—provided psychologists and sociologists with better means and added incentives to examine prejudice quantitatively.[13]

Focusing on prejudice did not preclude interest in how the social, economic, and political context, the immediate institutional setting, or the cultural milieu mattered to attitude development, however. In fact, one strand of psychological research on prejudice focused on "contextual effects." The earliest comprehensive social scientific study of prejudice, New York social worker Bruno Lasker's *Race Attitudes in Children* (1929), found that children were "born democrats" but their feelings toward other racial or ethnic groups reflected what they learned from the adults and institutional norms they encountered.[14] In a 1938 survey of literature on racial attitudes, Columbia-trained psychologist Eugene Horowitz (later Hartley) described "sociometric" analyses that assessed at what age school children exhibited preferences for their own racial group and studies of how "community pressures" contributed to prejudice in children.[15] Other psychological (and some sociological) work correlated demographic variables such as region, socioeconomic status, ethnicity, religion, or political affiliation with patterns of prejudice.[16]

Another strand of interwar research on prejudice investigated whether and how education could alter racial attitudes; this work tended to be less concerned with social or cultural context. Educators and religious or social welfare workers produced much applied work on prejudice, although many scientists who were well known for their "basic" scholarship, including University of Pennsylvania sociologist Donald Young, University of Chicago psychologist L. L. Thurstone, and Harvard University social psychologist Gordon Allport, also studied educational interventions. Published in education, social psychology, sociology, and psychology journals between the 1920s and the mid-1940s, much research tested subjects' racial attitudes before and after exposure to various types of education: factual material on the achievements of minority groups or "scientific facts" about the constructed nature of racial categories; emotional material such as movies or literature; college, high school, or elementary school courses; informational pamphlets; cultural performances; tours of minority neighborhoods; or planned interracial contacts. Drawing correlations between attitudes toward and knowledge about minority groups, assessing changes in racial attitudes over time, and comparing the effects of different types of "stimuli" were also popular research topics.[17]

Research on the malleability of prejudice emerged in step with educational and religious efforts to reduce prejudice. Although intercultural educator Rachel Davis DuBois recognized that economic inequality and disenfranchisement represented basic sources of racial injustice, she promoted a decidedly dispositional approach to fostering intergroup understanding that celebrated minority "cultural gifts." Focused largely on school children, the intercultural education movement that DuBois, Hilda Taba, and a few others led beginning in the late 1920s employed cultural performances, curricular interventions, and planned interracial contacts to encourage white tolerance and minority self-esteem.[18] Also gaining steam in the 1920s, religious organizations such as the National Conference of Christians and Jews, the American Jewish Congress, the American Jewish Committee, the Federal Council of Churches, the Fellowship of Reconciliation, and the American Friends Service Committee sponsored antiprejudice educational initiatives and research on their effectiveness.[19] Although professional networks linked researchers to this nascent movement for intergroup goodwill, the relationship between antiprejudice education and scholarship on prejudice was not always direct. Many well-known scholars of race—not only those who studied prejudice but also many who approached the issue from a social structural or political economic perspective—attended Race Relations Institutes run jointly by DuBois and the American Friends Service Committee at Swarthmore College in the 1930s, while others wrote instructional materials for the Bureau for Intercultural Education or pamphlets for the National Conference of Christians and Jews.[20] Research on prejudice often generated findings that were inconsistent or inconvenient for reformers, moreover, while many antiprejudice activists used social science only loosely or selectively.[21] Still, the simultaneous rise of research on and educational efforts to alter prejudice was hardly a coincidence. The psychology and sociology of prejudice and education for tolerance reinforced each other as activists frequently relied on scholarship to legitimize their programing and scholars claimed that activist groups needed their research. Together the two grew through the 1920s, 1930s, and 1940s. Each would generate much new interest as the nation entered World War II.

The individualism of interwar scholarship on prejudice is particularly evident when assessed alongside the broader range of social scientific work on race relations circulating in the 1920s, 1930s, and early 1940s. Prejudice-based theories of the race problem coexisted with robust alternative— systemic and relational—approaches in the interwar years and as war started in Europe. While sociologists and anthropologists had long defined race as a central interest, it was race relations, especially racial conflict and inequality, not prejudice, that these disciplines prioritized.[22] A number of debates divided proponents of the leading interwar approaches to the race issue, the Caste and Class school of social anthropology and the Chicago school of social ecology. Both frameworks, however, took cities, communities, or collectivities as units of analysis and shared a tendency—in contrast to scholarship on prejudice—to de-emphasize the causal importance of individual attitudes.[23]

A cohesive caste system that linked culture, politics, and social mores caused racial oppression and intolerance in Caste and Class theories. Associated with Lloyd Warner, John Dollard, and their students, social anthropologists produced many well-known community studies of southern race relations, including John Dollard's *Caste and Class in a Southern Town* (1937), Allison Davis, Burleigh B. Gardner, and Mary B. Gardner's *Deep South: An Anthropological Study of Caste and Class* (1941), and Hortense Powdermaker's *After Freedom: A Cultural Study in the Deep South* (1939). Warner argued that the American South exhibited the uncommon combination of a caste structure that existed alongside a class structure, while Davis, Powdermaker, Dollard, and the Gardners corroborated these findings empirically. The Caste and Class school described southern white supremacy as a "system of racial subordination" reinforced by "interlocking mechanisms of economic, political, and legal control" and further empowered by sexual taboos that became "ingrained" in the personalities of white and black southerners. Psychology played an important role in Caste and Class thinking, and John Dollard would move toward psychological frameworks by the 1950s, when he explicitly theorized the relationship between economic dislocation and prejudice in *Frustration and Aggression* (1950). In the social anthropology of the 1930s, however, prejudice was part of a multicausal system but not an independently acting, primary source of racial conflict or oppression.[24]

Chicago school social ecologists approached the race issue differently, presenting impersonal, large-scale, social-structural forces, namely technological, economic, and demographic transformations as key agents of change.[25] The University of Chicago's Department of Sociology led the discipline in the 1920s and early 1930s, and Robert Park and Ernest Burgess trained many prominent African American sociologists of race relations, including Charles S. Johnson, E. Franklin Frazier, and Oliver Cromwell Cox.[26] In Chicago school theories, the increasing interdependence of world society amid colonialism, international trade, and migration provided the basic sources of racial conflict and inequality. Arguing that "in the relations of races there is a cycle of events which tends everywhere to repeat itself," Park envisioned an "apparently progressive and irreversible" race relations cycle. Technological and economic changes, he suggested, produced migration, conflict resulting from competition over employment and space, race prejudice as a result of minority efforts to improve social status, and eventually accommodation, assimilation, and the development of a new social equilibrium.[27] The Chicago school did not dismiss attitudes entirely, especially since psychologist W. I. Thomas, social psychologist L. L. Thurstone, and sociologist Emory Bogardus (all of whom devised early quantitative attitude testing methods at the University of Chicago) ensured that their colleagues in the Department of Sociology were familiar with these techniques. Social ecologists, nonetheless, downplay the causal importance of prejudice.[28]

Since interwar social ecology and social anthropology provided tools for conceptualizing the macrosocial, economic, and cultural processes producing racial oppression and conflict, one might expect these views to lead seamlessly to calls for large-scale social restructuring or political economic reforms, as Myrdal did when synthesizing this work in 1944. And yet neither framework gave activists much help because each presented social, cultural, and political-economic structures as existing at such a large scale that they were resistant to change by individuals or the state. Since technological progress, demographic transformation, or closed cultural systems determined American race relations, social ecology and social anthropology frequently implied that gradualism was the best course of action. Park, who was strongly committed to distinguishing objectively produced social science from social reform, was largely untroubled by the fact that his theories suggested change in race relations would occur through the inevitable but gradual process of conflict and accommodation rather than government intervention.[29]

Between 1922 and 1945, however, a number of Park's African American students would root black subordination in what E. Franklin Frazier called "economic and social forces," reject Park's naturalizing of racial oppression, and question his political disengagement. Analyses of northern, urban racial violence by Charles S. Johnson (1922) and E. Franklin Frazier (1935) carefully chronicled evidence of African American exclusion from employment in public and private organizations and relegation to low-paid menial work. Both Johnson and Frazier's interwar analyses of urban rioting exemplified the slippery way discussions of discrimination could combine relational, systemic, and dispositional thinking. Frazier suggested that African American economic exclusion resulted not only from the impersonal social structures Park highlighted but also from many deliberate acts of discrimination that, when institutionalized in workplaces, unions, housing markets, health care systems, schools, and public policy, produced systemic obstacles to black progress. The "extraordinary record of discrimination against the Harlem Negro in the matter of employment" was especially destructive, he argued, since "a denial of the fundamental rights of a people to a livelihood," undergirded "every other problem in the community."[30] While Johnson and Frazier recognized that white racial attitudes were important since they motivated discriminatory actions, it was the institutionalized, systemic character of discrimination that mattered most. Both Park's gradualism and intercultural education were inappropriate responses in this view, since changing law and social policy, not attitudes, was necessary.[31]

Those with a relational leaning also put structures at the center of their causal models, but a focus on economic not social structures distinguished systemic from relational frameworks. In addition, political-economic thought on race emphasized the power, and often the violence, behind white supremacy more fully than Park's vision of naturally developing, inevitable processes of conflict and accommodation. Exploitation theories had a long history in African American social thought, and many scholars like Johnson, Frazier, and economist Robert Weaver integrated social ecological and political economic frameworks. Escalating during the Depression but continuing through World War II, a broad group of non-Marxist, left-leaning social scientists—including many involved with Fisk University's Race Relations Department and Howard University's *Journal of Negro Education*—described economic competition as the source of racial conflict; pointed to the roots of racialized labor exploitation in the histories of slavery, colonialism, and Jim Crow; and conceptualized interracial unionization as essential for racial progress.[32] Prejudice played a role in these theories, but not a primary causal role; instead, prejudice was a rationalization, a series of ideological justifications for exploitation whose primary motivations were economic and political.

In the two decades before Myrdal's *An American Dilemma*, most studies of prejudice acknowledged that larger-scale economic and political forces shaped the norms that contributed to bigotry, but these functioned beyond the range of the analytic lens. The political implications of the psychology and sociology of prejudice were also of a small scale. This was a benefit in the programmatic arena because much research on prejudice led to reform recommendations that were fairly easy to conceptualize, cheap to implement, and not very controversial. In contrast, while systemic and relational theories recognized racial attitudes to be one cog in larger sociological, cultural, and political economic systems, these approaches provided a much broader view that emphasized the causal importance of entities other than individuals. Systemic and relational frameworks also had much more complicated reformist implications. They suggested either that change in race relations could not be engineered or that reform was necessary on a much larger scale than dispositional theories acknowledged. The reforms systemic and relational theories suggested to be necessary included desegregation and civil rights legislation, around which many activists were mobilized but also considerable opposition in the 1930s and 1940s, as well as large-scale social engineering that would become even more fully associated with radicalism in the postwar years.

Political Economy and Racial Individualism in Myrdal's *An American Dilemma*

Gunnar Myrdal's *An American Dilemma* (1944) exemplified and aided a shift in research on the race issue that brought individual prejudice and discrimination to the center of analysis in much social scientific, as well as popular and social policy, discourse.[33] While the Swedish economist and social democrat was most familiar with political economy, *An American Dilemma* synthesized interwar sociology, anthropology, political science, economics, history, and to a limited extent psychology on the race issue. The project's sponsors, Carnegie Corporation leaders Newton Baker and Frederick Keppel, chose Myrdal to lead the giant undertaking on the assumption that neither white nor black Americans nor scholars from colonial countries would be sufficiently objective.[34] A "who's who list" of American scholars of race contributed, however, including sociologists E. Franklin Frazier, Charles S. Johnson, Horace Cayton, John Dollard, and Arnold Rose; anthropologists Lloyd Warner and Allison Davis; historians and economists of slavery and Reconstruction W. E. B. Du Bois, Rupert Vance, and T. J. Woofter Jr.; political scientist Ralph Bunche; and psychologists Kenneth Clark and Eugene Horowitz.[35] Like the research he integrated, and much wartime, foundation-promoted, team-based social science, Myrdal's final product was pulled in multiple directions.[36] Myrdal's central thesis linked psychological individualism and rights-based individualism. It did so by arguing that the denial of civil rights and economic opportunity to African Americans violated American democratic, egalitarian ideals and created much psychological and moral distress for white Americans. The bulk of the volume's evidence, however, as well as much of its theoretical framing and most reformist recommendations, conceptualized the race issue as a question of political economy.

Myrdal essentially presented the race problem as an issue of politics and economics, of power and exploitation. To do so, he synthesized work by economists, political scientists, historians, sociologists, and anthropologists on plantation economies, the Jim Crow South, and discriminatory northern housing and employment markets. The economist carefully described black disenfranchisement, lack of court protection, and exclusion from public services as essential components of southern white supremacy. Presenting a "structure of racial subjugation," he emphasized how vigilante violence enforced black political exclusion and economic exploitation, made clear that lynching was "only the most spectacular example of extralegal violence and intimidation" white southerners employed, and emphasized that African Americans could not depend on court protection.[37] The race issue essentially involved civil and political rights denied, but some of its most pernicious consequences were economic. "The economic situation of the Negroes in America is pathological," Myrdal proclaimed, beginning the discussion of economics, by far the longest segment of the book, by explaining that only a very small proportion of the black population could be considered upper or middle class and the vast majority of African Americans were "destitute."[38] When focusing on the South, he drew together economic literature on southern agriculture and tenancy by Rupert Vance and T. J. Woofter Jr. as well as studies of sharecropping by Charles S. Johnson, Will W. Alexander, and Edwin Embree. Much of this research, as historian Walter Jackson notes, used traditional economic explanations: soil erosion, the overproduction of cotton, short-term credit, little African American land ownership, and African American concentration in the depressed cotton economy. And yet discrimination, a concept economists rarely used before 1944 but that many of the African American sociologists whose work he synthesized employed, was central to Myrdal's analysis.[39]

Myrdal's vision for social engineering also pointed to political, economic, and legal levers for change. The architect of Sweden's welfare state called for the expansion of New Deal labor market regulations, social welfare provisions, and unionization among industrial and agricultural workers.[40] Emphasizing the national dimensions of the race issue, he recommended the planned migration of displaced black agricultural workers to industrial areas in the North and West and expressed hope about postwar full employment. He also envisioned New Deal labor legislation aiding black workers as well as white and antidiscrimination legislation being applied to unions.[41] *An American Dilemma* advocated legal mechanisms for combating discrimination in housing, voting, social services, and criminal justice and suggested increased federal oversight of education and public services in the South to ensure nondiscrimination. Myrdal also recommended the desegregation of northern public housing, challenged discriminatory federal housing policies like redlining, and supported the NAACP's legal efforts against Jim Crow.[42]

Despite Myrdal's political-economic orientation, *An American Dilemma* would be best known for bringing together rights-based individualism and psychological individualism while envisioning an American value consensus. These themes featured centrally in the volume's two most famous concepts: "the American creed" and "the American dilemma." Articulated clearly in the nation's founding documents, the "American creed," as Myrdal defined it, grew out of Enlightenment thinking, British law, American commitment to rationality, and Christianity. This political ideal emphasized individual dignity, equality of all men, and the inalienable rights of "freedom, justice, and a fair opportunity."[43] "The American dilemma" arose when white Americans confronted discrimination that violated the creed but to which they acquiesced and from which they benefited. The psychological and rights-based logics central to the dilemma thesis shared an astructural orientation. Both depicted the social world as the cumulative product of many individual actors' behaviors, suggested the social whole was best controlled by altering the beliefs and behaviors of discriminating individuals or protecting individual rights, and sat uncomfortably alongside Myrdal's political economic concerns.[44]

One place where this disjunction emerged involved Myrdal's treatment of rights. Although Myrdal's vision for social engineering echoed wartime calls for positive rights, the rights Myrdal saw at the heart of the American creed were negative ones.[45] "In principle the Negro problem was settled long ago," Myrdal argued, suggesting that political exclusion and the obstruction of equal opportunity, not economic inequality per se, violated the American creed, but "in practice . . . the Negro in America has not yet been given the elemental civil and political rights of formal democracy."[46] The American dream, Myrdal held further, promised only individual opportunity:

> The ordinary American does not, and probably will not within the survey-able future, raise the demand for full *economic equality* in the meaning of a "classless society" where individual incomes and standards of living would become radically leveled off. Such an ideal would be contrary to the basic individualism of American thinking. It could hardly be realized while up-holding the cherished independence of the individual. . . . It would thus bury the American Dream.[47]

Myrdal's concept of the American creed thus distanced his analysis from the Depression-era interracial left and contrasted with much of his political eco-nomic analysis. Suggesting that the race problem was separable from ques-tions of the inequality produced by capitalism, Myrdal argued that if equal opportunity were secured and negative civil rights were protected, "there would no longer be a *Negro* problem," though "many other pressing social problems would, of course, still remain."[48]

While Myrdal's attention to the white conscience also resonated amid wartime activism for tolerance, Myrdal actually paid relatively little atten-tion to reforming white attitudes. The dilemma thesis was largely evident in the introduction and conclusion of the enormous volume and had emerged late in the project's development. As Walter Jackson has shown, Myrdal de-veloped the thesis only after he had returned home to a Sweden braced for a German invasion. Since he was not familiar with psychological research on prejudice and did not have time to commission a full study, Myrdal only added an appendix by psychologist E. L. Horowitz.[49] Prejudice did play an important role in Myrdal's explicitly multicausal explanation of how racial injustice was perpetuated—the theory of the "vicious circle" that described a reciprocal relationship between prejudice, discrimination, and African American economic, social, and political conditions.[50] Still, prejudice was much more important to the volume's theoretical framing than to the ma-jority of the research it synthesized. Myrdal did call for publicity to make whites aware of employment discrimination and supported the expansion of antiprejudice efforts in American churches, schools, and media, at least in theory. He also criticized the "fatalism" of some sociologists who be-lieved education was irrelevant without far-reaching economic and political change and argued that a substantial and meaningful "*educational offensive against racial intolerance*" had never actually been tried. And yet education was a relatively small part of Myrdal's vision for reform. He recommended challenging prejudice by altering institutional norms rather than gearing antiprejudice efforts to individuals directly.[51] Myrdal's work would be best known for its moral dilemma thesis, but the social democrat and social engineer clearly believed that institutions, labor markets, and social welfare programs, not individual minds, were the best tools for producing needed changes in race relations.

In the postwar political and intellectual context, however, reviewers, policy makers, and social scientists interpreted the book as a call for further research and action on the white conscience. Even Myrdal's critics narrowed in on the American dilemma thesis. Oliver Cromwell Cox called Myrdal's focus on "the American Creed" a "mystification," while Marxist historian Herbert Aptheker appreciated the political economic components of Myrdal's analysis but argued that his individualistic framing was not simply ignorant but "vicious."[52] Ralph Ellison also drew attention to the dilemma thesis, suggesting the volume's main "virtue" was its attention to "how the mechanism of prejudice operates to disguise the moral conflict in the minds of whites produced by the clash on the social level between the American Creed and anti-Negro practices." He saw a "danger in this very virtue," however, since in a true democracy African Americans would not be at the mercy of white benevolence.[53] Among Myrdal's supporters, the project set the terms of discourse on race relations in social scientific, popular, and policy settings for the next two decades. While the American dilemma thesis was not the only factor encouraging individualistic shifts in the social science of race relations, much new research on race in the fifteen years following *An American Dilemma* tended to be social psychological in orientation. Even many sociologists and anthropologists leaned in psychological directions, emphasizing white hearts and minds rather than intergroup conflict, power relations, or the economic sources of racial inequality.[54]

The psychological and rights-based individualism in *An American Dilemma* may have resonated more strongly than Myrdal's political economic analysis because rightward shifts in American liberalism and civil rights politics had begun during and continued immediately following the war.[55] As support for New Deal liberalism declined and many civil rights activists dropped the class-oriented, redistributive notions of racial justice popular during the Depression, Myrdal's work reflected and helped to usher in a postwar racial liberalism that prioritized nondiscrimination, opportunity-based egalitarianism, and education for racial understanding, in addition to legal desegregation.[56] Since Myrdal's enormous, complicated blueprint for state-led social engineering drew on so many different theoretical paradigms, readers could choose which ones seemed most useful. For those who read *An American Dilemma* in a political context that was becoming more conservative than the setting in which Myrdal had written it, the American dilemma thesis likely appeared more actionable than his expansive blueprint for social engineering.

"To Control a Disease Even Though We Cannot Cure It": The Psychology of Prejudice and the Sociology of Race Relations after Myrdal, 1944–60

Research on prejudice and race relations expanded between the publication of *An American Dilemma* and the early 1960s but also narrowed in focus. The postwar years saw "a flood" of scholarship on prejudice by psychologists, sociologists, and a few anthropologists that initially addressed anti-Semitism but eventually came to focus on antiblack attitudes and African American psychology.[57] While much applied psychology and sociology continued to test antiprejudice education, basic psychology still explored the cognitive and emotional sources of racial attitudes. However, the presence of émigré scholars, wartime support for survey research methods, and activist concern with prejudice contributed to a major psychological innovation—personality-based theories of prejudice. This approach to the race question implied that racial animus originated in intertwined cognitive and emotional structures and could be examined regardless of social or political economic context. Concern with prejudice, a tendency to present discrimination as aberrational, and declining interest in the political economic sources and conflictual bases of race relations permeated important new sociological frameworks as well.[58] The decline of the Chicago school, debates over the scientific stature of the social sciences, and interest in social relations paradigms encouraged these shifts in the sociology of race relations in the immediate postwar years. By the late 1940s, McCarthyism and behavioralism provided added incentives for sociologists concerned with race to focus on prejudice and discrimination. Although theories of the prejudiced personality at times suggested that racial tolerance might be difficult to engineer, generally postwar psychological and sociological approaches to the race issue aided postwar racial liberalism.

The wartime institutionalization of survey research and this method's movement into universities immediately after the war provided financial and institutional incentives for scholars of race to focus on prejudice. The demands of war mobilization, the constraints of War Department work, and technocratic impulses associated with improving morale had all encouraged quantitative studies of attitudes during World War II.[59] When survey researchers returned to their universities after the war, they brought with them new experience in constructing measures, a new knowledge about how to secure federal support, new professional networks, and new appreciation for the ways applied work could enhance basic scholarship.[60] While sociologist Samuel Stouffer, who ran the War Department's production of *The American Soldier*, had warned that the volume might prove dangerous "if the survey methods on which it relies for so much of the data are regarded as the ideal," university-based survey researchers often engaged in a type of "sociologically (or demographically) informed applied psychology" that drew on statistical methods from applied psychology, polling, and market research.[61] And yet as postwar survey research centers received considerable foundation, federal, and industry support, some sociologists worried that these large-scale "number crunching" organizations too often depicted society as "'a mere aggregation of disparate individuals'" and turned attention away from important questions of social structure.[62] Organizations like Columbia University's Bureau of Applied Social Research (BASR, established 1940); the University of Chicago's National Opinion Research Center (NORC, established 1941); and the University of Michigan's Survey Research Center (established 1946) and Institute for Social Research (established 1949) only paid occasional attention to racial issues. Nonetheless, all exhibited the turn toward individual measures, quantification, and even a tendency to focus on attitudes rather than behaviors that would influence postwar psychological and sociological research on race.[63]

University and foundation support for interdisciplinary social science, social relations, and the behavioral sciences also aided the individualizing of the race issue and its separation from questions of political economy among psychologists, sociologists, and some anthropologists. Based on the assumption that "interdisciplinarity was closely related to creativity," many centers for interdisciplinary social science emerged during and after World War II, including at Harvard, Yale, Princeton, Berkeley, UCLA, Illinois, Minnesota, and Washington State.[64] As part of this war-generated enthusiasm for interdisciplinarity, concern with the study of social or human relations coalesced, most notably in Harvard's Department of Social Relations (DSR). Led by sociologist Samuel Stouffer, psychologist Gordon Allport, and sociologist Talcott Parsons, the DSR differed from most interwar experiments in interdisciplinarity in its commitment to theory generation (identifying comprehensive, generalizable, law-like patterns when describing the social world) and interdisciplinary theoretical integration.[65] And yet it was theoretical synthesis within a limited set of disciplinary perspectives that experiments in "social relations" pursued. As historian of sociology Howard Brick has shown, the emergence of social relations paradigms among sociologists represented a theoretical transition in which newer social scientific disciplines of sociology, cultural anthropology, and social psychology gained prominence at the expense of politics and economics.[66] Providing added institutional and financial support for theoretical tendencies already underway, the major foundations encouraged the behavioral shift the DSR exhibited. The Ford Foundation, which made the behavioral sciences one of its five program areas and established the Center for the Advanced Study of the Behavioral Sciences in 1949, took the lead, but the Carnegie Corporation, Social Science Research Council, and Rockefeller Foundation also aided interdisciplinary programs in human relations, social relations, or the behavioral sciences in the early 1950s.[67]

While the institutionalization of survey research, social relations, and behavioralism all provided postwar psychologists and sociologists with reasons to prioritize attitudes, wartime reformist concerns with prejudice and racial tensions legitimized much action-oriented psychological and sociological research on the race issue into the postwar years. Psychologists and sociologists of prejudice continued to investigate many of the applied topics that had occupied them in the 1920s and 1930s, examining school-based and mass media programs to fight prejudice and expressing new interest in planned interracial contacts.[68] As residential and school desegregation occurred in some northern communities and in the military during World War II, scholars, especially sociologists, also conducted "natural experiments" by studying integration in workplaces, housing projects, social service agencies, schools, and churches.[69]

Much applied psychology focused on the malleability of racial attitudes, but the discipline's predisposition to investigating individual minds also led psychologists with "basic" interests to root prejudice in cognitive and emotional processes that could be investigated with minimal reference to sociological, political economic, or historical contexts.[70] For example, Gordon Allport made clear in his 1954 *The Nature of Prejudice* that many large-scale political economic and social structural factors contributed to the race problem, aimed to highlight "plural causation," and noted that "realistic conflict of interests" motivated intergroup conflict. He nonetheless saw individuals as the most important—and explainable—causes of racial injustice and inequality.[71] *The Nature of Prejudice* defined prejudice as "an antipathy based upon a faulty and inflexible generalization" and excluded discrimination from the definition, though emphasizing that it was the most damaging result.[72] Allport claimed that "it is possible to hold the individualistic type of theory without denying that the major influences upon the individual may be collective," but some critics were not convinced.[73] Sociologist Arnold Rose worried that Allport naturalized prejudice by overemphasizing its acontextual cognitive and emotional roots.[74]

These theoretical commitments led Allport to contribute to the major new postwar development in psychological thinking on prejudice: theories of prejudiced personalities. The approach was most clearly exhibited in the American Jewish Committee–sponsored *The Authoritarian Personality* (TAP, 1950), which was coauthored by émigrés Theodor Adorno (a sociologist) and Else Frenkel-Brunswik (a psychologist), as well as US born psychologists Daniel Levinson and R. Nevitt Sanford. Another émigré, Frankfurt school sociologist Max Horkheimer helped conceptualize the project.[75] TAP drew on longitudinal, clinical research that some émigré psychoanalysts favored and new quantitative cross-sectional approaches in which investigators related prejudiced attitudes to other aspects of an individual's social outlook using scaling devices.[76] And yet reformist concerns shaped the project's origins as much as theoretical ones. When explaining why the Studies in Prejudice series focused on the personal and psychological rather than the social or political origins of prejudice, series editors Max Horkheimer and Samuel H. Flowerman suggested that the desire to improve popular antiprejudice educational techniques led researchers to a psychological approach. They admitted that they may have "placed undue stress upon the personal and the psychological rather than upon the social aspect of prejudice" but emphasized that this was not as a result of personal preference or "failure to see that the cause of irrational hostility is in the last instance to be found in social frustration and injustice." Instead they chose a psychological approach because their aim was to eradicate, not just to explain, prejudice. "Eradication means re-education, scientifically planned on the basis of understanding scientifically arrived at," Horkheimer and Flowerman noted, "and education in a strict sense is by its nature personal and psychological."[77]

Adorno and his colleagues de-emphasized the social, economic, or political context of prejudice, instead suggesting that the sources of racial attitudes lay in a coherent structure of personality. The authors established quantitative scales for measuring ethnocentrism, authoritarianism/fascism, and anti-Semitism and found that prejudiced individuals tended to express hostility toward many minority groups. They also emphasized the importance of hierarchical parenting styles to tendencies towards prejudice, adding this characteristic to the host of emotional and cognitive traits that prompted bigotry.[78] Prejudice in this view was not primarily a social problem but a psychic disorder, one that was closely tied to other personality traits and cognitive characteristics.[79] While some criticized its psychological structuralism (a term psychologists used disparagingly to denote theories that rooted belief and behavior entirely in the psyche), *The Authoritarian Personality* received widespread publicity and generated a wave of research on the topic.[80] In a 1953 survey of scholarship on racial and ethnic conflict, sociologist Robin M. Williams described work on the "personality correlates of prejudice" as the largest research area in this broad field.[81]

Synthesizing TAP, his own mid-1940s research on prejudice in college students, as well as studies of prejudiced children and adults by many other psychologists, Allport's *The Nature of Prejudice* also emphasized the importance of prejudiced and tolerant personalities.[82] The most critical finding of recent psychological research on prejudice, he argued, was that for those for whom prejudice served a crucial function within the personality structure, prejudice was interwoven into "a single and unitary style of life," and a "whole habit of thinking."[83] Theorists of the prejudiced personality made clear that not all individuals who exhibited prejudice could be characterized as prejudiced personalities; for some prejudice involved "blind conformity with prevailing folkways."[84] In addition, Allport's interest in prejudiced personalities may also have represented an effort to add factors like family and community socialization to arguments about the cognitive and emotional bases of prejudice. Still, since they generally focused on personality structure and family practices with only very limited attention to the social, political, or economic context, personality-based theories of prejudice represented the most individualistic of the range of approaches to the race problem circulating in postwar America.

At the same time, these theories actually disrupted the neat fit between psychological individualism and antiprejudice education. Neither Allport nor the TAP authors were willing to estimate the precise number of prejudiced personalities, but they suggested that change in racial attitudes would be very difficult to engineer for the most bigoted.[85] In fact, a great irony of *The Authoritarian Personality* is that though researchers chose a psychological approach in order to inform educational practices, they concluded that the most prejudiced were unlikely to respond to education. While Allport held out hope that psychotherapy might be useful, Adorno and his colleagues believed authoritarian personalities would not respond well to therapy and efforts to alter child-rearing patterns might also fail.[86]

Writing as committed racial liberals amid a flurry of antiprejudice activism and mounting progress toward desegregation, however, Allport and the TAP authors supported these central elements of racial liberalism. They maneuvered around complicated dilemmas of scale—in which their theories suggested that popular antiprejudice efforts were too limited to be effective at combating not only the full extent of the race issue but even individual prejudice—by compartmentalizing scholarly and political identities. The TAP authors noted that most of the measures employed by race relations organizations "are concerned with the treatment of symptoms or particular manifestations rather than with the disease itself." They still supported these partial solutions, however, because they did not want "a grasp of the true enormity of the fundamental problem" to discourage activists. "Some symptoms are more harmful than others," Adorno and his colleagues concluded, "and we are sometimes very glad to be able to control a disease even though we cannot cure it."[87] Allport also compartmentalized theoretical and practical priorities when supporting antiprejudice education. He produced antiprejudice pamphlets such as "Bigots in our Midst" (1944), "The ABC's of Scapegoating" (1948), and "The Resolution of Intergroup Tensions" (1952) for B'nai B'rith, the Anti-Defamation League, and the National Conference of Christians and Jews.[88] When surveying literature on prejudice for an NCCJ pamphlet, he acknowledged the utility of reforming attitudes, even by using facts (an approach he found theoretically faulty), as part of a broader civil rights agenda. "Change must begin somewhere," he explained, resisting "the irrationalist position that invites us to abandon entirely the traditional ideals and methods of formal education." "Facts may not be enough," he argued, "but they still seem indispensable."[89]

In the case of civil rights law and desegregation, theories of the prejudiced personality proved more useful than they did for advocates of antiprejudice education, though Allport was also strategic in linking research and activism on this issue. *The Authoritarian Personality* found that antidiscrimination laws might be effective in reducing prejudice since the prejudiced generally accepted authority.[90] Allport's support for legal desegregation was especially ardent. He helped prepare statements of social scientific evidence used in school desegregation litigation and dedicated a chapter of *The Nature of Prejudice* to the topic.[91] As evidence of his willingness to be theoretically strategic in the political realm, Allport largely drew on sociological and legal theories—not on his own research— to legitimize desegregation. He emphasized that antidiscrimination law and desegregation were necessary to secure African American rights not to reduce prejudice. He also cited sociological research on the negative effects of discrimination on minority groups, the tendency for resistance to civil rights law to be short-lived, and the possibility of smooth transitions to desegregation in military units and public housing.[92] When psychology provided ammunition in the battle for desegregation, he certainly emphasized this too. Allport suggested that segregation made equal status planned contacts impossible, that education might reduce prejudice in individuals who did not exhibit prejudiced personalities, and that law could affect "inner habits of thought and feeling" by controlling their outward expression.[93] Seeing some feasible reform as preferable to none at all, Allport and the TAP authors dismissed the challenges character structure theories of prejudice posed to antiprejudice education, especially when talking to reformers, and drew selectively on research when discussing legal desegregation.

Sociologists also directed increased attention to prejudice and discrimination, and revealed declining concern with the political economic sources of fraught race relations, in the decade and a half after the publication of *An American Dilemma*. A theoretical shift in the discipline was largely responsible for this new attention to the individual. Structural functionalism, the consensus-oriented framework associated with Harvard sociologist Talcott Parsons and his students, replaced Chicago school conflict-based theories of social change as the leading sociological paradigm by the early 1950s. Structural functionalism, as the name suggests, did have a systemic orientation since it presented discrete social processes in terms of their utility in and contribution to the functioning of a larger social system. When applied to racial issues, however, the approach tended to encourage individualism by minimizing intergroup conflict, obscuring political economy, and presenting prejudice and discrimination as individual aberrations to otherwise cohesive, integrated social systems.[94]

Although some sociologists had questioned social ecology in the 1930s, by the early 1950s sociologist more broadly moved away from the hallmarks of Chicago school approaches: attention to the intertwined nature of social structure and political-economy, community study methods, and the assumption that intergroup conflict was inevitable and necessary for progress in race relations. Historians debate why the Chicago school paradigm declined. Some point to problems of succession in the department, others emphasize wartime-generated demographic shifts among sociologists, and still others suggest Chicago school theories and methods were out of step with the emphases on scientism, quantification, and the search for general laws among federal and private funders.[95] The Society for the Study of Social Problems still provided a home for the "residue of reformists, ethnographers, radicals, and critics," but these thinkers functioned outside new centers of sociological power at Harvard, Columbia, and the big foundations.[96] Where Chicago school style social ecology did continue, as we will see, was in second-tier colleges and universities—a designation that for foundation executives included even the most elite HBCUs.[97] Still, by the early 1950s sociology's "self-proclaimed mainstream" of Talcott Parsons and Samuel Stouffer at Harvard and Robert Merton (a student of Parsons) and émigré Paul Lazarsfeld at Columbia "rejected ethnographic and institutional analysis and . . . embraced big project sociology . . . emulating the paradigm-shaping big science" of the emerging military-scientific establishment. This shift involved an embrace of large-scale quantitative survey research on the one hand and DSR style theory development on the other, both of which had implications for the study of race relations.[98]

A related factor contributing to growing interest in prejudice among sociologists by the late 1940s and early 1950s was that structural functionalism emerged in step with commitments to theoretical integration that brought sociologists and psychologists more fully into one another's theoretical orbit. Sociologists did not simply parrot social psychological approaches to racial issues after World War II, but social psychology influenced the postwar sociology of race relations more strongly than previously.[99] In the 1950s, two of the most widely cited volumes on race relations in sociology journals were Adorno and colleague's *The Authoritarian Personality* and Allport's *The Nature of Prejudice*.[100] At Harvard's DSR, Parsons's commitment to theoretical synthesis contributed to this interdisciplinary borrowing.[101] While Parsons had expressed concern with socioeconomics in the interwar years, by 1946 the sociologist had shifted his emphasis from the "region where politics and economics met sociology to that marked by the 'boundary' sociology shared with culture and personality."[102] Parsons wrote little about race early on, but his attention to the subject in the early 1950s drew strongly on Allport. The essay on race in *Toward a General Theory of Action*, the 1951 edited volume by Parsons and Edward Shils that stood as an attempt at theoretical integration by the DSR faculty, was an overview by Allport of many of the themes addressed in *The Nature of Prejudice*. Even as late as 1965, when Parsons and psychologist Kenneth Clark edited *The Negro American*, Parsons's analysis of racial issues began with a social psychological orientation and echoed Myrdal's dilemma thesis in suggesting that discrimination diverged from more characteristic American democratic values.[103]

Structural functionalism also had an individualistic tendency when turned to the race issue because the framework—in distinct contrast to Chicago school emphasis on conflict—postulated a consensual social order. Presenting social processes in terms of their utility in and contribution to the functioning of a larger social system, structural functionalism depicted society as a coherent and self-regulating system that "tended toward equilibrium."[104] The framework emphasized social stability, shared values, and integration as both the social norm and the objective.[105] Elements of the social order that defied integration—in this case prejudice and discrimination—were treated as exceptions to the norm. Functionalists therefore tended to assume that change in race relations was possible without substantial social disruption. Representing, as sociologist Howard Winant notes, "the *paradigmatic expression of the civil rights movement in the sociology of race*," functionalists suggested that racial stability and justice were possible with a reorientation of American values, a lessening of prejudice, and an end to discrimination, rather than a restructuring of the American economy or the relationship between social groups.[106]

The major contribution that functionalist sociologists made to the study of race relations in the late 1940s and early 1950s involved analyses of discrimination. Columbia sociologist Robert MacIver, who was partially identified with the paradigm, argued that discrimination, "the action itself," must be clearly distinguished from prejudice, "the disposition to act," since reforms in the "moral or ideological arena" were insufficient without legal and legislative change.[107] And yet MacIver, his Columbia colleague Robert Merton, and fellow functionalist Robin M. Williams Jr. all ultimately remained constrained by individualism. Merton sought to expand scholarly attention beyond the psychological focus on prejudice by showing that the prejudiced did not always discriminate, that some who engaged in discriminatory actions were not prejudiced, and that institutional context determined whether prejudice was translated into discrimination.[108] Williams's work, as we will see in chapter two, challenged Adorno's and Allport's narrow focus on personality by examining prejudice and discrimination with a careful eye to the ways different situational contexts shaped belief and behavior.[109] Still, this line of analysis, in contrast to interwar social ecology or political economy, ultimately sought to understand why individuals thought and behaved as they did. In fact, in its treatment of discrimination, structural functionalism exemplified broader shifts in postwar sociology toward noneconomic, apolitical "social relations" frameworks.[110]

One factor contributing to this noneconomic, apolitical leaning in the sociology of race relations involved economists' and political scientists' approaches to the race issue. With the notable exception of African American labor and housing economist Robert Weaver, who criticized his discipline's disengagement from racial questions, economists tended to be quiet on the topic in the late 1940s and 1950s. This reticence was due in part to anticommunism, in part to the field's turn toward macroissues, and in part to the discipline's retreat from historicism and institutionalism, approaches that had been popular in the 1920s and 1930s and might have been profitably applied to the study of discrimination.[111] Mainstream political scientists also disengaged from racial issues, again with some exceptions, such as African American political scientist Ralph Bunche.[112] In fact, developments in economics and political science combined with shifts away from Chicago school paradigms and the prioritizing of large-scale theoretical integration and quantitative survey work to create a situation that troubled many sociologists of the race issue. While many rejected Chicago school and social psychological models as insufficient and called for attention to social structure, power relations, and the foundational role of intergroup conflict, it was not until the mid-1960s that sociologists would successfully develop new systemic and relational frameworks.[113]

Theoretical currents that challenged racial individualism did exist in the 1950s, though these often circulated outside new centers of sociological power. One strand of thought built on Johnson and Frazier's interwar work on the urban North to articulate a budding concept of institutional discrimination in which harms could be perpetuated by institutions regardless of individual actions or intentions. MacIver's edited volume *Discrimination and National Welfare* highlighted the slipperiness of the concept of discrimination, since it included essays that treated discrimination through dispositional and systemic lenses. While Merton exemplified a dispositional approach, essays by Robert Weaver on housing discrimination and by anthropologist Ira de A. Reid on legal segregation exposed the ways many individual acts of discrimination functioned systemically—like a market—to exclude African Americans from whole sectors of the economy or entire neighborhoods.[114] A number of young sociologists associated with the University of Chicago's CETRRR would also, following Weaver's lead, emphasize the importance of collusion between real estate interests and federal housing loan programs that systematized housing discrimination.[115] Relational thinkers like sociologist Oliver Cromwell Cox and Marxist historian Herbert Aptheker continued to present the race problem as rooted in capitalist exploitation, though they worked from the margins of the academy. Like Cox, Aptheker criticized Myrdal for "deciding that the all-important item in the Negro question is the state of mind of the white man" and for ignoring the ways "the oppression and super-exploitation of the American Negro" as well as the prejudice it generated existed because it profited "America's propertied interests."[116] The main problem with *An American Dilemma*, Aptheker held, zeroing in on what distinguished structural functionalism from social ecology, was that Myrdal assumed "an identity of interests and values as between the Negro people and the 'accepted standards of the controlling class.'"[117] Although admitting communist sympathies was professional suicide in the early 1950s, as we will see, many non-Marxist social scientific proponents of civil rights also assumed that prejudice derived from political and economic sources and fundamental conflicts of interests.

Frazier had called for attention to the structural components of the race issue in 1948, Williams identified the problem of atomism in research on racial issues in 1947 and again in 1953, and Herbert Blumer raised the issue in 1958, but the tide of mainstream sociology would only begin to turn in the late 1950s. By then, Arnold Rose, Pierre L. van den Berghe, Lewis Killian, and R. A. Schermerhorn began criticizing psychological reductionism, called for sociologists to return to the field's traditional attention to structures and systems, and drew attention to power, revealing the direction the field would move in the mid-1960s.[118] Another factor that may have contributed to the return of structural thinking on racial issues by the mid-1960s among sociologists is that economists and political scientists reentered the conversation. After University of Chicago economist Gary Becker published *The Economics of Discrimination* in 1957, African American urban unemployment began gaining widespread national attention by the mid-1960s, and some economists started emphasizing the importance of "automation" to black joblessness, economists reemerged at the center of conversations about racial inequality.[119] It was not until the late 1960s that political scientists also reentered the debate in force.[120]

In the decade and a half following Myrdal's monumental work, institutional, methodological, and theoretical pressures converged with postwar antiradicalism to encourage racial individualism in psychology, where this emphasis was expected, and in sociology, where it was more surprising. The dynamics favoring racial individualism among psychologists and sociologists had sources in both wartime concern with prejudice and in models of interdisciplinary, survey research, whose quantifiable character proved appealing amid the maturing of postwar scientism. In the immediate postwar years, moreover, calls for theoretical integration from elite research centers like Harvard's DSR helped to explain why sociologists concerned with race increasingly took on psychological assumptions. Enthusiasm for noneconomic, apolitical social relations paradigms, combined with social ecology's decline, also shifted sociological attention away from the intersections of social structure and political economy so central to the interwar "Golden Age of Negro Sociology." Focused on individual prejudice and acts of discrimination, much postwar sociological and psychological thought on race fell neatly within new behavioral paradigms and provided a language for discussing the race issue that avoided anticommunist suspicion. Alternative currents persisted, especially in HBCUs, in interracial networks of activist social scientists, and among radical thinkers, but it would not be until the mid-1960s that social conflict, power relations, or the economic sources of racial injustice would permeate mainstream social scientific thought on race.[121] Although the fit between racial individualism and racial liberalism was not always seamless, generally psychological and sociological turns toward prejudice and discrimination aided a postwar racial liberalism that in its focus on white discrimination and violated black rights also leaned toward individualism.

While Allport clearly admitted his psychological leanings, *The Nature of Prejudice* warned against the dangers of all kinds of "structuralism" or "closed-system" theories.[122] Arguing for a "multi-causal" analysis and a "many-pronged attack" on both prejudice and discrimination, the social psychologist presented the relationship between different disciplinary approaches to the race issue as sequential:

> A person acts with prejudice in the first instance because he perceives the object of prejudice in a certain way. But he perceives it in a certain way partly because his personality is what it is. And his personality is what it is chiefly because of the way he was socialized (training in family, school, neighborhood). The existing social situation is also a factor in his socialization and may also be a determinant of his perceptions. Behind these forces lie other valid but more remote causal influences. They involve the structure of society in which one lives, long-standing economic and cultural traditions, as well as national and historical influences of long duration. While these factors seem so remote as to be alien to the immediate psychological analysis of prejudiced acts, they are, nonetheless, important causal influences.[123]

Allport suggested that dispositional, systemic, and relational frameworks did not necessarily compete, since most theories called attention to an important component or causal factor "without implying that no other factors are operating."[124] Instead, various theoretical frameworks, including the economic determinist's position, worked in a complementary, sequential fashion to explain a multifaceted problem. In contrast to Myrdal's interdisciplinary synthesis, however, Allport believed it was impossible to blend these alternative theories into one. "There is no master key," he argued. Instead, "what we have at our disposal is a ring of keys, each of which opens one gate of understanding."[125] What this view of theoretical complementarity did not acknowledge, however, was the ways some theories could obscure others. This could occur within the same work, as the reception of *An American*

Dilemma shows. This pattern could also emerge among hierarchically arranged and unequally funded scholars and disciplines. By presenting Oliver Cromwell Cox's relational approach, which received such scant attention when it was published in 1948, as simply one of many explanatory "keys" on a crowded ring, Allport obscured the political, financial, and institutional factors that favored some views over others.

Dispositional, systemic, and relational theories of the race issue all circulated in the interwar years and were brought together, albeit uncomfortably, in Myrdal's *An American Dilemma*. Highlighting the ways psychological individualism, rights-based individualism, and antiprejudice education reinforced one another, however, Myrdal's dilemma thesis had a wider influence than the political economy at the heart of his volume in the decade and half following the book's publication. Between 1944 and the early 1960s racial individualism expanded among psychologists and sociologists while conflict-oriented social structural paradigms and relational theories faced significant obstacles. The postwar setting in which *An American Dilemma* shaped subsequent research was as important to the volume's reception as the text itself. Intellectual pressures, including scientism, the decline of social ecology, support for social relations paradigms, concerns with theoretical integration, and behavioralism proved decisive in this setting. Political dynamics, notably antiradicalism and enthusiasm for antiprejudice education, were simultaneously important to racial individualism's expansion.

In fact, as the chapters that follow will reveal more precisely, the political and intellectual incentives favoring racial individualism frequently reinforced one another. In part this was because while not all causes of a social problem represented appropriate levers of change, assumptions about which levers were available often shaped research agendas.[126] The scale of reform that systemic and relational theories implied to be necessary did not seem feasible as congressional politics moved rightward and anticommunist sentiments raised questions about state-led redistribution and class-oriented politics in the late 1940s and early 1950s. Considerations related to scale also favored reforms, like antiprejudice education, that were uncontroversial because of their limited scope. Allport made clear in the conclusion to *The Nature of Prejudice* that American support for educational solutions to social problems ensured that these approaches might be effective, regardless of what social science found. As he explained:

> Americans, for example, seem to have great faith in the changeability of attitudes. The goliath of advertising in this country is erected on this faith; and we are equally confident in the power of education. Our system itself rejects

the belief that "you can't change human nature" . . . American science, philosophy, social policy incline markedly toward "environmentalism." While this
faith may not be entirely justified, the point is that the faith itself is a factor
of prime importance. If everyone expects attitudes to change through education, publicity, therapy, then of course they are *more likely* to do so than if no
one expects them to change. Our very gusto for change may bring it about, if
anything can.[127]

An increasingly popular strain in postwar thought on the race problem—
one that also generated considerable resistance—rested on this assumption.

TWO

"Data and Not Trouble": The Rockefeller Foundation and the Social Science of Race Relations

In 1930 Charles S. Johnson published a Rockefeller-funded survey of statistical material on African American life titled *The Negro in American Civilization*. The Chicago school–trained sociologist adhered carefully to standards of scientific objectivity. He presented enormous amounts of statistical data and de-emphasized the relationship between legal segregation, labor exploitation, and the social problems the research exposed. And yet not all readers considered Johnson's compilation apolitical. In "Mute Facts about the Negro," labor leader Benjamin Stolberg criticized Johnson's research for being "correlated to each other but to no social issue, and above all sterilized of all significance." Accusing Johnson of being "the ablest sociological diplomat in the country, certainly in the colored world," Stolberg knew the reason for Johnson's reticence. Having worked tirelessly to interest great foundations in the problems facing African Americans, Johnson was well aware that the "secretariat of this *noblesse oblige* wants data and not trouble."[1]

Between the 1920s and the early 1960s Rockefeller philanthropy struggled to delineate "data" from "trouble" by supporting social science and social reform on the race issue while avoiding involvement in racial politics. In the 1920s and 1930s, Rockefeller philanthropy encouraged applied social science and underwrote diverse disciplinary approaches to the study of race relations in part because a desire to confront the social problems affecting black communities influenced scholarly agendas. The foundation's long history of ties to southern moderates ensured that interwar Rockefeller philanthropy consistently accommodated segregation. Still, both the Laura Spellman Rockefeller Memorial (LSRM) and Social Science Research Council (SSRC), two Rockefeller subsidiaries, developed an action-oriented approach to race relations scholarship that generated careful investigations of the cultural, sociological, economic, and political forces affecting black life.[2] Rockefeller philanthropy also involved activists in scientific agenda setting and assumed interracial collaboration was essential.[3] And yet an organizational separation of social science and social reform within Rockefeller philanthropy, which the LSRM's disillusion made concrete in 1928, disrupted the interwar action-oriented model of race relations social science.[4]

The immediate post–World War II years saw behavioral frameworks and antiradicalism increasingly shape Rockefeller research agendas on race. Produced for the Rockefeller Brothers Fund (RBF) in 1946, the Creel Report recognized that multiple factors caused racial injustice, but assumed philanthropy could only appropriately intervene in apolitical issues. Widespread wartime concern with prejudice also led the RF to establish a Committee on Techniques for Reducing Intergroup Hostility in 1945 that employed Robin M. Williams Jr. to publish *The Reduction of Intergroup Tensions* (1947). Although this volume acknowledged that the sources of the race issue rested in politics, economics, culture, and social organization, Williams presented white racial attitudes as more easily amenable to reform than large-scale social or economic structures. Exposing the parallel trajectories of postwar behavioralism and antiradicalism, in the same years that Williams zeroed in on the psychological and interpersonal roots of prejudice, Dana Creel warned RBF leaders to maintain distance from civil rights groups making demands on government.

The RF's treatment of the race issue transformed even more markedly by the early 1950s when the social science of race relations was subsumed into the interdisciplinary, theoretically oriented, behaviorally focused field of "human relations." One reason for this shift in approach is that scientism took on newfound importance amid debates over social scientific inclusion in the National Science Foundation (NSF) and congressional investigations into foundation "subversion."[5] In addition, following Harvard's Department of Social Relations and the Ford Foundation, the RF joined the chorus of postwar sociologists, anthropologists, and psychologists enthusiastic about interdisciplinary behavioralism, an amorphous set of theories that tended to emphasize the causal importance of individual actors.[6] Both scientism and behavioralism ensured that leaders of a 1953 RF agenda-setting Conference on Research in Human Relations assumed only researchers at the most elite, white research universities should set scientific agendas and receive support. Conference leaders also prioritized theory generation and quantification—and overlooked the political economic theories and case-based methods that had been the hallmark of the interwar African American Chicago school. Of course some sociologists in the RF orbit urged the foundation to support work on the social structural sources of fraught race relations. Nonetheless, subsequent RF research on race generally avoided these suggestions. From the late 1940s through the early 1960s behavioralism, scientism, and antiradicalism worked alongside one another to ensure that the political economic concerns central to interwar Rockefeller research and reform on the race issue retreated almost entirely from view.

Applied Science and Multicausal Explanations: Race Relations and Interwar Rockefeller Philanthropy

The Negro in American Civilization developed out of research Johnson compiled for two Rockefeller-sponsored committees: the National Interracial Conference (NIC) and the Advisory Committee on Interracial Relations (ACIR). Established by the LSRM in 1926, the NIC brought together scholars and organizations working on African American social welfare or interracial relations to compile and publicize existing knowledge on the race problem.[7] Formed in 1925, the SSRC's interracial committee, the ACIR, set an agenda for social scientific research on interracial relations and African American social problems. Both deliberately interracial committees included scholars and activists in social scientific agenda setting. Alternatives to racial individualism were also centrally featured, as each committee brought varied theoretical approaches—including political economy—to bear on the race problem. A number of factors contributed to this action-oriented and multidisciplinary orientation of interwar Rockefeller-supported research on race: broader interwar enthusiasm for social science geared toward the amelioration of social problems, the importance of economic explanations of racial inequality to scholars who took an accommodationist stance toward Jim Crow, and the breadth of reformist issues under consideration. At the same time, the two committees exposed the challenges foundation leaders faced as they sought to explain "the race problem" while avoiding racial politics.

Rockefeller philanthropy's interwar approach to the race issue grew out of both the organization's long history of support for accommodationist black leaders in the South and concern with race relations as a national issue. Beginning in the 1880s, Rockefeller philanthropy built African American schools and universities in the South, supported social welfare and public health initiatives in black communities, and encouraged the development of moderate black leadership. Interwar Rockefeller leaders assumed segregation would be permanent and rejected civil rights activists' demands for legal and political action.[8] Instead, the Memorial (LSRM) and the General Education Board (GEB) largely addressed the race issue by urging the development of segregated African American economic, educational, and social institutions and supporting the pursuit of interracial understanding through groups like the Commission on Interracial Cooperation that accepted segregation.[9] The LSRM was especially careful when dealing with organizations, like the NAACP, with clear political agendas.[10] At the same time, the Great Migration and interwar racial violence in northern cities drew Rockefeller, and many other northern urban foundations, to acknowledge the national dimensions of the race issue by the 1920s.[11]

The NIC and ACIR's action-oriented approach to the race issue also drew on the LSRM's mission to encourage simultaneously empirically grounded and socially relevant social science. Established in 1918 to aid social and child welfare organizations, the Memorial emphasized the development of empirical work in psychology, economics, sociology, and anthropology and prioritized social science that could help "resolve pressing social problems." The LSRM supported university social science departments, worked to facilitate contact between social scientists and community settings, and advocated interdisciplinary research.[12] The LSRM was in good company in this effort. A tradition of social scientific research that, while committed to objectivity in method, focused on the amelioration of social problems and involved reformers actively in research efforts, flourished in leading interwar foundations.[13] Moderation on questions of segregation, however, affected the LSRM's stance toward African American educational institutions and scholars. While Rockefeller philanthropy supported the training of many leading African American social scientists at early points in their careers, LSRM leadership believed that true scientific research could only be produced at "the most elite white male universities."[14] The Memorial funded black colleges—extensively supporting Fisk's Department of Social Science, the study of law at Howard University, and programs in business at Morehouse College. But, historian John Stanfield argues, the LSRM generally aimed to train politically moderate black leaders not to further the production of rigorous scientific knowledge.[15]

The LSRM's National Interracial Conference exemplified the Memorial's action-oriented approach to social scientific agenda setting on the race issue. In addition to social scientists, representatives of leading religious, social welfare, and political organizations working in African American communities or involved in efforts to improve interracial relations—notably a group that included strong opponents of segregation and disenfranchisement like the NAACP and also those with more moderate political orientations like the Commission on Interracial Cooperation—were included on the NIC's executive committee.[16] The NIC prioritized dialogue between scholars and activists and emphasized the social utility of scientific research.[17] In preparation for the conference, the NIC conducted an exhaustive survey of research on the race issue. This survey, executive committee leaders hoped, would allow activists already working in the field of race relations to study existing social scientific findings, become accustomed to using scholarship to inform program development, and show the absence of data on pressing social questions.[18] And yet expertise would also move from activists to scientists, research director Charles S. Johnson noted, since activists would be able to "check the results of investigations by comparison with their own experience" at the same time that "their own experience and methods can be checked and improved by study of the results of investigations."[19]

The SSRC's ACIR also envisioned social science and social welfare as mutually dependent and included both scholars and activists when proposing a research agenda on interracial relations and African American social problems.[20] The ACIR focused more explicitly on directing the course of social scientific investigation than the NIC, but leaders assumed that social welfare and religious agencies should be involved. In addition to philanthropic organizations like the Phelps Stokes Fund and the Russell Sage Foundation, African American–led academic and social welfare organizations, such as the Association for the Study of Negro Life and History, the Urban League, and the National Association of Teachers of Colored Schools, represented important resources for producing new knowledge on interracial relations and black life.[21] A list the ACIR compiled of universities engaged in important work on race relations also prominently featured African American colleges and universities, while African American scholars were well represented on both the ACIR and NIC.[22]

In addition to being action oriented, the model of race relations social science the NIC and the ACIR developed promoted varied theoretical approaches to the study of interracial relations: psychological, sociological, anthropological, political, and economic. That both committees took the problems affecting black communities rather than a disciplinarily specific set of questions as their analytical starting point contributed to this theoretical diversity.[23] During a discussion of research goals in 1927, the NIC's executive committee emphasized that economic, political, psychological, and sociological views all needed to be brought to bear on the study of race relations because these factors produced the race problem concurrently.[24] Economic frameworks were especially well represented. Will Alexander of the Commission on Interracial Cooperation argued that "race trouble" derived from economic causes. "A great many of these things . . . that we dump into the general pile of race," he emphasized, "need to be restudied in a most thorough way . . . to discover the economic groups out of which they grew."[25] James Weldon Johnson of the NAACP, Eugene K. Jones of the National Urban League, Robert R. Moton of Tuskegee Institute, and Charles S. Johnson echoed Alexander's economic concerns. They raised questions about a possible "rural revolution" in the South and emphasized that economic patterns—especially southern industrialization, the displacement of agricultural workers, and the shift from tenancy to a wage system— were essential for understanding the race problem.[26]

The more scientifically minded ACIR also recommended studies of the political, economic, sociological, cultural, and legal forces affecting black life. In an attempt to establish a "logical arrangement" of the field of race relations, the ACIR recommended studies of a wide range of issues: African American culture and folk life; the social-ecological forces shaping black life; psychological approaches to African American families, child-rearing, and child welfare; "legal justice," criminal justice, prisons, reform schools, and African American lawyers; and economic issues such as agriculture, business, industry, credit unions, labor relations, financial institutions, and African American business. Racial attitudes were part of the SSRC's research interests, but only a small part.[27] Due to Rockefeller philanthropy's expertise in medical issues, the popularity of intelligence testing during World War I, and enduring interest in the relationship between race and biology, the ACIR also called for empirical analyses of public health and African American intelligence, which it proposed in conjunction with a National Research Council committee focused on "racial differences."[28] Even when the ACIR consolidated its interests in 1930, political and economic concerns remained central. Alexander outlined the three major fields in which the committee believed research on interracial relations was necessary: "the relation of Negroes to government and politics in this country"; a similar analysis of "negro economics"; and "psychological measurement of race characteristics."[29]

While the interwar NIC and ACIR supported many disciplinary approaches to the race problem, they also exposed the difficulty of avoiding racial politics while engaging in reform-oriented social science on such a controversial issue. Charles S. Johnson and the NIC compiled enormous amounts of data on African American life and race relations. Published as *The Negro in American Civilization: A Study of Negro Life and Race Relations in the Light of Social Research* (1930), Johnson's charts, graphs, and tables intended to provide an objective view but put African American oppression in bold relief.[30] Johnson cataloged many troubling aspects of black social, economic, medical, and cultural life. He exposed vast racial inequities in access to medical care and standards of living, the difficulties black workers faced in the labor market, and the inequalities that resulted from segregated housing and education.[31] *The Negro in American Civilization* even reprinted the conference proceedings, which at times ventured squarely into the political realm. For example, W. E. B. Du Bois (who reviewer Benjamin Stolberg described as "the only fly in the ointment") made a powerful case for the immediate need for African American voting rights and warned of the danger of interracial dialogue without political action.[32] "All of this is going to be of no avail in the crisis approaching," Du Bois concluded referring to the conference, "unless we take advantage of the present desire for knowledge . . . and attack the main problem, which is and has been the question of political power for the Negro citizens of the United States."[33]

Mary Van Kleeck, Russell Sage Foundation official, proponent of workers' rights, and chairman of the NIC's executive committee, took a middle position between Du Bois's bold political advocacy and Johnson's restrained objectivity in her foreword to the volume.[34] Writing for a public where many still blamed racial inequality on African American biology or psychology, Van Kleeck made clear that social policy could reverse the patterns of inequality and suffering Johnson exhibited:

> As to the findings and their significance, this book will speak for itself. One result only need be emphasized here. The synthesis of available data revealed a sound basis for planning programs of improvement. That the Negro is racially susceptible to disease, racially incapable of education or racially apt to violate laws, is a case not proved. . . . Change in conditions which produce ill health and crime and improvement in opportunities for education have demonstrated the capacity of the Negro to profit by these changes. . . . The causes of many of the unfortunate conditions which prevailed several years ago and still exist in some parts of the country, at least, are actually removable causes.[35]

She noted that economic opportunities were restricted, educational facilities for black children were inadequate, and disenfranchisement ensured that African Americans, in many states, were unable to "secure an equal measure of justice from the state" or share in "the responsibilities or the privileges of citizenship."[36] Still, perhaps because of the RF's hesitance on issues of segregation, Van Kleeck also failed to make clear policy recommendations, the oversight for which Stolberg criticized Johnson.[37]

The NIC's choice to publish Du Bois's conference paper must surely have angered Rockefeller-affiliated racial moderates, but Johnson's and

Van Kleeck's avoidance of policy recommendations offended some on the emerging interracial left. This stance of disinterestedness even raised questions among SSRC leaders. A September 1930 report on projects by the president of the SSRC suggested that Johnson's work was useful to SSRC leaders, "in view of our discussion of the importance of evaluating work and the impossibility of adequately discharging our obligations to policies if we are too scientific to be willing to evaluate."[38] The report provided a copy of Stolberg's review in which he accused Johnson of being "a very shrewd man who can make his facts shut up." According to Stolberg, *The Negro in American Civilization* exemplified "a certain type of very bad book," since "it deals with one of our major social issues exhaustively, very ably in its way, with a great air of scrupulous objectivity and 'scientific' modesty, without ever indicating or implying the reason for the problem."[39] "Like the Negro in reconstruction days," Stolberg accused Johnson of serving as "ward, in a more sophisticated relation, of big northern philanthropy."[40] Stolberg's review even encouraged some self-reflection among SSRC leaders, whose comments suggested they had urged Johnson's objective tone. In response to Solberg, SSRC officials wondered if they should, in the future, avoid "laying too much stress on fact-finding as against interpretation" since it might be "safer to let the competent investigator interpret his facts than to leave that to others."[41]

The NIC and the ACIR thus not only highlighted the multidisciplinary and action-oriented character of interwar LSRM- and SSRC-supported work on the race issue but also the complexity of attempts to sharpen the fuzzy line between social science, social reform, and racial politics. Beginning from an interest in addressing social problems in African American communities, the NIC and the ACIR promoted varied disciplinary approaches to the race issue, including political economy. Building on broader foundation interest in applied social science, they also included both African American scholars and representatives of activist groups in scientific agenda setting. At the same time, developing an applied but apolitical social science of race relations proved challenging. As *The Negro in American Civilization* revealed, evidence of African American social, economic, and political conditions raised politically troubling questions about causes whose implications for the politics of discrimination, disenfranchisement, and segregation were difficult to ignore. Even as the interwar NIC and ACIR embraced reform-oriented social science, commitment to scientific objectivity helped agenda setters like Johnson and Van Kleeck avoid the more politically controversial implications of their findings.

Efforts to use social science to shape social reform on the race issue proved relatively short-lived, moreover, within Rockefeller philanthropy. By 1932 both the NIC and the ACIR had been disbanded. Highlighting the close relationship between incidents of racial unrest and foundation responses, ACIR members lost interest in early 1931 partly due to a sense that the racial tensions of the mid-1920s had "quieted."[42] In addition, institutional restructuring among the different branches of Rockefeller philanthropy contributed to the shift away from applied social science on the race problem. After the LSRM was folded into the RF in 1928, the GEB took over its work on black education and social welfare while the RF took up its social scientific initiatives. This separation of applied and basic concerns largely undermined the action-oriented race relations social science the NIC and ACIR had promoted, especially because the RF avoided "projects involving the application of scientific knowledge to contemporary problems" and prioritized "top-notch white universities."[43] By the mid-1930s Rockefeller philanthropy had reduced support for social scientific initiatives at HBCUs. Neither the RF nor the GEB were involved in innovative social scientific analyses of African Americans in the 1930s, years when the Carnegie Corporation, Russell Sage Foundation, and Julius Rosenwald Fund helped produce "the Golden Age of Negro Sociology."[44]

Antiradicalism and Education, 1945–47

In the immediate postwar years, while the RF continued to remain aloof from racial issues, growing pressure to address prejudice and racial tensions amid Nazism, accelerating civil rights protest, and northern urban racial unrest drew other branches of Rockefeller philanthropy toward racial questions. Rockefeller Brothers Fund advisor Dana Creel's "The Negro in New York City" (1946) and Robin M. Williams Jr.'s SSRC-commissioned *The Reduction of Intergroup Tensions* (1947) each relied on multidisciplinary explanations of the race issue. Both pieces also highlighted tensions between scientific theories of the causes of the race problem and notions of the scope and scale of possible reform. Creel's sense of the limits of appropriate philanthropic reach and Williams's assumption that "structural reform" was of too grand a scale to be feasible, led each to recommend educational and social welfare initiatives, Rockefeller philanthropy's traditional specialty when it came to race.

Creel's "The Negro in New York City" chronicled the endurance of multidisciplinary explanations of the causes of racial injustice and the foundation's desire to improve African American status without stepping into the arena of racial politics. The foundation officer pinpointed African American poverty, delinquency, poor health, and low social, economic, and educational status as demanding intervention. Although Creel didn't cite his sources, he echoed social ecological and Myrdalian logic in suggesting that a variety of factors combined to produce these problems: individual prejudice; institutionalized discrimination in housing, employment, education, and health care; and social pathologies endemic to black communities.[45] Employment discrimination was especially important since Creel, like E. Franklin Frazier, recognized that "the Negro's ability to maintain himself as an individual, or as a family group or as a part of the community . . . depends upon his ability to obtain a job with a steady and adequate income."[46] As evidence of the shifting bounds of appropriate politics by 1946, Creel also held that black advancement in the South would only occur when legal barriers to political equality were dismantled. In New York City, however, he believed that there were few legal questions about "the Negro's political status" and that government already protected African American economic and political rights.[47]

Creel articulated a complex, interdisciplinary analysis of the causes of racial injustice, inequality, and black poverty. He nonetheless drew a sharp line between the social and the political and assumed that philanthropy could only successfully address social problems. The discrimination he identified as a key cause of many other social problems African Americans faced in Harlem lay outside the range of issues he believed philanthropists could productively tackle.[48] Instead, Creel thought the RBF should expand social welfare and health services in Harlem and work to improve African American education. Creel recommended the foundation fund vocational guidance and training for the unemployed, increase support for black colleges, expand church-based leadership development initiatives, combat child neglect and delinquency, and (echoing the more paternalistic components of the tradition of black uplift) improve the hygiene and behavior of black migrants.[49]

Worries about the radical potential of mainstream civil rights protest also motivated Creel's narrow attention to education and social welfare, despite his complex understanding of the sources of racial inequality. Among the new race relations organizations, Creel carefully distinguished between "aggressive and militant organizations exposing and attacking discriminatory barriers," which he did not recommend the foundation support because "discriminatory barriers, legal and practical, have been broken to such an extent in New York City that programs demanding drastic and immediate reforms are unnecessary and frequently harmful," and others. In contrast, "organizations conducting programs to determine the nature of inter-group tensions and develop techniques for the prevention of interracial and inter-cultural friction" might benefit from foundation backing.[50] The NAACP, the National Negro Congress, the Southern Conference for Human Welfare, the Southern Regional Council, and City-Wide Citizen's League of Harlem were "of such a radical nature" that he advised the RBF against supporting them.[51] One reason for this caution was that communist attempts to capitalize on black dissatisfaction worried Rockefeller leaders.[52] In fact, concern with off-setting communist gains in Harlem led Creel to recommend the RBF con-centrate much of its programming there. He also encouraged church-based leadership development and citizenship programs, based on the assump-tion that African Americans too frequently turned to government "as the immediate cure of the ills of the colored population, with little thought to the bilateral obligations of citizenship."[53]

The antiradicalism that shaped Creel's recommendations for racial re-form, which notably appeared six years before congressional investigations into foundation "subversion," substantially influenced postwar Rockefeller reform initiatives on race. While the RF, the RBF, and the Office of the Messrs. Rockefeller funded social welfare initiatives for African American commu-nities throughout the postwar period, all avoided supporting militant or-ganizations and treated activists seeking legislative change or engaged in "propagandistic" activities as aggressive. The Rockefeller family's direct in-volvement in the RBF (in contrast to its insulation from the SSRC) may have made the RBF especially wary of political controversy. After 1950 the RBF contributed to cultural, educational, and social welfare groups that served African American communities, including the National Urban League and the United Negro College Fund, but would not fund groups like the NAACP or the American Council on Race Relations that were "tending to look to federal and state legislative, executive, and judicial action as the most desir-able approach to the problems with which they are dealing."[54]

While the desire to distinguish its work from political agitation con-strained the RBF's approach to the race issue, a mid-1940s SSRC project revealed other factors encouraging Rockefeller leaders away from structural reform on the race issue. The SSRC's Committee on Techniques for Reduc-ing Group Hostility (1945–47) sponsored a study by sociologist Robin M. Williams Jr. of programming to reduce tensions between racial and cultural groups. This project, published as *The Reduction of Intergroup Tensions: A Sur-vey of Research on Problems of Ethnic, Racial, and Religious Groups* (1947), ex-posed not only the political but also the practical difficulties of translating structural or political-economic theories into feasible reform proposals.[55] The project stood on the precipice between interwar and early Cold War–

era approaches to the race issue. On the one hand the committee—which due to its applied orientation was under the direction of the SSRC not the RF—looked back to the action-oriented social science of race relations of the interwar ACIR and NIC. On the other hand its focus on interpersonal relations and the transformation of racial attitudes reflected the emerging behavioral orientation of much postwar RF research on human relations.

The SSRC's Committee on Techniques for Reducing Group Hostility emerged in 1945, prompted by widespread wartime efforts to improve intergroup understanding and enthusiasm for research at the intersection of psychology and sociology. The National Research Council originally forwarded a proposal to study psychological approaches to combating hostility between individuals and groups to the SSRC, but SSRC program officers accepted the proposal because they worried that "practically nothing" was being done to evaluate wartime efforts to reduce intergroup tension.[56] SSRC leadership were concerned, however, that psychological views "overemphasize the individual's tendency to hostility" and therefore appointed an interdisciplinary committee and chose sociologist Robin M. Williams Jr., rather than a psychologist, to conduct the study.[57] Nonetheless, the emerging importance of behavioralism was evident in the committee's acceptance of "the interpersonal approach," a view that assumed "that all conflicts and hostilities whether among individuals, groups, classes or nations may in part at least reduce to hostilities and conflicts on a personal level."[58] In addition, while the committee originally proposed two studies, one on techniques employed in industrial relations and one on techniques in intergroup relations, it dropped the more economically oriented project in favor of the behavioral study.[59]

Williams's 1947 synthesis of activist approaches to improving intergroup relations was also pulled between dispositional and systemic paradigms, though it ultimately erred toward the dispositional based on a sense of what kinds of reforms could be practically implemented. It was because "the efforts which go into education and propaganda constitute a very high proportion of all current activities" that Williams focused considerable scholarly attention there.[60] Williams set the tone of most postwar race relations research by focusing on racial attitudes, by attending to socioeconomic forces only when they helped to explain prejudice, and by suggesting that carefully planned intergroup interaction could reduce racial hostility.[61] And yet *The Reduction of Intergroup Tensions* acknowledged that intergroup conflict had roots in economic and social forces. "It is known," Williams argued, "that there is a minimum of group conflict, however difficult to specify, which arises from relatively permanent features of our society, such as the type of economic system, certain patterns of child training, and the way in which our distinctive family system is related to the competitive occupational structure."[62] Williams worried, however, about the practical implications of theories, especially sociological and economic, that rooted race relations in entrenched structures:

> An alternate reaction to the results of present action programs is the feeling that inter-group tensions are so deeply imbedded in the nature of our whole social system that only a major alteration of the system could bring adequate solutions. To this, again, the verdict of "not proven" is appropriate; and in some instances this "total" orientation toward the problem may block constructive action in the present. On the whole it appears that naïve optimism is becoming less and less a major handicap in the efforts being made to improve group relations in this country. Of greater import is the disillusionment which can come from frustrated effort and from unchecked judgments as to the possibilities of control.[63]

Since structural theories could not be translated into realistic reform agendas, psychological theories motivated the sociologist's recommendations for local "action programs," which advocated interracial cooperation around shared tasks.[64] In fact, *The Reduction of Intergroup Tensions* provided as clear a statement on the challenges of translating social science into reform as it did an agenda for progress in intergroup relations. As Williams noted in summary, "Research is not magic. It can not be expected invariably to produce solutions to immediate problems, nor to formulate panaceas for social ills." Well-conceptualized research generally involved extended time lines and produced "tentative, limited, and qualified findings," he explained, characteristics "not always appreciated by persons grappling with practical problems and strongly convinced of their seriousness and urgency."[65] While the committee's initial psychological and interpersonal framing of the issue in part explains why Williams leaned toward the individual, *The Reduction of Intergroup Tensions* also made clear that dilemmas related to the scale of practical—not simply politically acceptable—reform limited activist agendas.

Williams and Creel recognized that economic, political, and social-structural forces, as well as individual prejudice and acts of discrimination, produced intergroup tensions and disadvantaged African Americans. Both, however, avoided elaborating the programmatic implications of social structural, political, or economic theories of the race problem. Dana Creel's "The Negro in New York City" exposed how central the avoidance of divisive, militant racial politics was to Rockefeller philanthropy's midcentury ten-

dency to prioritize education and social welfare when fighting the race problem. In contrast, it was not a sense of limited political possibility or philanthropic reach but the assumption that large-scale political-economic reform
was programmatically unrealistic that constrained the reformist scope of
Robin M. Williams Jr.'s study of intergroup tensions.

Human Relations and the "Atomistic" Approach, 1950–53

By the early 1950s, not only reformist agendas but also the theoretical frameworks many Rockefeller associates used to examine the race issue narrowed
as the study of race relations was incorporated into the interdisciplinary field
of "human relations." A number of forces converged in the late 1940s and
early 1950s to separate Rockefeller scientific and reformist agendas on race,
to eliminate activist groups and scholars working outside the elite white
academy from scientific agenda setting, and to ensure that attention to the
political and economic sources of racial conflict and inequality nearly disappeared from debate within Rockefeller philanthropy. The postwar separation of scientific and reformist impulses had sources in the foundation's
1928 reorganization. In the early 1950s, however, behavioralism and the
Cold War's incentivizing of scientism exacerbated the apolitical and individualistic drift of RF-funded research on race.[66] Behavioralism encouraged
scholarly attention to individuals while pressures toward scientism led RF
leaders to prioritize theory generation and generalizability as scientific ideals,
to favor quantifiable research methods, and to remain aloof from applied
work. Two sociologists in the RF's orbit, Robin M. Williams Jr. and Arnold
Rose, questioned the individualistic orientation of midcentury research on
intergroup relations and the stark distinction between basic and applied
research. Nonetheless, few challenged the tendency to overlook political
economy. In addition, worries about generalizability left even critics of "atomism" unsure about how to produce studies of intergroup relations that
examined social structures while avoiding methodological "particularism."

Growing interest at the Ford Foundation and Carnegie Corporation,
and in leading research universities, in behavioral science and social relations paradigms that favored noneconomic visions of the social prompted
RF concern with human relations.[67] In fact, the SSRC had received a grant
from the Ford Foundation that led to the establishment of a Committee
on Social Behavior in 1951, an initial foray into many of the themes that
would occupy the RF at its 1953 Conference on Research in Human Relations.[68] However, Rockefeller philanthropy distinguished itself from its peer
institutions by sponsoring research on race relations as part of its behavioral

sciences initiative. Although the Carnegie Corporation encouraged the behavioral sciences after 1946, it avoided race relations and largely ignored *An American Dilemma* after it was published.[69] The Ford Foundation, the major supporter of the behavioral sciences between 1949 and the early 1960s, also distanced itself from (or at least avoided admitting to sponsoring) research on race relations—a topic Ford head Milton Katz described as "*Verboten* territory."[70] While the Julius Rosenwald Fund had remained supportive of racial research, the fund was dismantled shortly after World War II (due to an initial charter intended to avoid philanthropic funds existing in perpetuity), removing one of the largest twentieth-century supporters of African American social scientists from the philanthropic scene.[71]

RF leaders' inclusion of the race issue in the abstract, theoretical field of human relations also occurred in a context where the politics of desegregation were proving increasingly regionally divisive, where debate over social scientific inclusion in the National Science Foundation (NSF) encouraged postwar scientism, and where antiradicalism constrained foundations that supported liberal social science. The RF turned attention to human relations the year before the Supreme Court decision in *Brown v. Board of Education*, when southern segregationists were already threatening to resist a court decree and segregationist factions in the Democratic Party had inched both parties rightward on racial issues.[72] With its long history of support for segregated African American education and ties to southern moderates, it is little surprise that Rockefeller officials felt pressure to treat the race issue with care. In addition, debate over social scientific inclusion in the NSF between 1945 and 1950 had pitted SSRC-affiliated scientists who sought to convince Congress, natural scientists, and the public that the social sciences were as objective as the natural sciences against those who rejected the possibility and desirability of value neutrality and political disengagement.[73] Congressional opponents of social scientific inclusion often used scholarship on race and political economy as examples of the social sciences' inescapably political content. In fact, the NSF debate, historian Mark Solovey argues, ultimately "gave a central boost to the scientistic impulse and simultaneously helped to marginalize the trenchant critique of scientism that had emerged on the (noncommunist) political left."[74] Proponents of racial justice could also be branded as communists, an increasingly meaningful designation for RF leadership between 1952 and 1954 when the foundation was among the tax-exempt organizations under congressional investigation for "subversive activities." The Reece Committee assessed whether leading foundations like Carnegie, Rockefeller, and Ford had "used their resources for purposes contrary to those for which they were established," including "un-American," "subversive," or "political" purposes, or had "resorted to propaganda" to achieve their objectives. In fact, the committee's final report criticized Carnegie's funding of Myrdal's work, which it claimed "led to the publication of statements which were most critical of our Constitution."[75] When the RF and SSRC convened the 1953 human relations conference, pressure to treat any work on the race issue with care was palpable.

Theoretical ambitions shaped the conference's scholarly objectives and which participants were invited. Joseph Willits, director of the RF's Division of Social Sciences, planned the conference for twenty-five of the most well known scholars associated with the emerging interdisciplinary behavioral sciences (largely psychologists, anthropologists, and sociologists) to assess the state of the field and guide future RF programs.[76] In addition to a session on intergroup relations, topics included child socialization, communication and attitudes, the social organization of large and small groups, anthropological approaches to human relations, and research methods.[77] The roster differed markedly from the interwar NIC and ACIR, since RF leaders chose the attendees not to understand a social problem from a variety of scholarly and practical perspectives but to set a research agenda for a theoretically defined scholarly field. As a consequence, the group featured only scholars from elite, white research universities—including many from the new survey research centers, human relations labs, and social relations departments—already receiving foundation funds.[78] During a discussion of how foundations could foster scientific innovation, in fact, some of the participants noted the limited number of institutions represented at the meeting. "You people give too much money to the universities around this table," Harvard anthropologist Clyde Kluckhohn stated to the foundation officers, "and this, is, to use a cliché, a vicious circle."[79] It was "no coincidence," Columbia sociologist and head of the BASR Paul Lazarsfeld told Willits, that all of the conference participants "seem to know each other so well." Innovation in the social sciences "centers around a dozen institutions . . . the same names show up at all of these conferences." The RF's strong commitment to basic rather than applied work ensured, however, that little discussion occurred about the theoretical blind spots that might emerge if scientific agenda setting was not more inclusive.[80]

As race relations became a subset of foundation interest in human relations, moreover, scholars approached the issue through a more limited set of analytic lenses, though purely psychological approaches to the race issue generated criticism. Williams's paper on "race and culture conflict" criticized the "atomism" of research on prejudice, as he had in his 1947 *The Reduction of Intergroup Tensions*.[81] Much work on prejudice produced from the

1920s through the late 1940s had been "static and sheerly descriptive," treating "prejudice as an unanalyzed aggregate of individual attitudes, divorced from the functioning of real personalities and from enduring social relations and the structural properties of groups and communities." Between 1948 and 1953, individualistic approaches had expanded further, since the largest research area in the whole field of intergroup relations involved personality-based approaches to prejudice.[82] At the same time, the RF human relations conference provided a setting where an emerging sociological critique of the psychological drift of research on race relations reached foundation ears. This critique had two central tenets. One called for fuller elaboration of how personality and context interacted. The other built on E. Franklin Frazier's 1948 suggestion that sociologists return to the structural emphases of interwar sociology on the race issue.

Williams, whose own work used community study methods to examine attitudes in context, prioritized the first approach. He noted some movement—much of which involved sociological efforts to reclaim the race issue from psychologists—away from prejudiced personalities and toward "increased interest in patterns of discrimination (or differential behavior) as over against individual attitudes."[83] The work he praised did not completely reject individual units of analysis; instead, it situated individual belief, behavior, or interpersonal interaction in a situational context.[84]

The second approach, which suggested that the relations among social groups—not interpersonal interaction—served as the defining feature of race relations, revived a central tenet of interwar social ecological thought on race and even provided some room for an analysis of power and institutions. A sociologist at the University of Minnesota who had been a central contributor to *An American Dilemma*, Arnold Rose (who served as discussant for Williams's paper) called explicitly for analysis of the "structural" aspects of race relations. He recommended planning research such that it would "bring us back to an initial interest among sociologists in discovering the social conditions under which inter-group conflict arises and continues."[85] Williams agreed, suggesting that social structures—the ways social situations were set up, the process of social categorization, and the ways social settings encouraged behavior—had been defining elements of the study of race relations earlier but needed to be reintegrated into an increasingly psychologized field.[86] Traditionally, sociological interests in hierarchy and power relations, the two suggested, raised important questions about the social dynamics character structure theories of prejudice obscured. Williams's research on intergroup relations in Elmira, New York, had found, for example, that the most extremely prejudiced individuals tended to be uneducated, middle aged or older, and of low socioeconomic status. "Obviously the total situation would be very different," Williams emphasized, "were the 'bigots' to be found concentrated in positions of leadership and power."[87] Both sociologists also emphasized the importance of law and interest-group politics to the structural nature of intergroup relations, a development that was hardly surprising given civil rights activists' successes in the courts.[88] Williams cited sociologist E. Franklin Frazier's claim that race relations were most strongly shaped by the "organized actions of special-interest groups." He also pointed to analyses by Joseph Lohman and William C. Bradbury that exposed the importance of "power relationships as these determined law, administrative regulations, and formal operating practices" related to de facto segregation in many workplaces.[89] Thus when suggesting where the field of intergroup relations was and should be going, Williams and Rose applauded calls for a return to social structural analysis and noted some interest in law and interest-group politics.

At the same time, both Williams and Rose recognized that a number of factors impeded the research agenda they proscribed. Methodological considerations were paramount. Although Williams envisioned "an organized, interdependent series of studies moving from phenomena of individual personality through small groups to larger social structures, and permeated throughout by the incorporation of cultural content," available methods determined which questions could be effectively answered.[90] "In making the preceding review and appraisal, it is striking," he noted, "how frequently one finds that the fulfillment of crucial research needs depends upon *advances in research methods*—upon more valid and reliable measuring instruments, more ingenious and better controlled study designs."[91] In particular, while scholars knew how to examine the relationship between prejudice, discrimination, and individual personalities, they faced more difficulty measuring the social structural components of race relations. The challenges of observing "important real life situations" and relating survey data to actual lived situations, the "clumsiness" of available techniques for recording data on social interaction, and ethical dilemmas associated with contriving situations for the sake of research worried Williams.[92] Comparative studies of race relations in different communities or cultural settings appeared promising, but very large sample sizes were essential. Cross-community comparisons were often difficult to develop, Williams noted, "simply because there were not enough cases for statistical analyses."[93]

Williams's methodological worries were also related to commitment to theory generation, a clear priority at the RF's human relations conference. That Talcott Parsons had prioritized interdisciplinary theoretical integration when developing Harvard's new Department of Social Relations may have shaped this orientation, though the RF's long-standing focus on basic research also contributed. Historian Joel Isaac argues that while survey research centers, programs in area studies, and institutes like Stanford's Center for Advanced Study in the Behavioral Sciences (CASBS) encouraged interdisciplinarity without prioritizing theory development, what distinguished the DSR's approach was an "insistence that the widely touted integration of the social-scientific disciplines should be guided by a comprehensive system of *theory*."[94] Parsons was not at the RF 1953 conference, though his DSR colleague Samuel Stouffer and students Merton and Williams were a strong presence. Attention to theory generation was widely evident nonetheless. In fact, letters by participants in response to the conference described theory production as a first priority of foundation support for research on human relations. As psychologist Lee Cronbach put it, "Breakthroughs depend chiefly on conceptualization. When a single man or small groups succeeds in reorganizing his field so as to bring a point of view to bear, we get significant and coherent results."[95] Many conference participants recommended that in a context where government and business sponsored much applied work, the RF could help "balance the books" by funding explicitly theoretical research. Others emphasized that the RF should commit itself to fostering theoretical breakthroughs, not simply encourage a buildup of empirical work.[96]

In this context, a project's ability to abstract from rather than carefully explain the particular determined its scientific value, a consideration that incentivized quantifiable methods and raised questions about applied research. Although Rose and Williams tried to convince their colleagues that the line between applied and basic work was too stark, each still emphasized that the short-term demands of applied research did not encourage the cumulative work that would build theory.[97] While Rose was the strongest defender of applied research at the conference, even he argued that studies that were so wedded to the particular that they could not be generalized should be avoided. "There is much to be gained," he held, "by studying race and culture conflict in a broad context of group conflict generally, and of considering the processes involved in inter-group relations as characteristic sociological processes that apply in all sorts of human situations."[98] Williams emphasized that one should assess scholarship—basic or applied—based on its generalizability, that is, "whether the results of a study are dated and localized and specific and concrete to such a degree that you can't clamp them down anywhere else in the universal reality and have them work."[99] The most useful studies of race relations, both suggested, were the most abstract: those that elucidated universal patterns that could be applied to any type of intergroup relations. Eventually, Williams argued, scholars "shall not be studying Negro-white relations, Catholic-Protestant relations, Irish-Polish relations—but we shall be analyzing *the relations between differently situated and differently categorized persons*, and selecting our cases wherever found on the basis of strategic interest to social science."[100]

Of course, systemic or even relational theories of race relations could have also been made generalizable if scholars pursued them using large-scale, quantifiable methods. Scientism was combined with behavioralism at the 1953 conference, however. Together the two priorities obscured political and economic orientations to social problems and left the voices most likely to promote those approaches—the reformers who had been centrally included in the NIC and ACIR and scholars outside the behavioral sciences—out of scientific agenda setting on the race issue.[101] While interwar Rockefeller discussions of "the Negro problem" employed a wide range of disciplinary perspectives in part because thinkers examined concrete problems in African American communities, the 1953 conference started and ended with a behavioral orientation that elided the economic and the political. That Williams and Rose emphasized the need for research on the social structural and noted increased attention to the legal and political aspects of the race issue remains significant. The research agenda the RF would pursue, however, one chosen amid not only enthusiasm for scientism and behavioralism but also concerns with radicalism and increasingly divisive integrationist politics tended to ignore their suggestions. Moreover, even Rose and Williams agreed that the scale of viable available research methods—most notably the dangers of "particularism"—impeded the development of the structural approaches they recommended.

"One of the Major Social Changes of Our Generation": The RF and Race Relations, 1953–63

The one Rockefeller-funded initiative that took Williams's and Rose's critiques of atomism and calls for a social structural approach to the race issue seriously were the Cornell Studies in Inter-Group Relations. Led by Williams and his colleagues in the Department of Anthropology and Sociology, the Cornell projects received support from the RF between 1950 and 1956.[102] The initial research, begun in 1948, used Elmira, New York, as a case study to examine prejudice, discrimination, and the situational context of race relations. Reflecting Williams's concerns with generalizability and securing a large "N," by 1956 Cornell researchers had conducted detailed analyses of four mid-sized industrial cities and had surveyed race relations in twenty-five other cities, using this information to assess the typicality of the case studies. They also correlated their findings with questionnaires sent to community leaders in 250 cities.[103] In contrast to much midcentury research on prejudice, the projects examined racial attitudes in their "situational context" and prioritized nonwhite as well as white attitudes.[104] Despite Williams's concerns with the limits of applied work, research on intergroup relations at Cornell used "action programs" as a basis for scientific investigation, though Cornell researchers emphasized repeatedly that scientific analysis, not evaluation, was their primary goal.[105]

The Cornell studies both complicated and developed an individualistic approach to the study of intergroup relations. On the one hand, the projects distinguished clearly between racial attitudes and discriminatory behaviors and examined both within a social, cultural, and often institutional context.[106] Williams and his colleagues used attitude surveys to expose correlations between prejudice, socioeconomic status, and other demographic variables and devised questions that highlighted the differences between public and private attitudes. They also pointed to the ways individuals' perceptions of the attitudes of their family and friends affected prejudice and discriminatory behavior and, when possible, analyzed surveys alongside observational data.[107] In *Strangers Next Door: Ethnic Relations in American Communities* (1964), the synthesis of the projects' major findings, Williams emphasized that prejudice could not be considered "exclusively psychological" since prejudices were "saturated with, and presuppose, an elaborate cultural context, and they are both learned through and expressed in social interaction."[108] In addition, Williams suggested that action programs should restructure situations of intergroup contact rather than address attitudes directly.[109] On the other hand, the causes and nature of prejudice, not the social structural, economic, or political context of race relations, remained the Cornell researchers' primary object of analysis, perhaps helping to explain why the RF and the Ford Foundation funded the research. While Williams and his colleagues had considered focusing on "institutional structures in communities and the operating practices of these institutions," "the attitudes and opinions of . . . the adult population," or " the relationship of attitudes and behavior," they ultimately chose the last topic.[110] Where Williams and his colleagues tried to diverge from the atomism he criticized was in showing how many variables—culture, social systems, and personality systems—influenced prejudice.[111]

Despite the Rockefeller Foundation's tendency to subsume race relations within the behavioral field of human relations, some postwar Rockefeller-funded research began to challenge "atomism" by pursuing a "situational," if not a fully structural, approach to the study of race relations. The RF was only willing to support the Cornell projects to a point, however. By 1954, Williams and his colleagues believed that school desegregation provided an essential site where processes of change in race relations could be examined. Neither the RF nor the Ford Foundation would fund research on desegregation, however. Williams wrote RF official Leland DeVinney in July of 1954 asking for additional funds to adjust the Cornell intergroup relations study so that it could respond to the desegregation order. DeVinney refused, suggesting that this would divert attention from the original project, but noted that the Cornell team could request outside funds.[112] Edward Suchman, another leader of the Cornell project, explained in exasperation to Leonard Cottrell Jr. of the Russell Sage Foundation in December of 1954, that a "high level policy decision" at the Ford Foundation had "eliminated any chances of support from them for research on desegregation." Although the SSRC continued to debate the issue in 1955, RF resistance led Suchman to worry that "one of the major social changes of our generation may go unstudied."[113]

In the scope of postwar RF funding, moreover, the Cornell project was an exception. Williams's and Rose's 1953 calls for social structural and institutional approaches to race relations produced little response from the foundation. Between 1953 and 1955, the RF supported almost no new work on race relations, only following through on commitments it had made earlier. The scholarship on intergroup relations that it did fund was produced at major behavioral science research centers such as the University of Michigan's Research Center for Group Dynamics, the University of Chicago–affiliated National Opinion Research Center, and Harvard University's Laboratory of Social Relations. These organizations fell neatly within the human relations paradigm the RF had outlined in 1953, and the RF-funded work was generally quantitative and social psychological in orientation.[114] The RF Division of Social Sciences' appropriations for studies of "Human Behavior and Interpersonal and Inter-group Relations" (one of its six major program areas in the early 1950s) were smaller in 1954 than in 1953 and disappeared altogether by 1955.[115] Although some programs in area studies and foreign cultures sought to increase international understanding, RF programs in economics, law, and political science developed in directions unrelated to race relations while the SSRC's Committee on Social Stratification similarly overlooked the topic.[116] Between 1953 and 1963, the Rockefeller Foundation expressed little sustained interest in domestic race relations or African American life and even reduced support for the broader field of intergroup relations.

Late in the decade, RF avoidance of the race issue began to shift as be-havioralism declined in importance throughout the foundation world, McCarthyist pressures slowly retreated, and the civil rights movement chipped away at the legitimacy of the southern moderate's political stance.[117] In 1959 the RF funded a project by the Institute for Research in Social Science of the University of North Carolina on "the changing position of the Negro within the framework of a Southern society undergoing urban-ization and industrialization." As Johnson had in 1930, researchers paid careful attention to population growth, migration from rural to urban areas, changes in occupational patterns, and comparative interracial data.[118] When Rockefeller philanthropy did make racial issues a central component of its reform programming, however, it returned to its traditional ameliorative, apolitical, and noneconomic approach—focusing on higher education and leadership development in minority communities. "Toward Equal Oppor-tunity for All," a program that was launched in 1963, funded black colleges and graduate students, encouraged minority attendance in integrated uni-versities through financial aid, and developed summer programs to identify talented high school students of color. In fact, although the RF appeared more self-conscious than in earlier decades about its narrowly educational orientation to racial reform given accelerating African American demands for civil rights, the RF defended its fairly conservative focus on black educa-tion by citing its long experience in the area.[119] Thus despite Williams's and Rose's suggestions, Rockefeller philanthropy made few sustained contribu-tions to social structural or political economic research on race before 1959 and in 1963 returned to the ameliorative, educational reform approach that it had long favored.

At the 1953 Conference on Research in Human Relations, leading sociolo-gists interested in race relations noted with some surprise that research could be simultaneously socially relevant and theoretically innovative. Describing work produced by William C. Bradbury, Joseph Lohman, and Dietrich Re-itzes (which was sponsored by the National Committee on Segregation in the Nation's Capital [NCSNC]), Columbia University sociologist and lead-ing structural functionalist Robert Merton argued that in rare instances ap-plied research could lead to theoretical "breakthroughs." Merton, who had advised Bradbury at Columbia, explained:

> Now, I don't know whether this is called applied research or not, but I do
> know that it has provided the beginnings of fundamental insight in this

field of discussion of race prejudice and discrimination, which has become increasingly focused on the existence or non-existence of these attitudes as though those were all determinant of what is happening in social fact. These attitudes do or do not find expression under different social circumstances, and a key problem is to define the structural situation in which they do or do not. Applied to the Federal Government, it becomes an eminently practical problem. Looked at in terms of its theoretical import, it is a new insight to supplement the recent emphasis on attitudes.[120]

This new insight, that individual "attitudes will depend very greatly on the organizational context in which people behave," represented "a complete departure from what the man in the street and the man in government, incidentally, has assumed."[121] Applied research, a handful of leading postwar scholars admitted, could in rare instances move science toward "genuinely new insights."[122]

This insight, that applied work could be theoretically innovative, would not have struck scholars involved in the interwar NIC and ACIR as noteworthy. By the early 1950s, however, Merton and his colleagues were pleasantly surprised. For a few years in the late 1920s the LSRM and SSRC had supported an action-oriented, multidisciplinary approach to the race issue that included activists and scholars based in HBCUs in agenda setting. While accommodating segregation, the agenda the NIC and ACIR promoted prioritized political economic research on the race issue alongside studies of African American history, psychology, culture, and sociology. This approach was fairly short-lived within Rockefeller philanthropy, however, as the dissolution of the LSRM separated reformist and scientific agendas with implications for the foundation's treatment of the race issue.

When wartime concerns with prejudice and domestic unrest led both the RBF's Dana Creel and the SSRC's Committee on Techniques for Reducing Group Hostility to revisit the race issue in the mid-1940s, the separation of science and reform, the constraining force of antiradicalism, and turns from multidisciplinary to behavioral orientations on the race issue—trends that would accelerate by 1953—were starting to take form. Antiradicalism encouraged Creel to avoid involvement with organizations making demands on government and to reassert Rockefeller philanthropy's traditional educational and ameliorative approaches to the race issue in 1946. The next year, Robin M. Williams Jr.'s SSRC-sponsored *The Reduction of Intergroup Tensions* made clear that behavioral theories were more programmatically useful than political economic or social structural research on race.[123]

After 1950, RF research on the race issue continued to turn away from the applied concerns and the multidisciplinary, especially political economic, orientation that had characterized the interwar NIC and ACIR, patterns especially evident in the RF's 1953 Conference on Research in Human Relations. Enthusiasm for postwar behavioralism in and of itself turned researchers toward largely apolitical, noneconomic, and frequently individualistic views of the race issue. And yet, that behavioralism worked in tandem with scientism—a commitment the RF's long interest in basic research, congressional investigations into foundation subversion, and NSF debates made especially acute in the early 1950s—further encouraged individualism by prioritizing theory generation and generalizability. Scientism and behavioralism together ensured that key voices that might have challenged the separation of the study of race relations and the study of political economy (namely, activists working on social problems in African American communities or scholars outside the behavioral sciences) were not part of the discussion. It remains significant that Williams and Rose opposed the atomism of much postwar research on the race issue. At the same time, in his RF-funded research, Williams kept his analytic gaze on the individual (albeit the ways contexts and situations affected individuals) and remained perplexed by methodological dilemmas of scale that led to atomism on the one hand or particularism on the other.

The desire among postwar RF executives and the elite social scientists who advised them to develop human relations into a theoretically oriented field and to remain disengaged from racial politics shaped an intellectual landscape that many postwar scholars concerned with the race issue had to negotiate. The next chapter—on the University of Chicago's Committee on Education, Training, and Research in Race Relations—exposes the challenges structurally oriented scholar-activists faced as they sought to develop an action-oriented, multidisciplinary social science of race relations that cut against the grain of the RF's priorities.

THREE

The Individual and the "General Situation": Defining the Race Problem at the University of Chicago's Committee on Education, Training, and Research in Race Relations

In 1947, in the wake of a series of urban racial disturbances, Louis Wirth considered race relations the nation's most urgent problem. One of the University of Chicago's best-known urban sociologists, Wirth believed the race issue, if left untreated, would present "a formidable threat to our social order and a serious obstacle to the social progress of America."[1] What particularly troubled him was the widespread popularity of intergroup relations programs based on commonsense assumptions rather than scientific knowledge and the particularism that permeated much of this amateur research. As he explained:

> The tendency now is to intervene in problem situations that arise much as we call out a fire department when there is a report of a fire. In the field of race relations and minority problems, however, we call out the "fire brigade" without knowing whether we are dealing with a small fire calling for one set of equipment or a large conflagration calling for another, or even whether we have water in our fire hoses or gasoline.[2]

In response, Wirth advocated a version of instrumentalist scientism, in which he suggested that the scientific search for universally valid social laws was essential and that this search could and should inform social reform. In linking generalizability and application, the sociologist stood at odds with Rockefeller Foundation proponents of pure theory as well as with race relations reformers whose gaze turned only to the particular context they were trying to fix.[3]

The University of Chicago's Committee on Education, Training, and Research in Race Relations (CETRRR) emerged from Wirth's sense that an organization was needed to simultaneously bring coherence to the science of race relations and facilitate the dissemination of scientific expertise to reformers. Wirth established CETRRR, with support from the University of Chicago's Division of Social Sciences and the Carnegie and Rockefeller Foundations, to serve as a research center and to train scholars and practitioners. Composed of an interdisciplinary group of University of Chicago faculty, in which sociologists, anthropologists, and professors of education were best represented, CETRRR held national conferences, produced a quarterly review of scholarship, and published popular education materials between 1947 and 1954.[4]

As we have just seen, some sociologists worried about the atomistic drift in midcentury research on the race issue. This chapter investigates the institution that had been the home of the leading interwar systemic alternative to that atomism—Robert Park's social ecology—in the generation that followed Park. Given the Chicago school's theoretical emphasis on the causal importance of large-scale social structures and Wirth's systemic orientation to race relations in the interwar years, CETRRR was an unlikely location for individualistic theories of the race issue to take root. And yet, individualism made significant gains there. Even though the approach was contested, racial individualism's ultimate success at CETRRR exposes how concerns with urban racial unrest, wartime enthusiasm for individualistic research methods, and nascent behavioralism aided the paradigm's ascent in an unexpected institutional location.

As CETRRR took shape in 1947 and developed through the early 1950s, affiliated researchers had many reasons—political, institutional, and intellectual—to be attracted to not only the study of white attitudes but also individualistic reform agendas. The committee was situated at the crossroads of two intellectual networks: one that linked white social scientists like Wirth to the wartime federal research establishment and to elite foundations and the other that connected these same scholars to race relations and civil rights activists. In the wake of wartime Nazi atrocities and a series of urban racial disturbances—notably rioting in Detroit in 1943 that many feared would recur in Chicago—networks of religious and civic activists concerned with urban "racial tensions" created a demand for research to which CETRRR responded.[5] At the same time, the politics of wartime and postwar knowledge production determined the theoretical and methodological orientation of that response. The grand War Department–supported experiments with interdisciplinarity and attitude-based survey research methods of the early 1940s set the landscape in which CETRRR made theoretical and methodological decisions. By popularizing psychological theories, refining attitude testing and public opinion polling techniques, aiding the establishment of survey research centers (like the National Opinion Research Center (NORC) that moved to the University of Chicago in 1947), producing cadres of young social psychologists who spread their theoretical assumptions about race as they moved between institutions, and exposing sociologists and anthropologists to attitude-based methods, wartime survey research broadly influenced discussions of the race issue in the postwar years.[6] CETRRR was already moving toward individualistic theoretical and methodological orientations when the Ford Foundation launched its behavioral sciences initiative in 1949, but it is hard to imagine that a favorite of the foundations, like Wirth, did not see this development as further encouraging the individualistic approach CETRRR was pursuing.[7]

At the same time, and less frequently acknowledged by historians, the developments that favored racial individualism simultaneously created obstacles for advocates of systemic and relational approaches to the race issue. Most importantly, methodological tools for studying the social and economic context of race relations remained underdeveloped. CETRRR scholars who questioned the attitudinal focus of research on race were unsure about how to study "the general situation" from which racial tensions emerged. Concern with scientific application also dissuaded the pursuit of theoretical alternatives to racial individualism. Taking lessons from interwar social ecologists who suggested that large-scale demographic and historical forces were not amenable to reform, many at CETRRR assumed that the social structural causes of racial tensions could not be altered— and were thus unproductive objects of analysis.[8] Without viable, non-Marxist economic frameworks for envisioning racial inequality as both rooted in the structures of capitalism and shaped by systemic discrimination, many CETRRR researchers treated unequal interracial competition for resources as unalterable. Although CETRRR faculty rarely discussed the developing anticommunist context explicitly, the extent to which scholars approached class-based and economically oriented analyses of race relations with trepidation paralleled postwar antiradicalism.[9] Moreover, as CETRRR's attempts to improve race relations in the Chicago public schools reveal, reforming racial attitudes produced considerably less popular opposition than redistributing resources through desegregation. Theories of the race issue that examined social structure, political economy, and institutions continued to circulate at CETRRR between 1947 and 1952. Nonetheless, the concerns of activist groups focused on prejudice and racial tensions, methodological pressures shaped by wartime survey research, and the maturing of postwar scientism together ensured that racial individualism made considerable inroads, even in the institutional home of social ecology.

Applied Knowledge on "A Generic Problem": CETRRR's Origins

Wirth's vision for CETRRR emerged from long-standing intellectual and political interests. Trained by Chicago school social ecologists—including Park, Ernest Burgess, and W. I. Thomas—Wirth completed his doctorate in sociology at the University of Chicago in 1926 and was on the staff nearly continuously until his early death in 1952.[10] He had wide-ranging intellectual interests, but his major contributions were in the development of sociological theory, urban sociology, race relations, and the theory and practice of planning.[11] Wirth's intellectual trajectory exemplified broader shifts to individualism in midcentury sociological research on the race issue, while his attention to scientific applicability blurred distinctions between basic and applied research that were becoming increasingly stark in the early Cold War years.[12]

Given his Chicago school training, Wirth's concern with the ways socioeconomic systems and individual attitudes shaped race relations is no surprise. Although known for Park's structural approach to the race issue, Chicago school sociology featured both conceptual and methodological diversity during the school's height in the 1920s and 1930s.[13] Chicago school social ecologists, as we have seen, argued that impersonal, social-structural forces—technological development, demographic change, and economic competition—provided the agents of change in race relations.[14] The approach that Park and Burgess developed, which conceived of "the city as a 'social laboratory' or clinic in which human nature and social processes might be conveniently studied," generally took cities, communities, neighborhoods, or social groups as the object of study.[15] Still, Chicago school methodology was eclectic.[16] Informal interviews, participant observation, case records of social agencies, public documents, as well autobiographies, personal letters, and fiction provided Park's and Burgess's students with much of their research material.[17] In addition, Wirth's Chicago school training would have exposed him to attitude research since sociologists and psychologists at the University of Chicago (individuals who were not considered social ecologists but were important influences on the department) had expressed interest in the study of attitudes since the interwar period. In the 1920s, Emory Bogardus devised the widely used social distance scale for measuring racial attitudes, W. I. Thomas (who counted both as a social psychologists and social ecologist exhibiting the fluidity between disciplinary

2. Louis Wirth, courtesy of University of Chicago Photographic Archive, apf1-08915, Special Collections Research Center, University of Chicago Library.

paradigms still evident in the 1920s) produced some of the earliest attitude tests, and psychologist L. L. Thurstone embraced a statistical approach to attitudes.[18]

The Chicago school's theoretical and methodological diversity and the influence of Nazi racism on American social democratic thought were both evident in Wirth's view of the race problem, which shifted substantially between the 1930s and the late 1940s. In the interwar period, Wirth understood interracial conflict as the result of ecological and economic forces and believed developing a more robust social democracy as essential to improving race relations. According to historian Walter Jackson, however, Wirth's wartime intellectual and political development "strikingly illustrates the movement towards the psychological and social psychological emphasis in studies of race and ethnicity" that characterized postwar social thought.[19] After World War II, Wirth's attention shifted from groups to individuals, as he emphasized the importance of white attitudes to the race problem. He also increasingly treated antidiscrimination legislation, desegregation laws, and education, rather than expanded jobs, housing, and social welfare mechanisms, as first priorities in the struggle for racial justice.[20]

The approach to the race issue that Wirth developed at CETRRR also challenged the stance of scientific disengagement from politics that had met considerable opposition in the 1930s but was gaining authority in the postwar years. Debates over "values" and "objectivity" had especially divided sociologists in the 1930s. While interwar "champions of objectivity" like William F. Ogburn suggested social scientists could only provide reformers with technical guidance about how to achieve certain ends, not normative advice on what ends were best, scientific democrats such as sociologist Robert Lynd emphasized the inescapably ethical nature of scientific knowledge.[21] Both agreed that scientists' values should not bias data interpretation, but scientific democrats believed scientists should take the lead in applying their findings to social problems, a stance Lynd articulated boldly in *Knowledge for What?* (1939).[22] Questions of value continued to divide postwar sociologists, and Wirth was centrally involved in the debate. Wirth believed that values should shape the choice of, but not scholarly approach to, research problems but also envisioned scientists leading programs of social betterment. In fact, bridging the first generation of the Chicago school, which featured a laissez-faire approach to reform, and the second, which emphasized urban planning and the applied field of housing, Wirth helped lead Chicago's Department of Sociology as it lost stature partially due to its focus on application.[23] Along with other critics of "abstracted empiricism," Wirth found a home in the interdisciplinary, University of Chicago–based Society for the Study of Social Problems (SSSP).[24] However, as large-scale, quantitative sociological research received considerable resources, and many functionalists gained prominence by pursuing a scholarly detachment modeled on the natural sciences, Wirth and the SSSP each moved against the grain in their continued attention to social problems.[25]

Wirth did not reject abstraction, however, but sought to bring it together with commitment to scientific utility.[26] In its first two years, Wirth reported in 1949, CETRRR researchers surveyed "the enormous body of scientific and pseudo-scientific, literature in the field." He noted in 1951 that researchers sought to distinguish "the strategically important aspects" of race relations from "the traditional and common-sense conception of the field."[27] Too much existing scholarship did not consider race relations "in their general context" and tended "to treat each instance of each minority and virtually each area as a unique case," Wirth worried. Although at times activists tried to address the "minority problem in general," in these instances "they usually follow a single technique or aim at a relatively limited objective, such as education, community organization, stimulation of pressure groups, legal action, propaganda, etc."[28] CETRRR worked to correct this problem by encouraging scholars to study race relations "as a generic problem," by integrating knowledge about different social groups and activist perspectives, and by using conclusions from specific case studies to build "a more generally valid body of knowledge" and "more generally applicable techniques."[29]

In addition to illuminating universal laws of race relations, CETRRR would also help social scientists shepherd movements of social reform. Wirth was directly involved in much activism on race relations and urban social problems, authoring or advising countless federal, state, and local government reports, serving on boards of activist organizations, and giving speeches to political or activist groups so frequently that students complained about his absence from the classroom.[30] CETRRR held a yearly conference to facilitate "better coordination" between scholars and activists engaged in race relations work. The committee also responded to a growing demand for race relations practitioners from state and city commissions, private organizations, government departments, labor unions, and business personnel departments by training such experts.[31] The organization aimed to disseminate expertise to practitioners and political workers as well. The American Council on Race Relations (ACRR), the National Association of Intergroup Relations Officials, and the Chicago Council against Racial and Religious Discrimination were closely associated with CETRRR.[32] With the ACRR, which functioned as the committee's activist arm, CETRRR served as a "clearing house" for research on the race issue, and activist groups sent a flood of requests for information each year.[33] The two groups developed manuals for improved race relations for police officers, public administrators, housing officials, and journalists and prepared model bills and ordinances to help states and localities establish race relations agencies. They also published pamphlets, including *Race Riots Aren't Necessary*, *"To Secure*

These Rights" in Your Community, and *A Community Relations Manual: What to Do about Your Community's Problems of Intergroup Relations,* to educate the public about how best to improve race relations.[34]

CETRRR had close ties to political and civic groups on the front lines of the African American civil rights movement and the more nebulous race relations movement, but the committee took a top-down approach to scientific dissemination. In contrast to the "action research" in which Kurt Lewin and the American Jewish Congress's Commission of Community Interrelations engaged or even the commitment to dialogue between scholars and activists that Fisk's Race Relations Institutes promoted, Wirth urged scientists to conduct research independently before disseminating it to activists.[35] One of CETRRR's main functions was to serve as a "fact-finding" agency. Researchers collected material on minority unemployment rates used in national and local struggles for Fair Employment Practices Commission (FEPC) legislation and compiled information on the social implications of segregation that NAACP lawyers used in Supreme Court battles against restrictive covenants and segregated higher education.[36]

Wirth's vision of social science for social action on the race issue meshed well with wartime scientific instrumentalism when he initially envisioned CETRRR in 1944. By 1947, however, postwar anticommunism and scientism were beginning to put scientific democrats and social democrats on the defensive.[37] In this setting, Wirth's plan for generalizable but applied social science distinguished the organization from the disengaged social science that increasingly attracted federal and foundation support and from efforts to mold social science to political ends in which groups like the American Jewish Congress and the NAACP were engaged. CETRRR's focus on race relations specifically also distinguished it from other interdisciplinary initiatives like Harvard's Department of Social Relations, while its methodological diversity set CETRRR off from new university-affiliated survey research centers.[38] Moreover, Wirth's extensive ties to civil rights activists and the committee's emergence in what had been the institutional home of interwar social ecology positioned it well to serve as a holdout of social structural and political economic theorizing on race in the mainstream academy.

Attitudes versus "Situation Manipulating": Defining the Race Problem

Although a few researchers concerned with labor unions and antidiscrimination law employed political economic frameworks, racial individualism permeated research at CETRRR much more than one might expect given committee members' historic ties to social ecology. A desire to improve and inform existing activism—which had expanded substantially during the war and focused on changing white attitudes and encouraging racial tolerance in integrating settings—contributed to the individualistic tilt in much CETRRR research. The shifting methodological and theoretical landscape played a central role as well.

Wirth believed that activists needed information on racial attitudes to improve their programs and assumed foundations would be supportive of applicable social research. It was due to "the enormous expenditure of effort that goes into it," Wirth noted in 1947, that research on attitudes and their malleability was especially necessary.[39] In grant proposals and reviews of the committee's work sent to Carnegie and Rockefeller officers, the sociologist emphasized that one of the most pressing needs in the field of race relations was for a synthesis of existing research on the origins of racial and ethnic attitudes and how they could be altered.[40] To address this need, Wirth employed CETRRR-affiliate Arnold Rose to compile *Studies in Reduction of Prejudice* (1947), which synthesized work in the field to aid researchers and activists.[41] In his introduction to Rose's publication, Wirth explained that the report was motivated by a desire to provide race relations organizations with a scientific basis for their work, since most race relations programs rested on the assumption "that it is possible to change human behavior by teaching, preaching, propaganda and legislation or by exposing people to certain experiences and changing their conditions of life."[42]

A number of other research projects also made racial attitudes the unit of analysis in the hopes of informing activism. Prompted by reformist and methodological considerations, the "Tension Barometer Study" exemplified a dispositional approach to the race problem. This project, as we will see shortly, sought to predict racial violence by measuring changes in white attitudes in the face of African American movement into previously homogenous, white neighborhoods. Assuming that an understanding of the cultural and psychological factors that contributed to happy interracial marriages could explain successful integration in other social contexts, another CETRRR project examined marriages between American servicemen and Japanese or Filipino women.[43] At anthropologist Sol Tax's urging, CETRRR also provided money for an investigation of Native American–white interaction among the Sioux Indians and white neighbors of the Sioux reservation.[44] In addition, social psychologist Donald Campbell, who joined CETRRR in 1951, developed an "Information-Attitude Test" that assessed the relationship between individuals' knowledge about and attitudes toward minority groups.[45]

Even though Wirth was critical of the limited reach of intercultural education, some CETRRR research addressed schools-based efforts to alter racial attitudes. Given the prevalence of antiprejudice education during World War II, Wirth believed it was necessary to scientifically assess its methods and improve its techniques.[46] In conjunction with Chicago Public School representatives, CETRRR researchers conducted a "Survey of Problems and Projects in Human Relations in the Chicago Public Schools" that informed a summer human relations workshop.[47] As part of a program titled "Intergroup Relations in the Public Schools," research assistant Helen E. Amerman reviewed relevant social scientific work, critiqued common educational approaches to intergroup relations, and produced an extensive bibliography of material on intergroup relations, prejudice, and discrimination.[48] Finally, CETRRR researchers used the Chicago Public Schools as a "laboratory" to investigate how attitudes could be modified by educational interventions and "how modifications in the social situation and in the rules of the game affect intergroup relations."[49] Thus while the popularity of intercultural education convinced Wirth that researchers needed to better understand its effects, he also tried to direct concern with prejudice toward studies of the social context of race relations.

Because sociologists and anthropologists, not psychologists, were most strongly represented among CETRRR's faculty, research tended not to focus on personality but instead took an interpersonal approach.[50] Committee research on interracial interaction in integrated housing projects, workplaces, labor unions, and schools asked two related questions: what sorts of racial attitudes were necessary for successful integration and what kinds of social and institutional circumstances could create tolerant attitudes? In fact, because of its potential for informing integration efforts, Wirth explained that studying the processes by which successful integration took place "represents one of the most important problems in race relations that has developed in America since the days of emancipation and reconstruction."[51] Supported by the Field Foundation, a number of CETRRR studies examined the successes and failures of integration in varied institutional contexts: schools, labor unions, public and private housing, and heath care facilities.[52] For example, Bernard Rosenthall, a CETRRR graduate student, placed observers in interracial housing projects and held periodic interviews with residents to test whether, and how, interracial living altered racial attitudes.[53] He used a number of different methods, including interviews of participants, observation of interracial child interaction, and tenants' collection of behavioral data on interracial interaction to examine attitudes and assess their relationship to behavior.[54] While Rosenthall believed that the institutional setting would impact levels of prejudice, relied on some of the observational methods common among interwar Chicago sociologists, and assessed the relationship between attitudes and behaviors, the dispositional and interpersonal—not social structural or political economic—realm remained his focus.

Not all CETRRR research was dispositional or interpersonal in orientation. Analyses of employment discrimination and labor unions consistently showed that conflicts of interest and political maneuvering perpetuated racial inequality and intolerance. "Racial Integration in the Local Union and the Plant: The Role of the Local Union," a paper David Bisno, another graduate student, produced for the Field Foundation, suggested that integration must further an organization's primary interests to be successful.[55] Another investigation by William Kornhauser examined thirty-four of the largest national AFL, CIO, and independent unions to determine why specific unions approached race relations as they did. He also found that organizations largely acted to preserve their interests and remained unpersuaded by appeals to "interracial solidarity of all workers."[56] *The Dynamics of State Campaigns for Fair Employment Practices Legislation*, a pamphlet produced by Bernard Goldstein for CETRRR and the ACRR with funding from the Anti-Defamation League, highlighted the political sources of racial conflict.[57] Using newspaper clippings, questionnaires, interviews, and correspondence, Goldstein looked at efforts to pass FEPC legislation in twenty-seven states from 1944 to 1949.[58] While Goldstein examined social, economic, and demographic variables, he found "the political situation and the nature of the campaign" were decisive.[59] State-level politics allowed some interest groups to make legislation reflect their concerns more fully than others.[60]

Occasionally, CETRRR research examined the connections between economic systems and racial inequality. A project completed in 1952 by graduate student E. F. Schietinger, whose origins Robert Weaver's presence at the American Council of Race Relations from 1947 through 1948 likely influenced, examined the relationship between real estate values and African American migration into particular Chicago neighborhoods.[61] Begun under Wirth's supervision, the study used real estate transaction data from different Chicago neighborhoods as well as sales information to provide "the most extensive analysis yet made of the relations between Negro occupancy and real estate prices and financing."[62] As a reminder of the anticommunist context, which was infrequently mentioned outright, William Bradbury joked about having to certify Schietinger's loyalty on a Civil Service form, since his study was "obviously subversive."[63]

CETRRR researchers working closely with labor or civil rights groups produced a few studies that rooted the race issue in conflicts of interests or economic systems. In a postwar context where much activist concern—and some foundation attention—had recently turned to prejudice and urban racial "tensions," however, the desire to produce useful knowledge more frequently led CETRRR researchers to study the race issue through a dispositional and interpersonal lens. When making a case for the practical utility of CETRRR research, Wirth had an easy time defending studies of racial attitudes or interracial interaction, especially because he claimed that CETRRR could help reformers improve programs to which they were already committed. That CETRRR emerged in 1947, as anticommunism was putting civil rights activists and socially engaged academics on the defensive, was rarely discussed openly. While this silence as likely resulted from great caution among committee members as from lack of concern, it is hard to imagine that antiradicalism did not contribute to the general skewing of CETRRR research away from politics and economics. In addition, as debate over the tension barometer, to which we now turn, reveals, the postwar politics of knowledge production also gave researchers methodological reasons to ask questions that individuals could answer.

The "Tension Barometer" and the "Situational Vacuum"

CETRRR's interest in "racial tensions" exemplifies how two sets of pressures, one externalist and the other internalist (but strongly shaped by the politics of knowledge production), intersected to favor racial individualism, even in the face of substantial critique. From 1947 through 1950, researchers working on the tension barometer focused their attention on racial attitudes in part because they were concerned with the needs of agencies committed to preventing urban racial violence. At the same time, CETRRR researchers made methodological choices in a setting strongly shaped by the flowering of wartime, attitude-based survey research and the institutionalization of survey research centers at the outskirts of leading postwar universities.

Highlighting the importance of the institutionalization of survey research to the turn to the individual at CETRRR, Clyde Hart, a Chicago-trained sociologist who had learned public opinion techniques working for the Office of War Information and led the National Opinion Research Center (NORC), initially proposed the "tension barometer" project. One of the nation's leading survey research centers, NORC was founded in 1941 at the University of Denver but relocated to the University of Chicago in 1947. Hart envisioned the "barometric scale for the measurement of interracial tensions" being used, much like a meteorological barometer, to measure the intensity of racial tensions and to predict the likelihood of interracial violence in communities undergoing racial transition.[64] In addition to Hart, Shirley Star, a sociology student associated with CETRRR and NORC who had also learned survey research techniques through wartime service, and Bernard Kramer, a former student of Gordon Allport's working at the University of Chicago, developed multiple drafts of the barometer and completed an initial test run in 1948.[65]

The barometer exemplified an individualistic approach to the study of racial conflict since its producers assumed that racial tensions could adequately be measured and explained by studying white attitudes. While social ecological analysis framed the project, authors treated demographic and economic transformations as background factors that could not be controlled and whose role in contributing to urban race relations scholars already understood.[66] Instead, the barometer surveyed a random sampling of white households in communities experiencing African American in-migration—what researchers termed "racial invasion"—to assess white attitudes toward integration that was "involuntary on the part of the whites involved."[67] Researchers assessed white respondents' attitudes to their neighborhood, understanding of the extent of or potential for "invasion," perception of tension in the neighborhood and the city, and their general feelings about African Americans.[68] Attitudes were the focus, but how context shaped them was a central concern. Researchers used a "non-invaded" community as the control and divided the "invaded community" into zones based on proximity to "the site of invasion."[69] In addition, since "racial invasion" created temporarily integrated communities, researchers also claimed they would test the "contact hypothesis," that more contact fostered better racial understanding. They also proposed considering how negative attitudes could be altered.[70]

On the one hand, externalist considerations—namely, activist and civic leaders' fears of racial violence—explain the barometer's focus on racial attitudes and tensions. Race riots in Detroit, Harlem, and Los Angeles had attracted national attention in 1943. After white youth violently attacked an interracial group of civil rights activists in Chicago's Tuley Park in 1947, Chicago municipal authorities, members of the city's race relations committee, and ACRR leaders worried Chicago might see destructive riots as well.[71] As a consequence, the barometer's authors were motivated in part by applied concerns: they wanted to determine whether methods to anticipate racial violence could be devised that might aid in prevention. To this end, authors hoped the barometer could serve as a "tension scale" that would quantify levels of racial tensions over time and use that information to predict outbreaks of interracial hostility.[72] The study was necessary, authors explained, because "action agencies" needed systematic information on the state of racial tensions and the likelihood of violence in local communities.[73] In addition, Wirth criticized agencies in the field of racial and cultural relations that claimed that racial tensions were either increasing or decreasing but whose strategies were too often "based in these unauthenticated reports." Activists themselves wanted more reliable data, moreover, "to know whether or not their activities make any difference."[74]

Methodological considerations also motivated the tension barometer. Searching for units of analysis in the study of race relations, the barometer's authors hoped to find variables that could serve the same function as "volume of trade" or "exports" did for scholars measuring "the health of an economy."[75] That the study's producers were sociologists and social psychologists influenced by concerns with attitudes among some of the interwar Chicago school as well as by the postwar expansion of attitude-based survey research and opinion polling certainly colored this search for variables. In addition to the NORC-affiliated researchers, psychologist Donald Campbell, who joined the University of Chicago in 1951 after wartime service and quickly became involved in the project, was well versed in public opinion polling and attitude testing methods.[76] Given that fear of urban violence turned researcher attention to racial tensions while the wartime refining and institutionalization of attitude-based survey methods provided a popular new tool that could readily be applied to this reformist concern, CETRRR's dispositional approach to the topic was hardly surprising.

What was somewhat surprising is the debate that developed in response to the barometer. Throughout a CETRRR seminar held in the winter of 1949 that focused on the barometer, some students and faculty criticized the barometer's basic assumptions by asking whether white attitudes provided an adequate measure of racial tensions.[77] Critics of the barometer consistently demanded analysis of what they termed "situational pressures," "historical background" factors, or "controls." In a debate with Bernard Kramer, a seminar member (probably Dietrich Reitzes or Joseph Lohman, though the name was not recorded in the seminar minutes) got to the heart of the issue. "We have a problem in that people are not free to act—there are internal and external controls operating—thus where controls differ a person behaves differently although holding the same attitudes."[78] Knowledge of situational factors was necessary, critics argued, to make the intellectual leap from individual attitudes to individual and group behaviors.

Seminar participants had a hard time, however, defining the "situational factors" that should be included in the barometer and proposing concrete methods for studying "the general situation." C. M. Briggs, a CETRRR research assistant and graduate student, argued that knowledge of "the situational pressures and controls which influence the individual to acts of hostility or increase the tension between factions in a community" was necessary. His suggestions for developing "a wider frame of reference" were quite broad, though. Briggs recommended including questions about the rate of migration, the levels of segregation in recreational facilities and opportunities, the "age pyramid" of the area, changes in the delinquency rates in transition areas, the possibilities for housing loans, and the existence of "offensive and defensive organization activities."[79] Another student, Rose Helper, made suggestions about how the barometer could integrate "situational and background factors" that were also hard to implement. Helper called for a probe of the employment situation, dissatisfaction with the community over transportation and recreational facilities, institutions such as the church and clubs, patterns of community leadership, and the role of the family.[80] While John V. Lassoe argued that an attitude survey could not predict action because an individual "seldom finds himself in a situational vacuum," student Leo Shapiro's recommendation that African American attitudes be included because minority groups were keen students of racial tension was one of the more feasible proposals.[81] One recommendation was more specific than the others, reflecting an emerging line of research on the ways institutional context affected attitudes. Lewis M. Killian, Dietrich Reitzes, and John Lassoe argued that the barometer could not predict racial violence without an understanding of power relations and the actions of organized groups. They recommended supplementing the barometer with a social survey designed to reveal "the policies and practices of the organizations in the community," the interrelationships between significant community organizations and leaders, and an analysis of community leaders and the policies they advocated.[82] In general, however, seminar participants demanded that information on power relations, market forces, and patterns of systemic discrimination be integrated into the barometer, but they lacked theoretical frameworks or methodological models to make their suggestions concrete.

The ways the tension barometer's authors responded to criticism also reveals that uncertainty about how to productively study situational factors contributed to the barometer's individualistic focus. The barometer's defenders claimed first that one study could not be expected to take all factors into account since "a single instrument will not measure everything." The barometer authors also suggested that broadly defined historical forces, which had served as key agents of change in Chicago school sociology, were too difficult to predict or to measure.[83] In contrast, authors admitted that attitudes were the unit of analysis because scholars knew how to study them. When asked whether factors other than individual attitudes would be included in the study, Kramer replied, "we may need to refine our techniques and recognize more variables." He concluded, however, sounding like his mentor Gordon Allport, that "individuals are the only ones who can talk and we should stay with them."[84] Although the authors originally defended the barometer's social utility by suggesting that it would be useful for action agencies attempting to prevent racial violence, when questioned they retreated from this claim.[85] Kramer noted repeatedly that the barometer could only predict when used in combination with other studies. "It has never been said that a tension barometer was to be used in vacuo," researcher David Gold explained.[86] The barometer's authors recognized that knowledge of other factors would ultimately be necessary to predict racial violence but did not assess or define the situational factors that should be taken into consideration.[87]

Seminar participants fiercely debated the merits of an individualistic approach to the study of racial tensions, but this discussion had little impact on the final version of the tension barometer or on future scholarship at CETRRR. Shirley Star's dissertation, which most extensively tested the barometer, responded to the seminar debate only by emphasizing that demographic forces framed the analysis and by noting, in a retreat from earlier claims, that the barometer intended only to measure not to predict racial violence.[88] A subsequent investigation by Clyde Hart and Donald Campbell integrated behavioral indexes into the analysis of racial tensions. This study used newspaper accounts of racial violence and observations of public interracial activity (in stores, theaters, bars, and playgrounds) to assess whether racial interaction reached a tipping point where integrated public spaces rapidly became segregated African American contexts.[89] And yet neither Star nor Hart and Campbell's projects addressed seminar participants' calls for an analysis of power differentials, organized groups, market forces, or systemic discrimination.

Ideas articulated in the seminar did eventually develop into an early institutional approach to the study of race relations, however, one that prefigured contemporary concepts of "institutional racism." Joseph Lohman, a Park student and criminologist who was intermittently involved with CETRRR; graduate student Dietrich Reitzes; and William C. Bradbury elaborated on the 1949 critique of the tension barometer by attacking the sustained focus on individual attitudes in race relations research more broadly.[90] Because "deliberately organized groups . . . structure and define the situations for the individual," they argued, "the key to the situation and the individual's action is the collectivity."[91] It was not individuals, Lohman, Reitzes, and Bradbury argued, but formal institutions—such as labor unions, government agencies, corporations, or neighborhood clubs—and informal social collectivities that were the appropriate focus of race relations research. This institutional approach built on social ecological methods and on Charles S. Johnson and E. Franklin Frazier's interwar analyses of systemic discrimination.[92] Most importantly, this research grew out of empirical work conducted in association with Robert Weaver's National Committee on Segregation in the Nation's Capital (NCSNC), an organization that was associated with both CETRRR and the ACRR.[93] One line of institutional analysis, which focused on housing segregation, emphasized the ways discrimination by intersecting social institutions produced systemic barriers to African American opportunity. In research that informed *Shelley v. Kraemer*, the 1948 Supreme Court case that invalidated restrictive covenants, Lohman concluded that there was collusion between real estate interests, lending agencies, title companies, and government institutionalized segregation through private practices he termed "racial zoning."[94] Bradbury's work with the NCSNC exhibited a second concern: discrimination within discrete institutions. His comparison of three federal agencies showed that leadership, policies, and the enforcement of nondiscrimination statues produced social norms within particular institutions. It was these social norms—and, more importantly, the leaders and policies that produced them—that determined a person's behavior concerning race relations and an institution's level of segregation regardless of individual attitudes.[95]

Dietrich Reitzes's University of Chicago sociology dissertation, "Collective Factors in Race Relations" (1950), represented a third, slightly different approach. This project examined the ways formal institutions and informal social collectives differently affected the same individual's behavior, regardless of attitudes. This line of analysis also linked the study of "mass society," a popular topic in the 1950s, to emerging research on the differences between racial attitudes and behaviors that Robert Merton and Robin M. Williams Jr. were pursuing.[96] Individual behavior "cannot be understood by studying merely the individual and his generalized attitudes or verbalisms," Reitzes maintained, but "must be studied in terms of his participation in collectivities and of the definition of situations by these collectivities."[97] Analysis of a segregated white neighborhood, an integrated shopping context, and a racially liberal labor union revealed that the same white individuals behaved differently on racial issues depending on the context. "*It is the policy, strategy, and tactics of organized groups,*" Reitzes emphasized, "rather than community folkways or prejudices or individual racial attitudes which are the essential factors in conditioning what happens in specific situations."[98] While Lohman studied criminology and juvenile delinquency in the late 1950s and 1960s, Bradbury later turned attention to mass society by focusing on communist soldiers during the Korean War, and Reitzes later researched racial discrimination in the medical profession, their institutionalist approach remained a minority viewpoint among sociologists in the 1950s.[99] Still, as we have seen, some leading sociologists troubled by atomism in the study of race relations—including Robert Merton, Robin M. Williams Jr., and Arnold Rose—recognized Reitzes, Lohman, and Bradbury's theoretical innovations.[100]

Interest in the institutional sources of prejudice represented an exception to CETRRR's main theoretical trajectory, however. The issues the tension barometer debate illuminated—the lack of precision in CETRRR discussions of "situational factors," the inability of most critics of the tension barometer to recommend alternative research methods, and the ease with which the tension barometer's authors deflected critique—help explain racial individualism's unexpected success at CETRRR. While wartime federal and postwar private support for survey research methods incentivized attention to attitudes, less obvious but equally important disincentives discouraged scholars interested in alternative approaches. Most significantly, tools for measuring the social, economic, or political context of race relations—techniques for studying communities, social collectives, or patterns of interaction between groups in ways that could be quantified and generalized—remained underdeveloped. Although critics of the barometer called for analyses of systemic discrimination, competition for resources, and the relative distribution of power among social groups, CETRRR researchers were unsure how to turn their impulses into concrete research proposals. That the second generation of Chicago school sociologists never refined generalizable methods for studying communities or collectives partially explains this difficulty.[101] In addition, many at CETRRR assumed that Chicago school historical factors, including migration, intergroup competition, de facto segregation, and even systemic discrimination, had little relevance for reformers because these factors had the force of natural law.[102] Social ecological theories functioned at such a grand scale that they proved difficult to translate into concrete reform programs, a problem that both Myrdal and Williams had noted.[103] The state of economic research on the race issue also contributed to the theoretical imbalance at CETRRR. The historically grounded institutional economics of the interwar period might have provided scholars of race relations with tools for studying the ways inequality in access to jobs and housing contributed to racial tensions, but the abstract, market-focused neoclassicism that dominated postwar economics was not useful to this end. In fact, Weaver recognized that University of Chicago economists were unlikely to be interested in race relations but unsuccessfully urged Wirth to include an economist (whose interests were broader than Fred Harbison's focus on industrial relations) on CETRRR.[104] Significant methodological and institutional incentives encouraged postwar scholars concerned with race to focus on racial attitudes, while critics of the individualistic approach were less sure about what kinds of methods could elucidate the social, economic, and institutional context that shaped interracial interaction.

"The Situational Approach to the Reduction of Intergroup Tensions": Redistricting and the Chicago Public Schools

The case of the tension barometer shows how important internalist, in this case methodological, considerations were to the turn to the individual in the study of race relations at CETRRR. In contrast, CETRRR's work with the Chicago Public Schools (CPS) between 1947 and 1952 exposes the ways externalist pressures shaped the translation of research into reform. Carried out by a subcommittee, the Technical Committee for the Chicago Public Schools (TC), the educational reforms CETRRR affiliates proposed questioned racial individualism. TC leaders suggested that changing teachers' and students' attitudes was irrelevant if educational resources were not equalized, by desegregation if necessary. The TC's efforts to redistrict and surreptitiously desegregate portions of the Chicago Public Schools produced mixed results, however, while intercultural education simultaneously generated quiet success. While racial integration produced as much controversy as educational redistribution, even at the height of postwar McCarthyism, intercultural education's political innocuousness proved crucial to its success.

From the outset, public school officials and CETRRR leaders disagreed about the TC program's primary goals, especially regarding intercultural education. CPS superintendent Herold Hunt had read about CETRRR in the newspaper and asked Wirth if the committee would be interested in devising an "inter-group education program" for the schools.[105] The committee Wirth put together in response included some of the university's leading social scientists: anthropologist/educationalist Allison Davis; head of the University of Chicago's School of Education Ralph Tyler; sociologists Everett Hughes, Philip Hauser, and Joseph Lohman; legal scholar Robert Ming; NORC head Clyde Hart; and anthropologist Sol Tax.[106] Despite Hunt's interest in intercultural education, the TC program developed largely out of Wirth's critique of narrowly curricular interventions, a systemic leaning shared by many on the TC, especially the sociologists. "All of the problems of human aggression and conflict cannot be solved through teaching and preaching," Wirth emphasized, citing Rose's *Studies in Reduction of Prejudice.*[107] Allison Davis, one of the first African Americans to hold a full faculty position at a major white university when the University of Chicago's School of Education hired him in 1942, shared Wirth's skepticism of intercultural education.[108] Noting that intercultural educators had been struggling to attain professional status, Davis explained that some "schools with courses in race relations tend to have the worst conditions." "It was generally agreed," the TC minutes reported in 1949, "that there was an inverse correlation between formal programs in race relations and fundamentally good relations."[109] In fact, while Hilda Taba's Intergroup Education Project was also loosely affiliated with the University of Chicago Department of Education, Taba was one of the few scholars with ties to the university whose research proposals CETRRR rejected.[110]

Instead, the TC program made equal educational opportunity its central goal and addressed the complex array of "systemic" factors affecting school-based race relations.[111] Despite school personnel's interests in intercultural education, Wirth favored analysis of "school systems," in which researchers investigated how hiring practices, districting, distributions of educational resources, and school community relations reproduced educational inequality. A focus on redistricting, Wirth hoped, would reveal "how segregation comes about in a system where officially there is a no segregation policy."[112] While CETRRR researchers working on the tension barometer might have been unsure about how to measure the systemic and institutional forces contributing to racial tensions, those associated with the TC knew at least one clear way to fight systemic racial inequality in public schooling. The centerpiece of the TC's program was a massive redistricting project—what advocates described as a "situational approach to the reduction of intergroup tensions"—that sought to ease overcrowding and equalize the utilization of elementary school facilities. The theses that analyzed CETRRR's work with the CPS emphasized this situational orientation. Framed in social ecological assumptions, student theses made clear that African American migration into previously depopulating areas of the city, a reduction in school building due to the war and suburbanization, and overcrowded facilities provided the background context in which the problem of school race relations emerged.[113] While researchers treated these patterns as unchangeable, the TC proposed to alter not individual attitudes but "the social situation within which individuals must act."[114] The TC's program also aimed to avoid "the emotion-laden issue of race relations" by addressing systemic inequality in the schools without focusing directly on its racial dimensions.[115]

Despite these intentions, however, avoiding a dispositional approach to educational race relations proved difficult. Wirth emphasized to the school board that "intercultural education is not being neglected, but the committee is using this as an opportunity to take a fresh view of it." That "fresh view" involved adding institutional reforms to antiprejudice curricular and extracurricular efforts and expanding on existing antiprejudice programs. The TC did recommend adjustments to many noncurricular aspects of the school's program: administration, the distribution of personnel, teaching methods, recreational activities, and school-community relations. It also, however, suggested modest revisions to existing intercultural education programs, such as assigning more than one person to policy making on racial and cultural relations, going beyond curricular efforts that were simply additions to the current school program, and using all subject matter (not just social studies or civics) to foster "acceptable attitudes and behavior."[116] Implicit dispositional assumptions permeated TC research efforts as well. The committee, following sociologists who had examined racial attitudes and interpersonal interaction in integrated army units, public housing, and labor unions during World War II, used the newly redistricted schools as a social laboratory in which to investigate attitudes under conditions of desegregation.[117] Many of the conclusions student theses reached answered questions about the ways individuals responded to integrated contexts. One dissertation, for example, dedicated its last six chapters to teachers' attitudes toward race relations in the hopes of supporting the "contact hypothesis" and to make clear that school integration could occur without significant protest from teachers.[118]

One factor that pushed the TC toward an individualistic approach to research and reform was fear of popular resistance to its efforts. Surprisingly, given the Cold War context, it was desegregation not redistribution that the TC worried would generate the most resistance. This concern exposed how fraught the Chicago racial context was in the late 1940s and early 1950s and how educational redistribution generated less anticommunist resistance than other redistributive policies. TC scholars did not worry about the redistributive elements of the redistricting plan when pursued in isolation or about curricular antiprejudice efforts. They repeatedly debated, however, how transparent they should be with the school board about the fact that the inequality the plan sought to redress was racial and that the redistricting they proposed would involve desegregation. At a September 1948 meeting of a subcommittee of the TC, which did not include school officials, a research assistant "pointed out that those areas where the problem of overcrowding could not be solved by shifting district boundaries were mainly either on the periphery of, or in, the Negro district."[119] Recognizing that redistricting "involves a very touchy problem in public relations," one member believed the committee should "be cautious about urging changes where there may be only slight overcrowding."[120] Others, including Wirth, Sol Tax, and Everett Hughes, eventually suggested the TC be explicit about the racial dynamics of overcrowding. Concern with public and school committee resistance to integrative redistricting was so great that in publicly circulated documents and meetings with school officials CETRRR leaders generally avoided discussing the issue.[121] In privately circulated documents, however, researchers emphasized that redistricting reversed patterns of racial inequality produced by school district gerrymandering and by housing segregation.[122]

Still, the outcomes of the TC's reformist agenda and its intellectual legacy were mixed. The school board proceeded with the elementary redistricting plan, which altered the racial distribution of Chicago's elementary schools at least for a few years. The redistricting plan reduced overcrowding in redistricted schools and did not cause overcrowding in receiving schools, as some had feared it might.[123] At the same time, many individual schools failed to comply with TC requests, litigators associated with early 1960s Chicago school desegregation cases found that many schools had underreported available rooms to avoid redistricting, some white parents protested the plan, and school officials often impeded research by refusing to provide necessary documents.[124] Most significantly, the project, which Wirth had imagined as far-reaching and long-term, was short-lived. By late 1952, public school leaders lost interest in the program altogether. While CETRRR researchers remained eager to enact a redistricting program in Chicago's high schools, and developed elaborate proposals, maps, and surveys for a project they expected to undertake, Superintendent Hunt eventually backed out and the TC was disbanded.[125]

In the TC case, popular resistance to integration and school board disinterest ultimately stymied systemic reforms. Despite the centrality of social structural and political economic analysis to CETRRR understandings of how to improve race relations in the schools, intercultural education faced less protest and school board intransigence than systemic, integrative reform. While University of Chicago faculty members saw redistricting to reduce racially uneven overcrowding as the center of its proposal for reform, the integrative elements of this plan remained too provocative to discuss publicly and, when they became evident, generated resistance and school board inaction. Despite Wirth's consistent effort to distinguish the TC's "program to improve race relations through the public schools" from intercultural education, antiprejudice curricula had a more enduring legacy.[126] Limited in scale and in its demands on white parents and educators, intercultural education was much easier to implement and much less controversial than changing discriminatory hiring practices, building new facilities, or reducing uneven patterns of overcrowding by integration.

Whether attitudes or "situational factors" should be the unit of analysis in studies of race relations, and thus whether "individual therapy" or "situational change" should be the focus of reform, was a question that surfaced repeatedly during CETRRR's short history. The issue emerged so pointedly during the seminar on the tension barometer that a faculty member proposed a class on the question. The course would investigate "to what extent are problems of intergroup tension, discrimination, etc. to be thought of as residing in the souls of individuals, to be cured by 'changing attitudes' and to what extent are they to be thought of as residing in a social situation or social structure, to be cured by legislation or other forms of situation manipulating?"[127] The course proposal held that many dilemmas in the field of race relations would be clarified if social scientists carefully assessed the potential and limits of both frameworks and produced "a frame of reference into which they both might fit."[128] The relative significance of individual attitudes and the socioeconomic context of race relations was an ongoing point of contention for CETRRR researchers, but the committee never fully linked the two frameworks. In fact a failure of interdisciplinary integration may well have contributed to the committee's dissolution after Wirth's death in 1952. Although it is likely few other CETRRR faculty were as committed to the experiment in social science for social action as Wirth, sociologist William C. Bradbury suggested the committee fizzled out because little was accomplished by its interdisciplinary collaboration.[129]

And yet in ways that often remained unacknowledged, the emphasis on interdisciplinary experimentation that permeated the wartime and postwar politics of knowledge production help explain why CETRRR turned so much attention to the dispositional and interpersonal sources of fraught race relations. The blending of sociological and psychological approaches in wartime attitude-based survey work affected debate on race at CETRRR. As networks of scholars who had learned survey methods during the war, were associated with new survey research centers, or trained in social relations programs moved through the academy, individualistic methods and theories developed momentum. At the same time, the debate over the tension barometer simultaneously exposed how significant the absence of theoretical and methodological models for studying "situational factors" was to the emergence of an individualistic approach to the race problem. In addition, the social ecological tendency to naturalize unequal competition and systemic discrimination, the failure of the second generation of social ecologists to refine case and community study methods while avoiding "particularism," and economists' minimal involvement in postwar research on race all left CETRRR graduate students uncertain about how to measure "the general situation" in which race relations evolved. Still, externalist, political dynamics—especially widespread activist concern with urban racial tensions amid resistance to desegregation—simultaneously shaped research priorities and assumptions about what theories best translated into reform. In fact, despite Wirth's skepticism of activists' common sense, reformers' priorities were among the most important factors influencing individualistic research agendas at CETRRR.

This is not to say that social scientists who emphasized racial attitudes believed the socioeconomic context of race relations was irrelevant. Wirth, Hart, and Kramer all recognized that racial tensions emerged from a variety of intersecting factors, the Field Foundation studies assessed behavior as well as attitudes in integrated settings, and the TC prioritized systemic reform. In addition, a handful of CETRRR researchers challenged the individualistic approach by emphasizing the ways institutional context shaped behavior regardless of attitudes, studying the political context nurturing state FEPC laws, or focusing on the economics of housing segregation. While these challenges remain significant, they moved against the grain. At CETRRR, individualistic explanations competed, ultimately quite successfully, against alternatives, despite the systemic orientation of the interwar Chicago school of sociology and calls for attention to the "situational context" of race relations. Even researchers focused on the institutional setting assessed how institutions and collectives shaped individual behaviors. If we return to Wirth's fire brigade metaphor, scholars of race relations who used the individual as the unit of analysis had refined tools and a developed theory when they investigated a fire's cause and their strategy for fighting the fire could be easily implemented. Those who understood the race problem in social structural or political-economic terms, however, faced dilemmas of scale that were methodological and political in orientation. They were, on the one hand, unsure how to measure the systemic and relational sources of fraught race relations in ways that met standards of postwar scientific rigor. They also, as the next chapter on Fisk University's Race Relations Institutes also shows, faced considerably more opposition turning systemic and relational paradigms into viable reform proposals, especially in the rightward moving postwar political context.

FOUR

The Mature Individual or the Mature Society: Social Theory, Social Action, and the Race Problem at Fisk University's Race Relations Institutes

"Noisy frontal attacks on prejudice" would not bring progress in race relations, Fisk University sociologist Charles S. Johnson argued at the fourth annual Fisk University Race Relations Institutes in 1947. Instead, careful social science, which involved "getting the facts," "breaking the problem down into manageable parts," and "fully sharing a common interest in solving this or that detailed part of the general problem," were "the means by which necessary and durable changes in race relations will come."[1] Johnson's commitment to dissecting a social problem so as to view its "manageable parts" posited social science as an essential tool in the struggle for racial justice, while his skepticism of "noisy . . . attacks on prejudice" questioned antiprejudice education and moral exhortation. Both themes emerged centrally in the history of Fisk University's Race Relations Institutes, where leaders believed that social scientific knowledge should inform social action, that multidisciplinary dialogue would improve research and reform on the race issue, and that calls for racial goodwill were not enough.

With funding from Fisk University, the American Missionary Association, and the Julius Rosenwald Fund, Johnson established Fisk's Race Relations Department (RRD) in 1942 and initiated yearly Race Relations Institutes (RRI) in 1944. Like Johnson's interwar work with the Rockefeller Foundation, the three-week summer Institutes brought social scientists into dialogue with civil rights and labor activists, teachers, social workers, and government personnel.[2] The first week of the meetings presented varied social scientific frameworks for envisioning the race issue, generally sociological, anthropological, and psychological. The second two weeks addressed activist concerns, including employment, housing, education, the needs of returning veterans, court battles for civil rights, and the activities of urban race relations commissions, religious antiracist groups, and social welfare workers.

The Institutes provided an intellectual underground where the social scientific interracial left that had flourished during the Depression continued to theorize the intersections of race and class oppression, emphasize the causal significance of exploitation, and present prejudice as a rationalization.[3] While pronounced in 1944, this systemic and relational theoretical orientation continued even into the late 1940s and 1950s, when political economic and social structural explanations of the race issue declined in prominence in mainstream social scientific discourse.[4] In addition, between 1944 and 1947 RRI participants developed a redistributive racial liberalism that translated systemic and relational theories into reformist paradigms. From 1949 through the early 1960s, however, as RRI leaders turned political attention from race relations and redistribution to rights, theoretical and reformist languages increasingly diverged.

Systemic and relational theories of the race issue endured at the postwar RRI for a number of reasons. While the refining of wartime survey research methods, the expanding institutional power of psychology, and growing postwar commitment to scientism and behavioralism shored up racial individualism in some elite white research universities and foundations, these methodological and theoretical imperatives exerted less influence at Fisk University. In the still segregated mid-twentieth-century academy, that foundation-based academic agenda setters tended to assume that cutting edge social science would only emerge from a handful of elite, white research institutions allowed alternatives to racial individualism—the "normal sociological paradigms" of the 1920s and 1930s—to continue at Fisk.[5] Institutes participants' views of the race issue also reflected counterhegemonic traditions in African American thought that had roots earlier in the century, flourished in the 1930s, but continued through the 1940s and 1950s among African American intellectuals, especially Pan-Africanists and anticolonialists.[6] In addition, the economic concerns that the teachers, social workers, labor organizers, and religious leaders who attended the Institutes faced on a daily basis in African American communities shaped RRI debate.[7]

The Institutes' mission of using interdisciplinary social science to inform activism for racial justice, nonetheless, involved a number of tensions associated with the scale of feasible reform. Even though the social scientific interracial left that met at the RRI articulated economically informed, conflict-based, structural theories of the race issue from 1944 through the early 1960s, translating systemic and relational conceptual frameworks into seemingly realistic reform agendas proved difficult after 1949. Always a nimble political strategist, Johnson reformulated the Institutes' politics, often in ways unrelated to his scientific commitments, in terms that would be palatable in a rightward-moving political context. Despite brief efforts to demand "positive rights" and enduring skepticism of racial "goodwill," many at the Institutes embraced individualistic, rights-oriented agendas for racial reform by the early 1950s, regardless of their theoretical convictions.

This chapter begins by explaining the Institutes' origins, situating their approach to socially relevant social science in Johnson's intellectual trajectory, and addressing how Fisk's Department of Social Sciences (DSS, established in 1928), its RRD and RRI pursued this mission. The second section focuses on social scientific debate at the Institutes, pointing to the relatively limited role psychological individualism played in Institute theorizing and the robust combination of systemic and relational theories that emerged from Institute discussions throughout the RRI's history. The third section addresses RRI reform discourse, highlighting two distinct periods: one between 1944 and 1947 that featured a redistributive racial liberalism and one that emerged after 1949 that saw a shift in reformist emphasis from redistribution to rights.

"To Stimulate Action with Knowledge and Understanding": Social Science for Social Action at Fisk

The firm commitments to resisting segregation, addressing the intersections of economic and racial oppression, and using science in the service of social and political action that would characterize Fisk's Race Relations Department and Institutes after 1944 grew out of concerns that had emerged in student protests at Fisk in the 1920s and permeated the Depression-era African American and interracial lefts. Interwar protests against white philanthropic paternalism, white college leadership, and racially discriminatory parietal laws shaped the integrationist politics that emerged from Fisk University, the nation's leading African American liberal arts college, as it developed as a center for social scientific research on race in the late 1920s.[8] In addition, advocating what historian Jonathan Scott Holloway describes as the "Amenia ideal," the interwar African American and interracial lefts that coalesced in the 1930s included many social scientists who would attend the RRI in the 1940s and 1950s. This coalition of communists, socialists, and liberals brought to the civil rights mainstream assumptions that had seemed radical previously: that race and class were inseparably linked social categories, that class oppression was as responsible as racial discrimination for African American social, economic, and political problems, and that securing jobs and interracial unionization were crucial first steps in the movement for racial justice. This group tied concerns with racial justice to an emphasis

3. Charles S. Johnson, courtesy Fisk University, John Hope and Aurelia E. Franklin Library, Special Collections, Photographic Archives, Charles S. Johnson Papers.

on reforming capitalism, demands on the state to redistribute economic resources, and anticolonial struggles abroad.[9]

Johnson's careful treatment of issues of scientific objectivity also shaped the RRI's postwar approach to theory and reform on the race issue. When working with the Urban League in the 1920s, or on the LSRM-sponsored *The*

Negro in American Civilization (1930), Johnson always employed politically neutral, empirically based language.[10] His approach involved a cultivated strategy of "indirection" in which he let the facts of racial injustice generate anger and motivate action.[11] This tactic helped Johnson become a favorite of foundation leaders, as we saw at the RF, and of moderate HBCU administrators like Fisk president Thomas Else Jones, who recruited Johnson to the faculty to establish its Department of Social Sciences (DSS) in 1928. Johnson's racial diplomacy also aided the sociologist in becoming the first African American president of Fisk University in 1947.[12]

And yet Johnson's scholarly work often had radical political implications. Throughout the 1920s, 1930s, and 1940s, Johnson examined the social structural, and especially the economic, underpinnings of urban racial conflict in the North and of racial injustice and inequality in the Jim Crow South. As associate executive secretary of the Chicago Commission on Race Relations, which published the 1922 *The Negro in Chicago: A Study of Race Relations and a Race Riot*, Johnson chronicled the ways migration, interracial competition for space and jobs, systemic racial discrimination, and white bigotry combined to create the 1919 Chicago race riot.[13] In *Shadow of the Plantation* (1934) and *The Collapse of Cotton Tenancy* (1935) the sociologist combined community study methods, a focus on social structure, and attention to "social disorganization" characteristic of the Chicago school with the emphasis on exploitation and political economy of the interracial left.[14] Johnson never directly promoted alternatives to capitalism. His careful studies of southern black sharecroppers nonetheless exposed how racial oppression was bound up with economic exploitation and highlighted the social, cultural, and economic costs of white supremacy. "It is unquestionably the economic system in which they live," Johnson concluded in *Shadow of the Plantation*, a heart-wrenching depiction of economic dislocation and cultural pathology among black sharecroppers, "that is responsible for their plight."[15] Although Johnson addressed white prejudice when explaining urban racial unrest in the 1920s, his interest in plantation economies and his Chicago school training led him to explain the sources of the race problem through a combination of political economy and social ecology.[16]

The stance toward the integration of science and politics that emerged first at Fisk's Department of Social Sciences (DSS) and then its Race Relations Department reflected Johnson's simultaneous commitment to social scientific objectivity and utility. On the one hand, since Johnson believed that scientists would be most effective politically if they let the facts of racism speak for themselves, he sought to make Fisk's DSS a major research center specializing in the study of African Americans and race relations, especially in the

South. He also assumed, like Louis Wirth and Robin Williams Jr., that generalizability was necessary for scientific rigor.[17] On the other hand, Johnson did not believe that scientists should be disengaged, only that their politics should not color their methods, conclusions, or tone. Once the facts of racial injustice had been objectively ascertained, Johnson, like many proponents of the Amenia ideal, envisioned social scientists taking leadership roles in movements for change.[18] To this end, the RRD established a "data bank" that provided a "reservoir of information" on African American community life, social problems, and race relations that activists, philanthropists, and government officials regularly turned to in the 1930s and 1940s.[19] *The Monthly Summary of Events and Trends in Race Relations*, the RRD's regular publication between 1943 and 1948, recorded race relations developments nationwide for activist use.[20] Johnson also envisioned both the DSS and RRD as settings that would provide future race relations practitioners with a sound foundation in social scientific theory.[21] The RRD's mission of scientific dissemination and application was also combined with an explicit commitment to political advocacy. The department published many educational pamphlets intended to influence public opinion in favor of desegregation, including *If Your Next Neighbors Are Negroes* (1948); *Segregation: A Challenge to Democracy* (1950); and *Integration: Promise, Process, Problems* (1952).[22] At times, moreover, the RRD envisioned a reciprocal relationship between social scientific experts and community leaders, an approach Johnson had promoted at the Rockefeller-supported National Interracial Conference in the late 1920s. RRD leaders encouraged dialogue between scholars, activists, and practitioners on the race issue, most notably in "community self-surveys" where scholars both sought to inform and learn from lay experts.[23]

The RRD's summer Institutes embodied this dual stance toward expertise. Since Johnson believed there were too few settings where political activists could be exposed to social science, scientific presentations held a privileged position in the Institutes' weekly structure.[24] Between 1944 and 1951, the first week of Institute meetings outlined psychological, sociological, anthropological, and historical perspectives on the race problem in the United States to provide background for subsequent activist discussions.[25] Some of the nation's best-known sociologists, anthropologists, psychologists, historians, and, occasionally, economists and political scientists of race relations (a multiracial group) served on the faculty over the years.[26] And yet social scientists were not the only individuals recognized as experts at the Institutes. The civil rights activists, labor organizers, religious leaders, politicians, and government workers who also served on the Institutes' staff were a "who's who list" of the postwar civil rights world.[27] The second two weeks of the Institutes included sessions on employment, housing, education, community organizations, migration, urban racial conflict, national civil rights campaigns, and the role of religious institutions in improving race relations.[28]

Although the Institute participants embraced a variety of disciplinary orientations and political priorities, RRI leadership had definite political objectives. Johnson and his successor as Institute head Herman Long were especially skeptical of approaches that fostered interracial understanding without necessarily attacking legal segregation. They did not, however, reject moral exhortation or planned interracial contacts altogether. After the RRI held its first summer session, Johnson emphasized that being located in a southern city, especially given the interracial living arrangements, represented a significant accomplishment in and of itself. Promotional pamphlets depicted interracial fellowship prominently.[29] (See figure 4.) What RRD leadership did reject was interracialism as a sole strategy. Despite consistent efforts to appeal "to conscience and good will," the RRD's second director Herman Long emphasized in 1953, experience revealed that "exhortations to do justly and to act toward all men as brothers were not enough." Instead, the RRI used social scientific expertise and Christian ideals "to make a dent in the armor of segregation and discrimination."[30]

Fisk's Race Relations Institutes brought together groups that had comprised the Depression-era interracial left and were realigning as World War II came to a close: the nation's most renowned African American intellectuals and social scientists of race relations; leading liberal white social scientists concerned with race; scholars interested in "other minority groups"; many national labor and civil rights leaders who advocated the Amenia ideal; representatives of religious and philanthropic organizations committed to direct action, not just moral exhortation; and local activists concerned with race relations or African American social welfare. The Institutes' commitment to using interdisciplinary social science to inform social action, combined with the fact that some of its best-known participants were the leading voices articulating social structural and political economic theories of the race issue, left it poised to challenge postwar racial individualism.

"A Chicken-and-Egg Kind of Problem": Prejudice and Oppression in RRI Theorizing

The history of Fisk's Race Relations Institutes from its origins in 1944 through the early 1960s reveals that racial individualism did not set the terms of debate on the race problem in all postwar social scientific settings.

4. Race Relations Institutes, 1948, courtesy Fisk University, John Hope and Aurelia E. Franklin Library, Special Collections, Race Relations Institutes Collection.

Certainly, in these years the numbers of psychologists and psychiatrists presenting at the RRI increased while some sociologists and anthropologists took on the language and assumptions of the psychological sciences. Still, although the Institutes began a decade after the Depression-era height of the black and interracial lefts, many of the social scientists who convened there each summer continued, in their theoretical work at least, to envision the race issue in systemic and relational terms, as a problem of social structure, group relations, oppression, and exploitation. And yet, though Institutes participants touted the practical utility of interdisciplinary dialogue, the dispositional theories of the race issue that psychologists tended to promote were much easier to translate into programs for change than the social structural or political economic frameworks sociologists, anthropologists, economists, and historians advocated.

Psychologists concerned with prejudice had the easiest time aligning theoretical commitments and reform proposals. Most of the psychologists and psychiatrists who contributed to the Fisk Institutes, including Helen McLean, Gordon Allport, Nathan Ackerman, Smiley Blanton, Janet Rioch, and Sol W. Ginsburg, focused on white attitudes and identified the sources of prejudice in individual emotional needs and patterns of child rearing. They also debated whether prejudice was normal or pathological and, as early as 1946, reflected the field's growing interest in personality structure. Often their causal explanations dissociated prejudice from the social context, an issue they admitted was a problem common to their discipline.[31] At the 1947 RRI, for example, Nathan Ackerman, a Columbia University–trained psychiatrist, synthesized emerging work on anti-Semitism and the personality correlates of prejudice, including research that would make up *The Authoritarian Personality*. Rooted in psychological needs regardless of social context, prejudice, he argued, served crucial functions for "distorted personalities."[32] Smiley Blanton, a psychiatrist based in New York, claimed at the 1946 and 1949 Institutes that prejudice was a natural psychological tendency, often emerging from universally valid aging processes. Children "whether . . . reared in the South Sea Islands, or in an African tribe in the Congo, or in Park Avenue in New York," he held, made sense of the challenges of adolescence by stigmatizing others.[33] In 1951 Sol W. Ginsburg presented the prejudiced as highly anxious and "struggling with inner conflict," a view that, like Blanton's, implied that prejudice could be understood without taking the social context into account.[34]

RRI psychologists tried to incorporate the social into their analysis when they could. Rioch, Ackerman, and Ginsburg called explicitly for an exchange of ideas between psychologists and sociologists, though they offered few specific suggestions about how collaboration across disciplines might occur. Allport, who reported in 1946 on rumors and race riots, recommended research on the relationship between social processes, group norms, and individual beliefs.[35] Even Ackerman, whose work leaned toward psychological structuralism in its primary emphasis on the causal importance of emotional and cognitive factors, acknowledged that in some individuals prejudice "is related to social conformity to the dominant group."[36] Character structure theories of prejudice overlooked the ways human behaviors resulted from the interplay of mental, socioeconomic, and cultural factors, Ginsburg worried in 1951, noting, "too often a psychiatrist did not know if his patient was 'a baker or a dentist.'"[37] While drawing attention to the need for integrating context into psychological research—and despite the fact that presence at the Institutes indicated support for legal desegregation—the RRI psychologists' reform recommendations reflected their disciplinary orientation. Generally RRI psychologists suggested changing individual attitudes through education, planned interracial contacts, or psychotherapy.[38]

Sociologists and anthropologists who approached the race issue from a structural and relational, not a dispositional, angle faced more difficulty showing how their theories could inform agendas for change.[39] The combination of social structural and political economic analysis articulated most clearly in Institute sociological and anthropological sessions drew on a number of sources. Sociologists relied on social ecological frameworks when emphasizing the importance to contemporary race relations of transitions from plantation society to Jim Crow segregation in the South and migration and interracial competition in the North and West. RRI structuralists also challenged the sense of inevitability in Chicago school theories by highlighting the centrality of unequal power relations sustained by violence to white supremacy. Many sociologists also framed their discussions of contemporary race relations in the United States in discussions of the colonial context.[40] In addition, echoing the Depression-era interracial left, it was not only broad social structures but also the structures of capitalism that played central causal roles in RRI sociological and anthropological theories. Institute discussions in fact exposed how frequently scientists on the non-Marxist left in the 1940s and 1950s employed concepts like exploitation, oppression, and rationalization associated with Marxist thought.

RRI sociologists, anthropologists, historians, and the occasional economist who focused on the systemic and relational aspects of the race issue did not ignore prejudice altogether. Instead, they treated it as a rationalization, an ideology that helped to sustain but did not fundamentally determine the economic and political structure. Exposing the enduring shadow of biological racism that postwar social scientists still felt the need to dispel, at least one session each year (usually anthropological) explained the fallacy of biological conceptions of racial difference, often by pointing to international variations in racial categorization. Still, while acknowledging that ideas about race helped to sustain injustice, most RRI sociologists and anthropologists prioritized exploitation and oppression, suggesting that the real cause of the race problem rested in politics, demographic patterns, and economics.[41]

Charles S. Johnson elucidated the common wisdom—arguments that emerged not only in the mid-1940s when they were fairly common among the African American "popular front" but also into the mid-1950s when they had become muted in wider discourse—when suggesting that racial ideas derived from economic pressures.[42] At the 1945 RRI, he emphasized that European expansion and "colonialism imperialism" determined the character of American race relations, since colonization necessitated slavery, and later segregation, to locate "cheap and controlled labor."[43] A social ecological explanation with Marxist echoes, Johnson claimed that the concept of race existed because it justified economic exploitation. "Slavery is old," Johnson argued, "but the present-day conception of race as a justification for keeping a population group in bondage is new." Not only did "the theory of racial inferiority" justify slavery, but it also sustained segregation, which provided "a substitute method for maintaining the labor supply in some areas."[44] While he remained imprecise about how exploitation could be avoided, and despite his reputation for political moderation, Johnson understood class and racial oppression to be inextricably linked.[45] Even in 1949, though his political agenda would shift, systemic and relational theorizing permeated Johnson's RRI presentations. Johnson distinguished between "inter-individual relations" and "social relations" and argued that American race relations should be understood as the latter since interactions "based on the social functions performed by the related persons," produced racial conflict.[46]

Duke University sociologist Edgar T. Thompson also discussed prejudice as a justification for, not the root cause of, the race issue. Trained at the University of Chicago and the University of South Carolina, Thompson established Duke's Center for Southern Studies and was a leader in the comparative sociology of plantation societies. While he recognized that prejudice could be irrational and instinctual, he largely articulated a political economic vision of the race problem. The plantation system served as a "political institution" that determined "the norm for the definition of southern social classes and for movements of rebellion, reaction, and conformity." Ideas about race were powerful, but American race relations, Thompson held, could only be understood in terms of historically specific social and political systems.[47]

For a few RRI participants, American race relations involve violently enforced political oppression and exploitation, while progress in race relations necessitated large-scale shifts in power, economic restructuring, and social engineering. A Cambridge University sociologist interested in postcolonial Africa, Reginald Barrett revealed how far left RRI participants were allowed to go in their discussions of the race problem, even in 1951.[48] "Racial Ideology seeks to reconcile the harsh policy of imperialism with the conscience of democracy," Barrett maintained, insisting on fundamental economic changes.[49] Sounding quite a bit like Myrdal, Barrett held that "race relations in the South could be improved by a planned economy and by full employment," since social engineering could produce a higher standard of living and "a feeling of security." While he recognized that prejudice worsened economic dislocation, Barrett clearly saw the economy as the most important engine of change in race relations.[50] Perhaps because he was a European, he felt less constrained by the backlash against an expansive state and economic planning that marked American liberal politics in the early 1950s. Barrett's straightforward call for economic restructuring and social planning would have been to the left of the RRI even in 1944; it was a minority view in 1951. Still, his presence indicated the ongoing expansiveness of RRI theoretical discussion even at the height of American antiradicalism.

Even as late as 1955, Johnson relied on a systemic logic—albeit one whose class elements were muted—to explain why economic and social modernization meant that progress toward cultural and political change in southern race relations was possible.[51] Johnson held that movements against colonialism were making the myth of white supremacy obsolete abroad while southern modernization exhibited this process at home. In the South, dramatic but underrecognized patterns of industrialization, urbanization, migration, educational development, and economic integration with the rest of the nation were emerging, Johnson held, "against the very logic of the culture and its folkways."[52] Johnson used a social ecological approach to explain why, since the South was already on the way to social and economic modernization, southern liberals should demand desegregation immediately.[53]

In the same year, economist Robert Weaver provided one of the most clearly systemic and relational theories of the racial crisis in housing, exhibiting the crucial perspective economists brought to the race issue. Weaver argued that race-neutral market and demographic processes, histories of and ongoing discrimination against African Americans, and flawed public policies produced de facto housing segregation.[54] Ecological patterns, such as wartime migrations, had created African American demand for affordable housing, but, despite higher earnings among nonwhites and reduced prejudice, housing integration substantially lagged behind other sectors. The political context was decisive, since a discriminatory real estate industry and redlining prevented African Americans from accessing the housing they would otherwise naturally demand in the market. Recent "slum clearance and rehabilitation" programs were part of the problem because they eradicated "substandard housing" but did not provide sufficient new housing for displaced communities. Weaver's recommendations for change also prioritized the systemic and relational. They included producing housing policy sensitive to the social ecological patterns that shaped urban development, creating federal and local programming to ensure access to affordable housing, and designing urban redevelopment so it attended to the housing needs of displaced minority communities.[55]

And yet even before McCarthyism limited the civil rights agendas of many RRI activists, others who articulated systemic and relational theories recommend reforms that failed to reflect the complexity of those visions. Edwin Embree, head of the American Council on Race Relations and the Julius Rosenwald Fund, suggested in 1945 that violently enforced power relations and economic exploitation served as the source of the race problem but provided recommendations for action that were vague, conservative, and saw schools as the primary agent of change.[56] Park-trained sociologist Clarence Glick, who taught at Tulane, Brown, and the University of Hawai'i, argued in 1947 that race relations research should not take the individual as the unit of analysis since the race problem involved patterns of conflict between unequal social groups. Since intergroup conflict and prejudice was "rarely between equals," Glick emphasized, the "ideology of race relations" provided "justifications for whatever social isolation and discrimination may be imposed" and "rationalizations for maintaining another racial group in a subordinate status."[57] This view of racial ideology, which depicted individuals mired in economic, political, and especially cultural-ideological systems they could not control, ensured that "improving race relations" was more complicated than "modifying one's prejudices."[58] And yet Glick turned to reforms whose rationale he had criticized when recommending what to do next.[59] "If totalitarians can remake the human nature of adults in a very short time," Glick concluded, "there is no reason why democracies cannot make more headway than they do with this same tactic."[60] While education by no means provided a total solution, interracial workshops and educational programs in schools and the media were, he suggested, a place to start.

Another example of the challenge scholars concerned with exploitation and oppression faced when pushed for reform recommendations emerged in a session featuring sociologist Horace Cayton and psychologist Kenneth Clark. In 1947, the two well-known African American scholars of race relations discussed the psychological processes at work in systems of exploitation. Linking Marxism and psychology, they argued that white prejudice resulted from and justified a system of oppression sustained by force. Cayton, then working as director of a community center on Chicago's South Side, had just published *Black Metropolis* with St. Clair Drake. Cayton presented the race problem as fundamentally an issue of power deployed to protect white economic interests. "The Negro in the United States is an oppressed minority," he maintained. "This oppression, based in some sections of the country on law, is further reinforced by tradition and custom" and "finds its ultimate sanction in the application of force and violence."[61] As under slavery and colonialism, the American racial situation derived from violently enforced oppression, a situation that caused white people to suffer from "an oppressor's psychosis," which led them to fear "retribution" from those they had victimized.[62]

Kenneth Clark also linked Marxist and psychological theories to define the race issue as a situation of oppression for which prejudice served as rationalization. He broke with psychologists who saw prejudice as merely a personality distortion or neurosis and instead presented prejudice as a cultural norm—not a pathological exception—in the United States. "Prejudice," as he put it, "is as American as the Declaration of Independence."[63] While prejudice might meet individual emotional needs it also served broader sociocultural and political functions. Psychological mechanisms such as rationalization, identification, guilt, and aggression, Cayton and Clark each held, worked to "stabilize" an oppressive, hypocritical racial order. "Having in mind the stereotype that 'the negro is childlike and irresponsible by nature,'" Clark argued, "we can say there is no use trying to educate him, and we can assume it is not necessary to be courteous to him."[64] Stereotypes of black criminality, childlikeness, and intellectual inferiority provided "an elaborate façade of justification and rationalization" that helped white Americans avoid guilt.[65] Radicalizing Myrdal's American dilemma thesis and flipping the causal argument at the heart of personality-based theories of prejudice, Cayton and Clark agreed that prejudice represented a rationalization, a psychological mechanism that white individuals employed to avoid confronting the oppressive racial order that benefited them.

At the 1947 Institute, Cayton and Clark shied away, however, from translating their vision of the race problem into a program for action. A discussion between the two scholars and sociologist Arnold Rose highlighted the theoretical bind in which they found themselves.[66] Distinguishing between reducing prejudice and fighting its consequences, Clark explained, "You can't hope to get rid of prejudice as long as human personalities function on an immature level in an immature society or culture." An unidentified audience member then asked whether "mature personalities" could even exist under a capitalist system. "The problem," Clark noted, suggesting this was the crucial question, "is a 'chicken-and-egg kind of problem' of whether the mature individuals or the mature society are developed first."[67] Scholarship exposing the contours of such "chicken-and-egg" problems did not, however, provide good guidance on what activists should do. The session reached few conclusions about how to proceed, and Clark and Cayton retreated from making policy recommendations. Instead, they advised self-reflection by RRI participants, fearing that "talk about action" would lead members to be inspired without adequately questioning their own assumptions.[68] Although their critiques of the individualistic paradigm were especially thorough, Cayton and Clark were either unable to clearly articulate the reform implications of their theories or decided that the venue was not appropriate for doing so.

What Institute theoretical debates reveal is that the social scientific interracial left that had flourished in HBCUs in the 1930s was alive and well, even as mainstream federal and foundation-supported research on race embraced attitude surveys after 1944, noneconomic "human relations" paradigms after 1946, and behavioralism after 1949. Psychology influenced but did not undermine the common wisdom among sociologists, anthropologists, historians, and economists at the RRI: that the race problem was an issue of social structure and political economy, of what many described as oppression and exploitation. These theories, while not advocating socialist revolution, rooted racism in histories of capitalist and colonial exploitation and presented prejudice as not a cause of the racial oppression but as a supporting rationalization. Institute participants did not move away from these *theoretical* convictions even as systemic and especially relational assumptions became politically suspect beginning in the late 1940s. Much as Chicago school frameworks lasted in some "second tier" sociology departments even as the field's center of gravity shifted to Harvard and Columbia, paradigms popular during the "Golden Age of Negro Sociology" continued to circulate at the RRI even in the 1950s when they had declined elsewhere. In part this endurance occurred because the incentives encouraging "atomistic" frameworks in elite white research institutions were not important for many RRI participants working in less elite academic settings.[69] In addition, the intellectual community that coalesced at the RRI drew actively on radical, internationally oriented traditions associated with the interracial left and African American popular front in ways the RF or CETRRR did not.

Dilemmas associated with the scale of feasible reform ensured that activist-scholars had a hard time translating this combination of political economic and social structural explanations into reform proposals, however. Even at the height of the interracial left in the 1930s, to claim that economic exploitation and violent political oppression produced America's "dilemma" did not lead to clear and viable agendas for change. Whether projects of social engineering could alter the large-scale demographic transformations that social ecologists saw at the root of the issue remained unclear, even in Myrdal's hopeful treatment of the topic. One could call for workers' cooperatives, "industrial democracy," or interracial unionizing, as Du Bois and Bunche did during the Depression. One could recommend redistributive, New Deal–style social democratic programming, as Myrdal had and many Institute activists would between 1944 and 1947. And yet, given the grand scope of theories of exploitation and oppression, these solutions were partial, separatist, or compensatory. The real implications of political economic and social structural theories suggested that sustained challenges to capitalism and large-scale, imprecisely defined restructuring of power relations were necessary. While even in the 1930s such policy implications were challenging to define and difficult to implement, after 1947, much more moderate demands branded one as a communist.[70] Despite the Institute's mission to avoid narrow programs of "goodwill," from the mid-1940s through the early 1960s, how to reform a prejudiced personality was clearer than how to restructure a capitalist economy or reorganize an oppressive political or social system. Except, of course, when one turned to legal segregation and discrimination, issues on which Institute participants knew exactly what to do.

From Redistribution to Rights: The Evolution of Institute Politics

Even though the absence of the theoretical, methodological, and financial pressures that favored racial individualism elsewhere helped account for the persistence of systemic and relational theories at the RRI, the rightward-moving postwar political context affected how scientists translated theory into practice. Johnson founded the Institutes at a moment of particular optimism among racial liberals and social democrats, when civil rights had moved onto the liberal agenda but the postwar narrowing of New Deal liberalism was not yet complete. In the second half of the 1940s, the federal government was emerging as an ally for proponents of racial justice, northern African Americans were becoming swing voters, campaigns for open housing and fair employment practices were meeting some success, and the NAACP scored crucial victories on the road to *Brown*.[71] In the same years, however, the reformist New Deal waned, economic growth suggested government intervention in labor markets might be unnecessary, labor leaders shed their Depression-era radicalism in favor of alliances with an increasingly liberal Democratic Party, federal fair employment legislation failed, and McCarthyism emerged with force.[72] Reflecting this shifting context, two distinct phases are apparent in Institute political debate. Between 1944 and

1947 Institute participants articulated a redistributive racial liberalism that featured calls for New Deal–style programs of social provision and also pursued legal desegregation and nondiscrimination. After 1947—and most clearly after 1949 as both anticommunism and legal efforts against deseg-regation gained considerable momentum—Institute participants continued to emphasize nondiscrimination and desegregation but dropped demands for redistribution. While Johnson briefly embraced a language of positive rights, Institute politics coalesced by 1949 around the protection of negative, civil and political, rights and equal opportunity characteristic of postwar racial liberalism, until new tendencies emerged in the early 1960s.

From 1944 through 1947, the community activists, educators, social workers, labor organizers, and national civil rights leaders featured in the Institute's second two weeks of sessions, as well as some social scientists giv-ing reform-oriented presentations, articulated alternatives to psychological individualism and even to rights-based individualism. The racially relevant, redistributive liberalism that emerged in these years featured unwavering commitment to legal desegregation in the South. Institute activists also, however, made job creation and robust welfare state provisions central ele-ments of an agenda for racial justice. In so doing they reflected New Deal priorities already on the wane and the core reforms black workers and grass-roots activists had been pursuing in the urban North and West since the 1930s—access to jobs, housing, education, and social insurance combined with antidiscrimination legislation.[73]

Between 1944 and 1947 RRI discussions of jobs, housing, and social wel-fare reflected social structural and political economic theories. This debate echoed the interwar interracial left's calls for federal and state job creation programs, affordable housing, and expanded social safety nets and the com-mitment to social engineering that permeated Myrdal's work. For example, Willard S. Townsend, a member of the Congress of Industrial Organizations' (CIO's) executive committee and international president of the United Transport Service Employees of America, argued in 1945 that "the abolition of economic insecurity . . . should be of immediate concern to the people of our nation." Although it is hard to know if his ideas were influenced by social scientific research, his views represented the logical conclusion of much of the systemic and relational theorizing simultaneously circulating at the RRI. Townsend suggested "planning for full employment and a decent standard of living in peacetime." He also advocated public-works-based job creation programs that would become "a permanent and accepted agency of government," expanding federal unemployment insurance programs, and government provision of "adequate medical and surgical care" to secure a minimum standard of living for all.[74] Others embraced systemic logics in suggesting that social provision could help prevent racial violence, a growing concern given the race riots of the mid-1940s. CETRRR leader Louis Wirth, who was also a frequent RRI participant, made clear in 1945 that race relations could not be separated from concerns with economic security because insecurity so often underlay racial conflict. Like Townsend, Wirth argued that race relations programs must provide "a sound level of economic security" by ensuring the provision of adequate employment, housing, schooling, health care, and public safety.[75]

While most liberals celebrated "full employment" in the immediate postwar years, they tended to disagree on whether public policy was necessary to produce it.[76] RRI participants fell on the left of these discussions, emphasizing the need for government job creation to produce full employment alongside fair employment legislation. William Y. Bell, the southern regional director of the National Urban League, argued at the 1945 RRI that Americans should commit fervently to full employment and should develop concrete policies and programs to secure that end.[77] Another Institute participant suggested that since a scarcity of jobs created competition between workers, full employment represented "the only hope for nondiscrimination in employment."[78] From 1944 through 1947 alternatives to racial individualism circulated widely in reformist debates over how to produce full employment and ease the postwar economic transition.

In discussions of housing, Institutes participants also drew on systemic assumptions by suggesting that the availability of a resource was as important as the level of discrimination African Americans faced in securing it. In 1945, Robert Taylor, chairman of the Chicago Housing Authority, argued not only that full employment was a prerequisite to successful urban development but also that government provision of affordable housing, alongside challenges to restrictive covenants and antidiscrimination measures, were necessary. "If a decent home for every family cannot be made available through the ordinary channels," he explained, worried that the building industry could not make a profit on homes low income families could afford, "then government must step in."[79] Since housing was as important a concern as employment for returning veterans, Bell strongly supported the GI Bill's housing provisions and called for "locational" as well as vocational readjustment for black veterans.[80]

Since Institute leader, sociologist, and housing expert Herman Long and economist Robert Weaver were leading voices at the RRI, it is no surprise that the systemic mechanisms sustaining housing segregation emerged centrally in Institute discussions. Both scholars were actively involved in the legal case against restrictive covenants, and Weaver's commitment to applying economic perspectives to not only African American labor but also housing markets generated more support among activists at the RRI than at CETRRR. (As evidence of the marginalization of economic perspectives even at the RRI, however, Weaver never presented on "economic perspectives on racial issues" in early theoretical sessions.)[81] Still, systemic views of discrimination and the sources of housing segregation permeated discussions of restrictive covenants and public housing. In 1945, Frank Horne, race relations advisor to the commissioner of the National Housing Agency, pointed to the ways restrictive covenants and public housing policy confined African Americans to urban ghettos.[82] Reflecting Joseph Lohman's work with Weaver and the National Committee on Segregation in the Nation's Capital (NCSNC), RRI housing panels also pointed to the ways collusion between private real estate interests and federal loan programs combined with segregated public housing policies to ensure that African Americans had access to almost no new housing.[83] A view in which discrimination functioned systematically and impersonally—like a market—regardless of the intentions of individual perpetrators was also made vivid in educational pamphlets the RRD and NCSNC produced. A number of these pamphlets depicted restrictive covenants as "locks" or "shackles" forcing overcrowding in African American communities while housing was available in segregated white suburbs.[84] (See figure 5.) In discussions of housing and employment, RRI participants highlighted the systemic impact and the institutional mechanisms of discrimination. They concluded that federal job creation and the production of affordable, accessible housing were necessary in addition to laws preventing restrictive covenants and discrimination.[85]

Calls for antiprejudice education rooted in dispositional theories, as well as rights-based appeals for antidiscrimination law and desegregation, were also present in RRI reform discussion between 1944 and 1947. Psychologists and sociologists, as we have seen, often recommended antiprejudice education even as they articulated systemic social theories with more far reaching reform implications. A variety of Institute participants, including professional educators, religious workers, and members of urban race relations commissions, from whom such an approach was unsurprising, presented antiprejudice education, moral exhortation, and the fostering of interracial understanding as essential components of their reform strategies.[86] Many proponents of fair employment legislation also believed that educational programming would lay necessary groundwork for implementing nondiscrimination policies in workplaces.[87]

5. From "If Your Next Neighbors Are Negroes," courtesy of Fisk University, John Hope and
Aurelia E. Franklin Library, Special Collections, Race Relations Institutes Collection.

The immediate postwar years served as a time of political fluidity, however, when Institute participants articulated redistributive, provision-oriented
conceptions of how to produce progress in race relations alongside the individualistic approaches historians traditionally associate with racial liberalism. The networks of scholar-activists that came together at Fisk were crucial
to the endurance of these programmatic, not just theoretical, alternatives to
racial individualism. Between 1944 and 1947, even as antiprejudice activism flourished and many across the nation read Myrdal as a call for moral
and psychological reform, the scholar-activists at Fisk continued to highlight the economic bases and structural character of American racial conflict
and inequality. They suggested consequently that race relations could not be
improved by simply challenging white prejudice or even by securing black
rights; government provision of basic resources was also needed.

While Institute participants articulated systemic and relational theories
of the sources of the race issue into the 1950s, RRI reformist priorities narrowed perceptibly after 1949 as the political context evolved. As the Cold
War advanced, anticommunism expanded, and statist New Deal liberalism generated suspicion, RRI participants adjusted their political demands.
Johnson and Long tried to reframe demands for state-provided jobs, housing, and social welfare in more individualistic terms by using a language
of positive rights, but these efforts were short-lived. Between 1949—when
Johnson reframed the RRI's central concern from "race relations" to "human

rights"—and the early 1960s, Institute participants dropped redistributive racial politics in favor of the rights-oriented calls for nondiscrimination and legal integration characteristic of postwar racial liberalism.

Post-1949 shifts toward rights-based individualism represented a pragmatic response to an evolving political context in which rights discourse had become especially important to proponents of racial justice while redistributive politics were becoming politically unlikely and professionally dangerous. For the postwar interracial left that attended the Institutes, rightward shifts in American liberalism as civil rights became one of its central elements proved a double-edged sword. Congressional support for the New Deal had begun to wane during the war and faced substantial opposition after 1946.[88] After 1947, moreover, as the House Un-American Activities Committee (HUAC) investigated suspected subversion in universities, Hollywood, and the military, conservative efforts to brand liberals as communists accelerated.[89] The implications for civil rights activists—long accused of communist sympathies—were decisive. Civil rights groups and HBCUs, including Fisk, emphasized their anticommunist credentials and purged members suspected of communist affiliations.[90] At the same time, rights-based individualism appeared politically promising amid the NAACP's late 1940s successes in the courts and the anticommunist struggles for the hearts and minds of newly decolonized peoples. While the Cold War provided civil rights activists with new rhetorical tools, the struggle against domestic communism dramatically muted the redistributive political orientation that had flourished among the African American and interracial lefts in the interwar and wartime years.[91]

In a context where the interracial left was fighting an uphill battle, Johnson—who continued to understand race relations in social structural and political economic terms, but who was also a pragmatist and fervent integrationists—reframed Institute politics. In a 1949 document aptly titled "A New Frame of Reference for Race Relations," Johnson argued that "democratic human rights" would replace race relations as the Institute's organizing principle. "The position of minorities in America, both racial and religious, has been more often and more popularly associated with social pathology and social work," Johnson held, "than with anything inherent in our traditional democratic concept and philosophy." Since it was a dangerous time when "the cry for justice is treated as the plaintive protests of the weak," Johnson presented the "race relations" approach as counterproductive because it had become too tightly associated with charity, welfare, and appeals to conscience rather than democracy and justice. Consequently, the Institutes would no longer simply focus on the needs of "outraged and frustrated underdogs, or sympathetic friends of underdogs, supplicating for kind treatment."[92] Although the Race Relations Institutes did not go so far as to change its name, human rights replaced race relations as the Institutes' central emphasis. "We find ourselves concerned only incidentally with the relations between racial and cultural groups," Johnson explained in 1951, "and basically with the realistic process of democracy."[93] In 1953 Johnson and Long reiterated the importance of the shift in framework. A pamphlet advertising the tenth annual Institute described "a new perspective within which intergroup relations must be viewed," which involved "developing the positive means by which all segments of the population may finally secure the opportunity to exercise the rights and assume the responsibilities of full citizenship."[94]

The assumption that internationally popular human rights discourse might strengthen domestic calls for racial justice fueled the Institute's rhetorical turn from relations to rights. The nation's growing international responsibilities and the ideological conflict with the USSR, Johnson suggested in 1951, provided proponents of racial justice with the opportunity to join their cause to an international struggle.[95] Outlining the key tenets of the United Nations Declaration of Human Rights, Johnson argued that civil rights provided "the domestic counterpart" of the postwar international doctrine of human rights.[96] In addition, Johnson emphasized action to produce racial justice at home was essential in the struggle to gain allies abroad. "The failure of the peoples of the world to rush up and buy our product as we took it for granted they would do at the first opportunity" resulted, Johnson held, from America's treatment of its racial minorities. This was especially true since American segregationists were being heard around the world, "two thirds of whose inhabitants are colored."[97]

For a short time in the early 1950s Johnson and Long included positive rights (a framework that had been popular during the war but had largely declined by the 1950s in mainstream civil rights settings) in their rights-based framework. In so doing, they articulated an anticommunist anticolonialism with a redistributive undertone.[98] For example, in 1951 Johnson held:

> The human rights on which we place the highest value and which are embodied in our constitution are in the last analysis, negative rights—intended to protect the individual against certain kinds of action. But there has grown up in the modern world a more positive conception of human rights—economic and social rights. These include the right to a job, to certain social benefits, certain minimum standards of living. It is the Russian claim that such rights

as these are more important, and that they are developing a system which gives greater assurance of the protection of these rights.[99]

It was the absence of a conception of positive rights in the postwar United States, Johnson argued, that made much of the black and brown postcolonial world skeptical of American democratic rhetoric. Herman Long employed a similar strategy in 1953. The kind of democracy respected around the world, Long argued, involved "shared decisions and shared results," "a fairly widely shared standard of living," and "certain moral values regarding the worth, dignity, and capacity of all individuals, who are to be considered not as means, but as ends."[100] As redistributive social and economic policies moved outside the American liberal mainstream in the Cold War era, Johnson and Long tried to reassert their importance by framing them as rights and highlighting their international appeal in the anticommunist struggle.

This late articulation of positive rights largely proved an exception, however, especially after 1951. More commonly, the RRI's new concern with democratic human rights involved negative rights, a focus that was as strongly influenced by the evolving legal context as by anticommunism. Frustration with the pace of legal reform had led some RRI participants—most notably NAACP lawyer Charles Houston—to question the utility of the courts in the fight for improved race relations in housing and employment in 1945.[101] As the courts became more hospitable after 1948, however, the legal battle against segregation took an increasingly central place in RRI discussions. Momentum resulting from the NAACP's legal successes in higher education, voting, and interstate transportation, as well as anticipation as school segregation cases reached the Supreme Court, certainly drew RRI participants' attention to legal desegregation.[102] The titles of Institute summaries between 1949 and 1954 expose the importance of the rights framework and the legal battle against desegregation to Institute politics: "Implementing Civil Rights" (1949), "Segregation: A Challenge to Democracy" (1950), "Human Rights and Human Relations" (1951), "Integration: Promise, Process, Problems" (1952), "Next Steps in Integration" (1953), and "Meeting the Challenges of Integration" (1954). Rights remained central through 1963, the year before the passage of the landmark Civil Rights Act, when the Institutes celebrated the hundredth anniversary of the Emancipation Proclamation with the title: "Human Rights—The New Century."[103]

Rights discourse especially affected the ways participants discussed employment, which, after 1949, they increasingly treated not by focusing on job creation but by emphasizing legal and legislative approaches to nondiscrimination. Houston acknowledged in these years that fair employment issues had a structural basis rooted in "the Negro's economic function as part of the unskilled reserve labor pool." While he suggested that ideally an attack on employment discrimination would include legislation, executive decrees, pickets, and boycotts, he prioritized court-based strategies because rightward shifts in Congress by 1948 had made civil rights legislation less likely. Since "Negroes are not able to force federal legislation unaided," Houston argued, court strategies that were not "dependent upon mass support" were increasingly essential.[104] While never absent, attention to labor issues declined after 1950, reflecting in part shifts in NAACP legal priorities concerning school desegregation.[105]

The turn to rights and focus on legal integration also involved increasing attention to psychology and education. The assumption that education could effectively combat racial injustice that had emerged in sessions on schooling and the church (where one might have expected them) in the Institutes' first five years, increasingly seeped into sessions on labor, housing, and even national legal and political strategy after 1949. For example, in that year Lester Granger of the National Urban League argued that the struggle for FEPC legislation had an educational component, and Charles Houston suggested that court action provided an essential tool of public education.[106] After 1951, the RRI staff included more psychiatrists, as well as representatives of human relations, religious, and educational organizations, than it had earlier, and RRI leaders stopped using the first week to provide social scientific framing. Instead, the 1953 meeting began with a discussion of the new rights framework followed by sessions on "the dimensions of prejudice."[107] Especially hopeful about a positive decision on school desegregation, Institute leaders dedicated the bulk of the 1953 sessions to the roles public agencies and community organizations might play in fostering interracial harmony during the transition to desegregation.[108] School integration—a reform that could be justified by both dispositional and systemic logics—was the primary redistributive policy proposed between 1949 and the early 1960s.

The shift away from redistributive politics at the post-1949 RRI also reflected the fact that the postwar interracial left remained constrained by not only anticommunism and a broader rightward shift in congressional politics but also by congressional opponents of desegregation. Moderate Arkansas congressman Brooks Hays' defense of his compromise position on FEPC, presented in a panel titled "Civil Rights and Political Expediency," exposed the intersecting pressures shaping RRI politics in the early Cold War years.[109] He compared the fair employment fight to the struggle for public housing and argued that if one wanted to secure public housing at all, compromise on segregation was essential.[110] These concerns continued after *Brown* as well. In 1955, housing expert and urbanist Charles Abrams worried that linking redistributive housing programs to desegregation might prove counterproductive. When discussing whether to support a civil rights rider to a public housing bill, Abrams worried that to do so might kill the bill entirely, and thus "make the civil rights fight the tool of reaction instead of the bannerhead of liberalism."[111] From the late 1940s through the mid-1950s, then, that desegregation and social legislation might function at cross-purposes limited the redistributive racial liberalism of the early RRI. In this context, it is no surprise that scholar-activists like Johnson were hopeful that protecting black rights through the courts might be fruitful and adjusted their rhetoric and gathered the resources at their disposal to pursue that aspect of the multifaceted attack on Jim Crow.

Although the pressures sustaining individualism in RRI politics would change by the early 1960s, the 1963 RRI revealed the culmination of many of the political tendencies developing in the post-1949 years. RRI scholars continued to emphasize that exhortations toward goodwill were insufficient as a total paradigm for racial progress and to center rights-based strategies. In his introduction to the 1963 Institute, Herman Long argued that growing black political strength ensured African Americans were no longer required "to resort to persuasion, good behavior, nice manners, or whatever appeal the white community believes is necessary in order for changes and concessions to be made."[112] Rights-based individualism was also evident in concern with the enforcement of desegregation and civil rights legislation. In fact, the bureaucratization of legal, legislative, and direct action civil rights protest led to the increased presence on the RRI faculty of federal, state, and local government employees, what sociologist Lewis Killian termed the "race relations industry."[113]

The 1963 Institutes simultaneously exposed new theoretical and political shifts away from racial individualism that the social scientific interracial left would begin to embrace by the mid-1960s. Two new themes that would become especially important to social scientific discourse on the race issue in the mid-1960s were coming into relief. First, RRI scholars paid increased attention to a different sort of individualism, a view that situated African American social marginality in black culture and psychology.[114] And second, some participants began suggesting that while legal gains were essential, they were not sufficient as a total paradigm for racial progress. In particular, a number of federal and state race experts presenting at the 1963 Institutes made clear that while federal executive orders demanding nondiscrimination required better enforcement, state fair employment legislation too frequently put the burden of proof on the individual.[115] Instead, some began to emphasize that both challenges of implementation and structural changes to the economy like automation proved nondiscrimination insufficient as a comprehensive approach to securing equal employment. As a consequence, on the cusp of the Civil Rights Act, some RRI participants began to wonder whether equalizing employment necessitated not just nondiscrimination but also racial preferences.[116]

While the 1963 RRI exposed the return of challenges to racial individualism that would continue in the post Civil Rights Act era, between 1949 and the early 1960s, international and domestic political climates combined to substantially narrow Institute participants' sense of the possible. This narrowing in political discourse occurred even though systemic and relational theories of the race issue continued to circulate widely in these years. By 1949, waning congressional support for New Deal liberalism and anticommunism made the statist emphasis of the RRI's redistributive racial liberalism seem increasingly untenable. Civil rights successes in the courts and racially tinged Cold War anticolonial struggles simultaneously favored legal and rights-based strategies. The RRI embrace of individualistic politics after 1949 was not absolute, as Johnson's attempt to refashion a concept of positive rights into an agenda for social and economic progress in the Cold War era reveals. Still the scope and emphasis of Institute participants' visions of change had altered. The shift from race relations to human rights as a guiding framework only highlighted the individualistic turn in discussions of employment, housing, and social welfare policy. By the early 1950s, reforms that followed the logic of systemic or relational conceptions of the race problem largely fell out of Institute discussion. Instead, as elsewhere, two of the basic tenets of racial liberalism—the protection of African American rights through antidiscrimination legislation and opposition to the denial of equal rights embedded in legal segregation—occupied center stage.

The agenda the RRI pursued in the late 1940s and 1950s met many of its central legal and legislative goals in the mid-1960s and had some institutional and even structural impact in the following decade. *Brown* and the Civil Rights Act of 1964 produced bureaucratic structures focused on securing civil rights and equal opportunity at the federal, state, and local levels.[117] In some cases, as with southern voting rights, these new legal mechanisms effectively altered patterns of racial inequality.[118] In employment, federal and state civil rights laws not only established elaborate bureaucracies to process complaints of employment discrimination, but they also expanded African American access to public and state-related (private sector but dependent on public funding) jobs. This increased access became especially consequential when this sector grew during the Great Society, though subsequent retrenchment chipped away at African American employment in the 1970s and 1980s.[119] In other cases, however, as with housing, moral exhortation and civil rights legislation proved unable to budge stubborn patterns of segregation and inequality. Efforts to desegregate the suburbs constituted the northern civil rights movement's least successful component, Thomas Sugrue argues, since even when white attitudes became more tolerant, "persuading whites to stay in racially changing neighborhoods or creating integrated housing markets in the suburbs proved to be much more difficult." Levels of racial segregation in housing were almost as substantial in 1970 as they had been in 1940.[120] While the rights-oriented racial liberalism that the RRI endorsed met many of its goals, by retreating from the redistributive concerns articulated during and immediately after World War II, the RRI's ultimate approach left many of the systemic and political economic sources of racial oppression unchallenged.

Despite reframing the Institutes around the issue of democratic human rights after 1949, Johnson still embraced the combination of social structural and political economic theories that marked his interwar and wartime scholarship. "It should be kept in mind," he explained in 1951, "that there are powerful forces in operation in our society affecting race relations over which neither individuals nor organized groups have any control. Many of the situations described as racial are incidental to the sweep of larger historical, economic, and cultural forces."[121] African American scholar-activists like Johnson moved easily between scientific and political arenas, but a keen sense of the difference between science and politics—and an ability to compartmentalize—affected what they said where. RRI political agendas narrowed significantly, especially between 1949 and the early 1960s, but RRI participants felt constrained in action, not in theory.

Although Fisk's RRI embodied the competing pressures of social science and racial politics, they were a crucial postwar location where social scientists thought beyond the parameters of racial individualism. This was the case not only during World War II and the immediate postwar years, when systemic and relational theories continued to circulate among left-leaning sociologists, anthropologists, and a few economists concerned with race relations, but also through the 1950s.[122] A number of factors explain the theoretical endurance of the combination of Chicago school social ecology and political economic theorizing into the late 1940s and 1950s.

Dynamics associated with the politics of knowledge production were at work. Since HBCUs fell outside the federal and philanthropic funding streams increasingly shaping scholarship in elite postwar research universities, intellectual traditions associated with the African American Chicago school simply continued at the RRI. Systemic and relational theories persisted at the RRI even after the sociological center of gravity shifted to Harvard and Columbia, surveys research centers like the Bureau of Applied Social Relations or the National Opinion Research Center generated enthusiasm for survey methods in the mainstream academy, and the Ford and Rockefeller Foundations directed many scholars toward the behavioral sciences. The endurance of systemic and relational thought in the 1950s also reflected the fact that the RRI drew on traditions of black leftist thought that highlighted the intersections of politics and economics in sustaining racial oppression, traditions that were not fully quieted by postwar antiradicalism.[123] In addition, that the links between reformers and scientists were more reciprocal than at the RF or CETRRR may also have encouraged the endurance of systemic and relational theorizing at the RRI.

Translating systemic and relational theories of the race problem into realistic reform proposals proved complicated, however, especially after 1949. For a short time, between 1944 and 1947, popular RRI reform proposals reflected the logic of the Chicago school, the interwar interracial left, and the demands of African American workers, who tended to prioritize nondiscrimination, desegregation, *and* the provision of social and economic resources. And yet by 1949 and especially by 1951, anticommunism, continued rightward political shifts, civil rights successes in the courts, and emerging segregationist resistance all narrowed Institute reformist visions. Always attuned to the shifting political climate, Johnson and Long repackaged the Institutes for the Cold War world. Regardless of their actual understandings of the sources of racial injustice, after 1949 many at the RRI came to assume that the best way to fight the race problem was a rights-based approach that included antiprejudice education (though few ever presented this as a total solution), legal desegregation, and civil rights legislation. Despite the RRI's claim that it would draw on social science to inform social and political action, the large-scale reform systemic and relational theories suggested to be necessary seemed unrealistic in the rightward-moving 1950s.

Applied, interdisciplinary social science might have proven challenging for developing coherent reform agendas in any setting, since different disciplinary perspectives often led activists toward very different priorities. In the end, however, the theoretical contradictions that multidisciplinary discussion brought to light proved largely irrelevant when RRI scholar-activists turned their attention to the political arena. When discussing not the causes of the race issue but what to do about it, RRI scholars used science strategically, in ways that tiptoed around the dilemmas of scale systemic and relational theories raised. As the next chapter on Howard University's *Journal of Negro Education* also shows, in political as opposed to scientific debate, having many theoretical frameworks to draw on was an asset not a liability.

FIVE

"Education for Racial Understanding" and the Meanings of Integration in Howard University's *Journal of Negro Education*

Although systemic and relational theories of the race issue circulated in Howard University's *Journal of Negro Education* (*JNE*) throughout the mid-century decades, the journal dedicated its 1944 summer edition to "Education for Racial Understanding." Martin Jenkins, the series editor, explained this focus:

> The term *racial understanding* is used here for want of a better and more definitive term. We mean by this term not "tolerance" alone, for tolerance implies a superior-inferior relationship. Nor do we mean better race relations necessarily (at least in the short-term view), for . . . improvement in the status of a subordinate racial group frequently results in deterioration of good race relations. Nor do we mean, even, better understanding, exactly, since better understanding does not *necessarily* result in a modified attitude. What we do mean by racial understanding is the development of an attitude which will permit and favor the adjustment of a subordinate racial group on a higher level than previously obtained.[1]

Likely anticipating criticism from colleagues who prioritized legal, legislative, and direct action strategies, Jenkins distinguished his notion of racial understanding from groups that promoted tolerance without simultaneously challenging segregation. He made clear that the race problem must be fought "on many fronts," but contrary to much established wisdom at the *JNE*, suggested that white racial attitudes should be one of them.[2]

JNE authors from the 1930s through the 1960s debated over the sources of "the race problem" and how education could best be employed in its solution. In particular, *JNE* authors addressed whether and how three objectives—fairly distributing educational resources, combating white prejudice, and desegregating schools—could be combined. Although many *JNE* contributors, in step with Howard's Depression-era leftist politics, espoused class-based conceptions of racism and prioritized the redistribution of educational resources in the 1930s, the journal turned attention to psychology and antiprejudice education by the mid-1940s. *JNE* authors shifted focus again by the early 1950s to present segregation, not capitalism, as the root cause of racial oppression.

The *JNE* was a site where "the Amenia ideal," a vision of social scientific purpose that prioritized social scientists' commitment to political engagement, flourished.[3] The only journal committed explicitly to the scientific study of African American schooling, the *JNE* brought an interdisciplinary group of social scientists—in which sociological, anthropological, political scientific, philosophical, economic, and historical voices were well represented—into dialogue with civil rights litigators, national political activists, philanthropists, educators, and social workers beginning in 1932.[4] Like Fisk's RRI and the University of Chicago's Committee on Education, Training, and Research in Race Relations (CETRRR), contexts to which scholars writing in the *JNE* frequently also had ties, the *JNE* used social science to inform social action. And yet the journal focused as much on the struggle for civil rights broadly conceived as on African American education. Political activists—many like NAACP leaders Roy Wilkins, Walter White, and Thurgood Marshall who were nationally prominent—regularly assessed the state of race relations and offered recommendations for change.[5]

In the 1930s and early 1940s, the *JNE* also reflected the Amenia ideal in its attention to the political economic sources of racial injustice.[6] Building on Howard University's identity as *the* center of class-based thought on race, *JNE* scholars generally suggested that interracial competition, labor exploitation, and violently enforced political oppression intersected to produce America's race problem. In addition, although discussions of intercultural education surfaced occasionally, *JNE* thinkers frequently translated class-based theories of the race issue into political agendas in these years. Debates over school desegregation, in particular, reflected political economic views. While some worried school integration might psychologically harm black youth and others suggested desegregation was the only way to redistribute educational funds, interwar *JNE* contributors agreed that securing sufficient resources for black students was their primary aim.

Like Fisk University's Race Relations Institutes (RRI), the *JNE* provided a space where the postwar social scientific interracial left remained insulated—at least in its theorizing—from many of the institutional pressures incentivizing postwar racial individualism. From the mid-1940s through the early 1960s, *JNE* authors continued to challenge individualism—at least in theory—by emphasizing the political-economic and social structural roots of the race problem. During World War II, however, an exception to this pattern emerged as the psychology of prejudice made some advances. Although many remained skeptical that tolerance education constituted a sufficient *total* strategy for progress in race relations, a number of wartime *JNE* authors debated the benefits and drawbacks of antiprejudice education. The timing of this interest, which reached its high point in the summer edition of 1944, suggests that *JNE* authors were not led toward the psychology of prejudice by the trickle-down effects of foundation support for the behavioral sciences or interdisciplinary social relations. Instead, the *JNE* emphasized prejudice strategically in an effort to turn wartime enthusiasm for tolerance and national unity to the battle for school desegregation.[7]

And yet concern with "racial understanding" was always contested and relatively short-lived at the *JNE*. After 1950, *JNE* authors returned to their earlier concerns with the politics and economics of segregation. As a result of the NAACP's decision to attack *Plessy v. Ferguson* based on the argument that segregation would harm black children even if educational resources were equalized, *JNE* authors dropped calls for equalizing school funding.[8] At the same time, as McCarthyism muted the political economic analysis that had been the hallmark of *JNE* interwar debate, a number of *JNE* economists, political scientists, sociologists, and anthropologists found new theoretical uses for the concept of segregation. Described as an intertwined social structural, political, and economic system, segregation replaced capitalism as the crucial causal mechanism in *JNE* theories of racial oppression. This theoretical shift helped scholar-activists describe the structural aspects of racial oppression that racial individualism overlooked without directly criticizing capitalism.[9] Despite this theoretical expansiveness, the shifting postwar legal and political context pushed *JNE* authors toward racial liberalism and exposed how dispositional, systemic, and relational theories could all provide rationales for school desegregation.

"The Educational Slums of Every Community," 1932–39

The *JNE*'s Depression-era, political economic theories of and agendas for progress in race relations had intellectual and political sources. Concern with the availability of jobs and housing had been central to grassroots civil rights organizing throughout the twentieth century. In the 1930s in particular, leading Howard intellectuals, including sociologist E. Franklin Frazier, economist Abram Harris Jr., political scientist Ralph Bunche, legal scholars William Hastie and Charles Houston, philosopher Alain Locke, and professor of education Charles H. Thompson, reflected these broader political concerns and articulated class-based theories of racism that echoed the central interests of the interwar interracial left.[10] In addition, the legal context reflected and influenced the economic cast of many Depression-era theories of racial injustice. In the 1930s and 1940s, lawyers at the Department of Justice and the NAACP—many of whom were trained at Howard—understood civil rights partly through the lens of workers' rights. They envisioned Jim Crow as an intertwined political and economic system, highlighted the material not only the stigmatic harms segregation inflicted on black workers, and saw the right to unionize and "economic rights" (including "minimum subsistence, unemployment insurance, old-age assistance, housing, and education") as central to civil rights law.[11] These economically informed views of the race issue influenced discussions of how education could best be used to secure racial justice.

A setting where an expansive, radical vision of the links between class and race oppression was articulated, the *JNE* leaned so far left that it featured broad critiques of capitalism in the 1930s. A wide array of *JNE* contributors suggested that the exploitation of black labor and intergroup competition for resources were basic causes of racial conflict and inequality and made clear that disenfranchisement and exploitation reinforced each other. Racial attitudes were not inconsequential in this view, but served as rationalizations that emerged from and legitimized oppressive political economic systems.

In 1935, for example, Howard University political scientist Ralph Bunche, then a socialist, emphasized the economic foundations of America's race problem but acknowledged that capitalism, liberal democracy, and white prejudice reinforced one another. "Modern democracy," Bunche held, was "conceived in the womb of middle-class revolutions." In his view, democracy "was early put out to work in support of those ruling middle-class interests of capitalistic society which fathered it" and "remained their loyal child" ever since. Because African American political exclusion was economically productive for the ruling classes, black people had to struggle to participate in democratic processes. The political scientist recognized that racial attitudes wielded great power. Prejudice existed, nonetheless, Bunch held, because it advantaged those interested in maintaining an exploitable workforce and rationalized the low political and economic status of minority peoples.[12] Bunche's interwar economic determinism led him to criticize many popular approaches to civil rights protest, especially those that instantiated either rights-based or psychological individualism. The popular "'don't-buy-where-you-can't-work' movement" failed to acknowledge that African Americans were out of work not simply due to white prejudice, he held, but because the economic system demanded a marginal labor supply.[13] Even movements for securing individual rights for African Americans by political means were misguided, he held in the 1930s, since they failed to take account of the fact "that the political arm of the state cannot be divorced from its prevailing economic structure, whose servant it must inevitably be."[14] Religious groups, social welfare agencies, and interracial commissions engaged in attempts to create interracial fellowship were also "dubiously valuable" because they failed to challenge capitalist ideologies.[15] A civil rights activist who worked for the US Department of State and the United Nations in the 1940s and 1950s, Bunche's intellectual journey exemplified the movement away from economic explanations of racial oppression and toward liberal individualism that many midcentury black thinkers would undertake. And yet in the 1930s Bunche believed that only challenges to liberal capitalism were likely to improve African American status.[16]

W. E. B. Du Bois also criticized capitalism in the 1930s, though his commitment to Marxism, black nationalism, and pan-Africanism remained strong throughout the second half of his life, certainly after postwar McCarthyism encouraged many of his colleagues in the interracial left to soften their radicalism. In 1932, the *JNE* published "Education and Work," Du Bois's 1930 Howard University commencement address. The talk critiqued the immorality of capitalism and suggested that only a social order where none earned more than they needed would effectively solve the race problem.[17] Du Bois even applauded the Soviet Union (a less radical choice in 1930 than it would be two decades later) since they were the only nation that was "making a frontal attack" on the problem of capitalist privilege.[18] Even in the 1930s Du Bois's unapologetic materialism and his emerging skepticism of interracialism made him one of the more extreme voices published in the *JNE*. Such views would lead to a break with the NAACP over their unwillingness to develop a more radical economic policy in 1934.[19]

Although direct challenges to capitalism were exceptional in the *JNE*, even in the 1930s, many interwar *JNE* authors paid careful attention to the economic underpinnings of racial injustice.[20] Authors certainly saw white attitudes—especially when they produced discrimination in the provision of state and federal resources—and African American disenfranchisement as intertwined with the economics of American race relations. Nonetheless, economic readings of the sources of the race problem were common. Many *JNE* contributors focusing on the South presented segregation as a political and economic system and suggested that class and race oppression were impossible to separate. This framework had implications for discussions of the sources of and how to address school segregation.[21]

The *JNE*'s Depression-era tendency to envision educational justice in terms of access to resources was hardly surprising given the focus of legal efforts against educational Jim Crow in the 1930s and early 1940s and the financial crisis that most southern African American students faced. Despite *Plessy v. Ferguson*'s requirement of "separate but equal" education, educational inequality—and often the basic absence of public education for black children—was flagrant and ubiquitous in the Jim Crow South. For many southern black children between 1860 and 1935, public elementary schools were unavailable or parents endured "double taxation" for vastly inferior facilities and services. Access to public high schools was "virtually non-existent" for black southerners.[22] While opportunities were better in northern and western cities, "de facto" (though widely state sanctioned) segregation was common.[23] The interwar NAACP, which, given its limited resources, only brought suits it believed it had a good chance of winning, challenged the expansion of segregated schooling in northern states but assumed a direct attack on southern school segregation futile.[24] Instead, the NAACP brought cases that demanded the equity *Plessy v. Ferguson* promised be secured in facilities, teacher pay, and higher education.[25] NAACP leader Walter White and lawyers Charles Houston and Thurgood Marshall hoped that taxpayer suits to equalize educational funding within dual systems would be so prohibitively expensive that states would move toward abolishing segregated schools voluntarily.[26] In higher education the equalization strategy was producing some legal if not practical results by the late 1930s. The 1938 decision in *Missouri ex rel. Gaines v. Canada* deemed state programs that provided black students with scholarships for higher study out of state illegal, insisting that such programs must be available within state boundaries.[27]

In this context, it is little surprise that *JNE* authors thought in terms of the distribution of resources when addressing southern educational segregation. Throughout the 1930s, Charles H. Thompson, dean of Howard University's School of Education and *JNE* lead editor from the 1930s through the 1960s, highlighted the inseparability of race and class oppression. He emphasized in particular that the most pernicious effect of educational segregation was the inequality in resources it created. African Americans were "thrice penalized" in their ability to acquire education, Thompson often repeated, "first, for living in the wrong section of the country . . . second, for belonging to the wrong class . . . and third, for belonging to the wrong race."[28] In contrast to Bunche and Du Bois, Thompson, a fervent integrationist,

6. Charles H. Thompson, courtesy of Moorland-Spingarn Research Center, Howard University, Charles H. Thompson Papers.

suggested that disenfranchisement was a more important underlying cause of segregation and racial inequality than capitalism. Since African Americans in segregated communities had no control over the distribution of school funds, no ability to hold office, and no chance to vote for the individuals who made educational policy, they were powerless to improve their children's schooling through public channels.[29]

Ultimately, Thompson, like Bunche and Du Bois, believed that politics and economics were intertwined in a context where black disenfranchisement provided white school boards with a free hand to distribute resources. Thompson made clear that since many southern states were struggling to fund the education of white children, there was little chance that white parents would voluntarily sacrifice for African American youth.[30] The segregated schooling black political exclusion allowed in turn ensured "notorious discrimination in the provision of school facilities, so that Negroes always have poorer schools than the white schools in the same community."[31] Southern African Americans wanting adequate education faced four choices, as Thompson saw it in the 1930s. They could migrate. They could work to secure access to the vote. They could try to use the courts. Or they could continue to appeal to whites. While the last choice, Thompson believed, was used most frequently, he was skeptical that appeals to conscience would help African Americans secure "'a new deal' in education." Although he acknowledged in 1935 that "one of the most important problems in the education of Negroes is the education of white people," he believed firmly that "depending upon the sense of fairness of . . . white people . . . for an equitable distribution of school opportunities" was misguided. Although in the long run changing white minds was necessary, to provide black students with the resources essential for their education, legal pressure to equalize state funding for black schools and to prevent the extension of dual systems were essential first priorities.[32]

JNE authors considered initiatives at the federal, state, and local levels as ways to equalize educational resources in the 1930s. In 1932, David A. Lane Jr. discussed the relationship between African American schooling and the report of President Hoover's 1929 National Advisory Committee on Education.[33] Lane defined educational equality strictly in terms of financial redistribution, expressed alarm that the president's report suggested states administer federal grants, and derided the report's finding that private philanthropy might effectively replace federal aid. Instead, he agreed with a minority report that advocated federal action to equalize educational resources within and between states, especially in southern and border states.[34] Others emphasized that black educational backwardness resulted from rampant discrimination in the provision of educational resources at the state and local level. Myrtle R. Philips maintained in 1932 that discrimination by local school officials and African American exclusion from the political processes that determined school board leadership ensured that black schools failed to receive the resources they were due. Her research revealed startling inequalities between and within states and between localities, even for students of the same race. "The Negro schools suffer not only all of the disadvantages inherent in the national problem of school finance," Philips maintained, "but are further disadvantaged by the fact that they are not permitted to share *equally* in the educational advantages made possible by state and local funds."[35] Philips's data exposed widespread racial differences in expenditures per pupil, in capital outlay, in values of school property, and in teacher salaries within states that drastically limited African American children's opportunities to learn. As a consequence, she described African American schools as "the 'educational slums' of every community."[36] Many Depression-era authors thus integrated economic and political analysis to recommend increasing resources to African American schools through fairly administered federal grants, the reform of state tax systems, and altering the mechanisms by which educational funds were allocated in dual systems.[37]

The tendency to emphasize the equitable distribution of educational resources had implications for interwar debates over the merits—and drawbacks—of school integration. African American parents and community leaders frequently disagreed about whether to attack school segregation, since, despite its stigmatic and financial disadvantages, segregated schools provided jobs for black teachers, protected black students from the prejudice they would encounter in mixed schools, and served as sites where black history and culture were responsibly taught.[38] Although the *JNE* was weighted toward integrationists even in the 1930s, scholars who disagreed about whether school integration was an appropriate mechanism for equalizing educational resources agreed that equalization was their primary goal.

In a 1935 *JNE* debate over "the Separate School," Thompson represented the integrationist case. "It is no longer a question of whether Negroes *should* resort to the courts as a means of removing present abuses," he put it bluntly, "they have no other reasonable, legitimate alternative."[39] He believed that educators, as a realistic and hopefully temporary measure, should devise strategies for improving black schooling within a segregated system. The psychologist and education scholar also understood the arguments black parents and teachers made for separate African American schools. And yet Thompson repeatedly argued that integration was the best strategy for producing educational equality and that inequality was inevitable in segregated schools. The basic problem black educators faced in the 1930s, Thompson believed, involved providing African American children with an adequate education in "the separate school" at the same time that they "pave the way for its ultimate extinction."[40] Like Thompson, most authors contributing to the edition on "the separate school" agreed that challenging legal segregation was the only long-term mechanism for effectively equalizing educational resources.

Bunche appeared torn between economic determinism and the pull of political pragmatism. Fighting for African American rights in the courts was likely to produce few gains, the political scientist suggested in 1935, since the legal system could not be separated from the political economic system of which it was a part.[41] In fact, the fight for civil rights focused too narrowly, in Bunche's view, on "such impairments and deprivations of civil liberties as segregation."[42] Even though liberal capitalism not segregation remained Bunche's ultimate target, he supported the NAACP fight against segregated schools and emphasized that it was the courts' refusal to protect African American voting and citizenship rights that allowed Jim Crow schools and public accommodations to endure.[43]

Historian Horace Mann Bond's concern with the implications of segregation for the distribution of educational resources led him to make clear that segregated schools were not accidentally unequal. Segregationist school officials, he suggested, deliberately maintained educational inequality in order to stigmatize. Bond outlined the history of separate schools for African Americans in both northern and southern contexts and emphasized that educational segregation nearly always resulted from white decision making.[44] In southern communities inequality was "an almost inevitable feature of a separate school system," since "the causes for this consistent inferiority of Negro schools . . . are inherent in the very reason for their being."[45] It was essential to recognize the separate school "for what it is," the historian held: a tool for maintaining white status and advantage.[46] Bond certainly understood that black parents wanted to protect their children from the inevitable maltreatment they would encounter in mixed schools, but he argued that separate schools would always be unequal because they were intended to maintain racial hierarchies.

Alain Locke, Howard University philosopher and well-known Harlem Renaissance intellectual, also pointed to the stigmatic functions of educational inequality. Intended to produce not only separation but also inequality, segregation, Locke held, almost never coexisted with equal educational standards.[47] In addition, in many instances the inferior education an African American received "rationalize[ed] . . . his inferior capacity and social need."[48] As a result, even though African American children might experience short-term harm due to desegregation, Locke echoed Thompson in arguing that integration was the only realistic mechanism for producing equal education. Despite "inevitable conflict" between short-term and long-term goals, African Americans should determine their approach to segregation by "principle" and not "expediency," Locke argued.[49] The roots of the stigmatic harm arguments the NAACP would employ after 1950 when attacking *Plessy v. Ferguson* were present in the 1930s, but it was the stigma— and the material educational consequences—of inequality not the stigma of separation per se that most concerned Depression-era *JNE* authors.

Despite Thompson's, Bond's, and Locke's support for court-enforced desegregation, whether integration was the best strategy for improving African American education was a topic of debate in the Depression-era *JNE*. Notably, given the postwar *JNE*'s strongly integrationist leanings, the 1935 summer edition published critiques of integrationist politics. Mixed schools, Du Bois explained, not the segregated schools that would become the focus of *Brown v. Board*, were likely to damage black personalities.[50] Du Bois did not point explicitly to any psychological research, but his arguments for "the separate school" were based on assumptions about the conditions necessary for fostering healthy personalities. Schools were *not* an appropriate context to agitate for integration, Du Bois argued adamantly, criticizing integrationists for forcing black children into "hells where they are ridiculed and hated" and making clear that white prejudice ensured "most Negroes cannot receive proper education in white institutions."[51] "Using a little child as a battering ram" with which to open the doors locked shut by *Plessy v. Ferguson* was immoral, Du Bois maintained, since he was convinced that small children were not prepared for such a battle, which was likely to ruin "character, gift, and ability."[52] Since white prejudice was the problem with integration, in cases where white support for integrated schools existed, Du Bois believed agitating for mixed schools worthwhile. In the absence of white support, however, he encouraged black parents to press for increased funding for black public schools and universities and to strengthen black private institutions.[53] Although Du Bois was the most vocal *JNE* critic of desegregation, even in 1935, many *JNE* authors took seriously Du Bois's argument that "the separate school," if adequately financed, would psychologically protect black youth.[54]

While economic explanations of the sources of racial oppression and educational segregation took center stage in the interwar *JNE*, the beginnings of another argument for integration, one that also drew on psychology, emphasized interracial contact, and would gain widespread traction during World War II, were also visible in the 1930s. Alain Locke exemplified this nascent concern with intergroup understanding. Even though he largely called for integration to equalize resources, he also claimed that integration had other benefits. Desegregation was essential, the philosopher suggested in 1935, because public schools provided one of the few locations where interracial tolerance could be fostered and interracial understanding taught. The educational interaction of black and white students "under . . . advantageous circumstances" was a benefit of integrated schooling, since the school was the "logical and perhaps the only effective instrument" to foster positive intergroup contact.[55] Even Du Bois agreed that under ideal conditions the integrated school was favorable because of the educational advantages of diversity.[56] In addition, the 1930s *JNE* did publish some psychologists of prejudice, representatives of interracial organizations, and intercultural educators.[57]

Given the popularity of intercultural education programs in the 1920s and 1930s, and *JNE* authors' tendency to move in the same circles as leading intercultural educators such as Rachel Davis DuBois and Hilda Taba, one might have expected intercultural education to feature more prominently in the journal.[58] The *JNE*'s support for such programming was tempered at best in the 1930s. Thompson certainly believed that white prejudice presented obstacles to African American advancement, especially given white control of political and educational resources throughout the South.[59] And yet he and many of his colleagues assumed that dispositional approaches alone were insufficient in the fight for racial justice. In 1933 Thompson described the development of "race-relations programs" that held that "unsympathetic and antagonistic racial attitudes are due to misunderstanding, and that misunderstanding is due to lack of knowledge and proper contact with the object of antagonism." These assumptions had led to the development of programs to study "the Negro in our American civilization" as well as projects "embarking upon 'The Quest for [Interracial] Understanding'" in schools throughout the South.[60] There was little evidence, however, about whether these programs had actually increased access to educational resources for African Americans.[61] Moreover, Thompson made clear that the "race-relations ideal" presented many difficulties as "an *ultimate* solution of the problem of the Negro separate school," while educational programs to alter white attitudes were likely to have little effect on the "*immediate* problem of getting equitable provision of school facilities."[62] In fact, antiprejudice education tended to be associated with the accommodationist approach to interracial cooperation and appeals to the white sense of fairness that many *JNE* authors rejected in favor of political mobilization.[63]

Proponents of intercultural education who published in the *JNE* stood out from the norm in the 1930s. Instead, in both their social theories and their calls for educational reform, an interdisciplinary group of scholars in which sociologists, political scientists, and historians were especially well represented highlighted the intertwined political and economic character of Jim Crow. They joined *JNE* educators and civil rights activists in prioritizing the economic foundations of the race problem, in presenting integration as a tool for reversing educational inequality, and in carefully considering how to effectively provide educational resources to black children given black political powerlessness in the Jim Crow South. While prevailing interwar scholarly paradigms, especially social ecology and the political economy of slavery and sharecropping, encouraged *JNE* scholars to situate analyses of educational injustice in large-scale, systemic, and political economic patterns, the political commitments of the interwar interracial left favored the economic determinism evident in Depression-era *JNE* debate. The nature of the educational race problem in the Jim Crow South—in which African American disenfranchisement allowed flagrant inequality in the distribution of educational funds—also made political-economic analysis nearly impossible to avoid. Those publishing in the *JNE* debated whether integration was the best tactic for redistributing educational funds and argued over the psychological costs and benefits of desegregating schools before other sectors. Depression-era *JNE* authors stated with vivid clarity and unanimity, however, that what black students in the Jim Crow South most needed was more money.

"Education for Racial Understanding" and Its Critics, 1939–45

In their social scientific theorizing, wartime *JNE* authors, much like their colleagues at the Fisk Institutes, pointed to the political economic and social structural foundations of American racial injustice. Even as the influence of Chicago school sociology declined in the mainstream academy by the early 1940s, *JNE* authors continued to draw on its core assumptions, as well as on the political economic research Myrdal synthesized, to suggest that American racism originated in the structures of capitalism, the politics of colonialism, and intergroup competition for resources. Nonetheless, especially between 1939 and 1945—alongside wartime enthusiasm for survey research but before private funding for the behavioral sciences expanded after 1949—psychological theories seeped into *JNE* theoretical debate. In the process, the logic used to demand school desegregation changed in character. Critics of desegregation like Du Bois no longer published in the journal, and the emphasis on redistributing resources that had been the focus of the interwar *JNE* educational agenda declined. Instead, seeking to capitalize on wartime concern with prejudice, the *JNE* promoted antiprejudice education and presented integration as a tool for fighting intolerance.

During the war and in the immediate postwar years, systemic and relational theories continued to circulate widely in the *JNE*, especially in articles by anthropologists and sociologists. Many began their analyses by refuting biological arguments for racial difference. They then relied on social ecological and social anthropological frameworks to explore how demographic, economic, cultural, and historical factors shaped intergroup relations.[64] In the 1939 *JNE*, for example, Fisk University sociologist Charles S. Johnson outlined the social ecological framework with political economic leanings that characterized much of his thought. He argued that the values and meanings individuals gave to observable physical differences were determined largely by historically contingent social and economic factors. Asian American racial characteristics held different significance "according to their [Asian Americans'] position as economic competitors," he suggested. When their labor was needed on the West Coast, race relations were calm, but when Asians competed for jobs with white Americans, "the physical and cultural differences have been given acute racial significance." In this view, white workers used racism to gain advantage over economic competitors and employers used it to keep labor cheap.[65] Although Johnson certainly recognized that prejudice was intertwined with the political economy of race relations, prejudice emerged as a tool used in conflicts whose origins were economic or political.

Duke University sociologist Edgar T. Thompson, an expert on plantation societies who had been trained by Park, along with Scarritt College social anthropologist Ina Corinne Brown, also pointed to the historically determined nature of race relations. They emphasized that interracial competition—for space, authority, or status, not only for jobs or resources—led to the development of racial castes. Brown suggested viewing race relations in the United States as a particular kind of group relations, "in the context of the age-old and world-wide problem of self-conscious groups which occupy or compete for the same territory."[66] Following social ecologists, Brown held that how diverse groups reacted to meetings with one another depended on "the circumstances of the initial contact, the patterns set up by previous contacts of similar nature, or on the cultural patterns previously established." Echoing Lloyd Warner and the Class and Caste school of social anthropology, Brown also suggested that the history of colonial North America, the slave trade, and regional racial slavery in the United States revealed that white beliefs about African American inferiority functioned ultimately "to preserve status."[67] Although prejudice was a cultural norm, Brown followed Warner in suggesting that it could function long after the economic or political context that gave rise to it had passed.

Edgar Thompson was even more explicit in his suggestion that racist ideology developed from and sustained labor exploitation. Race was an idea shaped and employed in particular historical circumstances—in plantation societies, in employer-employee relationships, in cross-cultural trade, and in wartime, he held. Twentieth-century Americans' concepts of race, therefore, derived from interracial encounters that occurred under European colonialism, but racism took different forms depending on social and historical circumstances. Still, the American racial situation was formed out of the need for black labor, Thompson held, as "the idea of race developed as a working element in colonial areas as a means of effecting control over the Negro's labor and of fixing him in a permanent caste position."[68]

Radical sociologist Oliver Cromwell Cox, another Park student, also developed a theory of the race problem rooted in capitalist labor relations, bourgeois ideology, and exploitation. The furthest left of the *JNE* scholars, Cox, who criticized the Chicago school, Warner, and Myrdal for failing to sufficiently address class, revealed Howard's continued intellectual breadth in the mid-1940s. Race relations, Cox argued in 1943, depended on the economic, demographic, and sociological characteristics of a particular historical setting—population ratios, economic circumstances, and the nature of interracial contact.[69] Where Cox leaned further toward economic determinism than his colleagues was in his critique of the ideological function the concept of prejudice served. Cox rejected Myrdal's concept of the "vicious circle," the idea that white prejudice and African American status were mutually reinforcing, as a form of "mysticism" since it avoided acknowledging "that both race prejudice and Negro standards are consistently dependent variables. They are both produced by the calculated economic interests of the Southern oligarchy."[70] Instead, he directly challenged the psychology of prejudice by suggesting that bigoted attitudes did not cause racial oppression but rather the causal process proceeded in the opposite direction. Cox even implied that scientific attention to prejudice justified exploitation. And yet a toned down version of Cox's basic claim—that racial prejudice emerged from and continued to exist because it served white economic interests—ran through analyses of the race problem offered by many scholars who were not known as radicals. Integrating social ecology, Caste and Class theories, and Marxist theories of exploitation, a dominant strain in wartime *JNE* thought on race continued to develop key elements of the interwar "Golden Age of Negro Sociology." Both Johnson, the politically moderate favorite of the white foundations, and Cox, a well-known radical, agreed that the meanings given to racial characteristics differed based on the economic and political needs of those in power.[71]

Articulated between 1939 and 1945, such arguments were striking for their deviation from emerging racial liberalism and the psychology of prejudice.[72] Systemic and relational theories also directly challenged calls for "education for racial understanding," the organizing principle of the *JNE*'s 1944 summer edition. In contrast to the interwar years, however, wartime *JNE* contributors tended to shy away from the political implications of their more radical theoretical conclusions. Although they suggested that the idea of race had *historically* justified exploitation under slavery and colonialism, none of the social scientists, except Cox, went on to recommend interracial class-based politics or challenges to American capitalism as *JNE* authors like Bunche or Du Bois had in the 1930s.

Instead, the psychology of attitude formation appeared increasingly relevant to reformist discussions in the early and mid-1940s. Although the endurance of systemic and relational theories at the *JNE* makes clear that psychology did not drown out alternative disciplinary frameworks, psychological assumptions permeated discussions of the race problem by sociologists, anthropologists, historians, and a broad group of postwar religious, labor, civic, and educational workers. While, as we have seen, scholarly interest in prejudice would grow throughout the late 1940s and early 1950s outside the *JNE*, the timing of the *JNE*'s 1944 interest in "Education for Racial Understanding" suggests the importance of the wartime explosion of activist interest in prejudice to *JNE* concern with the issue. As many religious, educational, and civic groups that had previously only taken marginal interest in race relations turned attention to prejudice, many at the journal sought to turn this concern toward the integrationist cause.[73] In addition, the NAACP's legal campaign against segregation was in a state of flux in the mid-1940s, with lawyers shifting away from equalization strategies amid victories in higher education, voting rights, and transportation, while some local communities still pursued equalization.[74] While the evolving legal context did not necessarily push *JNE* authors toward support for "racial understanding," it does explain the growing optimism many brought to discussions of school integration as well as their declining acceptance of "separate but equal."

While only a few psychologists wrote for the *JNE* during World War II, psychological assumptions permeated many writers' conceptions of the race problem. And yet psychology did not always provide clear guides for advocates of improved race relations. Efforts to reduce prejudice by providing information about minority groups were rarely effective, a number of scholars revealed. Too often, sociologist Edgar Thompson, anthropologists Ina Corinne Brown and Hortense Powdermaker, and psychologist Eugene Hartley noted, scientific findings about the fallacy of racial categories failed to alter ordinary people's beliefs.[75] In fact, what psychology often revealed was the profound irrationality and rigidity of racial thinking. It was partly because the formation of racial attitudes occurred during early childhood, Hartley (formerly E. L. Horowitz) argued, that racial ideas proved so tenacious. Once attitudes were fixed, they determined what factual information an individual would accept or reject.[76] Prejudice was also difficult to fight because it was embedded in widely held cultural norms. According to Powdermaker, an anthropologist who had worked with John Dollard on community studies of race relations in the South, since racism was learned through family and community socialization, it was particularly difficult to change especially since racial beliefs were generally supported by social mores.[77] Although Martin Jenkins had turned attention to psychology in the hopes of finding good news for proponents of racial understanding, Powdermaker's and Hartley's work implied that schools could do little to limit racial prejudice when children learned racism in all of their daily encounters.

Despite the inconclusiveness of much psychological research on antiprejudice interventions, as well as the pervasiveness of political-economic and social structural theories of the race issue in the wartime journal, *JNE* authors increasingly presented educational programs to reduce prejudice as a necessary component of the fight for racial justice. Contributors to the 1944 summer edition—a group that included not only psychologists but also anthropologists, philosophers, historians, educationalists, and civil rights leaders—engaged in extended discussions of the best techniques for challenging prejudice through curricular and extracurricular activities. The best age at which to employ antiprejudice educational programming—among very young children or in high school—was one subject of debate for *JNE* authors.[78] The relative utility of emotional as opposed to factual material in antiprejudice education was another topic of disagreement. While some, like Hartley, emphasized that education for racial understanding must concern itself not with facts but with "the attitudes themselves, with the realities of the *understanding* process," Lindeman believed that all youth living in interracial settings should receive "factual" education about different cultures.[79] Powdermaker, who wrote a textbook for the Intercultural Education Association, recommended education at the "emotional level," including activities and planned situations "to break down mistrust, fear and other socially undesirable attitudes," though she also believed wider teaching of anthropology essential to combating prejudice.[80]

In addition, the psychology of prejudice provided a powerful weapon for opponents of legal segregation. By 1944, while *JNE* authors called ubiquitously for school integration, many demanded integration as a tool for promoting racial understanding. For example, J. Max Bond, director of the Tuskegee Institute's School of Education, argued that democratic education must be integrated because it must "strive courageously and honestly to free the minds of children and adults from the American psychosis of racial hate and all of its attendant evils."[81] Howard University historian Caroline Ware also critiqued the psychological and social implications of segregated schooling. "The experience of students, even more than their studies, will condition their ability to react constructively to racial situations," Ware contended. Education for improved race relations was impossible in segregated schools, she held, since one could never instruct children about the immorality of racial injustice when legal segregation undermined those lessons at every turn.[82] Both legal and de facto segregation, Ware emphasized, created "barriers to knowledge, to the development of habits of interracial action, and, especially, to the ability to cut through stereotypes and to recognize the individuality behind different exteriors." A segregated school system therefore presented "almost insuperable obstacles" to improved race relations.[83] Integrated education, in contrast, held great promise for fostering racial goodwill. Echoing arguments Alain Locke made in 1935 and research on the importance of intergroup contact to racial tolerance, Ware suggested school integration could engineer racial harmony. Fostering "the habit of association, rather than dissociation" and encouraging students to learn from differences in "values" and "backgrounds," integrated schooling could contribute to all Americans' emotional and intellectual growth.[84]

In addition to calling for an end to school segregation, many *JNE* authors maintained that schooling for racial understanding required curricular innovation, changes to the culture of school communities, commitment to racial equality by school administrators and teachers, a focus on racial issues in teacher training schools, and nondiscrimination in teacher hiring and the treatment of students.[85] Some capitalized on wartime democratic rhetoric to draw attention to the racist character of school curricula. Roy Wilkins of the NAACP argued that democratic, antiracist teaching should be systematized. He, along with historian and media expert L. D. Reddick, built on an important strain in African American political thought that recognized mass media as a site where the fight for racial justice must be waged.[86] Wilkins also, as W. E. B. Du Bois, Carter G. Woodson, and many black educators long had, envisioned African American history as a political and psychological resource. Changing textbook and curricular depictions of African Americans and integrating African American history into public school curricula were necessary first steps, Wilkins maintained, since "we will make little progress in education for racial understanding until the average boy and girl stops absorbing this poison from the first grade through high school."[87]

Moreover, recognizing that the effects of schooling were limited in a racist society, the 1944 summer edition assessed the educational activities of religious agencies, interracial committees, philanthropic foundations, organized labor, African American advancement organizations, government agencies, and mass media.[88] "Democracy in race relations will never be achieved until the minds of the people are changed," Reddick proposed, noting that "the direct route to these minds is through the great agencies of mass communications." Film, newspapers, magazines, radio, and public libraries, he held, were the "greatest educational agencies of the United States" and could not be overlooked in programs for "racial understanding."[89] *JNE* authors generally supported the antiprejudice work, all of which was based on dispositional assumptions, being conducted by labor unions, religious institutions, and civic associations.

Although wartime *JNE* authors expressed much more support for antiprejudice education than they had in the mid-1930s, they continued to treat the reformist technique cautiously. Jenkins explained this dilemma in a letter to the *JNE* editorial board when planning the summer edition:

> It is true that the "educational approach" is emotionally rejected by many because of the insistence by individuals and organizations *antagonistic* to the Negro that education *rather than* political pressure is the real solution of the problem. This emotional reaction, however, must be guarded against in the clear awareness that the problem of racial understanding must be attacked on many fronts rather than a single front. Education constitutes one, and I believe a tremendously important one, of these fronts.[90]

As Jenkins expected, some emphasized that antiprejudice education was a necessary but not sufficient strategy for racial progress. Margaret C. McCulloch, a religious extension worker for the Federal Council of Churches of America and active participant in Fisk's RRI, warned that lofty statements against prejudice could obscure a religious organizations' failure to desegregate.[91] In his conclusion to the 1944 issue, Alain Locke worried that antiprejudice rhetoric would prove empty. As support for desegregation and opposition to it were growing, Locke argued, "all our authors make us vividly aware that we have come to a crisis, where action and action alone can convince and count."[92] The call for action involved an only thinly veiled criticism of interracial dialogue as a sole technique for combating racial inequity and injustice. When considering discussion of racial injustice in the political realm, rather than the secondary school classroom, Lindeman expressed a similar concern. "We may talk our so-called race problem 'to death,'" he argued, since "among sophisticated people talk can and does become a substitute for action."[93]

In 1945, Reddick, who would work closely with Reverend Martin Luther King Jr. in the 1950s, emphasized the potential and the limits of antiprejudice education. While opinion polls revealed that Americans considered the race issue one of their top national problems, Reddick worried that educational interventions against prejudice might detract attention from legal and legislative change. He described, in jest, the various approaches to the race problem Americans considered: "'Revolution?' 'Oh, no!' 'New laws?' 'Maybe.' 'Education?' 'Yes, indeed!'"[94] Reddick believed education could be socially transformative but considered this project more complicated than many admitted:

> The notion that education is a cogent lever for promoting unity appears to be vague and formless in the public mind. It is in some degree an easy "out," a simple faith in a peaceable settlement of a vexing question, an inexpensive long-time shock-proof procedure, a magical formula. The average person who says "Education" with so much relief and satisfaction does not take the time to consider what is involved in his decision.[95]

While education could make progress against prejudice, too often, Reddick held, vague calls for education simply obscured the absence of more substantive change. Even in the mid-1940s, at the height of the *JNE*'s interest in "racial understanding," a number of authors expressed concern that antiprejudice education might serve as a replacement for the more sweeping legislative, direct-action, or court-based approaches that wartime *JNE* authors prioritized.

Despite these concerns, and *JNE* leaders' commitment to using social science to inform social action, wartime *JNE* calls for change often sidestepped the full complexity of the scientific findings they articulated. On the one hand, systemic and relational theories of the race issue continued to circulate widely. By the mid-1940s, the journal generally no longer featured explicit challenges to capitalism. Instead, with many wartime proponents of racial democracy, *JNE* authors tended to emphasize desegregation and civil rights legislation, calling, as Charles S. Johnson put it in 1944, for nothing more "than is theirs already in principle."[96] Since RRI and *JNE* communities substantially overlapped, many *JNE* authors were no doubt also supportive of the redistributive racial liberalism that circulated at the RRI from 1944 through 1947. Still, by suggesting that in addition to legal changes reforms at a very large scale were needed, systemic and relational theories raised troubling questions about political feasibility that *JNE* authors tended to leave unacknowledged. In addition, as the NAACP began moving away from school equalization cases, demands for redistributing educational resources that had so often followed interwar political economic analyses of school segregation were no longer politically useful. In contrast, although psychology pointed as often to the intractable as to the malleable nature of racial attitudes, *JNE* educators carefully explored the ways antiprejudice education could serve as a weapon in the struggle for racial justice. Many also sought to draw wartime anti-Nazi sentiments toward the integrationist cause. The 1944 summer edition did, in a limited way, broaden intercultural educators' narrowly curricular conceptions of how to improve race relations by recommending changes in school hiring policies, teacher education, and school administration and by warning of the dangers of "talk without action." And yet a leading voice of the Depression-era interracial left nonetheless moved decidedly toward racial individualism by 1944 by suggesting that antiprejudice education and school integration were essential fronts on which the fight for racial justice should be waged.

The Results of "Enforced Isolation," 1950

While the wartime moment led *JNE* authors to try to turn broader debates over the sources of prejudice and programs for fighting intergroup intolerance toward the integrationist cause, by 1950 other political factors encouraged a retreat from economic explanations for and redistributive approaches to the race issue. These included the rightward turn in national politics that began during the war, accelerated with Republican gains in the congressional election of 1946, and were cemented by McCarthyism.[97] In addition, the NAACP's 1950 decision to launch a direct assault on *Plessy*, which was based on the argument that segregated schools could never be equal because segregation caused psychological and stigmatic harm, also reshaped *JNE* rhetorical strategies.[98] Although the *JNE*, like many postwar sociology departments, shifted away from political economic analysis, the journal did not fully retreat from systemic theories.[99] Instead, a number of *JNE* sociologists, political scientists, and economists developed a language for explaining the causes of the race issue that did not reduce racism to individual acts of prejudice and discrimination but avoided implicating capitalism explicitly. These thinkers used the malleable concept of segregation to describe not only the legal structures of southern Jim Crow but also a social, economic, and political system that circumscribed African American opportunities regardless of the intentions of individual actors. By 1950, in much *JNE* analysis, segregation had edged out capitalist exploitation as the root cause of the race problem.

This framing of the race issue represented a clear bid for legal desegregation but also provided *JNE* authors with a systemic language for discussing the race problem that remained palatable amid McCarthyism. The tendency to avoid direct critiques of capitalism in the emerging Cold War context is hardly surprising, as the NAACP emphasized its anticommunist credentials and leading black thinkers like Du Bois and cultural icons like Paul Robeson faced accusations of subversion. By the end of World War II, the Howard University radicals of the 1930s had largely moved away from their Depression-era economic determinism due to ordinary African Americans' skepticism about the potential of interracial class-based politics and to the international context.[100] The JNE reflected this broader political shift. Du Bois published an article on the post–World War II colonial situation with communist leanings in the *JNE* in 1946, and this was his last in the journal. Oliver Cromwell Cox, who had published articles in the *JNE* nearly yearly since 1940, was not published in the *JNE* after 1951. By 1950 political scientist Ralph Bunche had moved substantially away from the economic determinism he expressed in the interwar years and instead fervently embraced a rights-oriented, individualistic variant of racial liberalism that took direct aim at legal segregation.[101] Celebrating "the things the American democratic creed stands for—the equality of man; individual rights and liberties; respect for the individual and for the dignity of the individual," Bunche presented his wish "only to be an American—in full,—with no ifs nor buts" clearly in terms of liberal individualism.[102] The journal provided little explicit discussion of the anticommunist context but moved with broader trends in the social sciences and civil rights politics by avoiding class analysis and embracing liberal individualism.[103]

At the same time, the *JNE* case makes clear that the changing focus of the battle for desegregation in the courts was as important as anticommunism in encouraging scholar-activists to rethink the sources of the race problem and its educational manifestations. Thompson's enthusiasm for legal desegregation took on an increasingly hopeful cast in 1950, when the NAACP won key victories against segregation in higher education and transportation. In *Sweatt v. Painter* (1950), the NAACP successfully challenged the constitutionality of a segregated black law school based on consideration of "intangible factors" (such as a school's prestige and the networks a student might develop). *McLaurin v. Oklahoma* (1950) held that segregation in classrooms impeded an African American graduate student's ability to adequately prepare for a profession.[104] *Henderson v. United States* (1950) made racial discrimination in luxury railroad accommodations unconstitutional under the Interstate Commerce Act and implicitly condemned the stigmatic function of legal segregation.[105] The three decisions suggested the court might be willing to rule against segregation broadly and that focusing on public primary and secondary schools might be productive. The decisions also led NAACP attorneys to embrace an "immaterial harm" strategy, the claim that segregation violated black rights because regardless of resource distribution the stigma of segregation damaged black children's self-esteem. As a result, in 1950 the NAACP stopped accepting primary and secondary school equalization cases.[106] In this context, one in which attempts at equalizing educational resources became tools segregationists used to stall desegregation, it is little surprise that calls for resource redistribution disappeared from *JNE* discussion.[107]

The NAACP's post-1950 immaterial harm strategy forced integrationists who were also concerned with the distribution of educational resources to adjust. At the *JNE*, desegregation unquestionably moved to center stage politically, as the titles of the journal's summer editions—"The Courts and Racial Integration in Education" (1952), "Next Steps in Racial Desegregation in Education" (1954), "The Desegregation Decision—One Year Afterward" (1955), "Educational Desegregation" (1956)—reveal. While the *JNE* continued to explore African American education broadly, after 1950 how to secure and, after *Brown v. Board*, how to implement court-ordered school desegregation received special attention.

The *JNE*'s shift in political priorities was coupled with a less obvious but also consequential change in theories of the race issue. While Depression-era *JNE* authors had suggested that capitalist exploitation and competition was the source of first slavery and then the Jim Crow social and legal structures that replaced it, by the 1950s authors reversed the equation. Segregation and institutionalized discrimination appeared not as products of the race problem but as intertwined, systemic causes of the economic dislocation and social pathologies researchers found in African American communities. In this view, segregation was a social structure that worked much like a market to circumscribe the life chances of the individuals it victimized without identifying particular perpetrators. While commitment to securing the desegregation of southern schools certainly prompted JNE authors to envision segregation as a legal and a social structure, wartime and postwar activism by northern open housing and fair employment activists also shaped this view. *JNE* visions of segregation as a social structure reflected understandings of the race problem that scholars of northern de facto employment and housing segregation, including Charles S. Johnson, E. Franklin Frazier, Robert Weaver, and Joseph Lohman, had articulated since the interwar years.

Using a language of "enforced isolation" and "racial proscriptions," *JNE* authors presented segregation as a structure that worked in concert with systematic patterns of discrimination to produce the social, cultural, and economic problems evident in African American communities. Using the Mid-Century Whitehouse Conference on Children and Youth as a backdrop, the *JNE*'s 1950 summer edition asked how minority status affected African American youth.[108] Thompson presented an argument that reappeared throughout postwar *JNE* discussions of the relationship between education and race relations. Although the economic, political, social, and cultural components of the race problem were intertwined, he held, segregation—not economic exploitation or labor competition—provided the root cause of the race problem. He explained:

> The Negro community in any section of the country is a world within a world, segregated by law or custom or both; and it is characterized by certain pathological features which are direct results of its enforced isolation. The economic status of the Negro is generally defined by the fact that the large majority of Negroes are restricted to the most insecure and poorly paid jobs in the community; and proscriptions because of race have served to keep them on this level. The education and cultural level of the Negro is lower than that of the population as a whole, and is due primarily to his inferior minority status and the proscriptions which go along with that status.[109]

In this "world within a world," segregation combined with institutionalized patterns of discrimination to impede African American economic and social advancement.[110] Although labor exploitation certainly continued to oppress African Americans, Thompson presented segregation and racial proscription as causes not consequences of this exploitation. This systemic analysis of discrimination and segregation led Thompson to recommend federal fair employment practices legislation and integration as the best ways to fight economic injustice. The 1950 summer edition exhibited this structural view of segregation by examining census data on population, economic conditions, and the social, political, and educational characteristics of black communities to assess the factors responsible for African Americans' "inferior status." The 1953 summer edition, which focused on "the facts which define the status of the Negro," also outlined African American social status and place in the social order by focusing on racial proscriptions.[111]

JNE discussions of de facto segregation also relied on structural frameworks in ways that prefigured late twentieth-century arguments about racial isolation concentrating poverty. Harry Walker, a sociologist from Howard University, built on economist Robert Weaver's studies of the economic and social consequences of residential segregation in the urban North to make clear that housing segregation compounded other social issues. By confining African Americans to "highly congested" communities with substandard educational, medical, sanitation, and recreational facilities, housing segregation explained why African Americans were disproportionately troubled by myriad social problems.[112] Like many of his colleagues, Walker believed that "a fundamental improvement in the Negro's social problems can be made only through the integration of the Negro into the general society."[113]

It was not simply residential segregation but the way it intersected with discriminatory labor markets that made the situation so dire. Weaver emphasized in 1950 how employment and housing segregation together locked African Americans into a low economic status. Like Depression-era *JNE* thinkers, the economist suggested that the race problem, during slavery, Reconstruction, and in the early twentieth century, served white economic needs.[114] At the same time, reflecting broader shifts in his thought from a focus on labor to concern with housing by the late 1940s, segregation appeared as the primary causal mechanism in Weaver's 1950 *JNE* discussion of the contemporary race issue. "Enforced segregation takes its place with continuing discrimination in employment as a principal impediment to the Negro's attainment of full and equal economic status," Weaver maintained. In fact, he suggested that it was residential segregation not employment discrimination that represented the "most economically oppressive expression of this negation of a competitive society."[115] Still this framing led Weaver to different policy recommendations than proponents of redistributive racial liberalism at the RRI. Since employment discrimination and residential segregation provided the primary obstacles to black economic advancement, Weaver held that the race problem could best be addressed not by creating more jobs or housing but by challenging both de jure and de facto segregation.

JNE authors also made clear that educational, housing, and employment segregation combined to produce not only economic and social problems but cultural and psychological ones as well. This focus on psychological damage would only increase in popularity as arguments about the cultural factors reinforcing poverty gained traction among liberal social scientists in the mid-1960s.[116] In 1950, many *JNE* authors built on E. Franklin Frazier's research on the black family to examine so-called cultural pathologies among black youth that stemmed from the intersection of "family disorganization" and racial isolation.[117] According to Walker, the isolation of African Americans from the larger American community created "cultural distortions and peculiar values" among black people, including consumerism, delinquency, and illegitimacy.[118] George N. Redd, head of the Department of Education at Fisk University, explained that some of the most "rigid patterns of racial segregation in any society" placed African Americans at a "disadvantage in competing with members of the white race for social and economic gains."[119] While Redd did not ignore inequality in school facilities, school terms, and teacher training, he emphasized that educational, residential, and employment segregation created racial isolation that produced the "cultural deficiencies of the American Negro."[120] While cracks in the "strong wall of racial segregation" were evident, Redd believed it would take a number of generations before the damage segregation inflicted on "the educational and cultural interests of the Negro" began to pass.[121]

African Americans had long been fighting Jim Crow as an intertwined economic and political system, and black intellectuals had long conceptualized legal segregation in the South and systemic discrimination in the North and West as nearly impermeable barriers to black advancement. While *JNE* thinkers in 1935 and in 1950 recognized that racial discrimination, segregation, and lower class status intertwined in complex ways, in 1950 segregation—"by custom and by law"—appeared as the basic causal factor whose detrimental results were not only economic and political but also cultural.[122] "In the case of the Negro in America," Redd held, "the limitations placed upon his area of mobility are so severe that complete realization of his potentialities has never been possible."[123] Segregation not capitalism, political scientist Ralph Bunche suggested in 1950, was the culprit. The elimination of legal segregation and the protection of African American civil and political rights were essential, he held, if "American society should cease requiring any of its citizens to run the race of life over a special obstacle course while all other citizens compete on the flat."[124] The constraints imposed by anticommunism and the possibilities embedded in the legal fight against *Plessy* led *JNE* authors to use the concept of segregation in new ways. Convinced that the race issue involved more than individual acts of prejudice or discrimination, but limited in their ability to discuss class and economic exploitation, Cold War–era *JNE* authors turned to the malleable and ever-critical concept of segregation to highlight the structural nature of racial oppression.

By 1968, more than ten years after his central political objective— overturning de jure segregation—had been secured, Charles H. Thompson still worried about how to integrate and equalize America's schools. Of course between 1954 and 1968, despite the effective stalling tactics of southern state and local officials, *Brown v. Board* effectively dismantled the legal, and much of the institutional, edifice of southern Jim Crow education. Once implemented, the decision altered the institutional organization, funding, hiring, and pupil placement plans of segregated school systems and transformed patterns of public resource distribution. Desegregation also brought the weight of federal authority into the struggle for civil rights in education and required racial moderates like President Eisenhower to bring federal power—and federal troops in cases like Little Rock in 1957—behind efforts to dismantle Jim Crow. After the passage of the Civil Rights Act (1964) and Elementary and Secondary Education Act (1965), moreover, the federal government had additional financial leverage with which to demand local compliance with desegregation mandates. Despite its individualistic rationale, *Brown v. Board* began to restructure southern public education, as Thompson had hoped it would.[125]

Nonetheless, when looking at school segregation outside the South in 1968, even ever-optimistic integrationists like Thompson were worried. The retired *JNE* editor responded to the arrival of formal equality, to James Coleman's *Equality of Educational Opportunity* (1966), and to the Kerner Commission Report's (1967) explanation of the racial unrest that had recently exploded in many American cities. In this setting, Thompson began to fear that the central premise on which much of his scholarly and political work had been based—that school desegregation could effectively equalize educational resources—had been flawed.[126] Thompson supported Coleman's focus on educational outcomes, saw compensatory education for poor and minority students as essential, and assumed that integration across class lines was necessary for improving African American schooling. He was coming to believe, however, that white flight made class integration nearly impossible to engineer.[127] In fact, Thompson began to articulate a point W. E. B. Du Bois had made in 1935 by arguing that alternatives to public education might be necessary for improving black schooling.[128] By the late 1960s, Thompson drew a new set of political lessons—that legal desegregation was not enough—from the combination of social structural and political economic theories that had suffused *JNE* debate since the journal's inception.

From the 1930s through the late 1960s *JNE* authors prioritized the systemic and relational sources of American racial oppression and injustice even though they took small steps toward racial individualism. Building on radical intellectual traditions associated with the African American and interracial lefts, Depression-era *JNE* authors emphasized the intertwined political and economic bases of racial oppression and depicted prejudice as a rationalization. They also, in keeping with the NAACP's interwar legal strategy against segregation, presented the redistribution of educational resources as a first priority. Wartime theoretical discussions continued to feature political economic and social structural frameworks. However, as World War II raised concern with prejudice among an expanded group of white liberals, *JNE* authors engaged with the psychology of prejudice and sought to turn national enthusiasm for tolerance toward support for legal desegregation. In so doing, the *JNE* downplayed earlier calls for the equitable distribution of educational resources. This tendency only grew in strength as McCarthyism took root after 1947 and the NAACP shifted to a direct attack on *Plessy* in 1950. In the early 1950s, *JNE* authors increasingly identified "enforced separation," not the structures of liberal capitalism, as the most important systemic cause of racial injustice and inequality. They replaced Depression-era economic determinism with a vision of segregation as an intertwined legal and socioeconomic structure and presented the latter as the most destructive and actionable source of racial inequality.

While the growing institutional power of psychology was evident in *JNE* debate, most authors never rejected systemic and relational theorizing or fully embraced behavioralism. The *JNE*'s historic ties to the African American popular front and the fact the journal fell beyond the reach of many new postwar funding streams ensured that the social structural and political economic theories that had circulated in the 1930s continued—albeit with their radical edges softened—in the postwar years. The central role political scientists, economists, and economically informed sociologists played in the *JNE* also helped theoretical alternatives to racial individualism endure in the emerging Cold War era. At the same time, however, many *JNE* authors also found dispositional theories and rights-based individualism politically useful. This was the case amid wartime celebrations of tolerance and democracy and after the political climate turned rightward in the late 1940s. In the two decades following *An American Dilemma*, *JNE* intellectuals and activists strategically embraced racial liberalism even though many of their theories suggested that negative rights and antiprejudice education were insufficient as a total paradigm for racial progress. In their qualified support for education for tolerance, *JNE* integrationists, somewhat surprisingly, found common ground with politically moderate groups like the National Conference of Christians and Jews that, as the next chapter shows, equivocated on commitment to desegregation.

SIX

"To Inoculate Americans against the Virus of Hate": Brotherhood, the War on Intolerance, and the National Conference of Christians and Jews

Drawing on unspecified social scientific evidence, a 1954 "Report of the National Conference of Christians and Jews" (NCCJ) held that "the religious and racial hostilities and discrimination which bring heartache and tragedy to thousands of Americans *are not born in people*." "If culture created them," the report explained, then "culture can correct and remake attitudes and folkways" since "it is not a matter of changing human nature but of *changing the training of human nature*." This key component of postwar racial individualism, the belief that educational programs could reduce intergroup conflict, had permeated NCCJ efforts to improve interfaith relations since the 1920s. When the NCCJ slowly and haltingly turned attention to racial intolerance during World War II, the group continued to assume that misguided attitudes caused discrimination and that "a far-flung and intensive educational effort" was needed. Tendencies towards educationalization were evident in the mid-1950s as well, when NCCJ leaders asserted that the group's more than two decades of work to improve interfaith relations through education prepared it for fostering better race relations amid massive resistance to *Brown v. Board of Education*.[1]

Established in 1927, the National Conference of Jews and Christians (NCJC, which became the National Conference of Christians and Jews [NCCJ] in 1938) was one of many religiously motivated associations seeking to produce tolerance in midcentury America. Supported, often imprecisely, by social scientific findings on the malleability of prejudices, the Conference was predisposed to using moral exhortation and educational techniques to challenge injustice. In fact, as religious, educational, and civic groups became committed to improving race relations during World War II, many drew on the techniques the interwar NCCJ had pioneered.[2] Even after the NCCJ included race relations in its purview during World War II, the group stood to the right of the religious movement for intergroup goodwill. In contrast to the American Jewish Congress, the Fellowship of Reconciliation, and the National Council of Churches—all of which made clear statements against racial discrimination and segregation during the war—the NCCJ was institutionally committed to avoiding politics.[3]

The organization's apolitical educational approach proved useful as leaders sought to remain aloof from the regionally divisive politics of desegregation but relevant to the fight for improved human relations. As controversy over school desegregation grew in the years leading up to and immediately following *Brown v. Board of Education* (1954), however, this effort produced much institutional hand-wringing. Conference officials perceived a moment of opportunity because the group was one of the few organizations in the intergroup relations field whose work in the South segregationists had not crushed. NCCJ leaders hoped to chart a moderate course on desegregation that would prove the organization's crucial national significance by promoting antiprejudice education in the short term and remaining imprecise about the institution's stance to legal desegregation in the long term. By separating two core components of racial liberalism, though, the group ultimately exposed the conservative political implications of racial individualism, since education to combat prejudice helped justify gradualism on legal desegregation.

"Humble Apologies and Kindly Resolutions": The NCCJ's Philosophy and Program

The movement for intergroup goodwill that gained significant momentum in the 1920s and again during World War II included organizations with different levels of interest in race relations and civil rights. Early twentieth-century immigration and nativism had prompted assimilationist programs in schools and community centers and intercultural educators' efforts to improve interethnic relations by celebrating immigrants' "cultural gifts."[4] The NCCJ emerged in 1927 as part of a broader effort to generate interfaith understanding at a time when anti-Jewish and anti-Catholic sentiments were running high; Jewish groups worried about conversion efforts in their communities; and liberal Protestants wanted to "put the brakes on hatred" and reclaim Christian rhetoric from the KKK.[5] Although some religious and educational proponents of intergroup goodwill such as the Federal Council of Churches (FCC) directed attention to racial issues in the 1920s, the NCCJ remained focused on interfaith concerns until the 1940s.[6]

Social scientific research on the malleability of prejudice supported and was legitimized by antiprejudice efforts like the NCCJ's.[7] While conceptions of the causes of intergroup prejudice shaped the Conference's educational mission, the organization at times relied specifically on social science and at other times made vague appeals to scientific authority. In the 1920s and 1930s, NCCJ director Everett Clinchy, who held a master's degree from Union Theological Seminary and a PhD in education from Drew University, often referred to Franz Boas, John Dewey, and anthropologist Clark Wissler in his writing. The NCCJ leaders' assumptions about how prejudices were acquired built on behaviorist psychology, Floyd Allport's discussion of habituated responses, Bruno Lasker's notions of children being "born without prejudice," and Horace Kallen's celebratory views of cultural pluralism.[8] Clinchy and many NCCJ members also appealed to scientific authorities with less precision, however. The most widespread assumption motivating NCCJ work was that prejudice derived from a lack of contact between and knowledge about individuals from different groups.[9] As an NCCJ 1931 bulletin explained, prejudices "are most often conditioned by notions carelessly picked up from others, or by one or two unfortunate experiences with annoying individuals on the fringe of another culture." As a result, stereotypes could be challenged, "some educators believe," by "having Protestants, Catholics, and Jews meet each other under fortunate conditions."[10] While these assumptions reflected emerging literature, they did not engage with the more nuanced arguments sociologists Arnold Rose and Robin M. Williams Jr. and social psychologist Gordon Allport brought to the topic, which suggested that only under certain conditions was contact likely to increase tolerance.[11]

Building on specific science and more general assumptions about the sources of intergroup conflict, the NCCJ promoted understanding using a variety of educational methods. These included "trio tours," where one priest, one rabbi, and one minister traveled the country together giving presentations about religious differences and the need for tolerance; round-table meetings, a discussion by individuals of different faiths that aimed to combat stereotypes by encouraging honest intergroup dialogue; interfaith institutes and clinics; teacher training programs; and mass mediated propaganda. Committed to teaching Americans about the danger of stereotypes and to convincing Americans of all cultural and religious groups of their shared interests, NCCJ leaders assumed that exposure to information about minorities and contact between members of different groups would foster understanding.[12] At the same time, the organization's interfaith character ensured that it resisted assimilation, made clear that it did not want to build an amalgamated religion or engage in missionary work, and even avoided direct programming for children whose religious beliefs might be vulnerable.[13] The NCCJ did encourage colleges to examine their curricula for unidentified prejudices and to establish interfaith organizations.[14] Another core component of the NCCJ's educational approach was its use of the mass media in a "nationwide effort for better human relations" and a "crusade for brotherhood."[15] The NCCJ's Religious News Service supplied news stories concerning interfaith issues to religious newspapers across the country. The NCCJ press department carefully counted how many people publications reached and boasted about the different types of media employed to "inoculate Americans against the virus of hate, prejudice and misunderstanding."[16] The group also encouraged film executives to address "brotherhood themes," claimed to have inspired *Gentleman's Agreement* (1947) (a film that dealt sensitively with anti-Semitism), and tried to regulate negative depictions of religious groups in the media.[17] Brotherhood Week, an annual media event featuring radio, newspaper, and screen programs that the NCCJ sponsored beginning in 1934, sought to foster widespread interest in improving human relations year-round.[18] (See figure 7.)

In part because of its interreligious focus, the NCCJ was institutionally committed to staying out of politics. Since the Conference, especially early on, had to convince potential members that it was not trying to challenge individual religious beliefs, it encouraged members "to come together to discuss our disagreements agreeably" and treated "differences in fundamentals . . . as a matter of course."[19] The NCCJ thus envisioned a pluralist ideal, one in which Americans from different religious backgrounds came to understand and to accept that they held fundamentally different articles of faith. Rhetoric of understanding, cooperation, brotherhood, and goodwill—a language that suggested that misunderstanding not power or competition underlay intergroup antagonism—motivated NCCJ efforts to secure "a Brotherhood of man under the Fatherhood of God."[20] While the organization's constitution clearly stated that it would "rely upon educational procedures in its work," Clinchy argued repeatedly that NCCJ would leave political agitation, including lobbying, litigation, or direct action protests, to other groups.[21]

The interwar NCCJ stood at the forefront of a religious movement for intergroup understanding that coalesced in response to interreligious and interethnic strife in the 1920s and relied loosely, though often imprecisely, on the psychology and sociology of prejudice. The organization developed an explicitly educational and deliberately apolitical approach to fighting prejudice and intergroup misunderstanding that members described as scientifically justified and modern. This pluralist ideal worked in the arena of religious ideology because one group's interests did not necessarily impinge on another's. When domestic and international political developments led

7. Brotherhood Week, courtesy Social Welfare History Archives, University of Minnesota, National Conference of Christians and Jews Records.

NCCJ leaders to the race issue, however, applying its approach to questions of racial justice proved complicated.

"Our Common Moral Concern for Racial Justice," 1940–54

During and in the decade following World War II international and domestic political developments forced the NCCJ to turn attention to the race issue and ultimately to confront tensions in the apolitical, educationally focused version of racial liberalism it embraced. The NCCJ had expressed fleeting concern with racial, not only religious, prejudice in the 1920s and 1930s, and some local roundtables supported fair employment efforts.[22] Nazi racial genocide, domestic racial violence, and mounting civil rights agitation during and immediately following World War II led to heated debate in the national office, however, about whether the organization's commitment to improving interreligious relations should be expanded to include interracial relations. The NCCJ did cautiously move to incorporate efforts against racial bigotry into its program during the war. After 1948, federal action in support of civil rights, mounting protests against segregation, and Cold War pressures forced the NCCJ to begin reconsidering whether its apolitical, educational orientation remained sufficient. Ultimately the Conference equivocated on the race issue, however, due to fear of detracting from its primarily interfaith orientation and worries that opposing segregation might regionally divide the national organization.

World War II, by mobilizing the NCCJ's peer institutions to address not just anti-Semitism but also black-white relations, pressured the Conference to decide whether it would include racial not just religious bigotry in its efforts. As Nazi atrocities were discovered, the American Jewish Congress, the American Jewish Committee, and the Anti-Defamation League of B'nai B'rith established the National Community Relations Advisory Council "to serve as a clearinghouse for information about anti-Semitism."[23] The American Jewish Committee and the Commission on Community Interrelations (CCI) of the American Jewish Congress also supported social science on anti-Semitism that generated interest in antiblack racism.[24] Religious proponents of racial goodwill took different approaches to political engagement, but wartime concern for prejudice translated for many into support for desegregation and civil rights legislation. The FCC issued a statement condemning segregation in 1946 and the American Missionary Association and the Julius Rosenwald Fund sponsored Fisk's integrationist Race Relations Department in the early 1940s.[25] The American Jewish Congress had long rejected "moral pleading" and instead combined efforts to protest and publicize anti-Semitism with litigation and lobbying for legal change.[26] Although the Fellowship of Reconciliation and FCC engaged in educational work, by the mid-1940s they also directly protested discrimination and segregation. With the Congress of Racial Equality, the Fellowship of Reconciliation's race relations secretaries helped to sponsor the first interracial sit-in in 1943 and the first "freedom ride" to test the court decision outlawing discrimination in interstate travel in 1947.[27]

As the NCCJ paid growing attention to the war abroad, it expanded its focus from interreligious to intergroup relations and began including interracial relations in this more generalized framework. In part because anti-Semitism was such a central element of its mission, the NCCJ closely followed and publicized Nazi atrocities beginning in 1938. Once the United States entered the war, the NCCJ sent "trio groups" to the troops overseas and sponsored a Human Rights Committee that helped gain approval from the United Nations for a convention on genocide.[28] In addition, local roundtables included racial issues in efforts to address wartime domestic intergroup relations before the national office took a stand on the issue. Shortly after the war started, the Chicago roundtable produced a pamphlet with the jarring title "No Ocean Separates Us from Our Enemies Within" that warned that the devastation in Europe might emerge at home if Americans did not attend to domestic disunity.[29] Interfaith understanding between the "trio" of Judeo-Christian religions was still the central concern, but the pamphlet presented racial relations within an expanded purview. "Enemies within, as dangerous as any of those without," the Chicago pamphlet held, "are propagating lies, suspicion, misunderstanding and intolerance among American citizens of every creed and race." In fact, like civil rights activists who engaged in Double V campaigns, many NCCJ branches treated World War II as a useful opportunity to emphasize the urgency of the message they had been articulating since the 1920s.[30]

And yet NCCJ leadership in the national office equivocated about whether the Conference should focus solely, or largely, on interfaith relations. For example, while a 1944 annual report, titled "An Idea Whose Time Has Come!" noted that religious persecution remained the organization's main concern, it explained (ironically under a picture of a "roundtable" discussion among six white men) that "the Conference . . . has one aim: harmonious teamwork among a united people of diverse racial origins, cultures and faiths."[31] A statement by Clinchy, which called for "respect for the rights of others, appreciation of people outside one's own group, civilized self-restraints implicit in a democracy of cultures" eluded to support for civil rights but did not mention race outright.[32]

By the late 1940s, accelerating civil rights politics at home and the importance of human rights rhetoric abroad pushed the NCCJ to clarify its stance
to race relations and led some Conference leaders to begin challenging the
organization's interreligious, apolitical orientation. In 1948, Truman's desegregation of the military, the Dixiecrat revolt, and the Republican and
Democratic Parties' addition of civil rights planks to their platforms ensured that the unavoidably political—and increasingly regionally divisive—
character of American race relations was difficult to escape. The NCCJ's
Commission on Educational Organizations began to clarify "the Commission's thought regarding interracial relations" in 1948. It stated on the one
hand that "the NCCJ believes that it must, in its functioning as the educational arm of a great national organization, concern itself with any problems having to do with the improvement of intergroup understanding and
relationships." On the other hand, the commission would not tell southern
chapters what to do regarding integration, since "any effective human relations program must adapt itself to the thinking and social pattern of a
particular local situation."[33] In addition, the NCCJ began noting the ways
southern segregation damaged the nation's reputation abroad and incor-
porating the language of international human rights that gained popularity
among civil rights and race relations activists in the early 1950s.[34] Although
leaders worried that the organization might lose its interreligious focus, by
1952 the NCCJ's Commission on Religious Organizations further worked
to clarify the organization's approach to the race issue. "As Catholics, Protestants and Jews interested in eliminating intergroup prejudices," this commission explained, "we once again would reaffirm our common moral concern for racial justice" and "must be courageous and forthright in seeing
that basic human rights are upheld regardless of race."[35] NCCJ leaders even
seemed to venture into the political realm when they suggested that Americans must eliminate interracial prejudice and secure human rights at home
and abroad to effectively fight communism.[36] "In an era when the two-thirds
of the earth's population who are colored want, and certainly should get, a
fair break in life's opportunities and values," Clinchy emphasized, sounding like Charles S. Johnson and Edwin Embree, "no one's dignity is secure
unless of the rights of all humans are respected."[37] Even after the Supreme
Court struck down *Plessy v. Ferguson* in 1954, Clinchy relied on rights discourse to urge the NCCJ to fight racial prejudice and discrimination because
"they are sinful; they play into the hands of Communism; and they slow
down the united action of the free world's development."[38]

Pressure from local branches in northern and border states also encouraged the national office toward racial issues and political engagement in

the early 1950s. Many local roundtables were making the struggle against discrimination and segregation—not simply against prejudice—the focus of their activity. In 1954, Philadelphia and Baltimore roundtables initiated training in human relations for police departments, the Washington, DC, chapter coordinated an intergroup relations project for the Recreation Department of the District of Columbia to prepare for implementing a desegregation policy, and the Detroit NCCJ helped a department store integrate its sales force.[39] In Tulsa, in connection with a Brotherhood Week tour by Jackie Robinson, the NCCJ worked with the Lions Club to hold the first interracial meeting in the area. The Saint Louis NCCJ chapter helped establish a Citizen's Committee on Human Rights to facilitate an orderly transition from separate to integrated schools and contributed to the desegregation efforts that integrated hotels, pools, parks, and some movie theaters.[40] Although the national office increasingly included language about fighting racial prejudice in its publications, local chapters were clearly taking the lead in actually combating discrimination and segregation.

Despite this local initiative, NCCJ leaders with a national view tried to take a compromise position on the race issue between World War II and *Brown v. Board*. While World War II provided the NCCJ with an opportunity to highlight the significance of its work, the increasingly regionally divisive civil rights struggle could simultaneously challenge and further NCCJ goals. The combination of mounting civil rights protest, federal action against segregation, and Cold War–era human rights rhetoric made inaction on the race issue seem contradictory and reactionary for an organization committed to intergroup tolerance. And yet outright support for civil rights and desegregation threatened to alienate the national organization's southern constituents. Essentially the Conference had to decide whether two key elements of postwar racial liberalism—antiprejudice education rooted in psychological individualism and rights-based individualism that demanded political action—could logically and ethically be separated. Even as civil rights activists appeared poised for legal success in 1954, the NCCJ's national leadership remained deliberately vague about whether it would oppose discrimination and segregation.

"Vindication for the Policy of Moderation We Have Been Urging": The NCCJ and *Brown v. Board of Education*

The compromise position on civil rights that the NCCJ had begun to develop between World War II and the early 1950s would become increasingly difficult to maintain as southern communities engaged in "massive resistance" in response to *Brown v. Board of Education*. As the direct action phase of the civil rights movement accelerated in the mid-1950s, a number of religiously motivated groups joined the fight against segregation and discrimination.[41] While the Fellowship of Reconciliation supported the Southern Christian Leadership Conference in the 1950s and 1960s, the National Council of Churches (formerly FCC) established a Department of Racial and Cultural Relations (1952) that sought "to secure full opportunity for all minority racial and cultural groups, in churches, education, employment, housing, recreation, health services, government, and all other aspects of American society."[42] Resistance to segregation by leading religious organizations committed to intergroup goodwill encouraged some NCCJ members to push their organization to do likewise. At the same time, for an organization with a regionally diverse membership, segregationist resistance to civil rights gains pulled the NCCJ in other directions.[43] In the early 1950s—and especially after *Brown*—the NCCJ's national office discussed the "race issue" incessantly in an attempt to determine the relationship between national and regional policy and the place politics would play in its mission.

As segregationists opposed mounting civil rights gains, the NCCJ worried about losing southern members and being branded as just another radical civil rights organization. In 1951, when the Commission on Religious Organizations debated joining the National Council of Churches in observance of "Race Relations Sunday," members worried how support for interracial pulpit exchanges might affect the NCCJ's "southern constituency." The commission recommended moving "slowly and with caution" and suggested the decision be made at the regional rather than the national level. All agreed that the organization's stance to the race issue must develop with sensitivity, caution, and considerable forethought.[44] In 1953, NCCJ national leaders worriedly anticipated the *Brown* decision, concluding that the best way to avoid being branded as militant was to quietly prepare to aid communities in the process of school desegregation without ever stating outright support for the court's ruling. The Conference had established a Committee on Desegregation, a subcommittee of the Commission on Educational Organizations, in early 1953 but renamed this body later that year, as the Committee on the Integration of Minority Groups in American Education, out of fear that the original name suggested the NCCJ's clear support for school desegregation.[45]

Essentially the NCCJ sought to make itself a resource to communities undergoing court-ordered desegregation without condoning integration outright—and its traditional apolitical, educational stance was a valuable resource in this endeavor. The Committee on Integration approached desegregation as a research problem and as an issue demanding widespread educational programming. It put together a "master list" of institutions where integration had already taken place, sent questionnaires to area officials investigating "strategies and techniques useful in an integration situation," recommended observation of the process of integration in key cities, and produced a bibliography on the topic.[46] It also prepared to offer services that communities facing a court order might request. The NCCJ published "a guide book of strategies that have worked in previous integration situations," provided lists of speakers, and sponsored workshops and in-service teacher trainings on human relations throughout the South.[47] The national office, at the same time, became increasingly emphatic that it would not engage in political propaganda or agitation. "Since the Committee was created neither to propagandize for integration nor to attempt its delay," the minutes of the initial meeting explained, "it was felt that the Committee should respond principally to requests for help rather than to take the lead in offering its services."[48] As a result, much to the dismay of integrationist northern members, the Conference's national office retreated from the gestures supporting civil rights that it had begun to make in 1952.

The actual *Brown v. Board* decision caused the NCCJ to outline the major tenets of the approach it would maintain toward desegregation until the mid-1960s. The NCCJ developed this stance as Supreme Court justices resisted the NAACP's "immediatist" demands, President Eisenhower claimed privately that he believed *Brown* would retard progress in the South by fifteen years, segregationist governors in Georgia and South Carolina refused to enforce the decision, and some southern communities closed their schools, or warned they might, rather than desegregate.[49] A week after the *Brown* decision, an NCCJ committee met in Nashville, Tennessee (deliberately in a southern city), to assess "the present role and activities of NCCJ in interracial matters" and make recommendations regarding a future course of action.[50] Worried about the potential for noncompliance in the South, this committee's main concerns were to prevent alienating southern "moderates" and to highlight the NCCJ's unique ability—in contrast to groups directly supportive of civil rights—to foster peaceful intergroup relations through educational means.[51] The approach to race relations the committee developed had three main tenets: the NCCJ would focus on interreligious relations not race relations, it would continue to take an educational as opposed to a political approach to social problems, and it would avoid regional favoritism.[52] Essentially, the NCCJ refused to express support for desegregation outright at the same time that it provided educational resources (from pamphlets describing successful integration to documents explaining the *Brown* decision to laypeople) to southern communities adjusting to new legal demands.[53]

The NCCJ's original mission to address tensions between religious groups provided a great resource in the NCCJ's mid-1950s efforts to steer a moderate course on desegregation. The committee suggested that the NCCJ's by-laws be revised to include a "Statement of Interracial Policy" and that a paragraph be added to the NCCJ's constitution that explained the organization would treat racial issues through an interreligious lens. NCCJ members' "religious motivation" left the organization "increasingly aware of the grave problems centering around race relations in the United States." Still, committee members agreed that the group had no desire to "depart from its original purpose," which was "to ameliorate, through an educational approach, inter-religious tensions."[54] At the same time, religious morality, the fact that so many church groups were engaging in interracial activities, and the practical concerns of NCCJ constituents demanded that the organization become involved in interracial relations in some capacity.[55] While the NCCJ's sense of moral obligation made some approach to race relations necessary, its religious origins provided a distinctive—and politically evasive—tool the Conference could use against racial bigotry.

The NCCJ's focus on educational rather than political methods also gave it a unique role to play in the South's adjustment to desegregation. Like the postwar Rockefeller Foundation, the NCCJ worried about the kind of relationships it should establish with civil rights organizations and "how to cope with the pressure methods of certain action agencies." Fearing that direct action tactics would lead to increased racial tension, the committee instructed local groups to adhere strictly to their position of aiding the process of desegregation by distributing information while refusing to endorse the Supreme Court decision outright.[56] "As often as necessary—and whenever possible—" the committee instructed, NCCJ spokesmen should reiterate that "the National Conference is not a militant, legalistic, direct social action agency leading the fight for integration." Instead, the organization was to continue to make clear that "it attempts through an educational approach—in the broadest sense of the word—to build good human relations by getting at the sort of things that make for prejudice." The Committee on the Problems of Integration instructed regional directors and NCCJ leaders to follow this party line, emphasizing, as President Eisenhower did, that its stance derived not from conviction or moralism but from "the necessity of obeying legal decisions."[57] While acknowledging that "there are many possible solutions to the problems of human relations" including direct action and pressure tactics, the committee emphasized that "such possible solutions, it must be stressed . . . *are not* those used by NCCJ."[58]

The Conference also went to great lengths to avoid regional favoritism. It sought to prevent the organization's northern voices from overshadowing its southern members by requiring that all NCCJ commissions that produced materials on desegregation have adequate southern representation and increasing national control over pro–civil rights northern offices. "*All Regional Offices of NCCJ*" were instructed to "move with considerable circumspection before agreeing to act as a convening agency for a meeting of local organizations concerned with problems of integration." The committee emphasized that a regional office should not hold a meeting regarding integration unless it had consulted with the National Program Department and with local NCCJ boards, refused to prevent meetings in segregated facilities, and postponed a survey of segregation in churches.[59] Although many northern roundtables and regional leaders pressured the national office to publicly support legal desegregation and civil rights legislation, in the year following *Brown* the NCCJ used its educational mission and its religious moorings to defend itself against the accusation that it was just another northern-dominated civil rights group.[60]

The NCCJ's caution would only become more acute as the politics of integration became increasingly violent between 1954 and the early 1960s and the Supreme Court issued the gradualist *Brown II* decision. The NCCJ's advocacy of gradualism on integration was in tune with the sympathies of many powerful Americans. After the Supreme Court's decision in *Brown*, the NAACP had pressed for the articulation of a clear completion deadline in the fall of 1956, but the president and the Supreme Court were against the "immediatists" on the issue of timing. The justices had never truly considered any other stance, since a flexible and gradual design had been a concession necessary to secure a unanimous verdict.[61] In fact, winning the allegiance of the southern "moderates" prompted some of the justices toward the vague timeline of *Brown II*, which called for "all deliberate speed" in implementing school desegregation.[62] Dr. Gordon Lovejoy, who was appointed as the director of the NCCJ's southern activities in 1955, responded to the *Brown II* decision in a way that made clear the reasons for his commitment to gradualism. "If the Supreme Court of the United States had had NCCJ in mind," Lovejoy argued, "I do not see how it could have issued a decree more favorable to our position and our work than its recent implementation decree on desegregation." Lovejoy of course knew that much of the NCCJ's pro–civil rights constituency would be disappointed. He maintained, however, that *Brown II* provided "vindication within the Court decree for the policy of moderation we have been urging," and that the decision "strengthened—and possibly clarified—NCCJ's position and role."[63]

The NCCJ supported gradualism on desegregation in part in response to violent resistance NCCJ workers experienced firsthand and in part because the group believed that they had a unique role to play in moving southern moderates toward tolerance without alienating them entirely. The opposition Lovejoy and other NCCJ workers in the South encountered certainly convinced the organization of the need for a slow timeline on desegregation. Lovejoy and David Hyatt, an NCCJ official who toured southern regional offices after *Brown*, each faced resistance to desegregation. As Lovejoy traveled through the South holding "Building Brotherhood in Your Community" institutes in 1955 he noted white supremacists "gaining steadily in strength and in audacity" while southern liberals and moderates were keeping quiet. While Hyatt presented a long list of the educational activities in which southern branches of the NCCJ were engaged, Lovejoy, Hyatt, and many regional directors were receiving threatening phone calls and "hate literature" from white citizens' councils. They were also experiencing poor turnout at events.[64] Since "anything smacking of human relations has been automatically equated as being race relations," southern roundtable directors worried that their programs might "cause trouble."[65] Like Lovejoy, Hyatt's travels convinced him that a recent Gallup poll suggesting only one in eighteen southerners supported desegregation had been accurate. This situation meant "a tremendous educational job is ahead," one that might require more than two decades to complete.[66]

And yet the dilemma of the southern racial moderate also, Lovejoy suggested, provided the NCCJ with a great opportunity. The NCCJ might play a crucial role in the long-term process of desegregation if it remained committed to gradualism, highlighted its interfaith not interracial focus, and stayed out of the political fray.[67] Civil rights organizations were facing significant obstacles in the South, he emphasized, noting that the NAACP's immediatist stance on desegregation caused it to lose so much southern support it was forced to "retreat if it is to remain effective." Having injured their reputations by issuing "Teaching Units on Desegregation," the Southern Regional Council and the Anti-Defamation League were also waiting for changes in southern opinion before resuming their efforts.[68] In contrast, the NCCJ's interfaith origins and educational methods, Lovejoy hoped, meant the group might avoid the direct opposition civil rights activists faced. To signify a neutral stance toward desegregation, Lovejoy deliberately described his programs as advocating better "human relations" rather than race relations.[69] Moreover, Lovejoy believed the NCCJ was in a unique position to contribute to long-term desegregation because the Conference's southern constituency was the southern elite.[70] By slowly pushing "our constituency forward," the NCCJ would be able to "move the entire South" since the Conference was better situated than all other organizations in the field of race relations to influence southern opinion makers. "To me the only course of wisdom is to work with these people at the point they have now reached," Lovejoy argued. "If the price we must pay is to drag our heels a bit, it is a cheap price considering the *ultimate* good we can do."[71] By eschewing politics and remaining evasive on integration in the short term, the NCCJ was one of the few organizations in the field that southern elites had not "labeled as 'too advanced'" and considered "'safe' to work with" as schools moved slowly toward integration.[72] In the long run, since NCCJ leaders were making "valuable contacts" in southern school systems, southern communities would be likely to ask the NCCJ for additional help when they were finally forced to integrate.[73]

In addition, Hyatt suggested that to show support for southern moderates, northern NCCJ leaders should avoid self-righteousness and regional blame. In response to northern members who wanted to "do something" about the South, he made clear: "If there is one thing Southerners resent most deeply it is Northerners telling them how to run the South." Instead, highlighting the systemic and extralegal sources of racial inequality in the North, he emphasized that, *"The shame of the North is as great as the South."* Since the worst segregated ghettos he'd witnessed were not in the South but in New York, Chicago and Detroit, Hyatt argued boldly that, *"The best way the North can help the situation in the South is to get its own house in order."* This required attending to northern "job discrimination, social color lines, housing restrictions and educational inequalities" and acknowledging that "even its so-called 'integrated' schools are in many cases segregated" due to districting and discriminatory housing markets.[74] When northern regional leaders were asked both privately and publicly about the NCCJ's role in southern "tension areas," they were to stress, Hyatt instructed, that racism was a national problem and that "all of us have a responsibility to wipe out this blot on our democracy."[75] While revealing the NCCJ's careful balancing act on desegregation, Hyatt also noted that the sources of much racial inequality outside the Jim Crow South were systemic not legal or dispositional, factors with which NCCJ's methods were poorly equipped to deal.

An internal evaluation produced in 1956 showed that while southern resistance and efforts to prove the group's long-term utility to southern moderates shaped the NCCJ approach, the Conference also held fast to its identity as an interfaith organization because this approach fit institutional needs. The evaluation committee had concluded that "the Conference must always remain an organization working in the areas that lie between the great religious organizations" and expressed concern that the NCCJ had moved away from its original mandate and engaged too fully in "the broad social field." In fact, since World War II, the evaluation noted, the NCCJ's interreligious relations work declined significantly, was underfunded, increasingly lacked innovation, and was "probably the most neglected area within its program spectrum."[76] Reinforcing the NCCJ's commitment to interreligious work was not intended to reduce the NCCJ's work fighting prejudice and discrimination directed at African Americans. Instead, the study's authors argued that a concern with interracial prejudice must instead emerge "from our mandate to deal with inter-religious tensions and prejudices."[77] The NCCJ spoke for engaging in the race issue not because it agreed with the Supreme Court's decision or with the "statements of social scientists" but because "one cannot debate the moral imperatives of our religious tradition."[78] Fighting racism by emphasizing the importance of interreligious relations—the approach that best fit institutional needs—also seemed realistic, NCCJ leaders argued, given the church's institutional power in the South. "The NCCJ as a race relations organization is a 'dead duck' in the South or Southwest," but since religious leaders had a captive audience and might be less vulnerable to economic or political threats than other southern professionals, addressing race relations through religious channels might be productive.[79]

The 1956 evaluation also provided strong justification for the NCCJ's desire to avoid overtly political work, not only due to southern resistance but also because this impulse served broader institutional needs. The evaluation framed itself against a rejected World War II–era report that recommended the NCCJ engage in direct action and launch "an active campaign against discrimination on all fronts." In 1956, however, NCCJ leaders defended the organization's decision to elide politics since, as George N. Shuster worried, "If we enter into the broad social field and deal with numerous problems, we run the risk of disappearing because of a lack of organizational unity." Had the earlier report been accepted, Clinchy added, "the Conference would become a kind of 'General League Against All Intolerance,' one more 'Pro-Democracy Committee,' of which the number is already legion."[80] This conviction led the authors of the evaluation to reject including a statement of support for *Brown v. Board* in its program manual. The Conference would gain little by making itself a "'me-too' organization" since "*A phrase does not make an organization; its program and activity do.*" The NCCJ was reducing prejudice in the South and improving African American status through its indirect, nonconfrontational approach, the evaluation concluded. It saw "*little profit in the addition of a phrase that, by itself, will yield few gains in the*

North but may seriously damage our great potential for productive work in the South."[81] The study went on to quote an African American religious leader from Dallas who argued that while the NAACP was just recovering from "scars of court battle" and Protestant organizations refused to take an effective stand on segregation, the NCCJ "without fanfare and without publicity" had become an invaluable ally for African Americans because it had "the respect of both sides."[82] On the issue of remaining apolitical, the NCCJ defended its stance by appealing to larger institutional interests, a sense of realism, and the conviction that engaging southern moderates was essential for real progress in race relations.

The NCCJ even turned, quite selectively, to social scientific authorities when defending regional variation in programming.[83] By appealing to the "power structure" of southern communities in support of "the 'American Creed' of brotherhood and fair play," the evaluation argued that the NCCJ was following Gunnar Myrdal's claim that "it is an essential strategy to evoke the powerful spiritual aid that inheres in the living conception of human brotherhood and in the democratic creed." The document also cited Robert MacIver, who it noted was allied with the "action-minded camp" but who the group read rather narrowly given *The More Perfect Union*'s emphasis on antidiscrimination legislation, to stress "the necessity of adapting programs to the prevailing mores."[84]

Throughout the postwar period, the NCCJ aimed to remain true to the group's interfaith focus but civil rights successes—and segregationist resistance—made divorcing educational programs to combat intolerance from racial politics particularly difficult. In striking contrast to many religious organizations that actively supported civil rights groups, however, the NCCJ remained stridently committed to its apolitical orientation. This was largely because the national organization worried that too militant a stance toward integration would alienate its southern membership. The desire to chart a moderate course on race relations also resulted, however, from assumptions about the organization's unique identity. After 1954, the NCCJ leadership was also convinced that the Conference, by addressing racism through human relations education and appeals to interreligious brotherhood, could make more long-term progress toward racial justice than civil rights groups that demanded desegregation immediately. As the NCCJ embraced the gradualist politics of racial moderates like President Eisenhower—whose calls for brotherhood the NCCJ often featured on promotional materials—Conference leaders found the group's interreligious origins and apolitical, educational orientation useful tools for attempting to stay above the political fray.

"As the National
Conference of Christians
and Jews seeks
to promote the welfare
of all people in the
Family of Man, it has my
complete support and
determined participation."

Dwight D. Eisenhower
Honorary Chairman, Brotherhood Week

8. Dwight D. Eisenhower, courtesy Social Welfare History Archives, University of Minnesota, National Conference of Christians and Jews Records.

The problems associated with attempts to depoliticize and educational-ize the race issue had been evident to some NCCJ members in the 1930s. It was only possible to ease differences by discussion, Dr. Felix Morrow, a roundtable participant with ties to the Communist Party explained in 1931, "where the differences are genuinely NOT differences, but misunderstand-ings." There were also many "irreconcilable differences" between religious groups—and presumably between races, classes, and ethnic groups—that would "make harmonious solutions gravely doubtful."[85] Other critics were not so conciliatory. In 1949 David Petegorsky and Leo Pfeffer of the American Jewish Congress emphasized that racial conflicts involved more than "differences of doctrine and belief," and the resolution of such con-flicts required more than education. In a scathing evaluation of the NCCJ program, they argued:

The kind of program which NCCJ practices was once perhaps harmful. It glosses over basic sources of inter-group conflict through a superficial agreement on slogans; it prevents democratic discussions and the resolution of genuine issues and it gives to many persons who might otherwise devote themselves to social activity in this field, a salve for their conscience by involving them in ineffective effort.[86]

The most important sources of intergroup antagonism, critics held, were those that the NCCJ avoided. On these issues the NCCJ was not only ill equipped to intervene but was also diverting financial resources and human energies toward unscientific and potentially harmful efforts.[87] For precisely the reasons critics flagged, translating the NCCJ approach to interfaith relations into a strategy for progress in race relations proved difficult. While misunderstandings could cause mistrust between members of different racial and religious groups, when conflict derived from blocked rights, exploitation, and oppression, it required political and legal action for its resolution. In these cases reliance on educational methods, as critics of interracialism had long maintained, was a form of accommodation.

The NCCJ remained committed to its apolitical educational techniques even when "massive resistance" to *Brown v. Board* brought the contradictions of the position to light because the group wanted to maintain its interreligious focus and did not want to lose its southern constituents. The organization's history ensured that it was better equipped for educational work than other types of activism. Conference leaders were also convinced they would profit institutionally by remaining in dialogue with elite southern gradualists. Moreover, NCCJ leaders believed they were uniquely situated in the racial field to chart a middle ground of conciliation and to avoid the allegations of radicalism launched at civil rights groups. Striving to balance the enthusiasm of northern, integrationist chapters and the concerns of southern gradualists, the NCCJ tried to reach a compromise position, one that represented the logical conclusion of their apolitical, understanding-oriented, educational framework for conceptualizing the race issue. Exposing key fault lines among postwar racial liberals, the civil rights movement broadly and school desegregation more specifically made the claim that the race issue could be depoliticized increasingly difficult for NCCJ leaders to promote. The NCCJ would eventually see the errors of its ways and by the mid-1960s opposed segregation and even published pamphlets on the dangers of de facto racial separation.[88] And yet before 1964, the NCCJ's halting and contradictory stance toward school integration exposed the conservative political implications of racial individualism and the utility of theories that obscured the centrality of self-interest to the race issue.

Conclusion

From Power to Prejudice has examined a collection of institutions where postwar social scientists who pursued racial justice sought to clarify what they were fighting against and what they were struggling for. In so doing, the book has historicized one subset of the assumption that social problems can be reduced to individual perpetrators and victims, an idea that has been especially influential in twentieth-century American thought and policy on race. From the 1930s through the mid-1960s, racial individualism—a set of social theories and paradigms for racial progress that presented white prejudice, discrimination, and legally denied civil rights as the most significant and remediable causes of racial injustice, conflict, and inequality—competed with systemic and relational frameworks. Between the publication of Gunnar Myrdal's *An American Dilemma* (1944) and the early 1960s, however, this competition occurred on an uneven landscape and produced unequal results.

In sites where racial individualism's influence was expected and in those where it proved surprising, the paradigm exhibited a fairly consistent postwar history. Individualistic frameworks circulated alongside systemic and relational views in the 1920s and 1930s. A period of transition occurred during the war and immediate postwar years, when individualistic approaches were on the rise but systemic and relational alternatives had not yet declined. Between1949 and the early 1960s, however, systemic and relational approaches to the race issue became considerably more muted. This trajectory confirms the importance of the familiar political pressures—namely, antiradicalism, rightward shifts in American politics, and the effectiveness of rights-based legal strategies—shaping postwar tendencies to separate racial and economic injustice. It also makes clear that other, largely intellectual, forces—scientism, enthusiasm for quantification, behavioralism, and faith in the socially transformative power of education—also helped to produce postwar racial liberalism's theoretical blind spots.

One crucial exception to this chronological pattern emerged, however, from some African American academic spaces to expose key fissures dividing the postwar social scientific interracial left: *theoretical* alternatives to racial individualism never substantially declined in the late 1940s and 1950s. Even as individualistic theories and agendas for racial progress reached their peak of influence in mainstream psychology, sociology, and civil rights politics in the early 1950s, a substantial group of scholars, one that extended beyond the cast of radicals whose critiques of liberalism historians usually identify, questioned the tendency to explain racial injustice in astructural, noneconomic terms, as a problem of individual perpetrators and victims. Many at Fisk University's Race Relations Institutes (RRI) and Howard University's *Journal of Negro Education* (*JNE*) viewed prejudice as a rationalization for, not a cause of, exploitation and saw legal segregation and state-sanctioned discrimination as only the most obvious components of more complex systems of racial injustice. They articulated economically informed visions of the race issue that reflected African American grassroots protest and suggested that political oppression and labor exploitation were fundamental elements of—not aberrations to—American democracy.[1] Dilemmas associated with the scale of feasible reform, nonetheless, constrained scholars who thought beyond the parameters of postwar racial individualism. Many had a difficult time translating systemic and relational theories into reform agendas that seemed realistic in the rightward moving postwar political context. In fact, despite widespread enthusiasm for politically relevant social science, scholars who leaned toward individualism and scholars who questioned it found efforts to use "social science" to inform "social action" to be quite complicated.

Racial individualism gained influence in the decade and a half after *An American Dilemma*, despite the endurance of systemic and relational frameworks in key African American–led intellectual sites, for a number of intersecting reasons. These included internalist pressures such as scientism, enthusiasm for quantifiable research methods, theoretical shifts toward personality study in psychology, and the waning of social ecology. The postwar politics of knowledge production was also influential, especially wartime federal support for attitude-based survey research techniques and postwar foundation backing of interdisciplinary behavioralism. Externalist factors, most importantly anticommunism, the widespread popularity of uncontroversial antiprejudice education, the utility of rights discourse and the courts to civil rights activists, and shifts in congressional politics that made redistributive policies unlikely, were at work as well.

At times, the political context did not fully account for racial individualism's expansion. Psychology's theoretical orientation toward individual units of analysis and the field's concern with the cognitive and emotional bases of personality are likely to have shaped the direction much postwar psychological research on racial issues took—as it did for Gordon Allport—regardless of wartime attention to Nazi racism or postwar McCarthyism. The replacing of Chicago school social ecology with structural functionalism among sociologists and postwar turns to interdisciplinary behavioralism did fail to violate Cold War ideological constraints.[2] Methodological and theoretical considerations were as important as antiradicalism, however, to declining enthusiasm for Chicago-school style case study methods, as Robin M. Williams's and Arnold Rose's concerns with particularism and CETRRR debates over the tension barometer reveal. That economists and political scientists' voices were muted in postwar discussions of the structural sources of racial inequality and segregation until the early 1960s, a factor that was related to but not reducible to antiradicalism, also encouraged postwar racial individualism.[3] The intellectual context was as important as the political, then, in explaining why many postwar scholars viewed the race issue in terms of individual prejudice and discrimination.

Still, the politics of wartime and postwar knowledge production frequently made methodological pressures toward individualism more acute. Wartime and postwar funding patterns—especially experiments in interdisciplinary, quantitative, attitude-based survey research and the movement of these methods into universities in the immediate postwar years—directly favored research that was both quantitative and dispositional.[4] By institutionalizing survey research in sites like the National Opinion Research Center, individualistic methods seeped into debates in nearby academic settings like CETRRR. Wartime methodological models also permeated privately funded scholarly initiatives like the American Jewish Committee's Studies in Prejudice series well after the war had ended. In some cases, moreover, scholars may not have fully acknowledged the factors pressing on their assumptions about methodological sophistication. Debate over social scientific inclusion in the National Science Foundation between 1945 and 1950 as well as congressional investigations into foundation support for "subversive," leftist social science in the early 1950s created a context in which many social scientists felt pressure to defend themselves against the accusation that their work was politically motivated and thus unscientific. That scholars like sociologist Robin M. Williams Jr. defined rigorous sociology as generalizable, theoretically oriented, and quantifiable—priorities that made a large data set essential and dismissed the relevance of case-based approaches—is hardly surprising in these years, since the objectivity of the "softer" social sciences was being questioned from many directions.[5] Of course research on race could be quantitative without being dispositional. Sociologists like W. E. B. Du Bois, Charles S. Johnson, and E. Franklin Frazier had quantified patterns of racial disadvantage since the early twentieth century.[6] However, while survey technologies created exciting new methods for studying the attitudinal causes of racial injustice, these tools provided little help for scholars seeking to measure the systemic or relational *causes* of (as opposed to the extent of) racial conflict or inequality. Especially between 1949 and the early 1960s, dilemmas of scale hampered the efforts of many sociologists who worried about atomism but were unsure how to avoid it methodologically.

The politics of postwar knowledge production also incentivized theoretical shifts toward racial individualism. Among sociologists, the combination of social structural and political economic analysis that characterized the African American Chicago school fell outside the behavioralist, "human relations," or "social relations" paradigms that wartime experiments in interdisciplinarity and foundation support for the behavioral science after 1949 greatly encouraged.[7] While the precise sources of postwar behavioralism are beyond the scope of this analysis, this theoretical drift had profound implications for social structural and political economic research on race.[8]

In addition to internalist pressures and the politics of knowledge production, externalist political dynamics also encouraged individualistic approaches to racial research and reform. The rightward moving political and ideological context, which involved turns away from redistributive, political economic reform as Congress became more conservative after 1946 and anticommunism limited academic and civil rights discourse after 1947, certainly contributed to racial individualism's postwar appeal.[9] The fact that legal and rights-based civil rights strategies proved effective in the shifting political climate was simultaneously of great significance. By the late 1940s, antiracist scholar-activists had to walk a fine line as they struggled against segregation, discrimination, and economic injustice while situating their demands within the rightward moving boundaries of postwar liberalism. Pragmatic social scientists like Charles S. Johnson and Charles H. Thompson adjusted to the limited political possibilities they faced by turning to psychological and rights-based languages and by prioritizing battles on the most promising reformist "fronts." This strategy proved both successful and inherently limiting.[10] While psychological and rights-based individualism aided antiracist scholar-activists facing a challenging postwar intellectual and political terrain, individualism faltered when reformist attention shifted from de jure to de facto segregation and from legally sanctioned discrimination to racialized economic inequality.

The history of antiprejudice education during and in the decade follow-ing World War II illuminates the ways another set of political dynamics—in this case political possibilities rather than impossibilities—shaped not only reform strategies but also research. The cheap, small-scale, and relatively in-nocuous character of antiprejudice education helped this reform appeal to a broad group that included both organizations like the Rockefeller Founda-tion (RF) and National Conference of Christians and Jews (NCCJ), which sympathized with the politics of southern gradualism, and avid integration-ists. Even the *JNE* embraced "education for racial understanding," though the fact that the journal did so only briefly during World War II suggests *JNE* leaders wanted to draw wartime antifascist concerns to the integrationist cause, but does not expose a sustained theoretical or political commitment. Still, that so many different constituencies viewed antiprejudice education as acceptable certainly aided the endurance of this core component of racial individualism. This apparent agreement may have also obscured the sub-stantial qualifications raised by those who considered tolerance education insufficient as a total paradigm for racial progress. In addition, antiprejudice education's reformist popularity encouraged some psychologists and soci-ologists, especially those like Allport and the authors of *The Authoritarian Personality* who already had theoretical and methodological reasons to study attitudes, to turn scholarly attention to prejudice. In fact, the relationship between social science and antiprejudice education exhibited a dynamic that advocates of the dissemination of scientific expertise like Louis Wirth hoped to avoid; a well-intentioned but narrowly conceived reform agenda generated much, also narrowly conceived, research. Between the mid-1940s and the early 1960s, externalist factors built on and frequently reinforced internalist, institutional, and financial pressures to support racial individu-alism as a social theory and as a program for racial progress.

Despite these intersecting pressures favoring racial individualism, inter-racial networks of scholar-activists continued to nurture systemic and rela-tional theories of racial injustice. Although the *JNE* and Fisk's RRI welcomed psychological analysis as part of their commitment to interdisciplinarity, in general wartime excitement for attitude measurement and postwar enthusi-asm for behavioralism had a fairly limited impact in these sites. A number of factors help to explain why. Foundation treatment of African American–led academic spaces as second tier allowed the combination of systemic and relational analysis that marked the African American Chicago school to continue into the late 1940s and 1950s, even when this approach became outdated in the elite white academic world.[11] In addition, that the African American "counter-public sphere," to which many of the leading voices at the RRI and *JNE* had close ties, had a robust history of questioning liberalism and supporting redistributive egalitarianism likely affected the endurance of oppression-oriented and exploitation-based theories of racism in these settings.[12] Moreover, given that many of the teachers, labor organizers, social workers, and race relations practitioners who attended Fisk's Institutes and wrote for Howard's *JNE* were engaged on a daily basis with African Americans struggling to find jobs, housing, and education, it is not entirely surprising that debates there were closely attuned to the economic concerns that permeated much grassroots civil rights activism.[13]

The endurance of structural and relational theories of the race issue in networks of scholar-activists tied to Fisk's RRI and Howard's *JNE* is important because these frameworks faced so many obstacles elsewhere in the late 1940s and 1950s. Certainly radical thinkers like Herbert Aptheker, Oliver Cromwell Cox, and W. E. B. Du Bois articulated structural and political economic theories of the race issue from the margins of the academy through the 1950s.[14] At times critiques of racial individualism reached the "mainstream" academic world, as when E. Franklin Frazier, the first African American president of the American Sociological Association, called on his colleagues to return to the study of race and social structure in his 1948 presidential address.[15] In addition, even if HBCUs were an intellectual underground, they still had close ties to the elite white academy. The postwar social scientific interracial left that moved through Fisk's Institutes and wrote for Howard's *JNE* included many white liberals like Gordon Allport, Louis Wirth, and Arnold Rose who were employed in leading, white research institutions. And yet it was the HBCUs they visited occasionally or the separate, action-oriented committees they established (like the American Council on Race Relations) not their home departments, where theoretical alternatives to racial individualism flourished most actively. This pattern suggests that African American–led intellectual spaces played an important role in sustaining non-Marxist, political economic and social structural alternatives to racial individualism in the postwar era. The precise connections between the intellectual underground the RRI and *JNE* nurtured and the radical theories of exploitation, oppression, and internal colonialism that reemerged in the late 1960s demands further investigation.[16] It is likely, however, that these sites help to explain why, when civil rights activists became frustrated with the limits of formal equality by the late 1960s, a language that rooted racial oppression in political economy, that highlighted exploitation, that applied to de facto segregation, and that exposed institutionalized discrimination was so readily available.

Whether based in HBCUs or in elite white research institutions, the postwar interracial social scientific left knew they had to tread lightly as they identified the elements of the race issue not encompassed by either the psychology of prejudice or rights discourse. To suggest that inevitable patterns of technological development, migration, and intergroup competition (as systemic, social ecological theorists suggested) or inherently oppressive political-economic systems that required cheap labor and a divided working class (which relational theories identified) caused mid-twentieth-century racial conflict and inequality did not lead to policy recommendations that could be easily implemented in any political climate. In the postwar years, when support for desegregation often raised anticommunist ire in the South, resistance to statism and class analysis generated suspicion of "subversion," and rightward turns in congressional politics meant that the redistributive elements of New Deal liberalism were on the decline, antiracist scholars carefully prioritized their political agendas.[17] It is little surprise, then, that many who identified interracial competition and labor exploitation as root causes of racial oppression nonetheless promoted reformist agendas that avoided (or at least postponed) the political implications of those theories.

By the mid-1960s a different set of theoretical and political pressures would nurture the return of systemic and relational frameworks among liberal social scientists focused on race and raise questions about the work postwar racial individualism left undone. The 1965 publication of two key volumes provides a fitting end point for a history of postwar racial individualism: Kenneth Clark and Talcott Parsons's *The Negro American*, a multidisciplinary edited collection of social scientific research on the race issue, and Kenneth Clark's *Dark Ghetto*, a community study that asked how Harlem's African American poor responded to oppression.[18] The two volumes marked a moment when a broad, interdisciplinary group of scholars questioned many of racial individualism's core assumptions and redirected attention to the systemic and relational theories that had occupied the interracial left of the 1930s and early 1940s.

Clark, Parsons, and their colleagues challenged basic elements of the postwar tendency to individualize the race issue. They questioned whether one must explain white prejudice to understand racial inequality, if pursuing white tolerance through education was productive, whether fostering racial understanding through integration was desirable, and if civil rights law and legal desegregation could create substantive racial equality without affirmative social provisions. They also suggested that equal opportunity was an insufficient goal. The two volumes responded to the new political and intellectual landscape of the mid-1960s, a context defined by the civil rights movement's success securing formal equality through legal desegregation and civil rights legislation, the specter of black power and urban rioting, widespread attention to the extralegal sources of segregation in the urban North and West, renewed possibilities for redistributive social and economic programming under Presidents Kennedy and Johnson, the waning of foundation enthusiasm for behavioralism, and the return of economists and political scientists to debate on racial questions.[19] Neither volume dismissed prejudice entirely, and all authors called for the enforcement of antidiscrimination legislation. Many scholars also promoted a different sort of individualism, damage theories that suggested that black poverty could be partly traced to African American psychology and behavior.[20] As evidence of racial individualism's evolution if not outright decline, however, *The Negro American*, which commentators described as a sequel to *An American Dilemma*, only devoted two of thirty chapters to the psychology of white prejudice.[21] Instead, the intersection of political economic systems and social structural patterns occupied center stage. By 1965, a broad group of sociologists, economists, political scientists, urbanists, and anthropologists identified worsening racial inequality and the crisis of northern and western center city black poverty as key elements of the racial crisis and saw de facto housing segregation and labor market exclusion as its prime causes. The key question was how these largely economic, institutional, and political mechanisms of exclusion functioned.[22]

The message that emerged clearly from *The Negro American* and *Dark Ghetto* was that while desegregation and civil rights laws had been important starting points of racial reform, they did not constitute a full or sufficient response to the ongoing racial crisis. St. Clair Drake may have been to the left of his colleagues in suggesting a national guaranteed income, but he set the tone for the volume in calling for "structural transformations" and in worrying that the civil rights movement might, as Whitney Young Jr. of the Urban League had put it, leave the black masses with "a mouthful of rights, living in hovels with empty stomachs."[23] A broad group of liberal social scientists suggested in 1965 that in addition to the protection of black rights, social engineering of labor markets, programs of job creation, "preferential treatment" for African Americans in employment, public programs to increase affordable housing, compensatory education, and expanded welfare provisions were necessary.[24] Relational theories were also centrally featured in *The Negro American* and especially in *Dark Ghetto*, though authors disagreed about whether racial conflict was inevitable, about whether African Americans should focus on securing "power," and about whether integration defined as intergroup understanding had any utility.[25] For example, Clark clearly exhibited relational logic when he described ghettos as "social, political, educational and—above all—economic colonies" and argued that the "invisible walls" of northern ghettos "have been erected by the white society, by those who have power, both to confine those who have *no* power and to perpetuate their powerlessness."[26] By the mid-1960s, the scholars who contributed to *The Negro American* generally agreed that fighting white prejudice and discrimination, erasing legal segregation, and protecting African American civil and political rights were insufficient for progress in race relations. In so doing, they joined a growing chorus of mid-1960s voices, which included black power insurgents, the Kerner Commission, President Johnson, and Reverend Martin Luther King Jr., in addressing the incompleteness of racial individualism as a total paradigm for securing racial justice and equality.[27]

Despite these criticisms, racial individualism accomplished a great deal, not only in the psychological and legal realm but also by initiating institutional and bureaucratic changes that made important dents in patterns of racial inequality. While it is unclear precisely what combination of factors contributed to shifts in racial attitudes—no doubt the combination of antiprejudice educational efforts, widely televised civil rights protests, and the educational functions of legal and legislative change were all at work—the expression of "overtly racist sentiments" became considerably less socially acceptable by the early 1970s than it had been earlier.[28] Theories of racism that centered individual perpetrators and victims also proved quite successful in the legal fight against segregation and discrimination, helping Americans transform a legally sanctioned apartheid society into one that was equal before the law.[29] As we have seen, legal desegregation and antidiscrimination legislation in turn had some structural and institutional effects, establishing extensive civil rights bureaucracies, enfranchising southern African Americans, expanding African American access to jobs (especially state-related when the public sector grew in the 1960s) and education (especially in the South between the late 1960s and the 1990s), and requiring the federal government to use its funds, influence, and at times its troops to enforce desegregation.[30]

However, as critics of racial liberalism have long noted, racial individualism's focus on psychology, rights, and education had inherent limitations as a paradigm for progress toward racial justice and equality, if one defines equality as more than formalized nondiscrimination. In addition, the mid-1960s return of systemic and relational rhetoric that *The Negro American* and *Dark Ghetto* evinced did not lead to the implementation of the structural reforms that the volume's authors prioritized. The story of enduring racial inequality and federal retreats from structural reform on racial issues in the four decades following the 1964 Civil Rights Act is well known. In employment, the job creation programs that most authors of *The Negro American* considered essential were never attempted, even at the height of Great Society liberalism. Johnson's celebrated War on Poverty was underfunded due to the Vietnam War and focused on training youth or retraining the unemployed.[31] While affirmative action measures rested on a redistributive logic in their outcome-oriented definition of racial equality and use of preferential mechanisms, the courts have been chipping away at "racial preferences" in employment and in higher education since the mid-1970s.[32] The War on Poverty's welfare agenda, while innovative in its willingness to bring poor people into decision making, rejected calls for "guaranteed income" and remained geared to the "deserving poor" of the disabled, elderly, and single mothers.[33] Although efforts to integrate and substantially expand African American access to housing were central civil rights goals, the 1968 federal Fair Housing Act lacked sufficient enforcement mechanisms and "placed the burden of investigation, exposure, and adjudication on private citizens."[34] Public housing and urban renewal initiatives did rest on structural logics, but they often destroyed cohesive African American communities and further concentrated racialized poverty.[35] The pervasiveness of urban/suburban residential segregation in the post–Civil Rights Act era also undergirded many other inequalities, in employment, health care, exposure to environmental hazards, wealth accumulation, and education.[36] In the educational realm, by the late 1960s the hopes of scholars like Charles H. Thompson, who believed that school integration would effectively redistribute educational resources, foundered in the face of rigid metropolitan housing segregation. *San Antonio v. Rodriguez* (1973), which denied poor students a right to an "equal education," and *Milliken v. Bradley* (1974), which deemed metropolitan busing unconstitutional, made educational equalization, with or without integration, even more difficult.[37]

Of course, many factors limited American commitment to racially relevant, redistributive economic and welfare policies in the second half of the twentieth century.[38] However, the combination of psychological individualism, rights-based individualism, and educational utopianism, whose postwar history this book has examined, implied—as Myrdal so clearly stated—that if one challenged prejudice and secured civil and political rights "there would no longer be a *Negro* problem."[39] By suggesting that racial injustice existed only when intentional racial animus was present and by obscuring the structural and institutional mechanisms sustaining racial inequality, racial individualism encouraged reformist paradigms that proved insufficient against the extralegal sources of residential and school segregation and against enduring racialized economic inequality in the second half of the twentieth century.

In addition, racial individualism reemerged in a new guise when the political climate turned more conservative in the 1970s and 1980s. Charting the precise connections between postwar racial individualism and late twentieth-century conservative attacks on desegregation and affirmative action is beyond the scope of this analysis. However, late twentieth-century racial conservatives have effectively employed key rhetorical elements of racial individualism in efforts to paint the race problem as already solved. On the basic question of whether racial injustice can exist without individual intention—which is at the heart of the distinction between dispositional, systemic, and relational frameworks—late twentieth-century courts have leaned toward dispositional views in ways that undermined school desegregation. In the 1970s, proponents of desegregation in northern and western cities had a difficult time if they could not prove a school board's intention to segregate, while in the 1990s legal attention to segregative intent even aided conservative efforts to retreat from desegregation in the South.[40] Components of racial individualism have also reemerged in a conservative language of "color blindness"—a paradigm that shares with racial individualism the tendency to present prejudice and discrimination as the full extent of racial injustice. Indeed, as historian Nikhil Singh argues of the last quarter of the twentieth century, "perhaps the greater success of post–civil rights conservatism was its ability to co-opt the discourse of civil rights liberalism and to make its arguments about racial conditions without endorsing racial inequality."[41] Conservative opponents of desegregation and affirmative action have been suggesting since the 1970s that because civil rights laws have been passed and "equal opportunity" secured, ongoing racial inequality must result from either a naturally functioning market or from failures of will, morality, or ability among African Americans.[42]

Synthesizing the research of a generation of social scientists committed to racial justice and equality, Gunnar Myrdal's *An American Dilemma* (1944) proposed reforms that would expand state power, restructure labor markets, redistribute resources, and integrate American schools, housing, and public spaces. Myrdal's proposals might have promoted "equality of results" but were likely, as King put it twenty years later, to "cost something."[43] Americans remembered Myrdal's far-reaching agenda for state-led social engineering and nascent social democracy, however, as a call for Americans to treat one another kindly and to protect black civil and political rights at least partly because the economist framed the race problem in those terms.[44] In foregrounding black rights and the white conscience, Myrdal was not the only postwar scholar of the race issue to pull (or in this case to obscure) his punches. Some members of the postwar interracial left continued to challenge racial individualism by calling for positive rights long after such language was popular, by emphasizing that the fight for racial justice must be fought "on many fronts," and by presenting de facto segregation as a social and political-economic structure that reproduced racial inequality. Still, many left-leaning postwar antiracists simultaneously acquiesced to reforms that seemed reasonable but did not reflect the full complexity of their understandings of racial injustice.

The intellectual and political tightrope that postwar scholar-activists walked exposes both the challenges of projects of "social science for social action" and how rightward political shifts combined with scientism and behavioralism to constrain antiracist political agendas. Even in settings like Fisk's RRI and Howard's *JNE*, where methodological individualism and behavioralism exerted less pressure than at the RF or CETRRR, a sense of political realism limited reformist visions in ways that some participants would later regret. Those who survived until the century's end were still fighting seemingly intractable racialized poverty and de facto segregation in the 1990s, when Kenneth Clark worried that his life had been "a series of glorious defeats."[45] Clark questioned the individualistic approach he and his colleagues had taken in the postwar years, arguing in 1993 that "I am forced to face the likely possibility that the United States will never rid itself of racism and reach true integration." "I look back and I shudder," he added, "at how naïve we all were in our belief in the steady progress racial minorities would make through programs of litigation and education."[46] Many postwar antiracists were not necessarily naive but acting strategically in the face of substantial constraints when they favored the programmatic implications of racial individualism. Their compromises proved to be both productive and at the same time inherently limiting.[47] A significant number of Clarks' contemporaries, including Frazier, Johnson, Wirth, Allport, and Rose, did not live to see much of the post–Civil Rights Act era. It is hard to imagine, however, that if faced with late twentieth-century racial inequality and segregation, they would not have shared a sense of mission incomplete or expressed frustration at the limited set of levers that had been at their disposal.

INTRODUCTION

1. While others have not used the term *racial individualism,* a number of historians of social science, social policy, law, and civil rights politics point to the growing significance of individualistic conceptions of the race issue in postwar America. Lani Guinier, "From Racial Liberalism to Racial Literacy: *Brown v. Board of Education* and the Interest-Divergence Dilemma," *Journal of American History* 91, no. 1 (2004): 92–118; Ellen Herman, *The Romance of American Psychology: Political Culture in the Age of Experts* (Berkeley: University of California Press, 1995), chaps. 7 and 8; Walter A. Jackson, *Gunnar Myrdal and America's Conscience: Social Engineering and Racial Liberalism, 1938–1987* (Chapel Hill: University of North Carolina Press, 1990); Alice O'Connor, *Poverty Knowledge: Social Science, Social Policy, and the Poor in Twentieth-Century U.S. History* (Princeton, NJ: Princeton University Press, 2001); Daryl Michael Scott, *Contempt and Pity: Social Policy and the Image of the Damaged Black Psyche, 1880–1996* (Chapel Hill: University of North Carolina Press, 1997); Stephen Steinberg, *Race Relations: A Critique* (Stanford, CA: Stanford University Press, 2007); and Thomas J. Sugrue, *Sweet Land of Liberty: The Forgotten Struggle for Civil Rights in the North* (New York: Random House, 2008).

2. On interwar social anthropological and social ecological approaches to the race issue, what O'Connor terms "black sociology's 'golden age' in the 1930s and 1940s," see Martin Bulmer, *The Chicago School of Sociology: Institutionalization, Diversity, and the Rise of Sociological Research* (Chicago: University of Chicago Press, 1984); James B. McKee, *Sociology and the Race Problem: The Failure of a Perspective* (Urbana: University of Illinois Press, 1993), 149–177; and O'Connor, *Poverty Knowledge,* 74 and chap. 3. For a survey of the pre–World War II and wartime economics of American race relations, focused largely on southern white supremacy, sharecropping, and tenancy, see Gunnar Myrdal, *An American Dilemma: The Negro Problem and Modern Democracy* (New York: Harper and Brothers Publishers, 1944), parts 4 and 5.

3. The postwar years, Walter Jackson argues, saw "the steering of social scientific research on race and ethnicity toward the study of intergroup contact and the psychodynamics of prejudice at the expense of analyses of how ethnic discrimination was rooted in institutions, social structure, and the economic system." Jackson, *Gunnar Myrdal and America's Conscience,* 283. On individualistic approaches to racial issues in postwar social psychology, see Jamie Cohen-Cole, "Thinking about Thinking in

Cold War America" (PhD diss., Princeton University, 2003); Herman, *Romance of American Psychology*, chap. 7; and Jackson, *Gunnar Myrdal and America's Conscience*, 279–93. On the individualistic turn in American race relations sociology, see McKee, *Sociology and the Race Problem*, chaps. 7 and 8; and Thomas F. Pettigrew, ed., *The Sociology of Race Relations: Reflection and Reform* (New York: Free Press, 1980), 133, 183. Postwar anthropology focused more on issues of racial identity than racial prejudice after World War II, but shifts toward the individual are evident among a number of anthropologists as well. Lee D. Baker, *From Savage to Negro: Anthropology and the Construction of Race, 1896–1954* (Berkeley: University of California Press, 1998); and Rebecca Lemov, *Word as Laboratory: Experiments with Mice, Mazes, and Men* (New York: Hill and Wang, 2005), chap. 6. On social relations and behavioralism, see Howard Brick, *Transcending Capitalism: Visions of a New Society in Modern American Thought* (Ithaca, NY: Cornell University Press, 2006); Joel Isaac, "The Human Sciences in Cold War America," *Historical Journal*, 50, no. 3 (2007): 725–46; and Mark Solovey, *Shaky Foundations: The Politics-Patronage-Social Science Nexus in Cold War America* (New Brunswick, NJ: Rutgers University Press, 2013), chap. 3.

4. On the "interracial left" and African American popular front, see Sugrue, *Sweet Land*, 18–31; Nikhil Pal Singh, *Black Is a Country: Race and the Unfinished Struggle for Democracy* (Cambridge, MA: Harvard University Press, 2004); and Jonathan Scott Holloway, *Confronting the Veil: Abram Harris, Jr., E. Franklin Frazier, and Ralph Bunche, 1919–1941* (Chapel Hill: University of North Carolina Press, 2002). Michael C. Denning, *The Cultural Front: The Laboring of American Culture in the Twentieth Century* (London: Verso, 1997), chap. 12, addresses the Depression-era "Popular Front" more generally. On "racial liberalism," see Jackson, *Gunnar Myrdal and America's Conscience*, 272–79; Ira Katznelson, "Was the Great Society a Lost Opportunity?" in *The Rise and Fall of the New Deal Order, 1930–1980*, ed. Steve Fraser and Gary Gerstle (Princeton, NJ: Princeton University Press, 1989); and Gary Gerstle, "The Protean Character of American Liberalism," *American Historical Review* 99, no. 4 (1994): 1043–73.

5. Sugrue, *Sweet Land*, 83. On antiprejudice education and moral exhortation, see Zoë Burkholder, *Color in the Classroom: How American Schools Taught Race, 1900–1954* (New York: Oxford University Press, 2011), chap. 3; Jackson, *Gunnar Myrdal and America's Conscience*, 279–83; Daryl Michael Scott, "Postwar Pluralism, *Brown v. Board of Education*, and the Origins of Multicultural Education," *Journal of American History* 91, no. 1 (2004): 69–82; Kevin M. Schultz, *Tri-Faith America: How Catholics and Jews Held Postwar America to Its Protestant Promise* (Oxford: Oxford University Press, 2011). On fair employment and open housing, see Anthony S. Chen, *The Fifth Freedom: Jobs Politics, and Civil Rights in the United States, 1941–1972* (Princeton, NJ: Princeton University Press, 2009); Wendell Pritchett, *Robert Clifton Weaver and the American City: The Life and Times of an Urban Reformer* (Chicago: University of Chicago Press, 2008); John David Skrentny, *The Ironies of Affirmative Action: Politics, Culture, and Justice in America* (Chicago: University of Chicago Press, 1996); and Sugrue, *Sweet Land*, esp. chaps. 2, 3, and 7.

6. Historians have pointed to many factors, such as the wartime Double V protests, rightward turns in Congress, the emergence of northern African American voting blocks, labor's declining strength, the broad popularity of rights discourse, and McCarthyism, that encouraged postwar racial liberalism at the expense of programs for racial progress that linked race and class oppression more explicitly. Michael Klar-

man, *From Jim Crow to Civil Rights: The Supreme Court and the Struggle for Racial Equality* (New York: Oxford University Press, 2004), chap. 4; and Jackson, *Gunnar Myrdal and America's Conscience*, chap. 7.

7. Risa L. Goluboff, *The Lost Promise of Civil Rights* (Cambridge, MA: Harvard University Press, 2007); Klarman, *From Jim Crow to Civil Rights*; Richard Kluger, *Simple Justice: The History of* Brown v. Board of Education *and Black America's Struggle for Equality* (1974; New York: Random House, 2004); Scott, *Contempt and Pity*; Mark Tushnet, *The NAACP's Legal Strategy against Segregated Education, 1925–1950* (Chapel Hill: University of North Carolina Press, 1987).

8. Guinier, "From Racial Liberalism," 96, 93. For the post-Brown history of school desegregation, and resegregation, see Gary Orfield, Susan E. Eaton, and the Harvard Project on School Desegregation, *Dismantling Desegregation: The Quiet Reversal of* Brown v. Board of Education (New York: New Press, 1996); and James T. Patterson, Brown v. Board of Education: *A Civil Rights Milestone and Its Troubled Legacy* (New York: Oxford University Press, 2001).

9. Guinier, "From Racial Liberalism," 96, 112, 116. Much of the literature on *Brown's* limitations emphasizes the negative impact of images of the "damaged black psyche" that reemerged in the 1960s and again in the 1980s in the guise of "cultural deprivation." Scott, *Contempt and Pity*; Herman, *Romance of American Psychology*, chaps. 7 and 8; O'Connor, *Poverty Knowledge*. On color blindness, see Lawrence D. Bobo and Ryan A. Smith, "From Jim Crow Racism to Laissez-Faire Racism: The Transformation of Racial Attitudes," in *Beyond Pluralism: The Conception of Groups and Group Identities in America*, ed. Wendy F. Katkin, Ned Landsman, and Andrea Tyree (Urbana: University of Illinois Press, 1998), 182–220; Kimberlé Crenshaw, "Race, Reform, and Retrenchment: Transformation and Legitimation in Antidiscrimination Law," in *Critical Race Theory*, ed. Kimberlé Crenshaw et al. (New York: New Press, 1995), 103–26; and George Lipsitz, *How Racism Takes Place* (Philadelphia: Temple University Press, 2011).

10. On durable inequality and the persistence of racial inequality in the twentieth century, see Charles Tilly, *Durable Inequality* (Berkeley: University of California Press, 1998); and Michael B. Katz and Mark J. Stern, *One Nation Divisible: What America Was and What It Is Becoming* (New York: Russell Sage Foundation, 2006), esp. chap. 3. My interest in racial individualism builds on critiques of the work racial liberalism left undone. For a few examples of this voluminous literature, see Bobo and Smith, "From Jim Crow Racism to Laissez-Faire Racism"; Kimberlé Crenshaw, "Race, Reform, and Retrenchment: Transformation and Legitimation in Anti-Discrimination Law," in *Critical Race Theory*, ed. Kimberlé Crenshaw et al. (New York: New Press, 1995) 103–26; Guinier, "From Racial Liberalism"; George Lipsitz, *The Possessive Investment in Whiteness: How White People Profit from Identity Politics* (Philadelphia: Temple University Press, 1998); Adolph Reed Jr., ed., *Without Justice for All: The New Liberalism and Our Retreat from Racial Equality* (Boulder, CO: Westview Press, 1999); Singh, *Black Is a Country*; and Stephen Steinberg, *Turning Back: The Retreat from Racial Justice in American Thought and Policy* (Boston: Beacon Press, 2001).

11. Robin M. Williams Jr., *The Reduction of Intergroup Tensions: A Survey of Research on Problems of Ethnic, Racial, and Religious Group Relations* (New York: SSRC, 1947), 41.

12. The relationship between race and class is, not surprisingly, a central theme in African American working-class history. A few key monographs include: Glenda Gilmore, *Defying Dixie: The Radical Roots of Civil Rights, 1900–1950* (New York: W. W. Norton,

2008); Tera Hunter, *To 'Joy My Freedom: Southern Black Women's Lives and Labors after the Civil War* (Cambridge, MA: Harvard University Press, 1997); Robin D. G. Kelley, *Hammer and Hoe: Alabama Communists during the Great Depression* (Chapel Hill: University of North Carolina Press, 1990); Robin D. G. Kelley, *Race Rebels, Culture, Politics, and the Black Working Class* (New York: Free Press, 1994); and Robert O. Self, *American Babylon: Race and the Struggle for Postwar Oakland* (Princeton, NJ: Princeton University Press, 2003). On race and class in African American intellectual history, see Kevin Gaines, *Uplifting the Race: Black Leadership, Politics, and Culture in the Twentieth Century* (Chapel Hill: University of North Carolina Press, 1996); Holloway, *Confronting the Veil*; Singh, *Black Is a Country*; and Adolph Reed Jr., *W. E. B. Du Bois and American Political Thought* (New York: Oxford University Press, 1997).

13. On the postwar politics of knowledge, see Ellen Condliffe Lagemann, *The Politics of Knowledge: The Carnegie Corporation, Philanthropy, and Public Policy* (Middletown, CT: Wesleyan University Press, 1989); Roger Geiger, *Research and Relevant Knowledge: American Research Universities since World War II* (New York: Oxford University Press, 1993); Isaac, "The Human Sciences in Cold War America," 725–46; O'Connor, *Poverty Knowledge*; and Solovey, *Shaky Foundations*.

14. On the "educationalization" of social problems, see Marc Depaepe, Frederik Herman, Melanie Surmont, Angelo Van Gorp, and Frank Simon "About Pedagogization: From the Perspective of the History of Education," in *Educational Research: The Educationalization of Social Problems*, ed. Paul Smeyers and Marc Depaepe (online edition: Springer, 2008); David Labaree, "The Winning Ways of a Losing Strategy: Educationalizing Social Problems in the U.S.," *Educational Theory* 58, no. 4 (2008): 447–60; Tracy Steffes, *School, Society, and State: A New Education to Govern Modern America, 1890–1940* (Chicago: University of Chicago Press, 2012), chap. 5; and David Tyack and Larry Cuban, *Tinkering toward Utopia: A Century of Public School Reform* (Cambridge, MA: Harvard University Press, 1995).

15. Charles Tilly, *Identities, Boundaries, and Social Ties* (Boulder, CO: Paradigm Publishers, 2005), 14–16; Tilly, *Durable Inequality*, 6–7, 24.

16. Tilly, *Identities, Boundaries, and Social Ties*, 14.

17. Donald Young, "Some Effects of a Course in American Race Problems on the Race Prejudice of 450 Undergraduates at the University of Pennsylvania," *Journal of Abnormal and Social Psychology* 22, no. 3 (1927): 235–42; John Dollard et al., *Frustration and Aggression* (New Haven, CT: Yale University Press, 1939); Hortense Powdermaker and Helen Frances Storen, *Probing Our Prejudices: A Unit for High School Students* (New York: Harper and Brothers, 1944); and Robert K. Merton, "Discrimination and the American Creed," in *Discrimination and National Welfare*, ed. Robert MacIver (New York: Institute for Religious Studies and Harper, 1949), 99–126.

18. Jean M. Converse, *Survey Research in the United States: Roots and Emergence, 1890–1960* (Berkeley: University of California Press, 1987); Jennifer Platt, *A History of Sociological Research Methods in America, 1920–1960* (Cambridge: Cambridge University Press, 1996), 13, 49–50.

19. Tilly, *Identities, Boundaries, and Social Ties*, 14–16.

20. Robert Park, "Our Racial Frontier on the Pacific," *Survey Graphic* 9 (May 1926): 192–96, in Robert Ezra Park, *Race and Culture: Essays in the Sociology of Contemporary Man* (Glencoe, IL: Free Press, 1950), 138–51. For a more critical view of social ecology, see Steinberg, *Race Relations*, 57–71.

21. Key case-based monographs include Charles S. Johnson, *Shadow of the Plantation* (1934; New Brunswick, NJ: Transaction, 1996); John Dollard, *Caste and Class in a*

Southern Town (Garden City, NY: Doubleday Anchor Books, 1937); and St. Clair Drake and Horace R. Cayton, *Black Metropolis* (New York: Harcourt, Brace, 1945). For examples of larger-scale studies of racial inequality, see Charles S. Johnson, *The Negro in American Civilization: A Study of Negro Life and Race Relations in the Light of Social Research* (New York: Henry Holt, 1930); and E. Franklin Frazier, *The Negro in the United States* (1949; New York: Macmillan, 1957).

22. On relational and transactional theories, see Tilly, *Identities, Boundaries, and Social Ties*, 14. Holloway, *Confronting the Veil*; Steinberg, *Race Relations*, part 3; Christopher A. McAuley, *The Mind of Oliver C. Cox* (Notre Dame, IN: University of Notre Dame Press, 2004).

23. Chicago Commission on Race Relations, *The Negro in Chicago: A Study of Race Relations and a Race Riot* (Chicago: University of Chicago Press, 1922); Mayor's Commission on Conditions in Harlem (MCCH), *The Negro in Harlem: A Report on Social and Economic Conditions Responsible for the Outbreak of March 19, 1935* (New York: Municipal Archives and Records Center, 1935); Drake and Cayton, *Black Metropolis*; O'Connor, *Poverty Knowledge*, chap. 3.

24. Brick, *Transcending Capitalism*; Herman, *Romance of American Psychology*, 133, 179, 184; Isaac, "The Human Sciences in Cold War America," 738; Jackson, *Gunnar Myrdal and America's Conscience*, 283 and chap. 7; McKee, *Sociology and the Race Problem*, 295–96; Pettigrew, *The Sociology of Race Relations*, xxxi–xxxii, 183; Solovey, *Shaky Foundations*, chap. 3; and Howard Winant, "The Dark Side of the Force: One Hundred Years of the Sociology of Race," in *Sociology in America*, ed. Craig Calhoun (Chicago: University of Chicago Press, 2007), 535–71, 556.

25. African American economist Robert Weaver and political scientist Ralph Bunche provide important exceptions to this pattern, and Weaver, revealingly, criticized his fellow economists for not engaging more fully with racial questions. Gary Becker's *The Economics of Discrimination* (1957) heralded economists' reentry into discussions of discrimination, but political scientists would not return to the issue until the mid-1960s. While he does not explicitly discuss postwar economists' stance toward racial issues, historian of economics Michael Bernstein's emphasis on the decline of interwar institutional economics in favor of macroeconomic concerns after World War II, on the crucial role objectivity played in economists' ability to secure federal and NSF funding in the 1950s, and on anticommunist constraints all suggest why Weaver's calls for economic analyses of segregation went largely unanswered. Robert Weaver, "A Needed Program of Research in Race Relations and Associated Problems," *JNE* 16, no. 2 (1947): 130–35; Donald Matthews, "Political Science Research on Race Relations," in *Race and the Social Sciences*, ed. Irwin Katz and Patricia Gurin (New York: Basic Books, 1969), 113–44, 113; Charles C. Killingsworth, "Job and Income for Negroes," in Katz and Gurin, *Race and the Social Sciences*, 194–273; Gary S. Becker, *The Economics of Discrimination* (Chicago: University of Chicago Press, 1957); Michael A. Bernstein, *A Perilous Progress: Economists and Public Purpose in Twentieth-Century America* (Princeton, NJ: Princeton University Press, 2001), 45–46, 88, 93–95, 101, 106–7, 117, 124–25, 139.

26. E. Franklin Frazier, "Race Contacts and the Social Structure," *American Sociological Review* 14, no. 1 (1949): 1–11; Robin M. Williams Jr., "Review and Assessment of Research on Race and Culture Conflict" Paper V, Conference on Research in Human Relations, (February 1953), folder 99, box 11, series 910, RG 3.1, RF, 2, 11; Drake and Cayton, *Black Metropolis*; Winant, "The Dark Side of the Force," 556.

27. Williams, *Reduction of Intergroup Tensions*, 9.

28. Theodor Adorno, Else Frenkel-Brunswik, Daniel Levinson, and R. Nevitt Sanford, *The Authoritarian Personality* (New York: Harper and Row, 1950); Gordon Allport, *The Nature of Prejudice* (1954; Reading, MA: Addison-Wesley, 1979). "Indeed, over the 1944–1968 period," Pettigrew notes, "two completely psychological volumes—T. W. Adorno, et al.'s *The Authoritarian Personality* and Gordon W. Allport's *The Nature of Prejudice*—were among the most cited books in sociological articles on race relations." Pettigrew, *The Sociology of Race Relations*, 133, citing H. M. Bahr, T. J. Johnson, and M. R Seitz, "Influential Scholars and Works in the Sociology of Race and Minority Relations, 1944–1968," *American Sociologist* 6 (1971): 296–98.

29. The volume would not generate substantial attention until the 1960s, and Cox spent most of his career in teaching heavy, small HBCUs at the margins of his discipline. McAuley, *The Mind of Oliver C. Cox*, 58; Pettigrew, *The Sociology of Race Relations*, 129.

30. I thank an anonymous reviewer for drawing my attention to the concept of "dilemmas of scale" to address this phenomenon.

31. Adorno et al., *The Authoritarian Personality*, vii, 974–75; Allport, *Nature of Prejudice*, 507.

32. Williams, *Reduction of Intergroup Tensions*, 9.

33. Cox, "An American Dilemma: A Mystical Approach to the Study of Race Relations," *JNE* 14, no. 2 (1945): 143; Herbert Aptheker, "The Negro People in America: A Critique of Gunnar Myrdal's *An American Dilemma*," in *Herbert Aptheker on Race and Democracy*, ed. Eric Foner and Manning Marable (Urbana: University of Illinois Press, 2006).

34. O'Connor, *Poverty Knowledge*, 26 and chap. 1.

35. Sarah E. Igo, *The Averaged America: Surveys, Citizens, and the Making of a Mass Public* (Cambridge, MA: Harvard University Press, 2007), 28; Dorothy Ross, *The Origins of American Social Science* (Cambridge: Cambridge University Press, 1991); and Mark Solovey, "Riding Natural Scientists' Coattails onto the Endless Frontier: The SSRC and the Quest for Scientific Legitimacy," *Journal of the History of the Behavioral Sciences* 40, no. 4 (2004): 393–422, 400.

36. Igo, *Averaged American*, 28.

37. Ibid. For tensions between objectivity and social reform in the Progressive Era, see Thomas L. Haskell, *The Emergence of Professional Social Science: The American Social Science Association and the Nineteenth-Century Crisis of Authority* (1977; Baltimore: Johns Hopkins University Press, 2000); Andrew Jewett, *Science, Democracy, and the American University: From the Civil War to the Cold War* (Cambridge: Cambridge University Press, 2012); and Mark C. Smith, *Social Science in the Crucible: The American Debate over Objectivity and Purpose, 1918–1941* (Durham, NC: Duke University Press, 1994).

38. Herman, *Romance of American Psychology*; and Igo, *Averaged American*.

39. Jewett, *Science, Democracy, and the American University*, 3.

40. Jill Morawski, "Psychologists for Society and Societies for Psychologists: SPSSI's Place among Professional Organizations," *Journal of Social Issues* 42, no. 1 (1986): 111–26; Stephen Park Turner and Jonathan H. Turner, *The Impossible Science: An Institutional Analysis of American Sociology* (Newbury Park, CA: Sage Publications, 1990), 192.

41. Solovey, *Shaky Foundations*, 109–10.

42. Ibid., 155, 160–62; Jewett, *Science, Democracy, and the American University*, chap. 11.

43. Jackson, *Gunnar Myrdal and America's Conscience*, 101; O' Connor, *Poverty Knowledge*, 74–98.

44. John H. Stanfield, *Philanthropy and Jim Crow in American Social Science* (Westport, CT:

Greenwood Press, 1985), 70, 79–90; Jonathan Scott Holloway and Benjamin Keppel, eds., *Black Scholars on the Line: Race, Social Science, and American Thought in the Twentieth Century* (Notre Dame, IN: University of Notre Dame Press, 2007), 12–23; Jackson, *Gunnar Myrdal and America's Conscience*, 379, n. 53.

45. Solovey, *Shaky Foundations*, 1. On the expansion of the postwar research university, see Geiger, *Research and Relevant Knowledge*; Christopher Loss, *Between Citizens and the State: The Politics of American Higher Education in the 20th Century* (Princeton, NJ: Princeton University Press, 2012); and Rebecca S. Lowen, *Creating the Cold War University: The Transformation of Stanford* (Berkeley: University of California Press, 1997).

46. James Capshew, *Psychologists on the March: Science, Practice, and Professional Identity in America, 1929–1969* (Cambridge: Cambridge University Press, 1999), 1, 3. Also see Herman, *Romance of American Psychology*, 17–18, 20; and Loss, *Between Citizens and the State*.

47. Herman, *Romance of American Psychology*. On expanding psychological interests in racial issues and the increasingly narrow set of topics behavioral research on race addressed, see ibid., chap. 7, especially 181–83.

48. Samuel A. Stouffer, *The American Soldier: Adjustment during Army Life* (Princeton, NJ: Princeton University Press, 1949); Andrew Abbott and James Sparrow, "Hot War, Cold War: The Structures of Sociological Action, 1940–1955," in Calhoun, *Sociology in America*, 281–313, 287–89; Converse, *Survey Research*, 217.

49. Ibid., 409–10, 392; Platt, *A History of Sociological Research Methods*.

50. Capshew, *Psychologists on the March*; Converse, *Survey Research*, chaps. 8–11; Isaac, "The Human Sciences in Cold War America," 725–46, 738.

51. Cohen-Cole notes that by the mid-1950s "there were interdisciplinary social science research and training programmes at Harvard, Michigan, Yale, Cornell, Berkeley, Columbia, Chicago, Stanford, Minnesota, Wisconsin and the University of North Carolina, among others." Jamie Cohen-Cole, "Instituting the Science of Mind: Intellectual Economies and Disciplinary Exchange at Harvard's Center for Cognitive Studies," *British Journal for the History of Science* 40, no. 4 (2007): 567–97, 576. Also see Craig Calhoun and Jonathan Van Antwerpen, "Orthodoxy, Heterodoxy, and Hierarchy: 'Mainstream' Sociology and Its Challengers," in *Sociology in America: A History*, ed. Craig Calhoun (Chicago: University of Chicago Press, 2007), 367–410, 386–87; and Lawrence T. Nichols, "Social Relations Undone: Disciplinary Divergence and Departmental Politics at Harvard, 1946–1970," *American Sociologist* 29, no. 2 (1998): 83–107, 83–86.

52. Isaac, "The Human Sciences in Cold War America," 738–39.

53. Brick, *Transcending Capitalism*, 172; Cohen-Cole, "Instituting the Science of Mind," 573; Herman, *Romance of American Psychology*, 132–33, 349, n. 29; Solovey, *Shaky Foundations*, chap. 3.

54. Solovey, "Riding Natural Scientists' Coattails," 394–95, 400–401; Solovey, *Shaky Foundations*, 20–55, 112–28; Herman, *Romance of American Psychology*, 348–49, n. 28; Ellen Schrecker, *No Ivory Tower: McCarthyism and the Universities* (New York: Oxford University Press, 1986).

55. Isaac, "The Human Sciences in Cold War America," 736–40. Also see Nils Gilman, *Mandarins of the Future: Modernization Theory in Cold War America* (Baltimore: Johns Hopkins University Press, 2003); Jewett, *Science, Democracy, and the American University*, 342–43; Solovey, *Shaky Foundations*, chap. 3.

56. This analysis draws on Joel Isaac's critique of "Cold War determinism" among American historians. Isaac, "The Human Sciences in Cold War America."

57. Myrdal emphasized this point in his "rank order of discrimination." Myrdal, *American Dilemma*, 60–67. Also see note 12.

58. Sugrue, *Sweet Land*, 34; Goluboff, *Lost Promise of Civil Rights*; Holloway, *Confronting the Veil*; Singh, *Black Is a Country*.

59. Alan Brinkley, *The End of Reform: New Deal Liberalism in Recession and War* (New York: Vintage Books, 1995), 73–74; Ira Katznelson, *When Affirmative Action Was White: An Untold History of Racial Inequality in Twentieth-Century America* (New York: Norton, 2005).

60. Sugrue, *Sweet Land*, 19, 23–31, 34–44; also see Holloway, *Confronting the Veil*; Pritchett, *Robert Clifton Weaver*; Anthony M. Platt, *E. Franklin Frazier Reconsidered* (New Brunswick, NJ: Rutgers University Press, 1991); and Singh, *Black Is a Country*.

61. Gary Gerstle, *American Crucible: Race and Nation in the Twentieth Century* (Princeton, NJ: Princeton University Press, 2001); and Barbara D. Savage, *Broadcasting Freedom: Radio, War, and the Politics of Race, 1939–1948* (Chapel Hill: University of North Carolina Press, 1999); Jacquelyn Dowd Hall, "The Long Civil Rights Movement and the Political Uses of the Past," *Journal of American History* 91 (2005): 1233–63. On the importance of the totalitarian menace to broader midcentury political and intellectual trajectories, see Benjamin Alpers, *Dictators, Democracy, and American Public Culture: Envisioning the Totalitarian Enemy, 1920s–1950s* (Chapel Hill: University of North Carolina Press, 2003); and David Ciepley, *Liberalism in the Shadow of Totalitarianism* (Cambridge, MA: Harvard University Press, 2006).

62. Charles S. Johnson, "The Present Status of Race Relations, with Particular Reference to the Negro," *JNE* 8, no. 3 (1939): 323–35; Alain Locke, "Whither Race Relations? A Critical Commentary," *JNE* 13, no. 3 (1944): 398–406; Edwin Embree, "World Patterns of Race Relations," in "Race Relations in Human Relations, Summary Report, Second Annual Institute of Race Relations, June 2–21, 1945, Fisk University, Nashville, TN" (Nashville: AMA and Fisk University, 1945), 2–4; Singh, *Black Is a Country*, chaps. 3 and 4; Penny Von Eschen, *Race against Empire: Black Americans and Anti-Colonialism, 1937–1957* (Ithaca, NY: Cornell University Press, 1997).

63. On shifts in federal civil rights policy under Roosevelt and Truman, see Sugrue, *Sweet Land*, 44–58, 75–77; Jackson, *Gunnar Myrdal and America's Conscience*, 234–37, 273–79; Klarman, *From Jim Crow to Civil Rights*, chap. 4.

64. Jackson, *Gunnar Myrdal and America's Conscience*, 279–93; Diana Selig, *Americans All: The Cultural Gifts Movement* (Cambridge, MA: Harvard University Press, 2008); Nicholas V. Montalto, *A History of the Intercultural Educational Movement, 1924–1941*, (New York: Garland, 1982); Schultz, *Tri-Faith America*.

65. Klarman, *From Jim Crow to Civil Rights*, 180, 185.

66. McKee, *Sociology and the Race Problem*, 257–58; Jackson, *Gunnar Myrdal and America's Conscience*, 280–81.

67. McKee, *Sociology and the Race Problem*, 258.

68. Chen, *The Fifth Freedom*; Sugrue, *Sweet Land*, 90–96 and 220–50. On the multiracial dimensions of these struggles and the "challenge of racial diversity to racial liberalism," see Mark Brilliant, *The Color of America Has Changed: How Racial Diversity Shaped Civil Rights Reform in California, 1941–1978* (New York: Oxford University Press, 2010).

69. Jackson, *Gunnar Myrdal and America's Conscience*, 281; Schultz, *Tri-Faith America*, chaps. 3 and 8; John Jackson Jr., *Social Scientists for Social Justice: Making the Case against Segregation* (New York: New York University Press, 2001), chap. 4.

70. E. Franklin Frazier, "The Negro and Non Resistance," *The Crisis* 27, no. 5 (1924):

213–14, 213. On the Commission on Interracial Cooperation, see Selig, *Americans All*, chap. 5; and Gilmore, *Defying Dixie*.

71. Allport, *Nature of Prejudice*; Adorno et al., *The Authoritarian Personality*.
72. Jackson, *Gunnar Myrdal and America's Conscience*, 281–84.
73. McKee, *Sociology and the Race Problem*, 259; Arnold Rose, *Studies in Reduction of Prejudice: A Memorandum Summarizing Research on Modification of Attitudes* (Chicago: American Council on Race Relations, 1947); Williams, *Reduction of Intergroup Tensions*; Robert M. MacIver, *The More Perfect Union: A Program for the Control of Inter-Group Discrimination in the United States* (New York: Macmillan, 1948).
74. Gordon Allport, *The Resolution of Intergroup Tensions: A Critical Appraisal of Methods* (New York: National Conference of Christians and Jews, 1952); Alfred McClung Lee and the ACRR, *Race Riots Aren't Necessary* (New York: Public Affairs Committee, 1945); Robert Weaver and the ACRR, *Community Relations Manual: What to Do about Your Community's Problems of Intergroup Relations* (Chicago: ACRR, 1946); RRD, AMA, *If Your Next Neighbors Are Negroes* (Nashville: RRD, AMA, and Fisk University, 1948), box 1, folder 7, RRIP.
75. Brinkley, *End of Reform*, 139, 171, 174, 213, 224; Sugrue, *Sweet Land*, 61–62; Jackson, *Gunnar Myrdal and America's Conscience*, 234–35; Self, *American Babylon*, 76.
76. Brinkley, *End of Reform*, 170–71, 263–64.
77. Sugrue, *Sweet Land*, 54–55, 82–84. Charles S. Johnson, "Keynote: Human Rights and Human Relations," RRI Summary 1951, 9–10; Herman Long, "Overview," Race Relations Department, American Missionary Association, RRI Summary 1953, 56. On the expansiveness of human rights language, see Carol Anderson, *Eyes off the Prize: The United Nations and the African American Struggle for Human Rights, 1944–1955* (Cambridge: Cambridge University Press, 2003); and Thomas Jackson, *From Civil Rights to Human Rights: Martin Luther King Jr. and the Struggle for Economic Justice* (Philadelphia: University of Pennsylvania Press, 2007). The tendency to frame collective obligations and resource distribution in terms of individual rights still underscored the power of individualistic descriptive and normative paradigms in postwar American social thought. Jewett, *Science, Democracy, and the American University*, 349.
78. Skrentny, *The Ironies of Affirmative Action*, 23–24, 27; Chen, *Fifth Freedom*; and Jewett, *Science, Democracy, and the American University*, 349. Although the literature on liberalism and republicanism in American political culture is too large to list here, a few key works include: Jefferson Cowie and Nick Salvatore, "The Long Exception: Rethinking the Place of the New Deal in American History," *International Labor and Working Class History* 74 (2008): 3–32; Louis Hartz, *The Liberal Tradition in America* (1955; New York: Harcourt, 1980); James T. Kloppenberg, "The Virtues of Liberalism: Christianity, Republicanism, and Ethics in Early American Political Discourse," *Journal of American History* 74 (1987): 9–33; and Daniel Rodgers, "Republicanism: The Career of a Concept," *Journal of American History* 79 (1992): 11–38.
79. Skrentny, *The Ironies of Affirmative Action*, chap. 2; Chen, *Fifth Freedom*; Jewett, *Science, Democracy, and the American University*, 349; Pritchett, *Robert Clifton Weaver*; Sugrue, *Sweet Land*, chap. 7.
80. Pritchett, *Robert Clifton Weaver*, Kindle edition, location 1677–80.
81. Chen, *Fifth Freedom*, 9, 12–13, 16; Skrentny, *Ironies of Affirmative Action*, 23, 27–29.
82. Thomas Borstelmann, *The Cold War and the Color Line: American Race Relations in the Global Arena* (Cambridge, MA: Harvard University Press, 2001); Mary Dudziak, *Cold War Civil Rights: Race and the Image of American Democracy* (Princeton, NJ: Princeton University Press, 2000); Von Eschen, *Race against Empire*.

83. Goluboff, *Lost Promise of Civil Rights*; Guinier, "From Racial Liberalism"; Scott, *Contempt and Pity*; Klarman, *From Jim Crow to Civil Rights*; Patterson, Brown v. Board.
84. Labaree, "The Winning Ways of a Losing Strategy"; Tyack and Cuban, *Tinkering toward Utopia*; Herman, *Romance of American Psychology*, 183.
85. Baker, *From Savage to Negro*, 176–77; and Holloway, *Confronting the Veil*.
86. Jackson, *Social Scientists for Social Justice*, chap. 4; Sugrue, *Sweet Land*, 83–84.
87. Manning Marable, *Race Reform and Rebellion: The Second Reconstruction and Beyond in Black America, 1945–2006*, 3rd. ed. (Jackson: University Press of Mississippi, 2007), chap. 2; Singh, *Black Is a Country*, chaps. 3 and 4.
88. Brilliant, *The Color of America*; Chen, *Fifth Freedom*; Pritchett, *Robert Clifton Weaver*; Self, *American Babylon*, chap. 2; Sugrue, *Sweet Land*.
89. Labaree, "The Winning Ways of a Losing Strategy," and Depaepe et al., "About Pedagogization."
90. Carl Kaestle and Marshall S. Smith, "The Federal Role in Elementary and Secondary Education, 1940–1980," *Harvard Educational Review* 52, no. 4 (1982); Patterson, Brown v. Board, chaps. 6–9; J. Harvie Wilkinson III, *From Brown to Bakke: The Supreme Court and School Integration, 1954–1978* (New York: Oxford University Press, 1979), 310.
91. Guinier, "From Racial Liberalism to Racial Literacy," 95–96; Sugrue, *Sweet Land*, 480–92; Orfield, *Dismantling Desegregation*, chaps. 1 and 2; Singh, *Black Is a Country*, 10; Crenshaw, "Race, Reform, and Retrenchment"; and Lipsitz, *How Racism Takes Place*.

CHAPTER ONE

1. Gunnar Myrdal, *An American Dilemma: The Negro Problem and Modern Democracy* (New York: Harper, 1944), li.
2. Walter A. Jackson, *Gunnar Myrdal and America's Conscience: Social Engineering and Racial Liberalism, 1938–1987* (Chapel Hill: University of North Carolina Press, 1990), chap. 5; David Southern, *Gunnar Myrdal and Black-White Relations: The Use and Abuse of An American Dilemma, 1944–1969* (Baton Rouge: Louisiana State University Press, 1987).
3. Jackson, *Gunnar Myrdal and America's Conscience*, 186–87; Myrdal, *American Dilemma*, li; Alice O'Connor, *Poverty Knowledge: Social Science, Social Policy, and the Poor in Twentieth-Century U.S. History* (Princeton, NJ: Princeton University Press, 2001), 95, 98; Thomas J. Sugrue, *Sweet Land of Liberty: The Forgotten Struggle for Civil Rights in the North* (New York: Random House, 2008), 59–63, 83; Ellen Herman, *The Romance of American Psychology: Political Culture in the Age of Experts* (Berkeley: University of California Press, 1995), 176–81.
4. Jackson, *Gunnar Myrdal and America's Conscience*, chap. 4; Howard Winant, "The Dark Side of the Force: One Hundred Years of the Sociology of Race," in Calhoun, *Sociology in America*, 535–71, 560.
5. Jackson, *Gunnar Myrdal and America's Conscience*, 283; Herman, *Romance of American Psychology*, 180; and Sugrue, *Sweet Land*, 62–63.
6. On wartime support for survey research, see Andrew Abbott and James Sparrow, "Hot War, Cold War: The Structures of Sociological Action 1940–1955," in Calhoun, *Sociology in America*. On the explosion of wartime and postwar interest in prejudice and antiprejudice education, see Jackson, *Gunnar Myrdal and America's Conscience*, 280–90; James B. McKee, *Sociology and the Race Problem: The Failure of a Perspective* (Urbana: University of Illinois Press, 1993), 257–58. On the importance of the avoidance of economics in postwar sociology, see Howard Brick, *Transcending Capitalism:*

Visions of a New Society in Modern American Thought (Ithaca, NY: Cornell University Press, 2006). On the intersections of postwar behavioralism and McCarthyism, see Joel Isaac, "The Human Sciences in Cold War America," *Historical Journal* 50, no. 3 (2007): 725–46, 738; Andrew Jewett, *Science, Democracy, and the American University: From the Civil War to the Cold War* (Cambridge: Cambridge University Press, 2012), chap. 11; and Mark Solovey, *Shaky Foundations: The Politics-Patronage-Social Science Nexus in Cold War America* (New Brunswick, NJ: Rutgers University Press, 2013), chap. 3.

7. John P. Jackson Jr., *Social Scientists for Social Justice: Making the Case against Segregation* (New York: New York University Press, 2001), 17–18; Diana Selig, *Americans All: The Cultural Gifts Movement* (Cambridge, MA: Harvard University Press, 2008), 19–20, 26–27, 29.

8. James Grossman, *Land of Hope: Chicago, Black Southerners, and the Great Migration* (Chicago: University of Chicago Press, 1989); Matthew Frye Jacobson, *Whiteness of a Different Color: European Immigrants and the Alchemy of Race* (Cambridge, MA: Harvard University Press, 1998); Daniel T. Rodgers, *Atlantic Crossings: Social Politics in a Progressive Age* (Cambridge, MA: Harvard University Press, 1998); and Robert Wiebe, *The Search for Order, 1877–1920* (New York: Hill and Wang, 1967).

9. Jean M. Converse, *Survey Research: Roots and Emergence, 1890–1960* (Berkeley: University of California Press, 1987), 55–57; Jackson, *Gunnar Myrdal and America's Conscience*, 99.

10. For contemporary overviews of interwar social science on the race issue, see Eugene L. Horowitz, "'Race' Attitudes," in *Characteristics of the American Negro*, ed. Otto Klineberg (New York: Harper, 1944), 139–44; Arnold Rose, *Studies in Reduction of Prejudice: A Memorandum Summarizing Research on Modification of Attitudes* (Chicago: American Council on Race Relations, 1947); Kenneth Clark, *Prejudice and Your Child* (Boston: Beacon Press, 1955), chap. 2. For historiographical overviews, see Jackson, *Gunnar Myrdal and America's Conscience*, 89–106; McKee, *Sociology and the Race Problem*, chaps. 2–6; and O'Connor, *Poverty Knowledge*, chap. 3.

11. Converse, *Survey Research*, 54–57, 86; Sarah E. Igo, *The Averaged American: Surveys, Citizens, and the Making of a Mass Public* (Cambridge, MA: Harvard University Press, 2007).

12. Converse, *Survey Research*, 20–21.

13. For summaries of these methods, see Converse, *Survey Research*, 63, 68–69, 72–73; and Rose, *Studies in Reduction of Prejudice*, part 4, pages 2–8.

14. Selig, *Americans All*, 32–35, 20.

15. Horowitz, "'Race' Attitudes," 159–65, 181–82; Eugene Horowitz and Ruth Horowitz, "Development of Social Attitudes in Children," *Sociometry* 1 (1938): 301–38.

16. Rose, *Studies in Reduction of Prejudice*, part 7, page 3.

17. Ibid., part 1, pages 8, 11–18; part 2; part 3, page 3.

18. Selig, *Americans All*, 14–15; Nicholas V. Montalto, *A History of the Intercultural Educational Movement, 1924–1941* (New York: Garland, 1982), 145–46; 53–54.

19. Jackson, *Gunnar Myrdal and America's Conscience*, 279–84; Kevin M. Schultz, *Tri-Faith America: How Catholics and Jews Held Postwar America to Its Protestant Promise* (Oxford: Oxford University Press, 2011); Selig, *Americans All*, chap. 4.

20. Katrina M. Sanders, *"Intelligent and Effective Direction": The Fisk University Race Relations Institute and the Struggle for Civil Rights, 1944–1969* (New York: Peter Lang, 2005), 34–36; Hortense Powdermaker and Helen Frances Storen, *Probing Our Prejudices: A Unit for High School Students* (New York: Harper and Brothers, 1944); Gordon

Allport, *The Resolution of Intergroup Tensions: A Critical Appraisal of Methods* (New York: National Conference of Christians and Jews, 1952); and Zoë Burkholder, *Color in the Classroom: How American Schools Taught Race, 1900–1954* (New York: Oxford University Press, 2011), chap. 3.

21. In *Studies in Reduction of Prejudice*, Rose expressed frustration at the contradictory and inconclusive character of much research on the topic produced by 1947. Rose, *Studies in Reduction of Prejudice*, part 1, pages 1, 19; McKee, *Sociology and the Race Problem*, 261–62; on the NCCJ's selective reliance on social science, see chap. 6.

22. McKee, *Sociology and the Race Problem*, esp. 296–300; Lee D. Baker, *From Savage to Negro: Anthropology and the Construction of Race, 1896–1954* (Berkeley: University of California Press, 1998).

23. McKee, *Sociology and the Race Problem*, 157–65; O'Connor, *Poverty Knowledge*, chap. 3, esp. 76–77.

24. O'Connor, *Poverty Knowledge*, 85; McKee, *Sociology and the Race Problem*, 153–76; John Dollard et al., *Frustration and Aggression* (New Haven, CT: Yale University Press, 1939); Rebecca Lemov, *Word as Laboratory: Experiments with Mice, Mazes, and Men* (New York: Hill and Wang, 2005), chap. 6. Also see Baker, *From Savage to Negro*; and Brick, *Transcending Capitalism*, 112–14.

25. O'Connor, *Poverty Knowledge*, 77–79. Martin Bulmer, *The Chicago School of Sociology: Institutionalization, Diversity, and the Rise of Sociological Research* (Chicago: University of Chicago Press, 1984); Fred H. Matthews, *Quest for an American Sociology: Robert E. Park and the Chicago School* (Montreal: McGill-Queen's University Press, 1977); Dorothy Ross, *The Origins of American Social Science* (Cambridge: Cambridge University Press, 1991), 305. On social ecology's assimilationist ideal and potential for justifying gradualism on civil rights issues, which generated considerable criticism by the 1960s, see O'Connor, *Poverty Knowledge*, chap. 3; Steinberg, *Race Relations*, parts 1 and 2; and Winant, "The Dark Side of the Force."

26. Jackson, *Gunnar Myrdal and America's Conscience*, 95.

27. Robert Park, "Our Racial Frontier on the Pacific," *Survey Graphic* 9 (1926): 192–96, in Robert Ezra Park, *Race and Culture: Essays in the Sociology of Contemporary Man* (Glencoe, IL: Free Press, 1950), 138–51, 150; McKee, *Sociology and the Race Problem*, 133–40; O'Connor, *Poverty Knowledge*, 76–84.

28. Jonathan Scott Holloway and Benjamin Keppel, eds., *Black Scholars on the Line: Race, Social Science, and American Thought in the Twentieth Century* (Notre Dame, IN: University of Notre Dame Press, 2007), 14–15; Bulmer, *The Chicago School*, 55–57, 176–77.

29. On Park's naturalizing of racial conflict and oppression, see O'Connor, *Poverty Knowledge*, 77–79; Steinberg, *Race Relations*, part 1.

30. The Mayor's Commission on Conditions in Harlem (MCCH), *Complete Report of Mayor LaGuardia's Commission on the Harlem Riot of March 19, 1935* (1935; New York: Arno Press, 1969), 43.

31. Chicago Commission on Race Relations, *The Negro in Chicago: A Study of Race Relations and a Race Riot* (Chicago: University of Chicago Press, 1922); MCCH, *Report on the Harlem Riot*; O'Connor, *Poverty Knowledge*, chap. 3.

32. Jonathan Scott Holloway, *Confronting the Veil: Abram Harris Jr., E. Franklin Frazier, and Ralph Bunche, 1919–1941* (Chapel Hill: University of North Carolina Press, 2002), 9, 15–17, 34; Sugrue, *Sweet Land*; Nikhil Pal Singh, *Black Is a Country: Race and the Unfinished Struggle for Democracy* (Cambridge, MA: Harvard University Press, 2004), chaps. 3–5.

33. While my focus in this chapter is largely on psychology, sociology, and the inter-disciplinary behavioral sciences, a number of historians present Myrdal as emblem and instigator of shifts from political economic toward behavioral approaches to the race issue in social science and social thought generally. Jackson, *Gunnar Myrdal and America's Conscience*, 283; Thomas F. Pettigrew, ed., *The Sociology of Race Relations: Reflection and Reform* (New York: Free Press, 1980), 183; O'Connor, *Poverty Knowledge*, 98; Herman, *Romance of American Psychology*, 184; and Sugrue, *Sweet Land*, 83-84.

34. Jackson, *Gunnar Myrdal and America's Conscience*, 26-35.

35. O'Connor, *Poverty Knowledge*, 95; Sugrue, *Sweet Land*, 59.

36. Abbott and Sparrow, "Hot War, Cold War," 295.

37. Myrdal, *American Dilemma*, 530; Jackson, *Gunnar Myrdal and America's Conscience*, 215-16.

38. Myrdal, *American Dilemma*, 205-6.

39. Jackson, *Gunnar Myrdal and America's Conscience*, 204-8.

40. Ibid., 208-10, 193; Sugrue, *Sweet Land*, 61; Myrdal, *American Dilemma*, 1011, 313.

41. Jackson, *Gunnar Myrdal and America's Conscience*, 204-11.

42. Ibid., 214-19; Myrdal, *American Dilemma*, 19-20, 828-36.

43. Myrdal, *American Dilemma*, 4, 8.

44. Skrentny, *The Ironies of Affirmative Action*, 27.

45. Jackson, *Gunnar Myrdal and America's Conscience*, 233; Sugrue, *Sweet Land*, 54; Barbara D. Savage, *Broadcasting Freedom: Radio, War, and the Politics of Race, 1939-1948* (Chapel Hill: University of North Carolina Press, 1999).

46. Myrdal, *American Dilemma*, 24. Jackson, *Gunnar Myrdal and America's Conscience*, 205, 193.

47. Myrdal, *American Dilemma*, 210.

48. Ibid., 24-25.

49. Jackson, *Gunnar Myrdal and America's Conscience*, 134, 200, and chap. 4; Winant, "The Dark Side of the Force," 560.

50. Myrdal, *American Dilemma*, 75-80.

51. Ibid., 383-84, 48-49, emphasis in original, 80; Jackson, *Gunnar Myrdal and America's Conscience*, 194-95.

52. Cox, "An American Dilemma"; Herbert Aptheker, "The Negro People in America: A Critique of Gunnar Myrdal's *An American Dilemma*," in *Herbert Aptheker on Race and Democracy*, ed. Eric Foner and Manning Marable (Urbana: University of Illinois Press, 2006), 185-86; and Ralph Ellison, "An American Dilemma: A Review," http://teachingamericanhistory.org/library/document/an-american-dilemma-a-review/, accessed November 12, 2013.

53. Ralph Ellison, "An American Dilemma: A Review" (1944).

54. Abbott and Sparrow, "Hot War, Cold War"; Baker, *From Savage to Negro*, 168-69, 180; Herman, *Romance of American Psychology*, chap. 7; Jackson, *Gunnar Myrdal and America's Conscience*, 283, 279-93; O'Connor, *Poverty Knowledge*, 98; Southern, *Gunnar Myrdal and Black-White Relations*, chaps. 5, 6, 8, and 10; Daryl Michael Scott, *Contempt and Pity: Social Policy and the Image of the Damaged Black Psyche, 1880-1996* (Chapel Hill: University of North Carolina Press, 1997); and Pierre L. van den Berghe, *Race and Racism: A Comparative Perspective* (New York: John Wiley, 1967), 7, cited in McKee, *Sociology and the Race Problem*, 13.

55. Sugrue, *Sweet Land*, 62; Jackson, *Gunnar Myrdal and America's Conscience*, 210-11; Brinkley, *End of Reform*; Gary Gerstle, "The Protean Character of American Liberalism," *American Historical Review* 99, no. 4 (1994): 1043-73, 1070, 1045.

206 / Notes to Chapter One

57. Herman, *Romance of American Psychology*, chap. 7, 181–82; Jackson, *Gunnar Myrdal and America's Conscience*, 279–93; McKee, *Sociology and the Race Problem*, 13.

58. Pettigrew, *Sociology of Race Relations*, 133; Stephen Park Turner and Jonathan H. Turner, *The Impossible Science: An Institutional Analysis of American Sociology* (Newbury Park, CA: Sage Publications, 1990), 125; Winant, "The Dark Side of the Force," 557.

59. Abbott and Sparrow, "Hot War, Cold War," 293–300; Platt, *A History of Sociological Research Methods*, 49–50.

60. Converse, *Survey Research*, 5, 234–36; Platt, *A History of Sociological Research Methods*, 49–50.

61. Platt, *A History of Sociological Research Methods*, 26; Turner and Turner, *Impossible Science*, 105.

62. Converse, *Survey Research*, 5, 253–57, citing Herbert Blumer, "Public Opinion and Public Opinion Polling," *American Sociological Review* 13 (1948): 542–49; and Turner and Turner, *Impossible Science*, 106–7.

63. Converse, *Survey Research*, chaps. 8–11, esp. 392, 409–10.

64. Jamie Cohen-Cole, "Instituting the Science of Mind: Intellectual Economies and Disciplinary Exchange at Harvard's Center for Cognitive Studies," *British Journal for the History of Science* 40, no. 4 (2007): 567–97, 573; Converse, *Survey Research*, chaps. 8–11.

65. Joel Isaac, "Theorist at Work: Talcott Parsons and the Carnegie Project on Theory, 1949–1951," *Journal of the History of Ideas* 71 (2010): 287–311, 290–92; Lawrence T. Nichols, "Social Relations Undone: Disciplinary Divergence and Departmental Politics at Harvard, 1946–1970," *American Sociologist* 29 (1998): 83–107, 83–86; Nils Gilman, *Mandarins of the Future: Modernization Theory in Cold War America* (Baltimore: Johns Hopkins University Press, 2003), 78.

66. Brick, *Transcending Capitalism*; Howard Brick, "Talcott Parsons's 'Shift Away from Economics,' 1937–1946," *Journal of American History* 87, no. 2 (2000): 490–514, 490; Joel Isaac, "The Human Sciences in Cold War America," *Historical Journal* 50, no. 3 (2007): 725–46, 738; Jewett, *Science, Democracy, and the American University*, chap. 11; Herman, *Romance of American Psychology*, chap. 7; and Solovey, *Shaky Foundations*, chap. 3.

67. Cohen-Cole, "Instituting the Science of Mind," 567–97; Herman, *Romance of American Psychology*, 133, 349; Solovey, *Shaky Foundations*, chap. 3; and Ellen Condliffe Lagemann, *The Politics of Knowledge: The Carnegie Corporation, Philanthropy, and Public Policy* (Middletown, CT: Wesleyan University Press, 1989), 175–79. On Rockefeller philanthropy, see chap. 2.

68. Gordon Allport, *The Nature of Prejudice* (1954; Reading, MA: Addison-Wesley, 1979), 480, 484–89, 491–99; Williams, *Reduction of Intergroup Tensions*, 8–21; Jackson, *Gunnar Myrdal and America's Conscience*, 279–93.

69. Arnold M. Rose, "Army Policies toward Negro Soldiers," *Annals of the American Academy of Political and Social Science* 244 (March 1946): 90–94; Rose, *Studies in Reduction of Prejudice*, part 1, page 10; Williams, *Reduction of Intergroup Tensions*, 22–23.

70. John D. Greenwood, *The Disappearance of the Social in American Social Psychology* (Cambridge: Cambridge University Press, 2004); and Katherine Pandora, *Rebels within the Ranks: Psychologists' Critique of Scientific Authority and Democratic Realities in*

New Deal America (Cambridge: Cambridge University Press, 1997); Allport, *Nature of Prejudice*, 504.

71. Allport, *Nature of Prejudice*, xviii, xv.

72. Ibid., 9, xv, 14–15.

73. Ibid., 41; Ian Nicholson, *Inventing Personality: Gordon Allport and the Science of Self-hood* (Washington, DC: American Psychological Association, 2003), 194–97, 219–21; Jamie Cohen-Cole, "Thinking about Thinking in Cold War America" (PhD diss., Princeton University, 2003), 103.

74. Arnold Rose, review of *The Nature of Prejudice* by Gordon Allport and *The Social Psychology of Prejudice* by Gerhart Saenger, *American Sociological Review* 19, no. 5 (1954): 608–10, 608.

75. Allport, *The Nature of Prejudice*, chaps. 25–26; Theodor Adorno, Else Frenkel-Brunswik, Daniel Levinson, and Nevitt Sanford, *The Authoritarian Personality* (New York: Harper and Row, 1950); Nevitt Sanford, "A Personal Account of the Study of Authoritarianism," *Journal of Social Issues*, 42, no. 1 (1986): 209–14; Franz Samelson, "Authoritarianism from Berlin to Berkeley: On Social Psychology and History," *Journal of Social Issues* 42, no. 1 (1986): 191–208, 199; Jackson, *Social Scientists for Social Justice*, 52.

76. Allport, *Nature of Prejudice*, 395.

77. Adorno et al., *Authoritarian Personality*, vii.

78. Ibid., 971.

79. Samelson, "Authoritarianism from Berlin to Berkeley," 193; Else Frenkel-Brunswik, "Tolerance toward Ambiguity as a Personality Variable," *American Psychologist* 3 (1948): 268; on the failure to address social variables, see Herbert H. Hyman and Paul B. Sheatsley, "The Authoritarian Personality—A Methodological Critique," in *Studies in the Scope and Method of "The Authoritarian Personality*," ed. Richard Christie and Marie Jahoda (Glencoe, IL: Free Press, 1954), 50–122, 50; Cohen-Cole, "Thinking about Thinking," 99, 103, 112–14; and Herman, *Romance of American Psychology*, 182.

80. Jackson, *Gunnar Myrdal and America's Conscience*, 288; on the dangers of psychological structuralism, see Allport, *Nature of Prejudice*, 504.

81. Robin M. Williams Jr., "Review and Assessment of Research on Race and Culture Conflict" Paper V, Conference on Research in Human Relations (February 1953), folder 99, box 11, series 910, RG 3.1, RF, 2, 11.

82. Allport, *Nature of Prejudice*, 408.

83. Ibid., 286, 174–75, 297. For the emergence of these ideas in Allport's work in the 1940s, see Gordon Allport and Bernard Kramer, "Some Roots of Prejudice," *Journal of Psychology* (1946): 22, 9–39, 32, 35. For details, see Allport, *Nature of Prejudice*, 298–99; 396–97; 404–9, 427.

84. Allport, *Nature of Prejudice*, 12.

85. Adorno et al., *Authoritarian Personality*, 973–76; Jackson, *Gunnar Myrdal and America's Conscience*, 288; Cohen-Cole, "Thinking about Thinking," chap. 2, 97–98.

86. Allport, *Nature of Prejudice*, 408, 495–96. On Allport's defense of civil rights legislation, see chap. 29. Adorno et al., *Authoritarian Personality*, 974–75.

87. Adorno et al., *Authoritarian Personality*, 9, 973–73. Indeed, the fact that the TAP authors explained support for reformist approaches they acknowledged to be only partially relevant by emphasizing that such reforms were doable suggests they may have had some qualms about advancing theories that undermined the antiprejudice educational efforts they had set out to bolster. Looking back on this conclusion from

1986, Sanford admitted its lack of precision as a call for action. Sanford, "A Personal Account of the Study of Authoritarianism," 209–14, 211.

88. Frances Cherry, "The Nature of *The Nature of Prejudice*," *Journal of the History of the Behavioral Sciences* 36, no. 4 (2000): 489–98, 495.

89. Allport, "The Resolution of Intergroup Tensions," 38–39, 18.

90. Jackson, *Gunnar Myrdal and America's Conscience*, 288, citing Adorno et al., *Authoritarian Personality*, 973–76.

91. Cherry, "The Nature of *The Nature of Prejudice*," 495; Jackson, *Social Scientists for Social Justice*, 171, 183–90; Allport, *Nature of Prejudice*, chap. 29.

92. Allport, *Nature of Prejudice*, 469–77, chaps. 14–16.

93. Ibid., 505–7, 472–73, 408, 479–97.

94. Pettigrew, *Sociology of Race Relations*, 183–84; Winant, "The Dark Side of the Force," esp. 559–60; Turner and Turner, *Impossible Science*; and McKee, *Sociology and the Race Problem*, chap. 7.

95. Turner and Turner, *Impossible Science*, chap. 3; Abbott and Sparrow, "Hot War, Cold War," 284; George Steinmetz, "American Sociology before and after World War II: The (Temporary) Settling of a Disciplinary Field," in Calhoun, *Sociology in America*, 314–66, 328–32.

96. Abbott and Sparrow, "Hot War, Cold War," 285.

97. Turner and Turner, *Impossible Science*, 125; Jonathan Scott Holloway and Benjamin Keppel, eds., *Black Scholars on the Line: Race, Social Science, and American Thought in the Twentieth Century* (Notre Dame, IN: University of Notre Dame Press, 2007), 12–23.

98. Abbott and Sparrow, "Hot War, Cold War," 285; Solovey, *Shaky Foundations*, chaps. 1 and 4.

99. McKee, *Sociology and the Race Problem*, 295–96; also see Pettigrew, *Sociology of Race Relations*, xxxi.

100. Pettigrew argues that much postwar sociology of race relations embraced a "psychological-reductionist model" that emphasized prejudice and dismissed social structure. Pettigrew, *Sociology of Race Relations*, 133, 183–84.

101. Craig Calhoun and Jonathan Van Antwerpen, "Orthodoxy, Heterodoxy, and Hierarchy: 'Mainstream' Sociology and Its Challengers," in Calhoun, *Sociology in America*, 386–87; Nichols, "Social Relations Undone," 83–86; Isaac, "Theorist at Work," 290–92.

102. Brick, *Transcending Capitalism*, 136.

103. Gordon Allport, "Prejudice: A Problem in Psychological and Social Causation," in *Toward a General Theory of Action: Theoretical Foundations for the Social Sciences*, ed. Talcott Parsons and Edward Shils (Cambridge, MA: Harvard University Press, 1951), 365–87; Talcott Parsons and Kenneth Clark, eds., *The Negro American* (1965; Boston: Beacon Press, 1967); Winant, "The Dark Side of the Force," 562.

104. "Sociology, Post-Parsonian America," *International Encyclopedia of the Social Sciences*, ed. William A. Darity Jr., 2nd ed., vol. 8 (Detroit: Macmillan Reference USA, 2008), 5–8, *Gale Virtual Reference Library*, September 29, 2012.

105. Gilman, *Mandarins of the Future*, 85; Winant, "The Dark Side of the Force," 557–60. In fact, while my emphasis on the centrality of political economy to Myrdal's *An American Dilemma* distances him from the functionalist paradigm, Winant is certainly right to suggest that the moral dilemma thesis exemplified the emphasis on consensus and values characteristic of functionalist thought.

106. Winant, "The Dark Side of the Force," 557–58, 561; Gilman, *Mandarins of the Future*,

85, 92, 557; Solovey, "Riding Natural Science's Coattails," 412–13; Calhoun and Antwerpen, "Orthodoxy, Heterodoxy, and Hierarchy," 394.

107. Robert M. MacIver, *The More Perfect Union: A Program for the Control of Inter-Group Discrimination in the United States* (New York: Macmillan, 1948), 89.

108. Robert K. Merton, "Discrimination and the American Creed," in *Discrimination and National Welfare*, ed. Robert MacIver (New York: Institute for Religious Studies and Harper, 1949), 99–128.

109. Robin M. Williams, *Strangers Next Door: Ethnic Relations in American Communities* (Englewood Cliffs, NJ: Prentice-Hall, 1964).

110. Brick, "Talcott Parsons's 'Shift Away from Economics,' 1937–1946," 490; Brick, *Transcending Capitalism*.

111. Robert Weaver, "A Needed Program of Research in Race Relations and Associated Problems," *JNE* 16, no. 2 (1947): 130–35; Michael A. Bernstein, *A Perilous Progress: Economists and Public Purpose in Twentieth-Century America* (Princeton, NJ: Princeton University Press, 2001), 45–47, 88, and chaps. 4 and 5.

112. Donald Matthews notes that the *American Political Science Review* only published thirteen articles (out of a total of 2,601) that included the words "race," "Negro," or "civil rights" in their titles between 1906 and 1963. Donald Matthews, "Political Science Research on Race Relations," in Katz and Gurin, *Race and the Social Sciences*, 113–44, 113.

113. Pettigrew, *Sociology of Race Relations*, xxviii; 183–84; McKee, *Sociology and the Race Problem*.

114. Robert C. Weaver, "Effect on Housing"; Ira de A. Reid, "What Segregated Areas Mean"; and Robert K. Merton, "Discrimination and the American Creed," all in MacIver, *Discrimination and National Welfare*. On Weaver's work on the systemic and structural sources of housing and employment discrimination, see Robert Weaver, *The Negro Ghetto* (1948; New York: Russell and Russell, 1967); Robert Weaver, *Negro Labor: A National Problem* (New York: Harcourt Brace, 1946); and Wendell E. Pritchett, *Robert Clifton Weaver and the American City: The Life and Times of an Urban Reformer* (Chicago: University of Chicago Press, 2008), chap. 6.

115. William C. Bradbury Jr., "Racial Discrimination in Federal Employment" (unpublished manuscript for PhD dissertation, Department of Sociology, Columbia University); and Joseph Lohman, "Residential Segregation: Discriminatory Housing in the Nation's Capital" (mimeographed) and "The Federation of Citizens Associations: Voice of the People?" (mimeographed), cited in Dietrich C. Reitzes, "Collective Factors in Race Relations" (PhD diss., University of Chicago, 1950). Also see McKee, *Sociology and the Race Problem*, 297–98.

116. Aptheker, "The Negro People in America," 191, 196, 185–86, 189–90.

117. Ibid., 188.

118. Herbert Blumer, "Race Prejudice as a Sense of Group Position," *Pacific Sociological Review* 1, no. 1 (1958): 3–7; E. Franklin Frazier, "Race Contacts and the Social Structure," *American Sociological Review* 14, no. 1 (1949): 1–11; and Robin M. Williams Jr., "Review and Assessment of Research on Race and Culture Conflict" Paper V, Conference on Research in Human Relations (February 1953), folder 99, box 11, series 910, RG 3.1, RF, 2, 11. Also see Pettigrew, *Sociology of Race Relations*, xxviii, 183–85; and McKee, *Sociology and the Race Problem*, 295–99.

119. Gary S. Becker's, *The Economics of Discrimination* heralded the return of mainstream economics to questions of racial discrimination in employment and housing, but it would not be until the early 1960s that political scientists and economists began regaining the central role in debates on race they exhibited in Myrdal's volume.

Gary S. Becker, *The Economics of Discrimination* (Chicago: University of Chicago Press, 1957); Charles C. Killingsworth, "Job and Income for Negroes," in *Race and the Social Sciences*, ed. Irwin Katz and Patricia Gurin (New York: Basic Books, 1969); Matthews, "Political Science Research on Race Relations."

120. Matthews, "Political Science Research on Race Relations," 113–44.

121. Pettigrew, *Sociology of Race Relations*, 183–84, 238–44; McKee, *Sociology and the Race Problem*, chaps. 8 and 9.

122. Allport, *Nature of Prejudice*, 514.

123. Ibid., 208.

124. Ibid., 207–8. Also see ibid., chap. 13 and part 4. On Allport's critique of "closed systems," see Jackson, *Gunner Myrdal and America's Conscience*, 289.

125. Allport, *Nature of Prejudice*, 207–8.

126. Williams, *Reduction of Intergroup Tensions*, 41.

127. Allport, *Nature of Prejudice*, 507.

CHAPTER TWO

1. Benjamin Stolberg, "Mute Facts about the Negro: The Negro in American Civilization," *New York Herald Tribune*, Books, June 22, 1930, quoted in "From Appendix XVI, Report on Projects by the President," in "P&P Aug–September 1930, Council September 1930," folder 998, box 174, series 1.19, RG 1, SSRC, 331.

2. On the LSRM's accommodationist stance to segregation despite this activist orientation to social science, see John Stanfield, *Philanthropy and Jim Crow in American Social Science* (Westport, CT: Greenwood Press, 1985).

3. On the inclusion of practitioners, social welfare workers, and other "lay" thinkers in scientific agenda setting in other Progressive Era and interwar settings, see Alice O'Connor, *Social Science for What? Philanthropy and the Social Question in a World Turned Rightside Up* (New York: Russell Sage Foundation, 2007); and Alice O'Connor, *Poverty Knowledge: Social Science, Social Policy, and the Poor in Twentieth-Century U.S. History* (Princeton, NJ: Princeton University Press, 2001), chaps. 1 and 2.

4. Walter A. Jackson, *Gunnar Myrdal and America's Conscience: Social Engineering and Racial Liberalism, 1938–1987* (Chapel Hill: University of North Carolina Press, 1990), 379, n. 53. On the conservatism and "basic" orientation of RF research, see Waldemar A. Nielsen, *The Big Foundations* (New York: Columbia University Press, 1972), 50–72; and Kenneth W. Rose and Thomas E. Rosenbaum, introduction to "A Survey of Sources at the Rockefeller Archive Center for the Study of African American History and Race Relations," http://archive.rockefeller.edu/publications/guides/afroam.pdf, accessed January 25, 2006, x.

5. On the maturing of scientism in the 1950s, see Andrew Jewett, *Science, Democracy, and the American University: From the Civil War to the Cold War* (Cambridge: Cambridge University Press, 2012), chap. 11; and Mark Solovey, *Shaky Foundations: The Politics-Patronage-Social Science Nexus in Cold War America* (New Brunswick, NJ: Rutgers University Press, 2013).

6. On postwar behavioralism and antiradicalism in universities, see Ellen Schrecker, *No Ivory Tower: McCarthyism and the Universities* (New York: Oxford University Press, 1986); Ellen Herman, *The Romance of American Psychology: Political Culture in the Age of Experts* (Berkeley: University of California Press, 1995), 132–36 and chap. 7; Joel Isaac, "The Human Sciences in Cold War America," *Historical Journal* 50, no. 3 (2007): 725–46; and Solovey, *Shaky Foundations*, chap. 3. On noneconomic social relations paradigms and the behavioral turn in sociology, see Howard Brick, "Talcott

Parsons's 'Shift Away from Economics,' 1937–1946," *Journal of American History* 87, no. 2 (2000): 490–514; and Howard Brick, *Transcending Capitalism: Visions of a New Society in Modern American Thought* (Ithaca, NY: Cornell University Press, 2006), 172.

7. "Survey of the Problems of the Negro Race in the United States, to be made by the National Interracial Conference," and letter from Charles S. Johnson to Director of Carnegie Corporation of New York, July 2, 1928, folder 998, box 98, series 3, LSRM; "P and P A," February 14–15, 1931, in "Advisory Committee on Interracial Relations," Minutes of the Committee on Problems and Policy (MCPP)—and of the Council," folder 998, box 174, series 1.19, RG 1, SSRC, 340; Mary Van Kleeck, foreword to Charles S. Johnson, *The Negro in American Civilization: A Study of Negro Life and Race Relations in the Light of Social Research* (New York: Henry Holt, 1930), v–vii.

8. Rose and Rosenbaum, "A Survey of Sources," iii, xi, xv, viii, x.

9. Stanfield, *Philanthropy and Jim Crow*, 73–74; Jackson, *Gunnar Myrdal and America's Conscience*, 31.

10. While LSRM staff member Leonard Outhwaite was happy to support the NAACP's research and welfare agenda, he wondered if funding the organization's general budget was appropriate due to the group's political orientation. Leonard Outhwaite to Edwin Embree, March 2, 1928; also see Edwin Embree to Leonard Outhwaite, February 29, 1928, folder 997, box 98, series 3.8, LSRM.

11. O'Connor, *Poverty Knowledge*, 74–75; Jackson, *Gunnar Myrdal and America's Conscience*, chap. 1.

12. Stanfield, *Philanthropy and Jim Crow*, 66–67.

13. O'Connor, *Social Science for What?*; Solovey, *Shaky Foundations*, 106; Ellen Condliffe Lagemann, *The Politics of Knowledge: The Carnegie Corporation, Philanthropy, and Public Policy* (Middletown, CT: Wesleyan University Press, 1989).

14. Stanfield, *Philanthropy and Jim Crow*, 70, 79–90. Whatever the intentions behind its funding, however, Rockefeller philanthropy helped train notable African American social scientists, including E. Franklin Frazier, J. Max Bond, L. D. Reddick, Ira de Augustine Reid, and even socialist Doxey Wilkerson at early points in their careers. Ibid., 70, 80–83. Also see, "Race Relations and Negro Work, 1926–1927," folder 996, box 98, series 3.8, LSRM, 1–2, 10–11. The following folders address GEB fellowships in the 1930s. On J. Max Bond, see folder 2404, box 238, series 400S, RG 1.2, GEB. On L. D. Reddick and Ira de A. Reid, see folder 2641, box 244, series 400S, RG 1.2, GEB. On Doxey Wilkerson, see folder 2477, box 246, series 400S, RG 1.2, GEB.

15. Stanfield, *Philanthropy and Jim Crow*, 80–81. Also see "Race Relations and Negro Work, 1926–1927," folder 996, box 98, series 3.8, LSRM, 1–2, 10–11.

16. Members included Dr. Will Alexander of the Commission on Interracial Cooperation; Walter White of the NAACP; Channing Tobias of the National YMCA; Eugene K. Jones of the National Urban League; John Hope and Bruno Lasker of *The Inquiry*; Charles S. Johnson of Urban League (who served as research secretary using time donated by the Urban League and then by Fisk University); George E. Haynes of the Federal Council of Churches; Mary Van Kleeck of the Russell Sage Foundation; Graham R. Taylor, formerly of the Chicago Commission on Race Relations and presently of the Commonwealth Fund; and Eustace Seligman. The research committee also included James Weldon Johnson, secretary of the NAACP; Monroe N. Work, editor of the *Negro Year Book*; a number of leading sociologists of the race issue, including Howard W. Odum and Robert Park; a number of statisticians and Census Bureau representatives; an economist associated with Amalgamated Clothing Workers of America; one historian; and two administrators of schools of social work. "Survey

of the Problems of the Negro Race in the United States, to be made by the National Interracial Conference"; "Minutes of Meeting of the Research Committee, National Interracial Conference, Held at Russell Sage Foundation Building," April 15, 1927; "Memorandum regarding Proposed Survey of Problems of the Colored Race in the United States, to be Made by the National Interracial Conference, December 16, 1927"; "Memorandum on Research, National Inter-Racial Conference," March 9, 1927; and Letter from Charles S. Johnson to Director of Carnegie Corporation of New York, July 2, 1928. All are located in folder 998, box 98, series 3.8, LSRM; also see Van Kleeck, foreword, *The Negro in American Civilization*, vi.

17. "Memorandum regarding Proposed Survey of Problems of the Colored Race in the United States, to be Made by the National Interracial Conference, December 16, 1927," folder 998, box 98, series 3.8, LSRM, 1–2.

18. "Letter from Mary Van Kleeck and George E. Haynes to Leonard Outhwaite," November 10, 1928; Charles S. Johnson, Research Secretary, Appendix B, "Memorandum on Proposed Field of Activity of the Research Committee of the National Interracial Conference, March 23, 1927," 1–5, and "Memorandum on Research, National Interracial Conference," March 9, 1927. All are in folder 998, box 98, series 3.8, LSRM.

19. "Survey of the Problems of the Negro Race in the United States, to be made by the National Interracial Conference," and Letter from Charles S. Johnson to Director of Carnegie Corporation of New York, July 2, 1928. Both in folder 998, box 98, series 3, LSRM.

20. This list, which overlapped with the NIC's membership, included Will Alexander of the CIC, UNC sociologist Howard W. Odum, Monroe N. Work of the *Negro Year Book*, Charles Johnson, and Carter G. Woodson of the *Journal of Negro History*; Leonard Outhwaite of the LSRM, Professor Guy S. Ford of the University of Minnesota, Professor Robert S. Woodworth of Columbia University, Professor Thomas Woofter Jr. of the University of North Carolina, Professor Robert M. Yerkes of Yale, John M. Glenn of the Russell Sage Foundation, and R. J. Terry of Washington University were also listed. "Advisory Committee on Interracial Relations, September, 1932: Appendix XII-48" of "Interracial Relations, 1925–1932," folder 998, box 174, series 1.19, RG 1, SSRC, 343; "Report of the Committee on Research Agencies and Resources Available for Committee Cooperation," in "Advisory Committee on Interracial Relations," MCPP—and of the Council, folder 998, box 174, series 1.19, RG 1, SSRC, 46–47.

21. Appendix A, "Research Agencies and Resources Available for Committee Cooperation," in SSRC, Minutes of the Advisory Committee on Interracial Relations, held at Dartmouth College, Hanover, NH, August 22–29, 1927, folder 998, box 174, series 1.19, RG 1, SSRC, 2–3.

22. Ibid., 2.

23. The NIC's 1926 outline of potential research areas, for example, exposed both attention to the concerns of African American communities and a tendency to employ varied frameworks of analysis—social, economic, cultural, political, and even, reflecting the RF's strong commitment to health issues and the endurance of eugenicist interests, biological. "Race Relations and Negro Work, 1926–1927," folder 996, box 98, series 3.8, LSRM, 11.

24. "Table of Contents, Proceedings of the Inter-Racial Conference," LSRM, Zeta Psi Fraternity House, December 19–21, 1927, New Haven, CT, folder 1001, box 98, series 3.8, LSRM ("Proceedings of the Interracial Conference").

25. "Proceedings of the Interracial Conference," 7.

26. Ibid., 13–14.

27. "Advisory Committee on Interracial Relations," MCPP—and of the Council, folder 998, box 174, series 1.19, RG 1, SSRC, 47; Appendix A, "Research Agencies and Resources Available for Committee Cooperation," in SSRC, Minutes of the Advisory Committee on Interracial Relations, held at Dartmouth College, Hanover, NH, August 22–29, 1927, folder 998, box 174, series 1.19, RG 1, SSRC; "Appendix F, Report on the Study of Racial Attitudes," in SSRC, Minutes of the Advisory Committee on Interracial Relations, held at Dartmouth College, Hanover, NH, August 22–29, 1927, folder 998, box 174, series 1.19, RG 1, SSRC, 64–73.

28. While the ACIR leaned firmly toward the environmentalist side of debates over the inheritability of racial propensities, concern with African American intelligence, physiology, and biology represents a reminder of the relatively recent emergence of Boasian environmentalism. The ACIR even jointly sponsored a Conference on Racial Differences with the National Research Council in which many of the nation's leading anthropologists and psychologists, including Franz Boas, Melville Herskovitz, Robert S. Lynd, and W. I. Thomas, participated. "Joint Conference on Racial Differences," from Agenda of Program and Policy Committee, April 6, 1928, in "Interracial Relations, 1925–1932," folder 198, box 174, series 1.19, RG 1, SSRC, 108–9.

29. "Advisory Committee on Interracial Relations, Appendix XII-48" of "Interracial Relations, 1925–1932," folder 998, box 174, series 1.19, RG 1, SSRC, 343–45.

30. Charles S. Johnson, *The Negro in American Civilization: A Study of Negro Life and Race Relations in the Light of Social Research* (New York: Henry Holt, 1930), v–vii; and "Abstract of the Report of the Research Committee to the National Interracial Conference," 1928, folder 999, box 98, series 3.8, LSRM.

31. Johnson, *The Negro in American Civilization*, xiii–xiv.

32. Benjamin Stolberg, "Mute Facts about the Negro: The Negro in American Civilization," *New York Herald Tribune*, Books, June 22, 1930, quoted in "From Appendix XVI, Report on Projects by the President," in MCPP—and of the Council, folder 998, box 174, series 1.19, RG 1, SSRC, 331.

33. W. E. B. Du Bois, "Chapter XXIX: The Negro Citizen," in Johnson, *The Negro in American Civilization*, 470.

34. On Van Kleeck's work on labor issues through the Russell Sage Foundation, see O'Connor, *Social Science for What?*, 42–43.

35. Van Kleeck, foreword, *The Negro in American Civilization*, ix–x.

36. Ibid., x–xi.

37. Ibid., xi.

38. "From Appendix XVI, Report on Projects by the President," in MCPP—and of the Council, folder 998, box 174, series 1.19, RG 1, SSRC, 330.

39. Benjamin Stolberg, "Mute Facts about the Negro: The Negro in American Civilization," *New York Herald Tribune*, Books, June 22, 1930, quoted in "From Appendix XVI, Report on Projects by the President," in MCPP—and of the Council, folder 998, box 174, series 1.19, RG 1, SSRC, 330.

40. Ibid., 330.

41. "From Appendix XVI, Report on Projects by the President," in MCPP, folder 998, box 174, series 1.19, RG 1, SSRC, 333.

42. In 1931, for example, ACIR member Edwin Embree had noted, "My own feeling is that unless Ruml is willing to take the chairmanship of this committee, it will do no harm to let the whole matter lie in abeyance for a year or two. Things are quiet at the moment. It seems to me there is much to be said for not multiplying committees unless and until there seems important work for them to do." Program and Policy

Minutes, February 14–15, 1931, in "Advisory Committee on Interracial Relations," MCPP—and of the Council," folder 998, box 174, series 1.19, RG 1, SSRC, 340.

43. On the conservatism and "basic" orientation of RF research, see Nielsen, *The Big Foundations*, 50–72, quote at 58; Rose and Rosenbaum, "Survey of Sources," x.

44. Jackson, *Gunnar Myrdal and America's Conscience*, 379 n. 53, and 31–32; Rose and Rosenbaum, "Survey of Sources," x.

45. Dana S. Creel, "Survey of Field of Negro Welfare," July 3, 1946, folder 353, box 32, series: OMR, subseries: Welfare, RG 2, RFA, 1, 3.

46. Ibid., 5.

47. Ibid., 1–2.

48. Ibid., 4–5.

49. Ibid., 2–9, 16, 19.

50. Ibid., 2, 11–12.

51. Ibid., 20.

52. John G. Simon, "The Regulation of American Foundations: Looking Backward at the Tax Reform Act of 1969," *Voluntas: International Journal of Voluntary and Nonprofit Organizations* 6 (1995): 243–54, 244–45; Nielsen, *Big Foundations*, 65.

53. Creel, "Survey of Field of Negro Welfare," RFA, 14.

54. "Project Memorandum, Rockefeller Brothers Fund, American Council on Race Relations," April 1949, folder 472, box 69, series 3, RBF quoting from "December 11, 1947 Docket Memorandum to the Rockefeller Brothers Fund"; Rose and Rosenbaum, "A Survey of Sources," xiii; Nielsen, *Big Foundations*, 75.

55. Grant in Aid, SSRC Committee on Techniques for Reducing Group Hostility, January 2, 1946, folder 4764, box 402, series 200S, RG 1.1, RF, and "Memorandum on the Study of Techniques for Reducing Group Hostility," no date, folder 4764, box 402, series 200S, RG 1.1, RF; Letter Charles Dollard to Joseph Willits, January 21, 1948, folder 4764, box 402, series 200S, RG 1.1, RF.

56. SSRC Program and Policy Minutes, December 9, 1944, folder 2071, box 348, series 8, RG 1, SSRC; Excerpt from Council Minutes, September 10–13, 1945, folder 2071, box 348, series 8, RG 1, SSRC, 1; Letter from Donald Young to Joseph Willits, December 5, 1946, folder 4764, box 492, series 200S, RG 1.1, RF.

57. SSRC Program and Policy Minutes, December 9, 1944, folder 2071, box 348, series 8, RG 1, SSRC. The committee included sociologist Leonard S. Cottrell Jr., who worked closely with Samuel Stouffer on *The American Soldier*; Charles Dollard, who would head the Carnegie Corporation in 1948; and psychologist Carl Hovland.

58. Excerpt from Council Minutes, February 24–25, 1945, folder 2071, box 348, series 8, RG 1, SSRC, 1.

59. "P and P Minutes Oct 27, 1945, E. Hostility and Conflict," folder 2071, box 348, series 8, RG 1, SSRC; Excerpt from Council Minutes, September 10–13, 1945, folder 2071, box 348, series 8, RG 1, SSRC, 1.

60. Robin M. Williams Jr., *The Reduction of Intergroup Tensions: A Survey of Research on Problems of Ethnic, Racial, and Religious Group Relations* (New York: SSRC, 1947), 21.

61. Jackson, *Gunnar Myrdal and America's Conscience*, 285–88.

62. Williams, *Reduction of Intergroup Tensions*, 5.

63. Ibid., 9.

64. Jackson, *Gunnar Myrdal and America's Conscience*, 286.

65. Williams, *Reduction of Intergroup Tensions*, 106.

66. On this rightward turn in RF funding generally, see Nielsen, *Big Foundations*, 56–66.

67. On the Cold War and behavioralism, see Herman, *Romance of American Psychology*,

132–36, 349, n. 29. On social relations frameworks, see Brick, *Transcending Capitalism*.

68. The Committee on Social Behavior included a number of members of the 1953 Conference on Research in Human Relations, including Robert R. Sears, Robin Williams Jr., and Leon Festinger. "Committee on Social Behavior, Notes on First Meeting," October 19, 1951, folder 1514, box 259, series 1.26, RG 1, SSRC.

69. Lagemann, *Politics of Knowledge*, 153–54, 166–70, 172, 146; O'Connor, *Social Science for What?*, 70.

70. H. Rowan Gaither Jr., director, "Report of the Study for the Ford Foundation on Policy and Program" (Detroit: Ford Foundation, 1949), 90–91; and Ford Foundation, *Annual Report* (New York: Ford Foundation, 1953), available at Ford Foundation Archives, New York City; Paul Ylvisaker, Oral History Transcript, September 27, 1973, Ford Foundation Archives, 20–23. Even in the early 1960s, the Ford Foundation used the euphemistic term "Gray Areas Project" to describe an urban redevelopment project that addressed black poverty.

71. Nielsen, *Big Foundations*, 340–42; Alfred Perkins, *Edwin Rogers Embree: The Julius Rosenwald Fund, Foundation Philanthropy, and American Race Relations* (Bloomington: Indiana University Press, 2011).

72. Michael Klarman, *From Jim Crow to Civil Rights: The Supreme Court and the Struggle for Racial Equality* (New York: Oxford University Press, 2004), 192–93.

73. Solovey, "Riding Natural Scientists' Coattails," 399, 394–95, 411.

74. Ibid., 408, 413–14. Solovey, *Shaky Foundations*, chaps. 1 and 4.

75. "The Report of Norman Dodd, Director of Research of The Special Committee of the House of Representatives to Investigate Tax Exempt Foundations, November 1, 1954–April 30, 1954" (New York: The Long House, 1954), http://www.scribd.com/doc/3768227/Dodd-Report-to-the-Reece-Committee-on-Foundations-1954, accessed February 25, 2013, 8, 15. Also see Herman, *Romance of American Psychology*, 348–49, nn. 28 and 29; Simon, "The Regulation of American Foundations," 244–45; Solovey, *Shaky Foundations*, chap. 3.

76. "Grant Action," Social Relations Conference, December 29, 1952, folder 96, box 10, series 910, RG 3.1, RF; also see "Inter-office correspondence" from Leland DeVinney to Joseph H. Willits, December 30, 1952, folder 96, box 10, series 910, RG 3.1, RF.

77. "Inter-office correspondence" from Leland DeVinney to Joseph H. Willits, December 30, 1952, folder 96, box 10, series 910, RG 3.1, RF.

78. The list included psychologists Robert Sears of Harvard's Graduate School of Education and Laboratory on Human Development, Carl Hovland of Yale, and Lee J. Cronbach of the University of Illinois; sociologists Kingsley Davis, Paul Lazarsfeld, and Robert Merton of Columbia University (including the BASR), Philip Hauser of the University of Chicago, Robin M. Williams Jr. of Cornell University, Samuel Stouffer of Harvard's Department of Social Relations, and Arnold Rose of the University of Minnesota; anthropologists Clyde Kluckhohn of Harvard's Russian Research Center, John Dollard of Yale's Institute of Human Relations, Alexander Leighton of Cornell, G. P. Murdock of Yale, and Rensis Likert of the University of Michigan's Survey Research Center. Leon Festinger of the University of Minnesota's Laboratory for Research in Social Relations as well as Frederick F. Stephan of Princeton's Department of Economics and Social Institutions also participated. Ibid.

79. "Conference on Research in Human Relations," Rockefeller Foundation, Volume I, Arden House, Harriman, New York, February 28–March 1, 1953, folder 100, box 11, series 910, RG 3.1, RF, 470.

80. Ibid., 478.

81. Williams noted that the paper he presented had been jointly produced by John P. Dean, Robert B. Johnson, Pauline Moller, and Edward A. Suchman. Robin M. Williams Jr., "Review and Assessment of Research on Race and Culture Conflict," Paper V, Conference on Research in Human Relations (February 1953), folder 99, box 11, series 910, RG 3.1, RF ("Review and Assessment").

82. Ibid., 2; James McKee, *Sociology and the Race Problem: The Failure of a Perspective* (Urbana: University of Illinois Press, 1993), chaps. 7 and 8.

83. Williams, "Review and Assessment," 2; McKee, *Sociology and the Race Problem*, chaps. 7 and 8.

84. Williams, "Review and Assessment," 2–3, 18, 28–30.

85. "Conference on Research in Human Relations" Rockefeller Foundation, Volume II, Arden House, Harriman, NY, February 28–March 1, 1953, folder 100, box 11, series 910, RG 3.1, RF (hereafter referred to as CRHR Summary, Volume II), 263.

86. Ibid., 274.

87. Williams, "Review and Assessment," 40, 28, 37.

88. CRHR Summary, Volume II, 270.

89. Williams, "Review and Assessment," 59; CRHR Summary, Volume II, 269.

90. Williams, "Review and Assessment," 69.

91. Ibid., 69, emphasis in original.

92. Ibid., 49.

93. Ibid., 12–13.

94. Joel Isaac, "Theorist at Work: Talcott Parsons and the Carnegie Project on Theory, 1949–1951," *Journal of the History of Ideas* 71 (2010): 287–311, 290–92, quote at 292; Lawrence T. Nichols, "Social Relations Undone: Disciplinary Divergence and Departmental Politics at Harvard, 1946–1970," *American Sociologist* 29 (1998): 83–107, 83–86; and Nils Gilman, *Mandarins of the Future: Modernization Theory in Cold War America* (Baltimore: Johns Hopkins University Press, 2003), 78.

95. Lee J. Cronbach to Leland DeVinney, March 9, 1953, folder 97, box 10, series 910, RG 3.1, RF, 2.

96. Kingsley Davis to Leland DeVinney, April 23, 1953, and Alexander Leighton, to Leland DeVinney, March 10, 1953, both in folder 97, box 10, series 910, RG 3.1, RF.

97. Williams, "Review and Assessment," 60, 67; CRHR Summary, Volume II, 275.

98. CRHR Summary, Volume II, 270–71.

99. Ibid., 278.

100. Williams, "Review and Assessment," 70.

101. Brick, *Transcending Capitalism*.

102. Grant Action 50104, Cornell University Inter-group Relations, November 19, 1950, and Extension to June 30, 1956, approved September 12, 1955, folder 4273, box 500, series 200S, RG 1.2, RF. See Letter from CW de Kiewiet, Acting President of Cornell University to Mr. Joseph H. Willits, September 27, 1950, folder 4273, box 500, series 200S, RG 1.2, RF.

103. The studies produced four books: John P. Dean and Alex Rosen's *A Manual of Inter-Group Relations* (1955); Edward A. Suchman, John P. Dean, and Robin M. Williams Jr.'s, *Desegregation: Some Propositions and Research Suggestions* (1958); Robin M. Williams Jr. and Margaret W. Ryan's (eds.) *Schools in Transition* (1954), and Robin M. Williams Jr.'s *Strangers Next Door: Ethnic Relations in American Communities* (1964). Individuals associated with the projects also produced over one hundred articles and

student theses. Robin M. Williams, *Strangers Next Door: Ethnic Relations in American Communities* (Englewood Cliffs, NJ: Prentice-Hall, 1964), vii–ix.

104. "Proposal for an Action Research Program in Inter-Group Relations, A research proposal submitted by Cornell University to the Rockefeller Foundation, September 1950," folder 4273, box 500 series 200S, RG 1.2, RFA, 7.

105. Ibid., 1–2; Williams, *Strangers Next Door*, 2.

106. "Proposal for an Action Research Program," 12.

107. Williams, *Strangers Next Door*, chap. 4, esp. 29–43 and 48–66.

108. Ibid., 111–12.

109. "Proposal for an Action Research Program," 3–4.

110. Williams, *Strangers Next Door*, 10.

111. Ibid., 26.

112. For discussion of possible extension of Cornell project to cover southern desegregation, see Letter from Robin M. Williams Jr. to Leland DeVinney, July 12, 1954; Letter from DeVinney to Williams, July 14, 1954; Letter from Robin M. Williams to Leland DeVinney, July 19, 1954; Letter from DeVinney to Williams, August 4, 1954; Letter from Williams to DeVinney, August 6, 1954, folder 4274, box 500 series 200S, RG 1.2, RF.

113. Letter from Edward A. Suchman to Leonard S. Cottrell Jr., Russell Sage Foundation, December 22, 1954, folder 4274, box 500 series 200S, RG 1.2, RF, 1. A group of southern sociologists with whom Suchman was working—a group led by Lewis Killian, who was then teaching at Florida State University, and that also included Clyde Hart of the NORC—had constituted themselves as a Planning Committee on Research on Educational Change in the South and produced the research proposal that the Ford Foundation rejected. Ibid., 1–2. Also see "Proposal for Coordinated Research on Educational Change in the South," December 30, 1954, folder 4274, box 500 series 200S, RG 1.2, RF, 1; "P and P Minutes, January 28, 1955, Intergroup Relations Research," folder 1517, box 259, series 1.26, RG 1, SSRC. McKee suggests that sociologists studied desegregation much less than one might have expected partially because of foundation reticence on the issue and partially because they had not devised methods for investigating conflict-filled social situations. McKee, *Sociology and the Race Problem*, 317.

114. Throughout the 1950s the RF continued to support "a program of methodological research in the field of human relations" at the Research Center for Group Dynamics at the University of Michigan, in which social psychologists researched "the development of a basic and applied science of the functioning of groups" and incorporated quantitative techniques and "graph theory" into its work. In 1953, the RF also funded Michigan-based social psychologist Theodore M. Newcombe, who was conducting a generalized social psychological study of the group. The RF provided resources for the University of Chicago–affiliated National Opinion Research Center to design questions "to measure the level of mental health and to determine attitudes toward mental illness and treatment for mental illness." Harvard University's Laboratory of Social Relations received a three-year appropriation to further its research on the functioning of small working committees, while Harvard's Laboratory of Social Relations and Graduate School of Education received funds to assess views about the appropriate responsibilities of school superintendents. A study by Rose of social disorganization did not address race relations but "the effects of varying degrees of social isolation on divergence in values, deviant behavior, and disorgani-

zation in both individuals and groups." The Cornell Inter-Group Relations Project, which Robin M. Williams led, and the University of Chicago's Committee on Education, Training, and Research in Race Relations are two exceptions to this trend. RF support for both projects was certainly related to the fact that both were being situated at leading research universities and that project leaders had close ties to foundation executives. Grant Action, University of Michigan Research Center for Group Dynamics, February 24, 1950, and Grant Action, University of Michigan Research Center for Group Dynamics, June 19, 1953, folder 4980, box 581, series 200S, RG 1.2, RF; Grant Action, University of Michigan Research Center for Group Dynamics, February 24, 1950, folder 4980, box 581, series 200S, RG 1.2, RF; and Grant Action, University of Michigan Small Group Study, September 1, 1953, folder 4028, box 581, series 200S, RG 1.2, RF; Grant in Aid, NORC Study of Mental Health and Prejudice, 1960, folder 4605, box 538, series 200S, RG 1.2, RF; Rockefeller Foundation, *Annual Report* (New York: Rockefeller Foundation 1953), 231–56.

115. Rockefeller Foundation, *Annual Report* (New York: Rockefeller Foundation, 1954), 207–9; and Rockefeller Foundation, *Annual Report* (New York: Rockefeller Foundation, 1955).

116. Rockefeller Foundation, *Annual Report* (New York: Rockefeller Foundation, 1956), 218 and 189–218. Also see UNESCO, Memo, Social Science Section, Preliminary Project outline of Project on Tensions Affecting International Understanding, Paris, May 12, 1947, folder 6736, box 565, series 1.89, accession 2, SSRC. Rockefeller Foundation, *Annual Report* (New York: Rockefeller Foundation, 1953); Committee on Social Stratification, Proposal, and letter from Nelson Foote to Elbridge Sibley, October 17, 1951, box 569, subseries 92 A and 93, series 1, SSRC.

117. On the decline of Ford's behavioral sciences initiative after 1957, see Solovey, *Shaky Foundations*, 140–45.

118. Rockefeller Foundation, *Annual Report* (New York: Rockefeller Foundation, 1959), 200–201.

119. Rockefeller Foundation, *Annual Report* (New York: Rockefeller Foundation, 1963), 17–18.

120. CRHR Summary, Volume II, 293.

121. Ibid., 293.

122. Ibid..

123. Williams, *Reduction of Intergroup Tensions*.

CHAPTER THREE

1. Louis Wirth, "Proposal for the Support of a Program on Education, Training and Research in Race Relations at the University of Chicago," April 2, 1947, University of Chicago, Committee on Education, Training, and Research in Race Relations Papers (box 2, folder 6), Special Collections Research Center, University of Chicago Library (hereafter referred to as CP), 2. Material from this chapter appears in Leah N. Gordon, "The Individual and 'the General Situation': The Tension Barometer and the Race Problem at the University of Chicago, 1947–1954," *Journal of the History of the Behavioral Sciences* 56, no. 1 (2010): 27–51.

2. Louis Wirth, "Proposal for the Support of a Program on Education, Training and Research in Race Relations at the University of Chicago," CP (box 2, folder 6), 5.

3. On instrumental scientism, see Mark Solovey, *Shaky Foundations: The Politics-Patronage-Social Science Nexus in Cold War America* (New Brunswick, NJ: Rutgers University Press, 2013), 109–10.

4. CETRRR, "Race Relations," December 4, 1947, box 3, folder 15, CP. In addition to Wirth, the core members included educationalist and anthropologist Allison Davis, anthropologist Fred Eggan, labor economist Frederick Harbison, sociologist Everett Hughes, anthropologist Robert Redfield, anthropologist Sol Tax, and educationalist Ralph Tyler. Also see CETRRR, "Minutes of Meeting of October 8, 1947," and CETRRR, "Minutes of Meeting of December 11, 1947," box 3, folder 15, CP.

5. On race relations activism see: Walter A. Jackson, *Gunnar Myrdal and America's Conscience: Social Engineering and Racial Liberalism, 1938–1987* (Chapel Hill: University of North Carolina Press, 1990), 280–85; Daryl Michael Scott, "Postwar Pluralism, *Brown v. Board of Education,* and the Origins of Multicultural Education," *Journal of American History* 91, no. 1 (2004); and John P. Jackson Jr., *Social Scientists for Social Justice: Making the Case against Segregation* (New York: New York University Press, 2001), chaps. 1–4.

6. On surveys and their postwar institutionalization, see Andrew Abbott and James Sparrow, "Hot War, Cold War: The Structures of Sociological Action 1940–1955," in Calhoun, *Sociology in America,* 281–313, 286–93; Jean M. Converse, *Survey Research in the United States: Roots and Emergence, 1890–1960* (Berkeley: University of California Press, 1987); Jennifer Platt, *A History of Sociological Research Methods in America, 1920–1960* (Cambridge: Cambridge University Press, 1996), 24–25, 48–52.

7. Solovey, *Shaky Foundations,* chap. 3.

8. Alice O'Connor, *Poverty Knowledge: Social Science, Social Policy, and the Poor in Twentieth-Century U.S. History* (Princeton, NJ: Princeton University Press, 2001), chap. 3, discusses this aspect of social ecology.

9. On the Cold War context see: Thomas Borstelmann, *The Cold War and the Color Line: American Race Relations in the Global Arena* (Cambridge, MA: Harvard University Press, 2001); Mary L. Dudziak, *Cold War Civil Rights: Race and the Image of American Democracy* (Princeton, NJ: Princeton University Press, 2000); Ellen Schrecker, *No Ivory Tower: McCarthyism and the Universities* (New York: Oxford University Press, 1986); and Penny Von Eschen, *Race against Empire: Black Americans and Anticolonialism, 1937–1957* (Ithaca, NY: Cornell University Press, 1997). Also see intro., note 25.

10. Roger A. Salerno, *Louis Wirth: A Bio-Bibliography* (New York: Greenwood Press, 1987), chap. 1, 26, 35–38. Also see Herbert Blumer, "In Memoriam: Louis Wirth, 1897–1952," *American Journal of Sociology* 58, no. 1 (1952): 69; E. Franklin Frazier, "Louis Wirth: An Appreciation," *Phylon* 3, no. 2 (1952): 167; Philip Hauser, "Louis Wirth, An Obituary," *British Journal of Sociology* 3, no. 4, (1952): 365–66; and Rupert B. Vance, "Louis Wirth, 1897–1952," *Social Forces* 31, no. 1 (1952): 96.

11. Blumer, "In Memoriam: Louis Wirth," 69; Hauser, "Louis Wirth, An Obituary," 365–66; Frazier, "Louis Wirth: An Appreciation," 167.

12. Jackson, *Gunnar Myrdal and America's Conscience,* 283–85.

13. Martin Bulmer, *The Chicago School of Sociology: Institutionalization, Diversity, and the Rise of Sociological Research* (Chicago: University of Chicago Press, 1984), 3; Andrew Abbott, *Department and Discipline: Chicago Sociology at One Hundred* (Chicago: University of Chicago Press, 1999), 6–7; James B. McKee, *Sociology and the Race Problem: The Failure of a Perspective* (Urbana: University of Illinois Press, 1993), chaps. 3 and 4; and Dennis Smith, *The Chicago School: A Liberal Critique of Capitalism* (New York: St. Martin's Press, 1988).

14. O'Connor, *Poverty Knowledge,* 49, 76–84; McKee, *Sociology and the Race Problem,* 158–65; and R. Fred Wacker, "The Sociology of Race and Ethnicity in the Second Chicago School," in *A Second Chicago School? The Development of a Postwar American Sociology,* ed. Gary Alan Fine (Chicago: University of Chicago Press, 1995), 136–61, 138.

15. Bulmer, *Chicago School of Sociology*, 92. Although Park and Burgess rejected reformist impulses as unscientific, their methodology had its origins in the early social survey that (in contrast to its postwar antecedent) measured social problems—levels of unemployment, the absence of playgrounds, or the number of bars—for ameliorative purposes. Converse, *Survey Research*, 37.

16. Wacker, "The Sociology of Race and Ethnicity in the Second Chicago School," 139; Bulmer, *Chicago School of Sociology*, 77, 108; Platt, *A History of Sociological Research Methods in America, 1920–1960*, 13.

17. Bulmer, *Chicago School of Sociology*, 92–93, 100–101.

18. Ibid., 56; 176–78; Dorothy Ross, *The Origins of American Social Science* (Cambridge: Cambridge University Press, 1991), 305; and Platt, *A History of Sociological Research Methods in America, 1920–1960*.

19. Jackson, *Gunnar Myrdal and America's Conscience*, 283–85, quote at 283.

20. Ibid., 283–85; Zane L. Miller, "Pluralism, Chicago School Style: Louis Wirth, the Ghetto, the City, and 'Integration,'" *Journal of Urban History* 18, no. 3 (1992): 251–79, 271; Salerno, *Louis Wirth: A Bio-Bibliography*, 30.

21. Andrew Jewett, *Science, Democracy, and the American University: From the Civil War to the Cold War* (Cambridge: Cambridge University Press, 2012), 273–76.

22. Ibid., 281.

23. Andrew Abbott and Emanuel Gaziano, "Transition and Tradition: Departmental Faculty in the Era of the Second Chicago School," in Fine, *A Second Chicago School?*, 221–72; Vance, "Louis Wirth, 1897–1952," 96; Miller, "Pluralism, Chicago School Style," 271; Salerno, *Louis Wirth: A Bio-Bibliography*, 35, 46; Louis Wirth, "Urbanism as a Way of Life," *American Journal of Sociology* 44 (July 1938): 1–24, 7–8. On the decline of the Chicago School more broadly, see Abbott, *Department and Discipline*; Fine, *A Second Chicago School*.

24. Marjorie L. DeVault, "Knowledge from the Field," in Calhoun, *Sociology in America*, 155–82, 168; Abbott, *Department and Discipline*, 78–79; Abbott and Gaziano, "Transition and Tradition," 257.

25. Abbott and Sparrow, "Hot War, Cold War," 296–97.

26. Solovey, *Shaky Foundations*, chap. 3.

27. Louis Wirth, "Report of Progress," CP (box 4, folder 2) (the date is not given, but this document was in a box marked 1949), 2; "Summary of Review of Activities of CETRRR," November 6, 1951, CP (box 3, folder 19), 2.

28. Louis Wirth, "Proposal for the Support of a Program on Education, Training and Research in Race Relations at the University of Chicago," April 2, 1947, CP (box 2, folder 6), 3.

29. Ibid., 3.

30. Frazier, "Louis Wirth: An Appreciation," 167; Salerno, *Louis Wirth, A Bio-Bibliography*, 26.

31. Louis Wirth, "Proposal for a Conference of Representatives of Educational and Research Institutions Conducting Programs in Race Relations," January 14, 1952, and Letter from Louis Wirth to Maxwell Hahn, Executive Vice President, The Field Foundation Inc. January 15, 1952, CP (box 2, folder 20); Pamphlet by Department of Sociology, University of Chicago titled "Training in Race Relations," July, 1946, CP (box 3, folder 20); CETRRR, Minutes of Meeting of October 8, 1947, CP (box 3, folder 15), 2–3; Memorandum from Harry Walker to Louis Wirth, December 4, 1947, CP (box 3, folder 15), 1–2; Letter from Louis Wirth to Donald Young, General Director, Russell Sage Foundation, May 8, 1940, LWP (box 29, folder 10); Letter from Louis Wirth to Leland DeVinney, January 3, 1952, LWP (box 29, folder 7); Letter from Charles

Dollard to Louis Wirth, January 6, 1947, LWP (box 20, folder 2); Letter from Charles Dollard to Louis Wirth, March 26, 1947, CP (box 1, folder 7). Also see McKee, *Sociology and the Race Problem*, 320–22.

32. See "Project Memorandum, Rockefeller Brothers Fund, American Council on Race Relations," April 1949, folder 472, box 69, series 3, RBF. Also see "Memorandum from Dana S. Creel to files," August 21, 1947, and "Memo from Dana S. Creel to files" May 20, 1947, folder 399, box 37, Series Welfare, RG 2, OMR, RFA. In addition, there were very close connections between CETRRR, the ACRR, and NAIRO. Louis Wirth was president of the ACRR from 1947 to 1951, and Robert Redfield served on the board between 1950 and 1952. Many individuals not associated with CETRRR or the University of Chicago, including many prominent white and African American intellectuals and civil rights workers, served on the ACRR rotating board between 1944 and 1951, including Charles H. Houston of the NAACP Legal Defense Fund; Mary McLeod Bethune of the National Council of Negro Women; Ralph J. Bunche of Howard University; Marshall Field; Charles S. Johnson of Fisk University; the Reverend John LaFarge, associate editor of *America*; Clarence E. Pickett of the American Friends Service Committee; P. L. Prattis, editor of the *Pittsburgh Courier*; Boris Shishkin, director of the American Federation of Labor; Channing H. Tobias, director of the Phelps-Stokes Fund; Walter White of the NAACP; and Donald Young of the SSRC.

33. For examples of requests for advice or materials from activist groups, see: Letter from Richard B. Anliot, Executive Secretary Committee on Discrimination in Higher Education, American Council on Education to Louis Wirth, September 18, 1950, CP (box 1, folder 1); W. Howard Bateson to Louis Wirth, August 29, 1947, CP (box 1, folder 1); Letter from Helen Amerman to Dr. Anna P. Burrell, New York State College for Teachers, Buffalo, New York, November 10, 1950. CP (box 1, folder 1); Letter from Helen Amerman to Phoebe Bridgman, Antioch College, Yellow Springs, Ohio, October 10, 1950, CP (box 1, folder 1); Louis Wirth to H. F. Hancox, Fellowship of Reconciliation, October 14, 1947, and H. F. Hancox to Louis Wirth, September 12, 1947, CP (box 2, folder 20); Letter from William Bradbury to Mr. Dan Bell, Research Consultant, Jewish Labor Committee, December 3, 1952, and letter from Mr. Dan Bell to William Bradbury, November 20, 1952, CP (box 1, folder 3); Letter from Frank S. Loescher, Executive Director, City of Philadelphia Commission on Human Relations to ACRR staff, April 14, 1952, CP (box 27, folder 6).

34. Louis Wirth, "Proposal for the Support of a Program on Education, Training and Research in Race Relations at the University of Chicago," April 2, 1947, CP (box 2, folder 6); Alfred McClung Lee and the ACRR, *Race Riots Aren't Necessary* (New York: Public Affairs Committee, 1945); Robert Weaver and the ACRR, *Community Relations Manual: What to Do about Your Community's Problems of Intergroup Relations* (Chicago: ACRR, 1946); and ACRR, *"To Secure These Rights" in Your Community: A Manual for Discussion, Fact-Finding, and Action in State and Local Communities* (Chicago: ACRR, June 1948).

35. Francis Cherry and C. Borshuk, "Social Action Research and the Commission of Community Interrelations," *Journal of Social Issues* 54, no. 1 (1998): 119–42, 124.

36. "Summary of Review of Activities of CETRRR," November 6, 1951, CP (box 3, folder 19), 2–4.

37. Jewett, *Science, Democracy, and the American University*, 311–12. On the NSF debate, see Solovey, "Riding Natural Scientists' Coattails." On the Cold War context, see Dudziak, *Cold War Civil Rights*; Joel Isaac, "The Human Sciences in Cold War

America," *Historical Journal* 50, no. 3 (2007): 725–46; Schrecker, *No Ivory Tower;* and Von Eschen, *Race against Empire.*

38. Lawrence T. Nichols, "Social Relations Undone: Disciplinary Divergence and Departmental Politics at Harvard, 1946–1970," *American Sociologist* 29 (1998): 83–107; Converse, *Survey Research.*

39. Louis Wirth, "Proposal for the Support of a Program on Education, Training and Research in Race Relations at the University of Chicago," April 2, 1947, CP (box 2, folder 6), 4.

40. Ibid., 4. Also see "Summary of Review of Activities of CETRRR," November 6, 1951, CP (box 3, folder 19), and Letter from Sol Tax, Chairman to Mr. Leland DeVinney, Rockefeller Found June 16, 1953; copy to Miss Florence Anderson, Associate Secretary, Carnegie Corporation of New York, CP (box 4, folder 3).

41. Arnold Rose, *Studies in Reduction of Prejudice: A Memorandum Summarizing Research on Modification of Attitudes* (Chicago: American Council on Race Relations, 1947).

42. Louis Wirth, Introduction to Arnold Rose, *Studies in Reduction of Prejudice.*

43. "Minutes, CETRRR, Meeting of November 3, 1952" CP (box 3, folder 19), 1; "Proposal for budget for Oriental-white intermarriage project" CP (box 3, folder 21).

44. Handwritten notes, "Future of Committee" and Minutes November 3, 1952, CP (box 3, folder 20).

45. Letters from Sol Tax, Chairman to Mr. Leland DeVinney, Rockefeller Found June 16, 1953; copy to Miss Florence Anderson, Associate Secretary, Carnegie Corporation of New York, CP (box 4, folder 3), 3.

46. Louis Wirth, Report to Dean Ralph Tyler and the Carnegie Corporation of New York, May 2, 1949, CP (box 3, folder 17), 3.

47. Letter from Sol Tax, Chairman to Mr. Leland DeVinney, Rockefeller Found June 16, 1953; copy to Miss Florence Anderson, Associate Secretary, Carnegie Corporation of New York, CP (box 4, folder 3), 3.

48. "The University of Chicago, CETRRR Memorandum, May 13, 1952," CP (box 3, folder 28), 3; "Selected List of General Intergroup Relations Materials Available from National Agencies," April 1952, CP (box 13, folder 3). On the extent of intercultural education work in the CPS, see "Newsletter on Workshopper's Intercultural Projects," CP (box 20, folder 6).

49. "The University of Chicago, CETRRR Memorandum, May 13, 1952," CP (box 3, folder 28), 3.

50. On this psychological leaning among sociologists concerned with race more broadly in the postwar years, see McKee, *Sociology and the Race Problem,* chap. 7, and Thomas F. Pettigrew, ed., *The Sociology of Race Relations: Reflection and Reform* (New York: Free Press, 1980).

51. Wirth letter quoted in Memorandum from William C. Bradbury to Sol Tax and Everett Hughes re: "Status of and Proposals for Carrying on the Field Foundation Integration Studies," November 14, 1952, CP (box 6, folder 7), and "The University of Chicago, Memorandum, May 13, 1952," CP (box 3, folder 28).

52. "Minutes, CETRRR, January 27, 1949," CP (box 3, folder 17).

53. "The University of Chicago, Memorandum, May 13, 1952," CP (box 3, folder 28), 3–6.

54. Ibid., 3–4. "Summary of Review of Activities of CETRRR," November 6, 1951, CP (box 3, folder 19), 4. Also see Letters from Sol Tax, Chairman to Mr. Leland DeVinney, Rockefeller Found June 16, 1953, CP (box 4, folder 3), 2.

55. David Bisno, "Racial Integration in the Local Union and the Plant: The Role of the Local Union," CP (box 11, folder 10).

56. Louis Wirth "Report of Progress" CP (box 4, folder 2), 5 (no date, but in 1949 box).

57. CETRRR, *The Dynamics of State Campaigns for Fair Employment Practices Legislation* (Chicago: American Council on Race Relations and The Anti-Defamation League of B'nai B'rith, 1950).

58. CETRRR, *Dynamics of State Campaigns*, 1.

59. Ibid., 12.

60. Ibid., 3–5, 36, 23.

61. Wendell E. Pritchett, *Robert Clifton Weaver and the American City: The Life and Times of an Urban Reformer* (Chicago: University of Chicago Press, 2008), chap. 6.

62. "The University of Chicago, CETRRR Memorandum, May 13, 1952," CP (box 3, folder 28), 2; Letter from Sol Tax, Chairman to Mr. Leland DeVinney, Rockefeller Found June 16, 1953, CP (box 4, folder 3), 2.

63. Letter to E. F. Schietinger from William C. Bradbury, November 24, 1952, CP (box 1, folder 5).

64. Paul B. Sheatsley, "Clyde Hart, In Memoriam," *Public Opinion Quarterly* (1970): 287–88; Shirley Star, "Interracial Tension in Two Areas of Chicago: An Exploratory Approach to the Measurement of Interracial Tension" (PhD diss., University of Chicago, 1950), 15–16.

65. On the tension barometer debate see Leah N. Gordon, "The Individual and 'the General Situation': The Tension Barometer and the Race Problem at the University of Chicago, 1947–1954," *Journal of the History of the Behavioral Sciences* 56, no. 1 (2010): 27–51.

66. In the dissertation that summarized the study, "Interracial Tensions in Two Areas of Chicago," Shirley Star cited Gunnar Myrdal, E. Franklin Frazier, Charles S. Johnson, Maurice Davie, St. Clair Drake, and Horace Cayton to suggest that urban racial tensions resulted ultimately from migration and African American confinement to segregated, overcrowded communities. Star, "Interracial Tensions in Two Areas of Chicago," 1–5.

67. Ibid., 147, 5–7.

68. Ibid., 149.

69. Ibid., 15–16.

70. Ibid., 147.

71. Thomas J. Sugrue, *Sweet Land of Liberty: The Forgotten Struggle for Civil Rights in the North* (New York: Random House, 2008), 157.

72. Star, "Interracial Tensions in Two Areas of Chicago," 147–48.

73. "Race Relations Seminar, February 28, 1949," CP (box 18, folder 4), 1–2.

74. Louis Wirth, "Proposal for the Support of a Program on Education, Training and Research in Race Relations at the University of Chicago," April 2, 1947, CP (box 2, folder 6), 5. "Race Relations Seminar, January 17, 1949," CP (box 18, folder 4), 1.

75. Ibid., 1.

76. Abbott and Sparrow, "Hot War, Cold War"; Bulmer, *Chicago School of Sociology*, 176–78.

77. "Race Relations Seminar, January 17, 1949," CP (box 18, folder 4); "Race Relations Seminar, January 31, 1949," CP (box 18, folder 4), 4.

78. "Race Relations Seminar, January 31, 1949," CP (box 18, folder 4), 3.

79. C. M. Briggs, "An Evaluation of NORC Questionnaire (Survey S-93), P1-Jan 20, 1949," CP (box 18, folder 6).

80. Rose Helper, "Course 403 Seminar in Race Relations, Winter Quarter, Feb 21, 1949, The Study of Intergroup Tensions. The Tension Barometer," CP (box 18, folder 6).

81. John V. Lassoe, "Race Relations Seminar, 432," CP (box 18, folder 6); "Race Relations Seminar, February 28, 1949," CP (box 18, folder 4); Leo Shapiro, "Comments on Proposed Pretest of Intergroup Tension Study," CP (box 18, folder 6).

82. Lewis M. Killian, John Lassoe, Dietrich Reitzes, "Report to Seminar on Barometer of Racial Tensions," no date, but 1949 box, CP (box 18, folder 6).

83. "Race Relations Seminar, February 14, 1949," CP (box 18, folder 4), 1.

84. "Race Relations Seminar, January 31, 1949," CP (box 18, folder 4), 4. Allport used similar language in *The Nature of Prejudice* in 1954. Gordon Allport, *The Nature of Prejudice* (1954; Reading, MA: Addison-Wesley, 1979), xviii.

85. "Race Relations Seminar, February 14, 1949," CP (box 18, folder 4); "Race Relations Seminar, February 28, 1949," CP (box 18, folder 4), 1.

86. "Race Relations Seminar, March 7, 1949," CP (box 18, folder 4), 1.

87. "Race Relations Seminar, February 14, 1949," CP (box 18, folder 4).

88. Star, "Interracial Tensions in Two Areas of Chicago," 8.

89. Donald T. Campbell and Clyde Hart, "Proposal: Exploratory Data Collection on Steepness and Asymmetry of Negro-White 'Boundaries,'" (no date) CP (box 3, folder 20).

90. Joseph D. Lohman and Dietrich C. Reitzes, "Notes on Race Relations in Mass Society," *American Journal of Sociology* 58 (November 1952): 240–46, 240. Also see McKee, *Sociology and the Race Problem*, 297–98.

91. Lohman and Reitzes, "Notes on Race Relations in Mass Society," 242.

92. Chicago Commission on Race Relations, *The Negro in Chicago: A Study of Race Relations and a Race Riot* (Chicago: University of Chicago Press, 1922); Mayor's Commission on Conditions in Harlem (MCCH), *The Complete Report of Mayor LaGuardia's Commission on the Harlem Riot of March 19, 1935* (1935; New York: Arno Press, 1969); O'Connor, *Poverty Knowledge*, chap. 3.

93. Kenesaw M. Landis, National Committee on Segregation in the Nation's Capital, *Segregation in Washington* (Chicago: NCSNC, 1948). For the organization's history, see Wendell E. Pritchett, "A National Issue: Segregation in the District of Columbia and the Civil Rights Movement at Mid Century," *Georgetown Law Journal* 93, no. 4 (2005): 1321–33, 1321.

94. Joseph Lohman, "Residential Segregation: Discriminatory Housing in the Nation's Capital" (mimeographed), and "The Federation of Citizens Associations: Voice of the People?" (mimeographed), both cited in Dietrich C. Reitzes, "Collective Factors in Race Relations" (PhD diss., University of Chicago, 1950), 18–21. This argument is presented in popular form in chapter six, titled "Segregation, Inc.," and chapter seven, titled "Negroes Are Americans," in Landis and NCSNC, *Segregation in Washington*, 30–38 and 39–47.

95. William C. Bradbury Jr., "Racial Discrimination in Federal Employment" (unpublished manuscript for PhD dissertation, Department of Sociology, Columbia University), cited in Reitzes, "Collective Factors in Race Relations," 18–21. This argument is presented in popular form in chapter 10, titled "Uncle Sam's Example," in Landis and NCSNC, *Segregation in Washington*, 60–74.

96. Robert K. Merton, "Discrimination and the American Creed," in *Discrimination and National Welfare*, ed. Robert MacIver (New York: Institute for Religious Studies and Harper, 1949), 99–128; McKee, *Sociology and the Race Problem*, 297–99. On mass society, see Sarah E. Igo, *The Averaged American: Surveys, Citizens, and the Making of a Mass Public* (Cambridge, MA: Harvard University Press, 2007).

97. Reitzes, "Collective Factors in Race Relations," 11.
98. Ibid., emphasis in original. For examples of these themes in Lohman's work on mass society, see Joseph Lohman, "Race Relations in Mass Society," in Race Relations Department, American Missionary Association, "Implementing Civil Rights, Summary Report, Sixth Annual Institute of Race Relations, June 27–July 9, 1949, Fisk University, Nashville, TN" (Nashville: AMA and Fisk University, 1949), 65–67.
99. Dietrich Reitzes, *Negroes and Medicine* (Cambridge: Commonwealth Fund and Harvard University Press, 1958).
100. Lohman and Reitzes, "Notes on Race Relations in Mass Society"; Joseph D. Lohman and Dietrich C. Reitzes, "Deliberately Organized Groups and Racial Behavior," *American Sociological Review* 19, no. 3 (1954): 342–44. "Conference on Research in Human Relations," Rockefeller Foundation, Volume II, Arden House, Harriman, New York, February 28–March 1, 1953, pp. 288–89, 293, folder 100, box 11, series 910, RG 3.1, RF.
101. On the methodological challenges of the second Chicago school, see Abbott, *Department and Discipline*, 62–65; Salerno, *Louis Wirth: A Bio-Bibliography*, 35, 38, 46; Marjorie L. DeVault, "Knowledge from the Field," in Calhoun, *Sociology in America*, 155–82, 163; Wacker, "The Sociology of Race and Ethnicity in the Second Chicago School."
102. On wartime pressures to downplay racial conflict see: Abbott and Sparrow, "The Structures of Sociological Action," 298, 301.
103. Jackson, *Gunnar Myrdal and America's Conscience*, 255; Williams, *Reduction of Intergroup Tensions*, 9; O'Connor, *Poverty Knowledge*, 49.
104. Letter from Robert Weaver to Louis Wirth, March 25, 1947, CP (box 2, folder 12); Robert Weaver, "A Needed Program of Research in Race Relations and Associated Problems," *JNE* 16, no. 2 (1947): 130–35. On Weaver's time at the ACRR, see Pritchett, *Robert Clifton Weaver*, chap. 6. On the decline of institutional economics, see Ross, *Origins of American Social Science*, esp. 419, and Michael A. Bernstein, *A Perilous Progress: Economists and Public Purpose in Twentieth-Century America* (Princeton, NJ: Princeton University Press, 2001), 44–48.
105. Herold C. Hunt, "After Two Years," *Chicago's Schools, Official Organ of the Citizens Schools Committee*, VXVI, October–November 1949, No. 1, pp. 3–4, CP (box 20, folder 6).
106. Ibid.; CETRRR, "Minutes of Meeting of December 11, 1947, University of Chicago," CP (box 3, folder 15); "CETRRR, University of Chicago in Cooperation with the Chicago Public Schools, Meeting of the Citizen's Advisory Committee on the Chicago Public Schools," April 14, 1948, CP (box 3, folder 16).
107. "CETRRR, University of Chicago in Cooperation with the Chicago Public Schools," Meeting of the Citizen's Advisory Committee on the Chicago Public Schools, April 14, 1948, CP (box 3, folder 16), 3; "Minutes, CETRRR, January 27, 1949," CP (box 3, folder 17), 2.
108. CETRRR, "Minutes of Meeting of December 11, 1947, University of Chicago" CP (box 3, folder 15), 4.
109. "Minutes, CETRRR, January 27, 1949," CP (box 3, folder 17), 2.
110. Ibid., 4. "Minutes, Meeting of CETRRR in Joint Session with Cooperating Members of the Faculty, November 8th, 1948," CP (box 3, folder 16), 1.
111. "Minutes, Meeting of CETRRR in Joint Session with Cooperating Members of the Faculty, November 8th, 1948," CP (box 3, folder 16).
112. "CETRRR, "Minutes of Meeting of December 11, 1947, University of Chicago," CP (box 3, folder 15), 3; Louis Wirth, "Committee on Education, Training, and Research

in Race Relations," CP (box 3, folder 15), 2; CETRRR, University of Chicago in Co-operation with the Chicago Public Schools," Meeting of the Citizen's Advisory Committee on the Chicago Public Schools, April 14, 1948, CP (box 3, folder 16), 3.

113. Polly Graham, Muriel Herson, Irene Jerison, and Ruth Weaver, "A Study of the Re-districting of the Chicago Public Elementary Schools" (master's thesis, University of Chicago, 1951), CP (box 9, folder 2), 1.

114. Ibid., 3.

115. Polly Graham, Ruth Weaver Halpern, Muriel Herson, and Irene Jerison. "An Investi-gation of the Chicago School Redistricting Program" (PhD diss., University of Chi-cago, 1952), 1, 18.

116. Louis Wirth, "Committee on Education, Training, and Research in Race Relations," no date, CP (box 3, folder 15), 5; "CETRRR, University of Chicago in Cooperation with the Chicago Public Schools," Meeting of the Citizen's Advisory Committee on the Chicago Public Schools, April 14, 1948, CP (box 3, folder 16), 4–5.

117. On work of this type in industry, public housing, and the army, see McKee, *Sociology and the Race Problem*, 309–10; Rose, *Studies in Reduction of Prejudice*, part 1, page 10; Williams, *Reduction of Intergroup Tensions*, 22–23.

118. Graham et al., "Investigation of the Chicago School Redistricting Program," 3–4, 52, 11–13, 15. On sociological interest in "natural experiments" of desegregation, see McKee, *Sociology and the Race Problem*, 307–19.

119. CETRRR, University of Chicago in Cooperation with the Chicago Public Schools "Minutes of the Meeting of the Technical Committee on Chicago Public Schools, University of Chicago, September 30, 1948" CP (box 20, folder 5), 2.

120. Ibid., 2.

121. Ibid., 2–3. "Report on the Chicago Public Elementary School Redistricting Program," CETRRR, April 1953, CP (box 12, folder 8); Muriel Herson and William C. Bradbury, "Report on the Chicago Public Elementary School Redistricting Program," CETRRR, April 1953, CP (box 12, folder 8), 4–5.

122. Graham et al., "Investigation of the Chicago School Redistricting Program," 1.

123. Ibid., 6–8.

124. The maps produced also proved useful in later integration struggles by proving that many white schools had undercounted their rooms to avoid integration. Letter from Harold Baron, Research Dept., the Chicago Urban League to Sol Tax, February 16, 1962, CP (box 2, folder 9). In a report to Wirth, Leonard Breen explained "the lack of readily available data on students as related to schools has been a constant source of difficulty and frustration to the many persons and departments concerned with planning for optimal school boundaries." Leonard Z. Breen, "Redistricting the Public Academic High Schools of Chicago: A Proposed Procedure," March 1953, CP (box 8, folder 16). For examples of schools failing to provide accurate informa-tion in an attempt to resist redistricting, see "Memorandum to Dr. Don C. Rogers and Dr. Paul R. Pierce from Thos. J. Higgins, Director Building Surveys, February 15, 1949," CP (box 8, folder 7). For an example of resistance to redistricting from a group of white parents, see "Memorandum from Louis Wirth, Chairman of the Committee on the Chicago Public Schools to Mr. John Christie, Secretary of the North-East Ogden Improvement Association," June 17, 1948, CP (box 8, folder 7). In her discussion of CETRRR attempts at redistricting, Kathryn Neckerman also found evidence of resistance from school officials. Kathryn M. Neckerman, *Schools Betrayed: Roots of Failure in Inner-City Education* (Chicago: University of Chicago Press, 2007), 98–105.

125. Leonard Breen, "A Proposed Methodology to Redistrict the Public Academic High Schools of Chicago, IL," and "Redistricting the Public Academic High Schools of Chicago: A Proposed Procedure," CP (box 8, folder 9). Surveys and maps prepared in anticipation of this project are also available in CP (box 8, folders 11, 12, 14, 16); "Minutes, CETRRR, Meeting of October 17, 1952," CP (box 3, folder 20); "Minutes: CETRRR, Meeting of November 3, 1952," CP (box 3, folder 20).

126. A 1949 newsletter reported a wide array of curricular and intercultural educational programs conducted in the schools, precisely the types of add-on curricular elements Wirth believed to be irrelevant. "Newsletter on Workshopper's Intercultural Projects," CP (box 20, folder 6).

127. "Faculty Seminar, University of Chicago, Division of the Social Sciences," February 22, 1949, CP (box 6, folder 6), 1.

128. Ibid., 1.

129. The termination of Rockefeller and Carnegie grants at the end of the allotted five years made CETRRR essentially defunct by 1954. "Minutes, CETRRR, Meeting of January 27, 1953," CP (box 3, folder 21), 4–5.

CHAPTER FOUR

1. Charles S. Johnson, "Review of the Fourth Institute of Race Relations," in AMA, "Race Relations in Human Relations, Summary Report, Fourth Annual Institute of Race Relations, July 1–19, 1947, Fisk University, Nashville, TN" (Nashville: AMA and Fisk University, 1947), viii.

2. For an institutional analysis of the Race Relations Institutes, see Katrina Marie Sanders, "Building Racial Tolerance through Education: The Fisk University Race Relations Institute, 1944–1969" (PhD diss., University of Illinois at Urbana-Champaign, 1997); Katrina M. Sanders, *"Intelligent and Effective Direction": The Fisk University Race Relations Institute and the Struggle for Civil Rights, 1944–1969* (New York: Peter Lang, 2005); and Patrick J. Gilpin and Marybeth Gasman, *Charles S. Johnson: Leadership beyond the Veil in the Age of Jim Crow* (Albany: State University of New York Press, 2003), chaps. 13 and 14.

3. On the interwar African American and "interracial lefts," see Thomas J. Sugrue, *Sweet Land of Liberty: The Forgotten Struggle for Civil Rights in the North* (New York: Random House, 2008); Jonathan Scott Holloway, *Confronting the Veil: Abram Harris Jr., E. Franklin Frazier, and Ralph Bunche, 1919–1941* (Chapel Hill: University of North Carolina Press, 2002); and Nikhil Pal Singh, *Black Is a Country: Race and the Unfinished Struggle for Democracy* (Cambridge, MA: Harvard University Press, 2004).

4. See chapter one.

5. Stephen Park Turner and Jonathan H. Turner, *The Impossible Science: An Institutional Analysis of American Sociology* (Newbury Park, CA: Sage Publications, 1990), 125; Jonathan Scott Holloway and Ben Keppel, eds., *Black Scholars on the Line: Race, Social Science, and American Thought in the Twentieth Century* (Notre Dame, IN: University of Notre Dame Press, 2007), 10, 18, 21; John H. Stanfield, *Philanthropy and Jim Crow in American Social Science* (Westport, CT: Greenwood Press, 1985).

6. Nikhil Singh's concept of the "African American counter-public sphere," George Lipsitz's focus on the "black spatial imaginary," and Robin Kelley's history of African American radicalism all illustrate the crucial critiques of American liberalism, individualism, materialism, and inequality that emerged from African American radical, and often more moderate, intellectual traditions. George Lipsitz, *How Racism Takes Place* (Philadelphia: Temple University Press, 2011); Singh, *Black Is a Country*, 102;

Robin D. G. Kelley, *Freedom Dreams: The Black Radical Imagination* (Boston: Beacon Press, 2002).

7.   On the centrality of economic issues to African American grassroots politics, especially in the North and West but also in the South, see Glenda Gilmore, *Defying Dixie: The Radical Roots of Civil Rights, 1900–1950* (New York: W. W. Norton, 2008); Robin D. G. Kelley, *Hammer and Hoe: Alabama Communists during the Great Depression* (Chapel Hill: University of North Carolina Press, 1990); Robin D. G. Kelley, *Race Rebels, Culture, Politics, and the Black Working Class* (New York: Free Press, 1994); Thomas F. Jackson, *From Civil Rights to Human Rights: Martin Luther King Jr., and the Struggle for Economic Justice* (Philadelphia: University of Pennsylvania Press, 2007); and Sugrue, *Sweet Land*.

8.   On protests at HBCUs, especially Fisk, in the 1920s, see Raymond Wolters, *The New Negro on Campus: Black College Rebellions of the 1920s* (Princeton, NJ: Princeton University Press, 1975), chap. 2; and James Anderson, *The Education of Blacks in the South, 1860–1935* (Chapel Hill: University of North Carolina Press, 1988), chap. 7.

9.   Sugrue, *Sweet Land*, 23, 34, 39–58; on the "Amenia ideal," see Holloway, *Confronting the Veil*, 15. That communists were some of the most vocal, visible, and controversial advocates of racial justice in the first three decades of the twentieth century, a role vividly exhibited in the Scottsboro trial, contributed to this pattern. Gilmore, *Defying Dixie*; James Goodman, *Stories of Scottsboro* (New York: Vintage Books, 1995); on the international implications of black leftist thought, see Singh, *Black Is a Country*; and Von Eschen, *Race against Empire*.

10. David Levering Lewis, foreword to Patrick J. Gilpin and Marybeth Gasman, *Charles S. Johnson: Leadership beyond the Veil in the Age of Jim Crow* (Albany: State University of New York Press, 2003); Gilpin and Gasman, *Charles S. Johnson*, x–xi.

11. Richard Robbins, *Sideline Activist: Charles S. Johnson and the Struggle for Civil Rights* (Jackson: University Press of Mississippi, 1996), 180–81, quoted in Sanders, *Intelligent and Effective Direction*, 47–48.

12. Gilpin and Gasman, *Charles S. Johnson*, 93–97; Sanders, *Intelligent and Effective Direction*, 105; O'Connor, *Poverty Knowledge*, 79–80.

13. Gilpin and Gasman, *Charles S. Johnson*, 78; Chicago Commission on Race Relations (CCRR), *The Negro in Chicago: A Study of Race Relations and a Race Riot* (Chicago: University of Chicago Press, 1922).

14. Lewis, foreword to Gilpin and Gasman, *Charles S. Johnson*; Gilpin and Gasman, *Charles S. Johnson*, xi.

15. Charles S. Johnson, *Shadow of the Plantation* (1934; New Brunswick, NJ: Transaction, 1996), 208, 212.

16. CCRR, *The Negro in Chicago*, chaps. 9 and 10; O'Connor, *Poverty Knowledge*, 80.

17. Gilpin and Gasman, *Charles S. Johnson*, 94–95.

18. "Democracy in Action," 1951, box 2, folder 2, RRIP, 1.

19. Gilpin and Gasman, *Charles S. Johnson*, 94–95, 117–24, 177.

20. Ibid., 176–77.

21. Ibid., 102–3.

22. RRD, AMA, *If Your Next Neighbors Are Negroes* (Nashville: RRD, AMA, and Fisk University, 1948), in box 1, folder 7, RRIP; Margaret C. McCulloch, *Segregation: A Challenge to Democracy* (Nashville: RRD, AMA, and Fisk University, 1950); and Margaret C. McCulloch, *Integration: Promise, Process, Problems* (Nashville: RRD, AMA, and Fisk University, 1952).

23. Gilpin and Gasman, *Charles S. Johnson*, 15, 175, 179–80. RRD, AMA Board of Home

Missions, Congregational Christian Churches, *This Is the Task: The Findings of the Trenton, New Jersey Human Relations Self-Survey, A Reporter's View Done by William Dwyer of the Trenton Times, Reprinted with the Generous Cooperation of That Newspaper* (Nashville: Fisk University, 1955).

24. Charles S. Johnson, foreword, "Race Relations in Human Relations," RRD, AMA, "Race Relations in Human Relations, Summary Report, Second Annual Institute of Race Relations, June 2–21, 1945, Fisk University, Nashville, TN" (Nashville: AMA and Fisk University, 1945), i–ii.

25. "Announcement of the First Institute of Race Relations, held under the auspices of the Race Relations Division of the AMA, held at the Social Sciences Institute, Fisk University, July 3–21, 1944," box 36, folder 9, JP. See RRD, AMA, "Race Relations in Human Relations, Summary Report, Second Annual Institute of Race Relations, June 2–21, 1945, Fisk University, Nashville, TN" (Nashville: AMA and Fisk University, 1945); RRD, AMA, "Race Relations in Human Relations: Summary Report: Third Annual Institute of Race Relations, July 1–20, 1946, Fisk University, Nashville, TN" (Nashville: AMA and Fisk University, 1946); RRD, AMA, "Race Relations in Human Relations: Summary Report: Fourth Annual Institute of Race Relations, July 1–19, 1947, Fisk University, Nashville, TN" (Nashville: AMA and Fisk University, 1947); RRD, AMA, "Implementing Civil Rights, Summary Report, Sixth Annual Institute of Race Relations, June 27–July 9, 1949, Fisk University, Nashville, TN" (Nashville: AMA and Fisk University, 1949); RRD, AMA, "Human Rights and Human Relations," A Report of Discussions of the Sixth Annual Institute of Race Relations (Nashville: AMA and Fisk University, 1951); RRD, AMA, "Next Steps in Integration, A Summary of Discussions of the Tenth Annual Race Relations Institute," Fisk University, June 29–July 11, 1953; RRD, Division of Higher Education and the AMA, "Human Rights—the New Century, Summaries of Presentations, 20th Annual Institute of Race Relations, Fisk U, Nashville, TN, June 24–July 6, 1963" (Nashville: AMA and RRD, 1963); RRD, AMA, "Race: The New Challenge, The 21st Annual Institute of Race Relations," June 29–July 11, 1964 (Nashville: AMA and Fisk University, 1964); RRD, AMA, "Human Rights in the Great Society," The 22nd Annual Institute of Race Relations, June 28–July 10, 1965 (Nashville: AMA and Fisk University, 1965). All of the institute summaries are available in either the JP or the RRIP. Unless a summary is only available at the Fisk Special Collections, I have cited it as a published document. (Throughout the rest of the notes, I will refer to the institute summaries as "Summary 1945," "Summary 1947," etc.) After 1951 the structure was somewhat altered, but laying out scientific agendas still took priority at the outset of the Institutes. On this 1951 shift, see Sanders, *Intelligent and Effective Direction*, 51.

26. The list included Harvard University social psychologist Gordon Allport, psychiatrist Kenneth Clark, sociologist Horace Cayton, Chicago anthropologist Allison Davis, Tulane sociologist Clarence Glick, psychologist Eugene Hartley, Columbia University psychologist Otto Klineberg, Chicago anthropologist Robert Redfield, Atlanta University sociologist Ira de. A. Reid, Rutgers biologist/anthropologist M. F. Ashley Montagu, Howard University professor of education Charles H. Thompson, Duke University sociologist Edgar T. Thompson, historians Eric Williams and C. Vann Woodward, Chicago sociologist Louis Wirth, and economist Robert Weaver.

27. AMA secretary Fred L. Brownlee, president of the Julius Rosenwald Fund Edwin Embree, and director of schools for the AMA Ruth Morton helped organize the yearly meetings. Executive director of the National Urban League Lester Granger, NAACP lawyers Charles H. Houston and Thurgood Marshall, NAACP leader Roy Wilkins,

director of the Southern Regional Council Guy B. Johnson, president of the United Transport Service Employees of America Willard Townsend, and intercultural educator Rachel Davis DuBois regularly gave presentations and led sessions.

28. "Announcement of the First Institute of Race Relations, held under the auspices of the Race Relations Division of the AMA, held at the Social Sciences Institute, Fisk University, July 3–21, 1944," box 36, folder 9, JP.

29. "A New Century a New Day" (1946), box 29, folder 1, JP, esp. 14. Sanders, *Intelligent and Effective Direction*, 51; Charles S. Johnson, "General Statement by the Director of the Race Relations Division of the AMA," November 30, 1943, box 29, folder 3, JP.

30. Charles S. Johnson, "General Statement by the Director of the Race Relations Division of the AMA, November 30, 1943," box 29, folder 3, JP. Also see Herman H. Long, director, RRD, "Ten Years Perspective on Our Work in Race Relations: Report to the Joint Meeting of the AMA Divisional Committee and the Policy and Planning Committee of the Board of Home Missions of the Congregational and Christian Churches," Deering, New Hampshire, June 16–17, 1953, box 33, folder 9, JP, Fisk University Special Collections, Fisk University, Nashville, TN, 3.

31. Charles S. Johnson, "Review of the Fourth Institute of Race Relations," Summary 1947, ii.

32. Nathan Ackerman, "The Psychiatrist and Race Relations," Summary 1947, 26–27. For a brief biography of Ackerman, see Donna R. Kemp, *Mental Health in America: A Reference Handbook* (Santa Barbara, CA: ABC-CLIO, 2007), 148.

33. Smiley Blanton, "The Basis of Brotherhood," Summary 1946, 21; Smiley Blanton, "An Analysis of Prejudice," Summary 1946, 18–19; Smiley Blanton, "Managing Your Love and Hate," Summary 1949, 2.

34. Sol W. Ginsburg, "Psychiatry and Group Relations," Summary 1951, 22.

35. Gordon Allport, "Some Roots of Prejudice," Summary, 1946, 19.

36. Nathan Ackerman, "The Psychiatrist and Race Relations," Summary 1947, 26–27.

37. Sol W. Ginsburg, "Psychiatry and Group Relations," Summary 1951, 22.

38. Still, since the RRI were a self-selecting group, presumably most intellectuals willing to attend were, like Allport, firm supporters of legal desegregation. Helen McLean, "Frightened People," Summary 1945, 19; Helen V. McLean, "Some Unconscious Aspects of Racial Conflict," Summary 1945, 21, Gordon Allport, "The Psychology of Rumor," Summary 1946, 17; Gordon Allport, "Some Roots of Prejudice," Summary, 1946, 19; Smiley Blanton, "The Basis of Brotherhood," Summary 1946, 21; Smiley Blanton, "An Analysis of Prejudice," Summary 1946, 18–19; Nathan Ackerman, "The Psychiatrist and Race Relations," Summary 1947, 26–27; Smiley Blanton, "Managing Your Love and Hate," Summary 1949, 2; Janet McKenzie Rioch, "A Theory of Interpersonal Relations," Summary 1951, 20–21; Sol W. Ginsburg, "Psychiatry and Group Relations," Summary 1951, 22.

39. I have included psychologist Kenneth Clark, who focused on black psychology rather than white prejudice, in this group because his RRI presentations theoretically aligned more closely with it.

40. Von Eschen, *Race against Empire*; Gilpin and Gasman, *Charles S. Johnson*, 99–104.

41. Ina C. Brown, "Race Anthropologically and Socially Defined," Summary 1945, 11; Ina C. Brown, "Race Defined Anthropologically and Sociologically," Summary 1947, 9–10; Ina C. Brown, "Race Defined Anthropologically and Sociologically," Summary 1951, 15–17. For a broader discussion of these anthropological frameworks, especially as they emerged from Franz Boas, Margaret Mead, and Ruth Benedict, see Zoë

Burkholder, *Color in the Classroom: How American Schools Taught Race, 1900–1954* (New York: Oxford University Press, 2011).

42. On the wartime African American popular front and its decline in the McCarthy era, see Singh, *Black Is a Country*, chaps. 4 and 5; and Von Eschen, *Race against Empire*.
43. Charles S. Johnson, "World Patterns of Race Relations," Summary 1945, 16.
44. Ibid., 16.
45. Ibid., 18.
46. Johnson, "A New Frame of Reference for Race Relations," Summary 1949, vi.
47. Edgar T. Thompson, "Race and Race Relations," Summary 1945, 12; Edgar T. Thompson, "The Plantation and Other Racial Situations," Summary 1945, 14–15.
48. Gilpin and Gasman, *Charles S. Johnson*, 103.
49. Reginald Barrett, "The Changing Context of Race Relations," Summary 1951, 24.
50. Ibid., 25.
51. Charles S. Johnson, "Equity and Eventualism," Introductory Address, Twelfth Annual Institute of Race Relations, June 27, 1955, box 38, folder 11, JP.
52. Ibid., 8
53. Ibid., 8–12.
54. Robert Weaver, "Recent Developments in Urban Housing and Their Implications for Minorities," Twelfth Annual Institute of Race Relations, June 29, 1955, box 38, folder 11, JP.
55. Ibid., 3–4
56. Edwin Embree, "World Patterns of Race Relations," Summary 1945, 2–4; Gilpin and Gasman, *Charles S. Johnson*, 186–189; Edwin Embree, "Education for the New World," Summary 1945, 4.
57. Clarence Glick, "Racial Attitudes and Group Tensions," Summary 1947, 36–37. Also see Clarence Glick, "A Sociological Approach to the Understanding of Race Relations" and "Discussion," Summary 1947, 10–16. Clarence Glick, "Racial Attitudes and Group Tensions," Summary 1947, 36–37.
58. Ibid., 38–40.
59. Ibid., 40; Clarence Glick, "A Sociological Approach to the Understanding of Race Relations" and "Discussion," Summary 1947, 11.
60. Clarence Glick, "Racial Attitudes and Group Tensions," Summary 1947, 40.
61. Horace Cayton, "The Psychological Approach to Race Relations," Summary 1947, 21.
62. Ibid., 23.
63. Arnold Rose, Kenneth Clark, and Horace Cayton, Panel Discussion, Summary 1947, 28; Kenneth Clark, "Psychological Aspects of American Race Relations," Summary 1947, 24.
64. Kenneth Clark, "Psychological Aspects of American Race Relations," Summary 1947, 24.
65. Horace Cayton, "The Psychological Approach to Race Relations," Summary 1947, 23.
66. Arnold Rose, Kenneth Clark, and Horace Cayton, Panel Discussion, Summary 1947, 29.
67. Ibid., 30.
68. Ibid., 31.
69. Turner and Turner, *The Impossible Science*, 125; Holloway and Keppel, *Black Scholars on the Line*, 10, 18, 21.
70. As evidence of the challenges thinkers discussing exploitation faced amid anticommunism, RRI participant M. F. Ashley Montagu would, in 1954, be dismissed from his post at Rutgers University and be unable to find a subsequent university appointment due to communist leanings. J. Marks, "Race across the Physical-Cultural Divide

in American Anthropology," in *A New History of Anthropology*, ed. Henrika Kuklick (Malden, MA: Blackwell, 2008).

71. Jackson, *Gunnar Myrdal and America's Conscience*, 234–45; Michael Klarman, *From Jim Crow to Civil Rights: The Supreme Court and the Struggle for Racial Equality* (New York: Oxford University Press, 2004), chap. 4.

72. Alan Brinkley, *The End of Reform: New Deal Liberalism in Recession and War* (New York: Vintage Books, 1995) 139, 171, 212–26, 263–64; Sugrue, *Sweet Land*, 92–96, 101–2, 110–11.

73. Brinkley, *End of Reform*, 139, 171; Mark Brilliant, *The Color of America Has Changed* (Oxford: Oxford University Press, 2010); Chen, *Fifth Freedom*; Sugrue, *Sweet Land*.

74. Willard Townsend, "The Road to Peace," Summary 1945, 124–25.

75. Louis Wirth, "City Planning and Racial Policy," Summary 1945, 31–32; Louis Wirth, "Positive and Negative Aspects of Present Day Race Relations," Summary 1945, 121–22.

76. On full employment, see Brinkley, *End of Reform*, chap. 10; and David Ciepley, *Liberalism in the Shadow of Totalitarianism* (Cambridge, MA: Harvard University Press, 2006), 84, 171.

77. William Y. Bell, "Lay-Offs, Reconversion, Reemployment, and the Future Status of the Negro Industrial Worker," Summary 1945, 52.

78. "Panel: Employment and Labor Problems and Race Relations," Summary 1945, 57.

79. Robert R. Taylor, "The American City Faces the Future," Summary 1945, 57–58.

80. William Y. Bell, "Lay-Offs, Reconversion, Reemployment and the Future Status of the Negro Industrial Worker," Summary 1945, 52.

81. Robert Weaver, *The Negro Ghetto* (1948; New York: Russell and Russell, 1967); Wendell E. Pritchett, *Robert Clifton Weaver and the American City: The Life and Times of an Urban Reformer* (Chicago: University of Chicago Press, 2008).

82. Frank Horne, "Federal Housing and Race Relations," Summary 1945, 59.

83. Frayser T. Lane, Herman Long, Robert Taylor, R. Maurice Moss, DeHart Hubbard, Frank Horne, Robert Weaver, "Panel: Housing Problems and Race Relations," Summary 1945, 68–70.

84. RRD, AMA, *If Your Next Neighbors Are Negroes* (Nashville: RRD, AMA, and Fisk University, 1948), in box 1, folder 7, RRIP, and Kenesaw M. Landis, National Committee on Segregation in the Nation's Capital, *Segregation in Washington* (Chicago: NCSNC, 1948), 30–38 and 39–47.

85. See Herman H. Long, "The Restrictive Covenant and Race Relations," Summary 1945, 66–68; Frayser T. Lane, Herman Long, Robert Taylor, R. Maurice Moss, DeHart Hubbard, Frank Horne, Robert Weaver, "Panel: Housing Problems and Race Relations" Summary 1945, 68–70; Corinne Robinson, DeHart Hubbard, Frayser T. Lane, and Herman Long, "Community Adjustment Problems in Housing," 48–50, Summary 1947.

86. Fred Brownlee, "The Church and Race Relations," Summary 1945, 24–25; Samuel Kinchelee, "The Personal vs. the Categorical in Race Relations," Summary 1945, 27–28. Supporters of intercultural education such as Rachel Davis DuBois were frequently on the Institute faculty as well. Rachel Davis DuBois, "Intercultural Education and Race Relations," Summary 1945, 88–89.

87. Lucy Randolph Mason, George L. P. Weaver, William Y. Bell, and R. Maurice Moss, "Panel: Employment and Labor Problems and Race Relations," Summary 1945, 56. For examples, see Sarah Southall, "A Management Program of Fair Employment," Summary 1947, 47; Sarah Southall, "Special Community Problems in Effecting Fair

Employment Policy in Border and Southern States," Summary 1947, 47–49; and Willard Townsend, Jerome Holland, George Weaver, Panel, Summary 1947, 55–57.

88. Sugrue, *Sweet Land*, xvii, 54; Brinkley, *End of Reform*, 140–41, 170–71, 219, 263–64; Ciepley, *Liberalism in the Shadow of Totalitarianism*, 8.

89. Brinkley, *End of Reform*, 141.

90. Sugrue, *Sweet Land*, 23; Gilmore, *Defying Dixie*. Like white research universities, HB-CUs often terminated members with proven communist sympathies. Johnson fired two faculty members for supposed communist leanings, one in 1949 and one in 1955. Marable, *Race, Reform, and Rebellion*, Kindle edition, location 394–414 of 4724; Von Eschen, *Race against Empire*, 135.

91. Brinkley, *End of Reform*, 10, 170–71; Sugrue, *Sweet Land*, 54–56; Borstelmann, *Cold War and the Color Line*; Dudziak, *Cold War Civil Rights*; Von Eschen, *Race against Empire*.

92. Johnson, "A New Frame of Reference for Race Relations," Summary 1949, i; Johnson, "Human Rights and Human Relations," Summary 1951, 6.

93. Johnson, "Human Rights and Human Relations," Summary 1951, 5; Johnson, "A New Frame of Reference for Race Relations," Summary 1949, i; Herman Long, "Overview," Summary 1953.

94. "Next Steps in Integration," pamphlet advertising the 10th Annual Institute of Race Relations, June 29–July 11, 1953, box 2, folder 4, RRIP, 3.

95. Johnson, "Human Rights and Human Relations," Summary 1951, 5–6.

96. Ibid., 8–10; Carol Anderson, *Eyes off the Prize: The United Nations and the African American Struggle for Human Rights, 1944–1955* (Cambridge: Cambridge University Press, 2003).

97. Johnson, "Keynote: Human Rights and Human Relations," Summary 1951, 9–10. Herman Long, "Overview," Summary 1953, 56. Johnson and Long's international human rights rhetoric reflect the opportunities Cold War pressures provided civil rights activists with a domestic focus, which Mary Dudziak describes, as well as the costs of the Cold War paradigm, which Glenda Gilmore is right to note "swept economic and public policy issues off the table and forced limited change only within the system." Gilmore, *Defying Dixie*, Kindle edition, location 274–88; Dudziak, *Cold War Civil Rights*.

98. Jackson, *From Civil Rights to Human Rights*; Anderson; *Eyes off the Prize*; Von Eschen, *Race against Empire*.

99. Johnson, "Keynote: Human Rights and Human Relations," Summary 1951, 9–10.

100. Herman Long, "Overview," Summary 1953, 56; also see Ruth Morton, "The Institute in the A.M.A.'s Program," Summary 1949, xi; and Fred L. Brownlee, "The Institute and the AMA," Summary 1951, 12–13.

101. "Panel: Federal Agencies and National Racial Policy," Summary 1945, 45–46. Charles Houston, "Recent Trends in Civil Rights," Summary 1945, 42–44; Klarman, *From Jim Crow to Civil Rights*, 213. For examples of the focus on FEPC, restrictive covenants, and court strategies in the 1945–47 years, see Charles Houston, "Recent Trends in Civil Rights," Summary 1945, 44; Charles Houston, "The Fair Employment Practice Committee," Summary 1945, 39–40; Robert C. Weaver, "Race Relations and the Federal Government," Summary 1945, 37–39; "Federal Agencies and National Racial Policy" and "Employment and Labor Problems and Race Relations" in the Summary 1945; "Employment and Labor"; "Community Programs and Techniques in Race Relations, Summary 1946; and "Management, Labor, and Employment Problems," "Legal Protections and Minority Rights," and "Politics and Labor," Summary 1947.

102. Gilpin and Gasman, *Charles S. Johnson*, 169. Klarman, *From Jim Crow to Civil Rights*, 290–92, 253–61.

103. Summary 1949; Summary 1951; Summary 1953; Summary 1954; Summary 1963; Margaret C. McCulloch, *Segregation: A Challenge to Democracy* (Nashville: RRD, AMA, and Fisk University, 1950); and Margaret C. McCulloch, *Integration: Promise, Process, Problems* (Nashville: RRD, AMA, and Fisk University, 1952).

104. Charles Houston, "Legal Aspects of Industrial Democracy," Summary, 1949, 29–31.

105. This decline at the RRI parallels patterns Risa Goluboff emphasizes in which labor-based civil rights doctrine was eclipsed by the NAACP's post-1950 shift in strategy leading to *Brown v. Board*. Risa L. Goluboff, *The Lost Promise of Civil Rights* (Cambridge, MA: Harvard University Press, 2007).

106. Lester Granger, Panel, Summary 1949, 48g; Charles Houston, "Legal Aspects of Industrial Democracy," Summary 1949, 29–31.

107. In response to criticism that there was too much repetition in the presentations, the staff altered the institute structure and replaced the first week of presentations on "Race and Racial Theories" with similar material presented in introductory addresses after 1951. Sanders, *Intelligent and Effective Direction*, 51.

108. Summary 1953.

109. Brooks Hays, "Civil Rights and Political Expediency," Summary 1949, 25–30.

110. Ibid., 27–28.

111. Charles Abrams, "The Limits of Law in Housing and Social Action," speech delivered at the Twelfth Annual Institute of Race Relations, June 29, 1955, box 38, folder 9, JP, 4–5.

112. Herman Long, "Human Rights—The New Century," Summary 1963, 7–11, 10.

113. In 1963, for example, government officials made up a significant proportion of the Institutes faculty, including individuals working for the US Office of Equal Economic Opportunity; the Office of Education of the US Department of Health, Education, and Welfare; the US Department of Labor; the Department of Justice; and the US Commission on Civil Rights, as well as many state human relations commissions. Summary 1963. On the bureaucratization of civil rights protest, see McKee, *Sociology and the Race Problem*, 347.

114. At the same time that "greater advances are made toward equal rights and opportunities," Long believed that the personal and psychological dimensions of African American identity, which he noted James Baldwin's literature and Robert Park's interwar work on the consequences of social "marginality" illuminated—were likely to "become a part of the orientation and the meaning of life in the Negro community." Long, "Human Rights—The New Century," 11. On the political implications of damage imagery in the twentieth century and especially from the 1960s through the 1980s, see Daryl Michael Scott, *Contempt and Pity: Social Policy and the Image of the Damaged Black Psyche, 1880–1996* (Chapel Hill: University of North Carolina Press, 1997); O'Connor, *Poverty Knowledge*; Michael B. Katz, *The Undeserving Poor: From the War on Poverty to the War on Welfare* (New York: Pantheon, 1989); and Michael B. Katz, *The Undeserving Poor: America's Enduring Confrontation with Poverty*, 2nd ed. (New York: Oxford University Press, 2013).

115. Hobart Taylor, "Federal Instrumentation of Equal Job Opportunity," 57–61; Eliot Shirk, "State Action for Equal Opportunity," 62–66.

116. Shirk, "State Action for Equal Opportunity," 65–67. On this focus on outcomes in President Johnson and Martin Luther King Jr.'s thought, see: http://www.lbjlib.utexas .edu/johnson/archives.hom/speeches.hom/650604.asp, accessed February 14, 2013;

Ira Katznelson, *When Affirmative Action Was White: An Untold History of Racial Inequality in Twentieth-Century America* (New York: Norton, 2005); Rev. Dr. Martin Luther King Jr., "Seventh Annual Gandhi Memorial Lecture, Howard University," November 6, 1966, cited in Thomas F. Jackson, *From Civil Rights to Human Rights: Martin Luther King, Jr. and the Struggle for Economic Justice* (Philadelphia: University of Pennsylvania Press, 2007), 299.

117. On the limited impact these structures had on actual patterns of discrimination, see McKee, *Sociology and the Race Problem*, 347.

118. Pettigrew, *The Sociology of Race Relations*, 240–41.

119. Michael B. Katz and Mark J. Stern, *One Nation Divisible: What America Was and What It Is Becoming* (New York: Russell Sage Foundation, 2006), 91–92.

120. Sugrue, *Sweet Land*, 247–49, chap. 7, quote at 247.

121. Charles S. Johnson, "Interpretive Summary of Institute Discussions," Summary 1951, 88.

122. Singh, *Black Is a Country*, chaps. 3 and 4.

123. Ibid., 102; Michael C. Dawson, *Black Visions: The Roots of Contemporary African-American Political Ideologies* (Chicago: University of Chicago Press, 2001); Lipsitz, *How Racism Takes Place*; Kelley, *Freedom Dreams* address varieties of black leftist thought.

CHAPTER FIVE

1. Martin D. Jenkins, "Editorial Comment: Education for Racial Understanding," *JNE* 13, no. 3 (1944): 266–67.

2. Ibid.

3. On the "Amenia ideal" and the political milieu at Howard in the 1930s, see Jonathan Scott Holloway, *Confronting the Veil: Abram Harris Jr., E. Franklin Frazier, and Ralph Bunche, 1919–1941* (Chapel Hill: University of North Carolina Press, 2002).

4. "Editorial Comment, Why a JNE," *JNE* 1, no. 1 (1932): 1–4.

5. Prominent civil rights activists and black intellectuals—philosopher Alain Locke; political scientist Ralph Bunche; economist Robert Weaver; sociologist Charles S. Johnson; NAACP leaders Roy Wilkins, Walter White, and Thurgood Marshall; president of Atlanta University Rufus Clement; media specialist and future advisor to Martin Luther King Jr. L. D. Reddick; and director of Tuskegee Institute's School of Education J. Max Bond—published regularly in the *JNE*.

6. Holloway, *Confronting the Veil*.

7. On wartime enthusiasm for unity and concern with prejudice, see Mark Brilliant, *The Color of America Has Changed: How Racial Diversity Shaped Civil Rights Reform in California, 1941–1978* (New York: Oxford University Press, 2010), chap. 1; Walter A. Jackson, *Gunnar Myrdal and America's Conscience: Social Engineering and Racial Liberalism, 1938–1987* (Chapel Hill: University of North Carolina Press, 1990); and Barbara D. Savage, *Broadcasting Freedom: Radio, War, and the Politics of Race, 1939–1948* (Chapel Hill: University of North Carolina Press, 1999).

8. On the NAACP's "immaterial harm" strategy, see Risa L. Goluboff, *The Lost Promise of Civil Rights* (Cambridge, MA: Harvard University Press, 2007), chap. 9; Michael Klarman, *From Jim Crow to Civil Rights: The Supreme Court and the Struggle for Racial Equality* (New York: Oxford University Press, 2004); and Mark Tushnet, *The NAACP's Legal Strategy against Segregated Education, 1925–1950* (Chapel Hill: University of North Carolina Press, 1987).

9. On the postwar and Cold War contexts, see Mary L. Dudziak, *Cold War Civil Rights:*

Race and the Image of American Democracy (Princeton, NJ: Princeton University Press, 2000); Ellen Schrecker, *No Ivory Tower: McCarthyism and the Universities* (New York: Oxford University Press, 1986); and Penny Von Eschen, *Race against Empire: Black Americans and Anticolonialism, 1937–1957* (Ithaca, NY: Cornell University Press, 1997).

10. For historiography that points to African Americans' linking of race and class, see Michael C. Dawson, *Black Visions: The Roots of Contemporary African-American Political Ideologies* (Chicago: University of Chicago Press, 2001), chap. 5; Goluboff, *Lost Promise of Civil Rights*; Holloway, *Confronting the Veil*; Robin D. G. Kelley, *Hammer and Hoe: Alabama Communists during the Great Depression* (Chapel Hill: University of North Carolina Press, 1990); Nikhil Pal Singh, *Black Is a Country: Race and the Unfinished Struggle for Democracy* (Cambridge, MA: Harvard University Press, 2004); and Thomas J. Sugrue, *Sweet Land of Liberty: The Forgotten Struggle for Civil Rights in the North* (New York: Random House, 2008). On Howard intellectuals, see Holloway, *Confronting the Veil*, esp. 48–49.

11. Goluboff, *Lost Promise of Civil Rights*, esp. 9, 15–17, 34.

12. Ralph J. Bunche, "A Critical Analysis of the Tactics and Programs of Minority Groups," *JNE* 4, no. 3 (1935): 308–20, 308, 309–11.

13. Ibid., 313.

14. Ibid., 315; for examples of Bunche's embrace of individualism and rights-based liberalism by 1950, see Ralph Bunche, "Democracy a World Issue," *JNE* 19, no. 4 (1950): 431–38; and Ralph Bunche, "Equality without Qualifications," *Phylon*, 12 no. 3 (1951): 209–18.

15. Bunche, "A Critical Analysis," 316.

16. For a thorough discussion of Bunche's intellectual and political transformation, see Holloway, *Confronting the Veil*; and Ben Keppel, *The Work of Democracy: Ralph Bunche, Kenneth B. Clark, Lorraine Hansberry, and the Cultural Politics of Race* (Cambridge, MA: Harvard University Press, 1995).

17. W. E. B. Du Bois, "Education and Work," *JNE* 1, no. 1 (1932): 60–74, 63.

18. Ibid., 69.

19. Manning Marable, *Race Reform and Rebellion: The Second Reconstruction and Beyond in Black America, 1945–2006*, 3rd ed. (Jackson: University Press of Mississippi, 2007), Kindle edition, location 322–24.

20. For some examples, see Eleanor Roosevelt, "The National Conference on the Education of Negroes" *JNE* 3, no. 4 (1934): 573–75; J. Scott McCormick, "The Julius Rosenwald Fund," *JNE* 3, no. 4 (1934): 605–26.

21. On these arguments in the legal context, see: Goluboff, *Lost Promise of Civil Rights*.

22. James Anderson, *The Education of Blacks in the South* (Chapel Hill: University of North Carolina Press, 1988), 285, 235–37.

23. On educational segregation and inequality in northern cities in the first half of the twentieth century, see Jack Dougherty, *More Than One Struggle: The Evolution of Black School Reform in Milwaukee* (Chapel Hill: University of North Carolina Press, 2004); James Grossman, *Land of Hope: Chicago, Black Southerners, and the Great Migration* (Chicago: University of Chicago Press, 1989); Kathryn M. Neckerman, *Schools Betrayed: Roots of Failure in Inner-City Education* (Chicago: University of Chicago Press, 2007); Sugrue, *Sweet Land*.

24. Klarman, *From Jim Crow to Civil Rights*, 147–48.

25. Tushnet, *NAACP's Legal Strategy*, 14.

26. Ibid., 14.

27. Klarman, *From Jim Crow to Civil Rights*, 204–5.

28. Charles H. Thompson, "Editorial Comment: Federal Aid to Education and Negro Separate Public Schools," *JNE* 18, no. 4 (1949): 445–51, 445–46.

29. Charles H. Thompson, "Editorial Comment: Race Relations and the Education of Negroes," *JNE* 2, no. 2 (1933): 121–27, 121.

30. Ibid., 121–27, 121–22.

31. Ibid., 121.

32. Ibid., 121–24; Charles H. Thompson, "Court Action the Only Reasonable Alternative to Remedy Immediate Abuses of the Negro Separate School," *JNE* 4, no. 3 (1935): 419–34.

33. David A. Lane Jr., "The Report of the National Advisory Committee on Education and the Problem of Negro Education," *JNE* 1, no. 1 (1932): 5–15.

34. Ibid., 6–7.

35. Myrtle R. Philips, "Financial Support," *JNE* 1, no. 2 (1932): 108–36.

36. Ibid.

37. Ibid., 118–20.

38. Adam Fairclough, "The Cost of *Brown*: Black Teachers and School Integration," *Journal of American History* 91, no. 1 (2004): 43–55. On the extension of these sentiments into the 1950s, see Vanessa Siddle Walker, *Their Highest Potential: An African American School Community in the Segregated South* (Chapel Hill: University of North Carolina Press, 1996).

39. Charles H. Thompson, "Court Action the Only Reasonable Alternative to Remedy Immediate Abuses of the Negro Separate School," *JNE* 4, no. 3 (1935): 419–34, 422.

40. Charles H. Thompson, "Introduction," *JNE* 1, no. 2 (1932): 102; Charles H. Thompson, "Some Aspects of Higher Education for Negroes in the United States," in Race Relations Department, American Missionary Association, "Race Relations in Human Relations, Summary Report, Second Annual Institute of Race Relations, June 2–21, 1945, Fisk University, Nashville, TN" (Nashville: AMA and Fisk University, 1945), 91–92.

41. Ralph J. Bunche, "A Critical Analysis of the Tactics and Programs of Minority Groups," *JNE* 4, no. 3 (1935): 308–20, 318.

42. Ibid., 317, 319.

43. Ibid., 320.

44. Horace Mann Bond, "The Extent and Character of Separate Schools in the United States," *JNE* 4, no. 3 (1935): 321–27, 325–26.

45. Ibid., 324.

46. Ibid., 326–27.

47. Alain Locke, "The Dilemma of Segregation," *JNE* 4, no. 3 (1935): 406–11, 407.

48. Ibid., 409.

49. Ibid., 406.

50. W. E. B. Du Bois, "Does the Negro Need Separate Schools?" *JNE* 4, no. 3 (1935): 328–35, 329.

51. Ibid., 331, 328–29.

52. Ibid., 331.

53. Ibid., 331–32.

54. For examples, see Mary Crowley, "Cincinnati's Experiment in Negro Education: A Comparative Study of the Segregated and Mixed School," *JNE* 1, no. 1 (1932): 25–33; Rayford W. Logan, "Education Segregation in the North," *JNE* 2, no. 1 (1933): 65–67; Paul E. Baker, "Negro-White Adjustment in America," *JNE* 3, no. 2 (1934): 194–204, 203.

55. Alain Locke, "The Dilemma of Segregation," *JNE* 4, no. 3 (1935): 406–11, 411.

56. Du Bois, "Does the Negro Need Separate Schools?" 329.
57. On the intercultural education movement in the 1930s and 1940s, see Diana Selig, *Americans All: The Cultural Gifts Movement* (Cambridge, MA: Harvard University Press, 2008); Nicholas V. Montalto, *A History of the Intercultural Educational Movement, 1924–1941* (New York: Garland, 1982); Walter Jackson, *Gunnar Myrdal and America's Conscience*, 279–84; and Jackson, *Social Scientists for Social Justice*, chap. 4. For examples, see Paul E. Baker, "Negro-White Adjustment in America," *JNE* 3, no. 2 (1934): 194–204; Walter C. Reckless and Harold L. Bringen, "Racial Attitudes and Information about the Negro," *JNE* 2, no. 2 (1933): 128–38; W. D. Weatherford, "Changing Attitudes of Southern Students," *JNE* 2, no. 2 (1933): 147–50; Maude Carmichael, "A Program for 'A Better Understanding between the Races,'" *JNE* 2, no. 2 (1933): 151–56.
58. Letter from Charles S. Johnson to E. Franklin Frazier, July 11, 1933, and Letter from Charles S. Johnson to E. Franklin Frazier, February 26, 1934. E. Franklin Frazier Papers, box 131–11, folder 15, Manuscript Division, Moorland-Spingarn Research Center, Howard University.
59. Charles H. Thompson, "Introduction," *JNE* 1, no. 2 (1932): 101–7, 101; and Charles H. Thompson, "Editorial Comment: Race Relations and the Education of Negroes," *JNE* 2, no. 2 (1933): 121–27, 121, 126.
60. "Editorial Comment: Race Relations and the Education of Negroes," *JNE* 2, no. 2 (1933): 121–27, 124.
61. Ibid., 124.
62. Ibid., 125–26.
63. On the Commission on Interracial Cooperation, see Selig, *Americans All*; and Gilmore, *Defying Dixie*.
64. Hortense Powdermaker, "The Anthropological Approach to the Problem of Modifying Race Attitudes," *JNE* 13, no. 3 (1944): 295–302, 296–97; and Edgar T. Thompson, "Race in the Modern World," *JNE* 13, no. 3 (1944): 270–79, 270–71.
65. Charles S. Johnson, "The Present Status of Race Relations, with Particular Reference to the Negro," *JNE* 8, no. 3 (1939): 323–35, 324.
66. Ina Corinne Brown, "Race Relations in the United States," *JNE* 13, no. 3 (1944): 280–86, 281.
67. Ibid., 281, 284.
68. Thompson, "Race in the Modern Word," 275.
69. Oliver C. Cox, "Race Relations," *JNE* 12, no. 2 (1943): 145. Also see O'Connor, *Poverty Knowledge*, 77.
70. Oliver C. Cox, "An American Dilemma: A Mystical Approach to the Study of Race Relations," *JNE* 14, no. 2 (1945): 132–48, 143.
71. Johnson, "The Present Status of Race Relations," 324.
72. Jackson, *Gunnar Myrdal and America's Conscience*; Southern, *Gunnar Myrdal and Black-White Relations*; Scott, "Postwar Pluralism"; O'Connor, *Poverty Knowledge*; and McKee, *Sociology and the Race Problem*.
73. On the increased wartime stature of psychologists, see Ellen Herman, *The Romance of American Psychology: Political Culture in the Age of Experts* (Berkeley: University of California Press, 1995). On the postwar explosion of research on prejudice, see Jackson, *Gunnar Myrdal and America's Conscience*, 279–93.
74. Klarman, *From Jim Crow to Civil Rights*, 196–235; Tushnet, *NAACP's Legal Strategy*; Goluboff, *Lost Promise of Civil Rights*.
75. Thompson, "Race in the Modern World," 270.

76. Eugene L. Hartley, "Psychological Investigations and the Modification of Racial Attitudes," *JNE* 13, no. 3 (1944): 287–94, 289.

77. Powdermaker, "The Anthropological Approach to the Problem of Modifying Race Attitudes," 300.

78. Hartley, "Psychological Investigations and the Modification of Racial Attitudes," 293; Edward C. Lindeman, "Next Steps in Education for Racial Understanding: A Philosophical Approach," *JNE* 13, no. 3 (1944): 409.

79. Hartley, "Psychological Investigations and the Modification of Racial Attitudes," 291; Lindeman, "Next Steps in Education for Racial Understanding: A Philosophical Approach," 407–13, 409.

80. Powdermaker, "The Anthropological Approach to the Problem of Modifying Race Attitudes," 300–301.

81. J. Max Bond, "Educational Programs for the Improvement of Race Relations: The Schools," *JNE* 13, no. 3 (1944): 390–97, 391.

82. Caroline Ware, "The Role of the Schools in Education for Racial Understanding," *JNE* 13, no. 3 (1944): 421–31, 421.

83. Ibid., 422, 424.

84. Ibid., 423.

85. Ibid., 424; Bond, "Educational Programs for the Improvement of Race Relations: The Schools," 390–92; Hartley, "Psychological Investigation and the Modification of Racial Attitudes," 292–94; Powdermaker, "The Anthropological Approach to the Problem of Modifying Racial Attitudes," 300–302; Ware, "The Role of the Schools in Education for Racial Understanding," 432–24, 429–31; and Wilkins, "Next Steps in Education for Racial Understanding," 435–38.

86. Savage, *Broadcasting Freedom.*

87. Roy Wilkins, "Next Steps in Education for Racial Understanding," *JNE* 13, no. 3 (1944): 432–40, 437; L. D. Reddick, "Educational Programs for the Improvement of Race Relations: Motion Pictures, Radio, the Press, and Libraries," *JNE* 13, no. 3 (1944): 367–89, 367.

88. Jenkins, "Editorial Comment: Education for Racial Understanding," 267; Rufus E. Clement, "Educational Programs for the Improvement of Race Relations: Interracial Committees," *JNE* 13, no. 3 (1944): 316–28, 319.

89. Reddick, "Educational Programs for the Improvement of Race Relations," 389, 367.

90. Martin D. Jenkins, "A Preliminary Outline of the Proposed Thirteenth Yearbook (July 1944) of the JNE," October 21, 1943, in box 12, folder "JNE," Charles H. Thompson Papers, Moorland-Spingarn Research Center, Howard University, Washington, DC (TP), 1–2.

91. Margaret C. McCulloch, "Educational Programs for the Improvement of Race Relations: Seven Religious Agencies," *JNE* 13, no. 3 (1944): 305–15, 314.

92. Alain Locke, "Whither Race Relations? A Critical Commentary," *JNE* 13, no. 3 (1944): 398–406, 400–401.

93. Lindeman, "Next Steps in Education for Racial Understanding," 407.

94. L. D. Reddick, "Adult Education and the Improvement of Race Relations," *JNE* 14, no. 3 (1945): 488–93, 488.

95. Ibid., 489.

96. Charles S. Johnson, "The Next Decade in Race Relations," *JNE* 13, no. 3 (1944): 441–46, 441.

97. Klarman, *From Jim Crow to Civil Rights,* chap. 4; Brinkley, *End of Reform,* 139, 171, 174, 213, 224.

98. Goluboff, *Lost Promise*, 228; Tushnet, *NAACP's Legal Strategy*, 135; and Klarman, *From Jim Crow to Civil Rights*, 289.

99. Howard Brick, *Transcending Capitalism: Visions of a New Society in Modern American Thought* (Ithaca, NY: Cornell University Press, 2006).

100. Holloway, *Confronting the Veil*, 34, 15–17.

101. For examples, see Ralph Bunche, "Democracy a World Issue," *JNE* 19, no. 4 (1950): 431–38; and Ralph Bunche, "Equality without Qualifications," *Phylon* 12, no. 3 (1951): 209–18.

102. Ralph Bunche, "Democracy a World Issue," 431–38, 435–36.

103. Dudziak, *Cold War Civil Rights*; Von Eschen, *Race against Empire*; Marable, *Race, Reform, and Rebellion*, chap. 2.

104. Klarman, *From Jim Crow to Civil Rights*, 207–8.

105. Ibid., 217–19.

106. Ibid., 289; Tushnet, *NAACP's Legal Strategy*, 135; Goluboff, *Lost Promise of Civil Rights*, 228, 4–5, 12.

107. Klarman, *From Jim Crow to Civil Rights*, 311–12. Even after *Brown*, President Eisenhower's efforts to provide federal funds to the states for needed school construction became embroiled in desegregationist politics. After New York congressman Adam Clayton Powell attached the Powell Amendment, which prevented the federal government from providing money to schools that remained segregated in defiance of court order, Eisenhower's school construction bill was defeated in Congress. James C. Duram, *A Moderate among Extremists: Dwight D. Eisenhower and the School Desegregation Crisis* (Chicago: Nelson-Hall, 1981), 213–34.

108. Charles H. Thompson, "Editorial Comment: The Relative Status of the Negro Population in the United States," *JNE* 22, no. 3 (1953): 221–31.

109. Charles H. Thompson, "Editorial Comment: The Negro Child in the American Social Order," *JNE* 19, no. 3 (1950): 215–18, 215, 216–17.

110. Ibid., 217–18.

111. Thompson, "The Negro Child in the American Social Order" (1950), 216–17. Charles H. Thompson, "Editorial Comment: The Relative Status of the Negro Population in the United States," *JNE* 22, no. 3 (1953): 225–26.

112. Harry J. Walker, "The Nature and Characteristics of the Negro Community," *JNE* 19 no. 3 (1950): 219–31, 221–22, 230; Walker builds on Robert Weaver, *The Negro Ghetto* (New York: Russell and Russell, 1948). Walker's analysis parallels some of the claims about the cultural and economic effects of the concentrated poverty that segregation creates that Massey and Denton made in the 1990s. Douglas Massey and Nancy Denton, *American Apartheid: Segregation and the Making of the Underclass* (Cambridge, MA: Harvard University Press, 1993).

113. Walker, "The Nature and Characteristics of the Negro Community," 231.

114. Robert C. Weaver, "The Economic Status of the Negro in the United States," *JNE* 19, no. 3 (1950): 232–43, 232; Robert Weaver, *Negro Labor: A National Problem* (New York: Harcourt Brace, 1946).

115. Weaver, "The Economic Status of the Negro," 243.

116. On the rise of cultural analyses of poverty in the postwar years, see O'Connor, *Poverty Knowledge*; Michael B. Katz, *The Undeserving Poor: From the War on Poverty to the War on Welfare* (New York: Pantheon, 1989); Michael B. Katz, *The Undeserving Poor: America's Enduring Confrontation with Poverty*, 2nd ed. (New York: Oxford University Press, 2013); and Daryl Michael Scott, *Contempt and Pity: Social Policy and the Image*

of the Damaged Black Psyche, 1880–1996 (Chapel Hill: University of North Carolina Press, 1997).

117. E. Franklin Frazier, "Problems and Needs of Negro Children and Youth Resulting from Family Disorganization," *JNE* 19, no. 3 (1950): 269–77, 269. On the significance of arguments about the "culture of poverty" and on the Moynihan Report's complex relationship to Frazier's scholarship, see Herman, *Romance of American Psychology*, 200–207, chap. 2; O'Connor, *Poverty Knowledge*, chaps. 3, 4, and 8; and Anthony M. Platt, *E. Franklin Frazier Reconsidered* (New Brunswick, NJ: Rutgers University Press, 1991).

118. Harry J. Walker, "The Nature and Characteristics of the Negro Community," *JNE* 19, no. 3 (1950): 219–31, 231, 228.

119. George N. Redd, "The Educational and Cultural Level of the American Negro," *JNE* 19, no. 3 (1950): 244–52, 252.

120. Ibid., 252.

121. Ibid., 248–49.

122. Ibid., 249, 252.

123. Ibid., 252.

124. Ralph Bunche, "Democracy a World Issue," *JNE* 19, no. 4 (1950): 431–38, 436.

125. Gary Orfield, Susan E. Eaton, and the Harvard Project on School Desegregation, *Dismantling Desegregation: The Quiet Reversal of* Brown v. Board of Education (New York: New Press, 1996); J. Harvie Wilkinson III, *From Brown to Bakke: The Supreme Court and School Integration: 1954–1978* (New York: Oxford University Press, 1979).

126. Charles H. Thompson, "Race and Equality of Educational Opportunity: Defining the Problem," *JNE* 37, no. 3 (1968): 191–203, 194.

127. Ibid., 194, 198, 201–2.

128. Ibid., 202–3.

CHAPTER SIX

1. NCCJ, "One Nation under God, Report of the National Conference of Christians and Jews," 1954, W2 Annual Reports, 1950–59 folder, box 1, National Conference of Christians and Jews records, 1927–89, Social Welfare History Archives, University of Minnesota (NCCJ), 15.

2. Walter A. Jackson, *Gunnar Myrdal and America's Conscience: Social Engineering and Racial Liberalism, 1938–1987* (Chapel Hill: University of North Carolina Press, 1990), 279–81; and Kevin M. Schultz, *Tri-Faith America: How Catholics and Jews Held Postwar America to Its Protestant Promise* (Oxford: Oxford University Press, 2011).

3. Diana Selig, *Americans All: The Cultural Gifts Movement* (Cambridge, MA: Harvard University Press, 2008), 115; Schultz, *Tri-Faith America.*

4. Jane Addams, "The Public School and the Immigrant Child" and "Immigrants and Their Children," in *Jane Addams on Education*, ed. Ellen Condliffe Lagemann (New York: Teachers College Press, 1985), 136–42, 162–71; Selig, *Americans All.*

5. On the emergence of the "tri-faith idea" in the 1910s and 1920s, see Schultz, *Tri-Faith America*, Kindle edition, Location 160–70. On the NCCJ's early history, see Chris Cominel, "A Triumphant Crusade against Religious Bias," reprinted from the *World-Telegram-Sun Saturday Feature Magazine*, 1957, History folder, box 1, NCCJ, 1–2.

6. Selig, *Americans All*, 115–19; Jackson, *Gunnar Myrdal and America's Conscience*, 279–81.

7. See chapter one.

8. Selig, *Americans All*, 121–22, 130.

9. Ibid., 120, 123–24; "Report of the Director, NCCJ," November 2, 1939, W2 Annual Reports folder, box 1, NCCJ, 2–3.

10. NCCJ, Information Bulletin, No. IX, July 1931, Historical folder, box 1, NCCJ records, SWHA, 2.

11. Jackson, *Gunnar Myrdal and America's Conscience*, 286; Allport, *Nature of Prejudice*, chap. 16 and 485–89; Arnold Rose, *Studies in Reduction of Prejudice: A Memorandum Summarizing Research on Modification of Attitudes* (Chicago: American Council on Race Relations, 1947); Robin M. Williams Jr., *The Reduction of Intergroup Tensions: A Survey of Research on Problems of Ethnic, Racial, and Religious Group Relations* (New York: SSRC, 1947), 69–73.

12. Chris Cominel, "A Triumphant Crusade against Religious Bias"; "Report of the Director of the National Conference, May 31, 1938, W2 Annual Reports, 1928–32 folder, box 1, NCCJ, 3.

13. Selig, *Americans All*, 124; Bernard C. Clausen, "The Syracuse Seminar, 1931," reprinted from *The Baptist*, May 16, 1931, in NCCJ, Information Bulletin, No. IX, July 1931, Supplement, Historical folder, box 1, NCCJ, 2. The NCCJ supported intercultural education teacher training initiatives by Rachel Davis DuBois and Hilda Taba through Columbia University's Teachers College and the University of Chicago beginning in 1948. In 1953 the conference's programs "to keep prejudice out of our schools" educated teachers, administrators, parents, and clergymen who could shape young people's intergroup attitudes. Selig, *Americans All*, 131–32.

14. For overviews of some of its educational and teacher training efforts, see NCCJ, Information Bulletin, No. IX, July 1931, Historical folder, box 1, NCCJ; "Report of the Director of the National Conference, May 31, 1938, W2 Annual Reports, 1928–32 folder, box 1, NCCJ, 3; "Report of the Director, NCCJ," November 2, 1939, W2 Annual Reports folder, box 1, NCCJ, 4; "This Year: A Report of the Director, NCCJ," May 1940, W2 Annual Reports folder, box 1, NCCJ; NCCJ, 20th Annual Report, 1948, W2 Annual Reports 1940–49 folder, box 1, NCCJ; NCCJ, "This Year in the National Conference of Christians and Jews, Inc., 1952," W2 Annual Reports 1940–49 folder, box 1, NCCJ, 3; NCCJ, "Because Some Men Hate," pamphlet, 1953, History folder, box 1, NCCJ, 2.

15. NCCJ, "Because Some Men Hate," 2.

16. NCCJ, Information Bulletin, No. IX, July 1931, Historical folder, box 1, NCCJ, 2–3; "Report of the Director of the National Conference," May 31, 1938, W2 Annual Reports, 1928–32 folder, box 1, NCCJ, 2–3, quote on page 2; NCCJ, "Because Some Men Hate," 2.

17. Cominel, "A Triumphant Crusade against Religious Bias," 3.

18. NCCJ pamphlet, "An Idea Whose Time Has Come!" no date (handwritten note, 1944), W2 Annual Reports, 1940–49 folder, box 1, NCCJ, 19.

19. Clausen, "The Syracuse Seminar, 1931," 3.

20. NCCJ, "Because Some Men Hate," 1.

21. Constitution of the National Conference of Christians and Jews, Adopted at Executive Committee Meeting, November 2, 1939, Constitution, By-Laws folder, box 1, NCCJ, 1; "Report of the Director, NCCJ," November 2, 1939, W2 Annual Reports folder, box 1, NCCJ, 2.

22. NCCJ, Information Bulletin, No. IX, July 1931, Supplement, Historical folder, box 1, NCCJ, 4; Clausen, "The Syracuse Seminar, 1931"; "Report of the Director of the National Conference, May 31, 1938, W2 Annual Reports, 1928–32 folder, box 1,

NCCJ, 3; "This Year: A Report of the Director, NCCJ," May 1940, W2 Annual Reports folder, box 1, NCCJ, 16; Cominel, "A Triumphant Crusade against Religious Bias," 4.

23. John P. Jackson Jr., *Social Scientists for Social Justice: Making the Case against Segregation* (New York: New York University Press, 2001), 64–65.

24. Herman, *Romance of American Psychology*, 181–82; Jackson, *Gunnar Myrdal and America's Conscience*, 280–83; Jackson, *Social Scientists for Social Justice*, chap. 4.

25. Patrick Gilpin and Marybeth Gasman, *Charles S. Johnson: Leadership beyond the Veil in the Age of Jim Crow* (Albany: State University of New York Press, 2003), chaps. 13 and 14. Richard Deats, "The Rebel Passion: Eighty-Five Years of the Fellowship of Reconciliation," http://www.forusa.org/nonviolence/0900_63deats.html, accessed April 13, 2008. Also see http://www.forusa.org/about/history.html, accessed April 13, 2008.

26. Jackson, *Social Scientists for Social Justice*, 64–66.

27. Deats, "The Rebel Passion."

28. NCCJ, "Because Some Men Hate," 3.

29. Chicago Roundtable of the NCCJ, pamphlet, "No Ocean Separates Us from Our Enemies Within," no date, W2 Annual Reports 1940–49 folder, box 1, NCCJ, 1–3.

30. Ibid., 3.

31. NCCJ pamphlet, "An Idea Whose Time Has Come!" 6.

32. Ibid., 20.

33. On the shifting political context see Sugrue, *Sweet Land*, 44–58, 75–77, and Jackson, *Gunnar Myrdal and America's Conscience*, 234–37, 273–79. "Interracial Relations: Statement of the Commission on Educational Organizations," January 1948, copy included in "Minutes, NCCJ Evaluation Committee, May 21, 1956, Yale Club, NY," NCCJ Evaluation Committee, 1958 folder, box 7, NCCJ, 7.

34. Michael J. Klarman, *From Jim Crow to Civil Rights: The Supreme Court and the Struggle for Racial Equality* (New York: Oxford University Press, 2004), 182–89; Mary L. Dudziak, *Cold War Civil Rights: Race and the Image of American Democracy* (Princeton, NJ: Princeton University Press, 2000); and Penny Von Eschen, *Race against Empire: Black Americans and Anticolonialism, 1937–1957* (Ithaca, NY: Cornell University Press, 1997).

35. "Interracial Relations, Statement of Commission on Religious Organizations Released February 10, 1952," copy included in "Minutes, NCCJ Evaluation Committee, May 21, 1956, Yale Club, NY," NCCJ Evaluation Committee, 1958 folder, box 7, NCCJ, 12. Schultz, *Tri-Faith America*, chap. 3.

36. On civil rights activists' use of Cold War rhetoric, see Von Eschen, *Race against Empire*; and Dudziak, *Cold War Civil Rights*.

37. NCCJ, "This Year in the National Conference of Christians and Jews, Inc.," 1952, W2 Annual Reports 1940–49 folder, box 1, NCCJ, 7. For an example of this rhetoric from 1954, see NCCJ, "One Nation under God, Report of the National Conference of Christians and Jews," 1954, W2 Annual Reports, 1950–59 folder, box 1, NCCJ, 1–2. On the universalist ethos Clinchy expressed, see David Hollinger, "Postethnic America," in *Beyond Pluralism: The Conception of Groups and Group Identities in America*, ed. Wendy F. Katkin, Ned Landsman, and Andrea Tyree (Urbana: University of Illinois Press, 1998), 51, 60.

38. NCCJ, "One Nation under God, Report of the National Conference of Christians and Jews," 1954, W2 Annual Reports, 1950–59 folder, box 1, NCCJ, 2.

39. Ibid., 3–5.

40. Ibid.

41. While the literature on the civil rights movement in the South in the 1950s and

1960s is too voluminous to list here, a few key volumes include: William Chafe, *Civilities and Civil Rights: Greensboro North Carolina and the Black Freedom Struggle* (Oxford: Oxford University Press, 1980); John Dittmer, *Local People: The Struggle for Civil Rights in Mississippi* (Urbana: University of Illinois Press, 1994); Thomas F. Jackson, *From Civil Rights to Human Rights: Martin Luther King Jr., and the Struggle for Economic Justice* (Philadelphia: University of Pennsylvania Press, 2007); Charles Payne, *I've Got the Light of Freedom: The Organizing Tradition and the Mississippi Freedom Struggle* (Berkeley: University of California Press, 1995); Harvard Sitkoff, *The Struggle for Black Equality* (New York: Hill and Wang, 1993).

42. Deats, "The Rebel Passion"; Schultz, *Tri-Faith America*, chap. 8; http://www.history.pcusa.org/finding/phsncc18.xml, accessed April 13, 2008; http://www.history.pcusa.org/finding/phsncc6.xml, accessed April 13, 2008. Kevin Schultz shows that in 1963, the NCC's group created a Commission on Religion and Race that helped sponsor Martin Luther King Jr.'s March on Washington and was actively engaged in litigation and direct action for civil rights throughout the 1960s.

43. For the context of segregationist resistance to *Brown v. Board*, see Patterson, Brown v. Board, 73–79, 81–82; Klarman, *From Jim Crow to Civil Rights*, 314.

44. "Minutes of the Meeting of the Executive Committee of the Commission on Religious Organizations, Union House of Living Judaism, NYC, December 11, 1951," "Inter-Commission Committee on the Problem of Integration in Education and Community Life" folder, box 2, NCCJ, 1.

45. Minutes, Committee on Integration of Minority Groups in American Society, Commission on Educational Organizations, NCCJ, St. Louis, Missouri, October 30–31, 1953, Desegregation and Integration folder, box 23, NCCJ, 1.

46. Ibid., 1.

47. Ibid., 2.

48. Ibid.

49. Patterson, Brown v. Board, 73, 78–79, 81–82; Klarman, *From Jim Crow to Civil Rights*, 314.

50. Minutes, Inter-Commission Committee on the Problems of Integration in Education and Community Life, NCCJ, Nashville, TN, May 24–25, 1954, Desegregation and Integration folder, box 1, NCCJ.

51. Ibid., 1–2; Klarman, *From Jim Crow to Civil Rights*, 352.

52. Historian Kevin Schultz has also noted how advocates of "tri-faith America" often took an "illogical" stance toward segregation since while "the organizations promoting the tri-faith ideal had solid, if uneven, records fighting racial discrimination," they simultaneously "chose not to insist on racial equality as part of their mission, as part of their call for 'brotherhood.'" Schultz, *Tri-Faith America*, Kindle edition, Location 4026–30.

53. Minutes, Inter-Commission Committee on the Problems of Integration in Education and Community Life, NCCJ, Nashville, TN, May 24–25, 1954, Desegregation and Integration folder, box 1, NCCJ. Ibid., 2, 4–5.

54. Appendix A, Suggested Revision to NCCJ Statement of Interracial Policy, Minutes, Inter-Commission Committee on the Problems of Integration in Education and Community Life, NCCJ, Nashville, TN, May 24–25, 1954, Desegregation and Integration folder, box 1, NCCJ.

55. Minutes, Inter-Commission Committee on the Problems of Integration in Education and Community Life, NCCJ, Nashville, TN, May 24–25, 1954, Desegregation and Integration folder, box 1, NCCJ, 2.

56. Ibid., 5.

57. Minutes, Inter-Commission Committee on the Problems of Integration in Education and Community Life, NCCJ, Nashville, TN, May 24–25, 1954, Desegregation and Integration folder, box 1, NCCJ, 2.

58. Ibid., 2.

59. Ibid., 3–5.

60. Ibid., 2.

61. Klarman, *From Jim Crow to Civil Rights*, 313–15.

62. Ibid., 316–17.

63. Letter from Gordon Lovejoy to Herbert L. Seamans, director of the Commission on Educational Organizations, NCCJ, June 2, 1955, Desegregation and Integration folder, box 23, NCCJ, 1.

64. These activities included establishing biracial committees that "would give the moderates a vehicle through which to speak out in a unified voice," holding institutes that would help school systems plan for desegregation, leading programs on brotherhood in schools, churches, and civic organizations, and distributing Brotherhood Week literature. Memo from Dave Hyatt to All Regional Directors, June 15, 1956, Desegregation and Integration folder, box 23, NCCJ, 1–4.

65. Memo from Gordon W. Lovejoy to Dumont F. Kenney re: Building Brotherhood in Your Community—A Series of Experimental Institutes, July 11, 1956, Desegregation and Integration folder, box 23, NCCJ, 1–2.

66. Memo from Dave Hyatt to All Regional Directors, June 15, 1956, Desegregation and Integration folder, box 23, NCCJ, 6.

67. Letter from Gordon Lovejoy to Herbert L. Seamans, June 2, 1955, Desegregation and Integration folder, box 23, NCCJ, 1–2.

68. Ibid., 1.

69. On the development of the field of human relations in the wartime and postwar eras, see Elizabeth Lasch-Quinn, *Race Experts: How Racial Etiquette, Sensitivity Training, and New Age Therapy Hijacked the Civil Rights Revolution* (New York: Norton, 2001).

70. Letter from Gordon Lovejoy to Herbert L. Seamans, June 2, 1955, Desegregation and Integration folder, box 23, NCCJ, 2.

71. Ibid., 2.

72. Ibid., 1.

73. Ibid., 2.

74. Memo from Dave Hyatt to All Regional Directors, June 15, 1956, Desegregation and Integration folder, box 23, NCCJ, 5–6 (emphasis in original).

75. Ibid., 6.

76. "NCCJ Evaluation Study, 1956–1959," NCCJ Evaluation Study, 1956–59 folder, box 7, NCCJ, 17–20.

77. Ibid., 33–34.

78. The study then (ironically given that it just stated that social scientific expertise did not shape its stance toward desegregation) quoted Gunnar Myrdal on the importance of the "American Creed" to its strategy against racial bigotry. Ibid., 34–36.

79. Ibid., 35–36.

80. Ibid., 16–17.

81. Ibid., 42.

82. Ibid., 43.

83. Ibid., 52–53.

84. Ibid., 11, 52.

85. Bernard C. Clausen, "The Syracuse Seminar, 1931," 2.
86. Summary of interview of January 26, 1949, with Dr. David Petegorsky, Executive Director, American Jewish Congress, and Mr. Leo Pfeffer, Assistant Director, Commission on Law and Social Action, American Jewish Congress," NCCJ Evaluation Study 1956–59 folder, box 7, NCCJ, 24–25.
87. Ibid., 24–25.
88. Arnold Rose, *De Facto School Segregation* (New York: the National Conference of Christians and Jews, 1964).

CONCLUSION

1. On the centrality of economic issues to African American working-class politics, see Robin D. G. Kelley, *Hammer and Hoe: Alabama Communists during the Great Depression* (Chapel Hill: University of North Carolina Press, 1990); Robin D. G. Kelley, *Race Rebels, Culture, Politics, and the Black Working Class* (New York: Free Press, 1994); Thomas Jackson, *From Civil Rights to Human Rights: Martin Luther King Jr., and the Struggle for Economic Justice* (Philadelphia: University of Pennsylvania Press, 2007); Robert Self, *American Babylon: Race and the Struggle for Postwar Oakland* (Princeton, NJ: Princeton University Press, 2003); and Thomas J. Sugrue, *Sweet Land of Liberty: The Forgotten Struggle for Civil Rights in the North* (New York: Random House, 2008).
2. On behavioralism and the Cold War, see Joel Isaac, "The Human Sciences in Cold War America," *Historical Journal* 50, no. 3 (2007): 725–46, 737–39; Andrew Jewett, *Science, Democracy, and the American University: From the Civil War to the Cold War* (Cambridge: Cambridge University Press, 2012), 342–43; and Mark Solovey, *Shaky Foundations: The Politics-Patronage-Social Science Nexus in Cold War America* (New Brunswick, NJ: Rutgers University Press, 2013), chap. 3. On shifts from the Chicago school to structural functionalist paradigms among postwar sociologists, see Andrew Abbott, *Department and Discipline: Chicago Sociology at One Hundred* (Chicago: University of Chicago Press, 1999); Andrew Abbott and James Sparrow, "Hot War, Cold War: The Structures of Sociological Action, 1940–1955," in Calhoun, *Sociology in America*, 281–313; Gary Alan Fine, ed., *A Second Chicago School? The Development of a Postwar American Sociology* (Chicago: University of Chicago Press, 1995); Stephen Park Turner and Jonathan H. Turner, *The Impossible Science: An Institutional Analysis of American Sociology* (Newbury Park, CA: Sage Publications, 1990); and Howard Winant, "The Dark Side of the Force: One Hundred Years of the Sociology of Race," in *Sociology in America*, ed. Craig Calhoun (Chicago: University of Chicago Press, 2007), 535–71.
3. Robert Weaver, "A Needed Program of Research in Race Relations and Associated Problems," *JNE* 16, no. 2 (1947): 130–35; Charles C. Killingsworth, "Job and Income for Negroes," in *Race and the Social Sciences*, ed. Irwin Katz and Patricia Gurin (New York: Basic Books, 1969); Donald Matthews, "Political Science Research on Race Relations," in Katz and Gurin, *Race and the Social Sciences*, 113–44.
4. Abbott and Sparrow, "Hot War, Cold War," 287–89; Jean M. Converse, *Survey Research in the United States: Roots and Emergence, 1890–1960* (Berkeley: University of California Press, 1987), 217.
5. Robin M. Williams Jr., "Review and Assessment of Research on Race and Culture Conflict," Paper V, Conference on Research in Human Relations (February 1953), folder 99, box 11, series 910, RG 3.1, RF, 12–13. On the NSF debates, see Solovey, *Shaky Foundations*, chaps. 1 and 4. On congressional investigations into foundation "subversion" and the retreat from racial issues at the Ford and Carnegie Foundations, see Ellen Herman, *The Romance of American Psychology: Political Culture in the Age of*

Experts (Berkeley: University of California Press, 1995), 348–49, notes 28 and 29; Ellen Condliffe Lagemann, *The Politics of Knowledge: The Carnegie Corporation, Philanthropy, and Public Policy* (Chicago: University of Chicago Press, 1989), 146, 185; Waldemar A. Nielsen, *The Big Foundations* (New York: Columbia University Press, 1972), 353; Alice O'Connor, *Social Science for What? Philanthropy and the Social Question in a World Turned Rightside Up* (New York: Russell Sage Foundation, 2007), 70; and Solovey, *Shaky Foundations*, chap. 3.

6. W. E. B. Du Bois, *The Philadelphia Negro* (1899; New York: Cosimo Classics, 2007); Charles S. Johnson, *The Negro in American Civilization: A Study of Negro Life and Race Relations in the Light of Social Research* (New York: Henry Holt, 1930); E. Franklin Frazier, *The Negro in the United States* (1949; New York: Macmillan, 1957).

7. On social relations frameworks see: Howard Brick, *Transcending Capitalism: Visions of a New Society in Modern American Thought* (Ithaca, NY: Cornell University Press, 2006).

8. Solovey, *Shaky Foundations*, chap. 3; Isaac, "The Human Sciences in Cold War America"; Herman, *Romance of American Psychology*, chap. 7; and Jewett, *Science, Democracy, and the American University*, chap. 11 point to those intersecting sources.

9. Thomas Borstelmann, *The Cold War and the Color Line: American Race Relations in the Global Arena* (Cambridge, MA: Harvard University Press, 2001); Mary L. Dudziak, *Cold War Civil Rights: Race and the Image of American Democracy* (Princeton, NJ: Princeton University Press, 2000); Manning Marable, *Race, Reform, and Rebellion: The Second Reconstruction and Beyond in Black America, 1945–2006* (Jackson: University Press of Mississippi, 2007), chap. 2; Singh, *Black Is a Country*, chap. 4; and Von Eschen, *Race against Empire*.

10. This argument builds on Kimberlé Crenshaw's analysis of civil rights strategists' reliance on rights discourse more broadly. She argues that there were "both risks and dangers involved in both engaging in the dominant discourse and in failing to do so." Kimberlé Crenshaw, "Race, Reform, and Retrenchment: Transformation and Legitimation in Anti-Discrimination Law," in *Critical Race Theory*, ed. Kimberlé Crenshaw et al. (New York: New Press, 1995), 103–26, 112.

11. Stephen Park Turner and Jonathan H. Turner, *The Impossible Science: An Institutional Analysis of American Sociology* (Newbury Park, CA: Sage Publications, 1990), 125; Jonathan Scott Holloway and Benjamin Keppel, eds., *Black Scholars on the Line: Race, Social Science, and American Thought in the Twentieth Century* (Notre Dame, IN: University of Notre Dame Press, 2007), 12–23.

12. While African American thought had both liberal and conservative traditions, this claim builds on scholarship in African American intellectual history that points to the importance of African American "counter-hegemonic" social imaginaries, an African American "counter-public sphere," and enduring critiques of liberalism in African American political thought. Singh, *Black Is a Country*, esp. 102; Michael C. Dawson, *Black Visions: The Roots of Contemporary African-American Political Ideologies* (Chicago: University of Chicago Press, 2001); Lipsitz, *How Racism Takes Place*.

13. Kelley, *Race Rebels*; Self, *American Babylon*; and Sugrue, *Sweet Land* all highlight this element of black grassroots politics.

14. Eric Foner and Manning Marable, eds., *Herbert Aptheker on Race and Democracy* (Urbana: University of Illinois Press, 2006); Christopher A. McAuley, *The Mind of Oliver C. Cox* (Notre Dame, IN: University of Notre Dame Press, 2004); Marable, *Race, Reform, and Rebellion*, chap. 2; Singh, *Black Is a Country*, chap. 4.

15. E. Franklin Frazier, "Race Contacts and the Social Structure," *American Sociological Review* 14, no. 1 (1949): 1–11.

16. Certainly many late 1960s theorists of black power and internal colonialism also drew explicitly on radical views of exploitation and oppression that circulated quite widely among the Depression-era interracial left and African American counter-public sphere of the 1930s and early 1940s. On these connections, see Singh, *Black Is a Country*, chap. 5; and Sugrue, *Sweet Land*, chaps. 10–12.

17. Borstelmann, *The Cold War and the Color Line*; Dudziak, *Cold War Civil Rights*; Von Eschen, *Race against Empire*.

18. Talcott Parsons and Kenneth Clark, *The Negro American* (Boston: Beacon Press, 1965); Kenneth Clark, *Dark Ghetto: Dilemmas of Social Power* (New York: Harper and Row, 1965).

19. On the mid-1960s intellectual and political context, see Michael B. Katz, *The Undeserving Poor: From the War on Poverty to the War on Welfare* (New York: Pantheon, 1989), chaps. 1–4; Michael B. Katz, *The Undeserving Poor: America's Enduring Confrontation with Poverty*, second edition (New York: Oxford University Press, 2013); Jackson, *From Civil Rights to Human Rights*; Alice O'Connor, *Poverty Knowledge: Social Science, Social Policy, and the Poor in Twentieth-Century U.S. History* (Princeton, NJ: Princeton University Press, 2001), chaps. 5–8; Singh, *Black Is a Country*, chap. 5; and Sugrue, *Sweet Land*, part 3. On the decline of behavioralism by the early 1960s, see Solovey, *Shaky Foundations*, chap. 3. On the return of economics and political science to the race issue in the mid-1960s, see Killingsworth, "Job and Income for Negroes," and Matthews, "Political Science Research on Race Relations."

20. For a few of many examples of the combination of concern with white prejudice and discrimination and attention to African American family and community pathology in *The Negro American*, see Philip M. Hauser, "Demographic Factors in the Integration of the Negro," 79–102; Rashi Fein, "An Economic and Social Profile of the American Negro," 102–33; and Daniel Patrick Moynihan, "Employment, Income, and the Ordeal of the Negro Family," 134–59 in Parsons and Clark, *The Negro American*. For historical accounts of the debates over deficit models and the "culture of poverty," see Michael B. Katz, ed., *The Underclass Debate: Views from History* (Princeton, NJ: Princeton University Press, 1993); Katz, *The Undeserving Poor*; James T. Patterson, *Freedom Is Not Enough: The Moynihan Report and America's Struggle over Black Family Life—From LBJ to Obama* (New York: Basic Books, 2010); O'Connor, *Poverty Knowledge*; Mical Raz, *What's Wrong with the Poor? Psychiatry, Race, and the War on Poverty* (Chapel Hill: University of North Carolina Press, 2013); and Daryl Michael Scott, *Contempt and Pity: Social Policy and the Image of the Damaged Black Psyche, 1880–1996* (Chapel Hill: University of North Carolina Press, 1997).

21. Paul B. Sheatsley, "White Attitudes toward the Negro," in Parsons and Clark, *The Negro American*, 303–24; Thomas Pettigrew, "Complexity and Change in American Racial Patterns: A Social Psychological View," in Parsons and Clark, *The Negro American*, 325–62. On shifts in sociology, by the mid-1960s, away from the focus on attitudes that characterized the field in the 1950s, see Thomas Pettigrew, ed., *The Sociology of Race Relations* (New York: Free Press, 1980), 183; James B. McKee, *Sociology and the Race Problem: The Failure of a Perspective* (Urbana: University of Illinois Press, 1993), 350–51.

22. *The Negro American*'s structural leaning is especially evident in the following articles, although some also pointed to the causal importance of African American family "disorganization" and discrimination: St. Clair Drake, "The Social and Economic Status of the Negro in the United States"; Philip Hauser, "Demographic Factors in the Integration of the Negro"; Rashi Fein, "An Economic and Social Profile of the

American Negro"; Daniel Patrick Moynihan, "Employment, Income, and the Ordeal of the Negro Family"; Lee Rainwater, "Crucible of Identity: The Negro Lower-Class Family"; James Tobin, "On Improving the Economic Status of the Negro"; Robert Dentler, "Barriers to Northern School Desegregation"; John H. Fisher, "Race and Reconciliation: The Role of the School"; Charles Abrams, "The Housing Problem and the Negro"; Everett C. Hughes, "Anomalies and Projections"; and Talcott Parsons, "Full Citizenship for the Negro American?" in Parsons and Clark, *The Negro American.*

23. Drake, "The Social and Economic Status of the Negro," 41, 19, 36; Drake is quoting Whitney Young cited in James Reston, "The Ironies of History and the American Negro," *New York Times,* May 15, 1964.

24. Hauser, "Demographic Factors," 95; Fein, "An Economic and Social Profile," 128–30; Moynihan, "Employment, Income, and the Ordeal of the Negro Family," 153; Rainwater, "Crucible of Identity: The Negro Lower-Class Family," 196–97; Tobin, "On Improving the Economic Status of the Negro," 456, 468; and Clark, *Dark Ghetto,* 36.

25. Some contributors to *The Negro American,* like Philip Hauser and Talcott Parsons, saw racial progress as possible without substantial conflict and encouraged integration, meaning, in Hauser's case, racial understanding and acculturation. Hauser, "Demographic Factors," 95–96, 99–100; Parsons, "Full Citizenship for the Negro American?"

26. Clark, *Dark Ghetto,* 11. In addition to emphasizing the need for structural change in labor and housing markets, Clark and Drake made clear that oppression was unlikely to be effectively challenged without conflict and that African Americans must "seize power" to promote racial justice. Clark, *Dark Ghetto,* 22–36, 48; Drake, "The Social and Economic Status of the Negro in the United States," 4, 41.

27. *Report of the National Advisory Commission on Civil Disorders* (New York: Bantam Books, 1968), 407. On black power and late 1960s debates over "internal colonialism," see Sugrue, *Sweet Land,* chaps. 10–12, esp. 315, 342–43; Singh, *Black Is a Country,* chaps. 5 and 6; and Katz, *The Undeserving Poor,* 52–65. On King's increasing reliance on systemic and relational logics by the mid-1960s, see Jackson, *From Civil Rights to Human Rights,* 276–77; Singh, *Black Is a Country,* 13; Lipsitz, *How Racism Takes Place,* Kindle edition, location 224–82. For a careful analysis of the sources—and implementation failures—of Johnson's "equality of results" rhetoric, see Ira Katznelson, *When Affirmative Action Was White: An Untold History of Racial Inequality in Twentieth-Century America* (New York: Norton, 2005).

28. Sugrue, *Sweet Land,* 540.

29. Crenshaw, "Race, Reform, and Retrenchment," 118.

30. Pettigrew, *The Sociology of Race Relations,* 240–41; Michael B. Katz and Mark J. Stern, *One Nation Divisible: What America Was and What It Is Becoming* (New York: Russell Sage Foundation, 2006), 91–92; Clayborne Carson, "Two Cheers for *Brown v. Board of Education,*" *Journal of American History* 91, no. 1 (2004): 26–31; Carl Kaestle and Marshall S. Smith, "The Federal Role in Elementary and Secondary Education, 1940–1980," *Harvard Educational Review* 52, no. 4 (1982): 384–408; Gary Orfield, Susan E. Eaton, and the Harvard Project on School Desegregation, *Dismantling Desegregation: The Quiet Reversal of* Brown v. Board of Education (New York: New Press, 1996); and James T. Patterson, Brown v. Board of Education: *A Civil Rights Milestone and Its Troubled Legacy* (New York: Oxford University Press, 2001), chaps. 5–10.

31. Sugrue, *Sweet Land,* 366.

32. John David Skrentny, *The Ironies of Affirmative Action: Politics, Culture, and Justice in America* (Chicago: University of Chicago Press, 1996); Anthony S. Chen, *The Fifth*

Freedom: Jobs Politics, and Civil Rights in the United States, 1941–1972 (Princeton, NJ: Princeton University Press, 2009); Patterson, Brown v. Board, 183–85, 191–205.

33. Katz, *The Undeserving Poor*, 79–123; O'Connor, *Poverty Knowledge*, 125–36.

34. Lipsitz, *How Racism Takes Place*, Kindle edition, location 471–73.

35. George Lipsitz, *The Possessive Investment in Whiteness: How White People Profit from Identity Politics* (Philadelphia: Temple University Press, 1998), introduction and chap. 5; Sugrue, *Sweet Land*, 432, 503–5.

36. Lipsitz, *How Racism Takes Place*, Kindle edition, introduction, esp. location 95–108.

37. Orfield, *Dismantling Desegregation*, chap. 1; Sugrue, *Sweet Land*, chap. 13; Patterson, Brown v. Board, 170–83.

38. On the sources of late twentieth-century conservatism on questions of race and poverty, see Katz, *Undeserving Poor*; Katz, *Underclass Debate*; Lipsitz, *Possessive Investment in Whiteness*; O'Connor, *Poverty Knowledge*, chaps. 10 and 11; and Sugrue, *Sweet Land*, part 3.

39. Gunnar Myrdal, *An American Dilemma: The Negro Problem and Modern Democracy* (New York: Harper, 1944), 24.

40. On the "erasure of intention" in debates over northern school and housing segregation, see Sugrue, *Sweet Land*, 183–84, 197–98, 480–92. On retreats from southern desegregation in the 1990s, see Lani Guinier, "From Racial Liberalism to Racial Literacy: *Brown v. Board of Education* and the Interest-Divergence Dilemma," *Journal of American History* 91 (2004): 92–118, 96, 93; Orfield, *Dismantling Desegregation*, chaps. 1 and 2.

41. Singh, *Black Is a Country*, 10.

42. For thoughtful critiques of this conservatism, see: Lawrence D. Bobo and Ryan A. Smith, "From Jim Crow Racism to Laissez-Faire Racism: The Transformation of Racial Attitudes," in *Beyond Pluralism: The Conception of Groups and Group Identities in America*, ed. Wendy F. Katkin, Ned Landsman, and Andrea Tyree (Urbana: University of Illinois Press, 1998), 182–220; Lipsitz, *How Racism Takes Place*, Kindle edition, location 21–30; Crenshaw, "Race, Reform, and Retrenchment"; and Singh, *Black Is a Country*, esp. 10–12.

43. Myrdal, *An American Dilemma*; King, "Seventh Annual Gandhi Memorial Lecture, Howard University," 3, quoted in Jackson, *From Civil Rights to Human Rights*, 299.

44. Walter A. Jackson, *Gunnar Myrdal and America's Conscience: Social Engineering and Racial Liberalism, 1938–1987* (Chapel Hill: University of North Carolina Press, 1990), chap. 5.

45. Kenneth Clark, "Racial Progress and Retreat: A Personal Memoir," in *Race in America: The Struggle for Equality*, ed. Herbert Hill and James Jones Jr. (Madison: University of Wisconsin Press, 1993), 18.

46. Ibid., 18.

47. On these compromises in the legal arena see: Crenshaw, "Race, Reform, and Retrenchment," 112.

INDEX

Abrams, Charles, 127
Ackerman, Nathan, 111
Adorno, Theodor, 10–11, 42–45, 184
Advisory Committee on Interracial
  Relations. *See under* Rockefeller
  philanthropy
affirmative action, 189
African Americans: employment of,
  35; housing of, 35, 114–15, 120–22;
  lynchings of, 35; migration of, 18, 28, 56,
  90; rights of, 1, 16, 20, 105, 119, 122–28,
  181; stereotypes of, 116; and violence in
  northern cities, 56, 79
After Freedom (Powdermaker), 31
Alexander, Will W., 35, 57–58
Allport, Floyd, 163
Allport, Gordon, 1, 8, 18, 30, 40–41, 111,
  182, 184
Amenia Conference, 17
Amenia ideal, 105, 108–9, 133
American Council on Race Relations, 63–
  64, 88, 115
American Dilemma, An (Myrdal), 22, 26–
  27, 34–39, 48, 51, 67, 116, 159, 180–81,
  187, 190
American Friends Service Committee, 30
American Jewish Committee, 30, 42, 166
American Jewish Congress, 18, 30, 84, 166,
  178
American Missionary Association, 18, 103,
  166
American Soldier, The (US War Department),
  14, 40
Amerman, Helen E., 87

Anthropological Study of Caste and Class
  (Davis, Gardner, and Gardner), 31–32
anthropology: Caste and Class school, 2, 9,
  21, 31, 145–46; of race relations, 28
anticommunism, 5–7, 15, 22, 47, 85, 89,
  119, 122, 125–26, 128, 130, 153, 157,
  181, 183, 190. *See also* antiradicalism;
  McCarthyism
Anti-Defamation League, 18, 88, 166
antidiscrimination legislation, 3, 7, 20, 36,
  44, 83, 85, 119–21, 128, 177, 187–88, 190
antiprejudice education, 3–5, 7, 10, 11, 16,
  22–25, 27, 30, 39, 42–45, 51, 87, 107,
  103, 121, 126, 133–34, 148–52, 162,
  181, 183
antiradicalism, 7, 10, 12, 15–16, 20, 22–
  23, 34, 49, 51, 54, 55, 61, 63, 67, 72,
  76, 80, 89, 114, 118, 130, 136, 179,
  180, 182, 190. *See also* anticommunism;
  McCarthyism
Aptheker, Herbert, 12, 38, 48, 185
Association for the Study of Negro Life and
  History, 57
attitude-based survey research. *See under*
  social scientific research
Authoritarian Personality, The (Adorno,
  Frenkel-Brunswik, Levinson, and
  Sanford), 11, 42–45, 184

Baker, Newton, 34
Barrett, Reginald, 113
Becker, Gary, 49
behavioral sciences, 2, 10, 12, 14, 27, 40–
  41, 67–68, 71–72, 77, 80, 130, 134, 144